**Ageing in Singapore**
Service needs and the state
*Peggy Teo, Kalyani Mehta,*
*Leng Leng Thang and Angelique Chan*

**Security and Sustainable Development in Myanmar**
*Helen James*

**Expressions of Cambodia**
The politics of tradition, identity and change
*Edited by Leakthina Chau-Pech Ollier*
*and Tim Winter*

**Financial Fragility and Instability in Indonesia**
*Yasuyuki Matsumoto*

**The Revival of Tradition in Indonesian Politics**
The deployment of *adat* from
colonialism to indigenism
*Edited by Jamie S. Davidson and*
*David Henley*

**Communal Violence and Democratization in Indonesia**
Small town wars
*Gerry van Klinken*

**Singapore in the Global System**
Relationship, structure and change
*Peter Preston*

**Chinese Big Business in Indonesia**
The state of the capital
*Christian Chua*

**Ethno-religious Violence in Indonesia**
From soil to God
*Chris Wilson*

**Ethnic Politics in Burma**
States of conflict
*Ashley South*

**Democratization in Post-Suharto Indonesia**
*Edited by Marco Bünte*
*and Andreas Ufen*

# Democratization in
# Post-Suharto Indonesia

**Edited by Marco Bünte and Andreas Ufen**

Routledge
Taylor & Francis Group

LONDON AND NEW YORK

First published 2009
by Routledge
2 Park Square, Milton Park, Abingdon, Oxon, OX14 4RN

Simultaneously published in the USA and Canada
by Routledge
270 Madison Avenue, New York, NY 10016

*Routledge is an imprint of the Taylor & Francis Group,
an informa business*

Transferred to Digital Printing 2009

© 2009 Editorial selection and matter, Marco Bünte and Andreas Ufen;
individual chapters, the contributors

Typeset in Times by RefineCatch Limited, Bungay, Suffolk, UK

*British Library Cataloguing in Publication Data*
A catalogue record for this book is available from the British Library

*Library of Congress Cataloging-in-Publication Data*
A catalogue record for this book has been requested

ISBN10: 0–415–43893–4 (hbk)
ISBN10: 0–415–57427–7 (pbk)
ISBN10: 0–203–93476–8 (ebk)

ISBN13: 978–0–415–43893–3 (hbk)
ISBN13: 978–0–415–57427–3 (pbk)
ISBN13: 978–0–203–93476–0 (ebk)

# Contents

# Contributors

**Marco Bünte** is a Senior Research Fellow at the Institute of Asian Studies in the German Institute of Global and Area Studies (GIGA) in Hamburg, Germany. His main research interests lie in the field of comparative politics, especially in democratization, decentralization and political violence. Bünte has been lecturer for Southeast Asian politics at the University of Helsinki and for comparative politics in Hamburg and Münster University. He obtained his PhD from the University of Münster in Germany in 2002 with a dissertation on regional autonomy in Indonesia (*Regionale Autonomie in Indonesien*, Hamburg, Institute of Asian Affairs 2003). In conjunction with this he carried out fieldwork in West Sumatra and Central Java for seven months in 2001/2002.

**Christian Chua** received his PhD in Sociology from the National University of Singapore. He currently works as organizational development expert for Deutsche Bank and lectures at the Humboldt University Berlin and Frankfurt University. His publications include *Chinese Big Business in Indonesia. The State of Capital* (Routledge 2008), *Indonesia's Chinese* (Hamburg, Institute of Asian Affairs 2002, in German) and articles on ethnicity and the political economy of Chinese business.

**Bob Sugeng Hadiwinata** is Associate Professor at the Department of International Relations, University of Parahyangan, Bandung, Indonesia, and former Alexander von Humboldt Fellow at University of Giessen, Germany. He is the author of *The Politics of NGOs in Indonesia* (RoutledgeCurzon 2003) and co-editor (with Christoph Schuck) of *Democracy in Indonesia: The Challenge of Consolidation* (Nomos 2007).

**Felix Heiduk**, born in 1976, is currently a research associate at the German Institute for International and Security Affairs (SWP) in Berlin. He has written his PhD thesis on the Aceh conflict at Free University Berlin. His main research interests include civil wars, transitions to democracy, security sector reform and terrorism in Southeast Asia. His latest publications include 'Indonesien – die gefährdete Transition' in Ulrich Schneckener (ed.) *Fragile Staatlichkeit – States at Risk zwischen Stabilität und Scheitern*

(Nomos 2006) and 'Conflict Analysis Province of Aceh/Indonesia', Series of Country-Related Conflict Analysis, Friedrich Ebert Stiftung, Bonn, October 2006.

**Jun Honna** is Associate Professor in the Faculty of International Relations at Ritsumeikan University, Japan. He obtained his PhD in 1999 at the Australian National University. His recent publications include *Military Politics and Democratization in Indonesia* (RoutledgeCurzon 2003), 'Local Civil-Military Relations during the First Phase of Democratic Transition, 1999–2004: A Comparison of West, Central and East Java', *Indonesia* (October 2006) and 'The Dilemma of Transnational Crime and Human Insecurity in Southeast Asia', in G. Shani *et al.* (eds) *Protecting Human Security in a Post-9/11 World: Critical and Global Insights* (Palgrave Macmillan 2007).

**Marcus Mietzner** is currently Lecturer in Indonesian Studies, Faculty of Asian Studies, ANU, Canberra. He holds a PhD from the Australian National University, and is the author of numerous articles and book chapters on Indonesian politics. Most recently, he published a monograph entitled 'The Politics of Military Reform in Post-Suharto Indonesia: Elite Conflict, Nationalism, and Institutional Resistance' (2006) at the East West Center in Washington.

**Mikaela Nyman** is currently Manager for International Engagement at the Department of Labour (Immigration New Zealand). Her interests include civil society development and democratization, human security, as well as the nexus between migration and development. In the past she has worked with civil society groups in overseas development aid in various countries. She is the author of *Democratising Indonesia: The Challenges of Civil Society in the Era of Reformasi* (2006) and has an MA in Asian Studies from the University of Southern Queensland.

**Sofie Arjon Schütte** studied Southeast Asian Studies, Economics and Sociology at the Rijksuniversiteit Leiden, the University of Melbourne and the University of Passau where she wrote her master thesis *Korruptionsbekämpfung in Indonesien seit dem Rücktritt Soehartos in Gesetzgebung und Praxis* and obtained a Magister Artium degree in early 2004. Since April 2004 she has worked in Jakarta, first under UNDP and CIM (Centrum für internationale Migration und Entwicklung) as advisor to the anti-corruption programme of the Partnership for Governance Reform in Indonesia, and since November 2006 as CIM integrated advisor to the Indonesian Corruption Eradication Commission (KPK).

**Petra Stockmann** is a political scientist and has worked as project officer at the Berlin-based human rights organization Watch Indonesia!, focusing on constitutional and human rights law. She graduated from the Free University of Berlin and received her PhD from Hong Kong Baptist

University. Among her publications are *Indonesian Reformasi as Reflected in Law. Change and Continuity in Post-Suharto Era Legislation on the Political System and Human Rights* (LIT-Verlag 2004) and *The New Indonesian Constitutional Court. A study into its beginnings and first years of work* (published by the Hanns Seidel Foundation and Watch Indonesia! 2007).

**Dirk Tomsa** is an Associate Lecturer at the University of Tasmania, Australia, where he holds a joint appointment at the School of Government and the School of Asian Languages and Studies. He was awarded a PhD at the University of Melbourne in March 2007. His main research interests include Indonesian politics and society, democratization and party politics in Southeast Asia, the role of political Islam in Southeast Asia, as well as international politics of the Asia Pacific. His works have been published in *Contemporary Southeast Asia, Indonesia* and *Inside Indonesia.*

**Andreas Ufen** graduated from the Free University of Berlin as a political scientist and completed his PhD in 2000 with a dissertation on *Herrschaftsfiguration und Demokratisierung in Indonesien (1965–2000)* ('Configuration of Power and Democratization in Indonesia (1965–2000)', Hamburg: Institut für Asienkunde 2002) at the University of Hamburg. He is Senior Research Fellow at the Institute of Asian Studies in the German Institute of Global and Area Studies (GIGA) in Hamburg and focuses on political parties, democratization, and Islamization in Southeast Asia. From July 2004 until December 2006 he led a research project on Islam and politics in Southeast Asia (Indonesia and Malaysia) sponsored by the German Research Foundation.

**Patrick Ziegenhain** is Senior Research Fellow at the department of political science at the University of Trier in Germany. He earned his PhD from Albert Ludwigs University in Freiburg, Germany with a dissertation on the Indonesian parliament ('From Rubber Stamp to Superbody? The Role of Parliament during the Democratization Process', Singapore: ISEAS 2008). His main research areas are systems of government, regime transitions, political parties and elections in Southeast Asia.

# Abbreviations and glossary

| | |
|---|---|
| *Abangan* | nominal Muslim or syncretist |
| ABRI | Angkatan Bersenjata Republik Indonesia (Indonesian Armed Forces) |
| *adat* | custom, tradition |
| ALDERA | Aliansi Demokrasi Rakyat (People's Democracy Alliance) |
| *aliran* | religio-political stream |
| AMPG | Angkatan Muda Partai Golkar (Young Generation of Golkar Party) |
| AMPI | Angkatan Muda Pembaruan Indonesia (Young Generation for Indonesian Renewal; Golkar youth organization) |
| APKASI | Asosiasi Pemerintah Kabupaten Seluruh Indonesia (Inter-Indonesia Regency Government Association) |
| APPSI | Asosiasi Pemerintah Propinsi Seluruh Indonesia (Inter-Indonesia Provincial Government Association) |
| *arisan* | rotating savings group |
| *asas (azas) tunggal* | *Pancasila* as the exclusive base for mass organizations |
| *Baligate* | Bank Bali scandal during the presidency of B.J. Habibie |
| *bapak* | father |
| Bapepam | Badan Pengawas Pasar Modal (Indonesia Capital Market and Financial Institution Supervisory Agency) |
| Bappenas | Badan Perencanaan Pembangunan Nasional (National Development Planning Agency) |
| *basah* | wet |
| BIN | Badan Intelijen Negara (State Intelligence Agency) |

| | |
|---|---|
| Bina Swadaya | Self Reliance Development Foundation, NGO, supporting rural self-help groups |
| BPK | Badan Pemeriksa Keuangan (State Audit Board) |
| BPKP | Badan Pengawasan Keuangan dan Pembangunan (Financial and Development Supervisory Board) |
| Bulog | Badan Urusan Logistik (State Logistic Agency) |
| *bupati* | district head |
| CEADAW | Convention on the Elimination of All Forms of Discrimination against Women |
| CMI | Crisis Management Initiative |
| CPI | Corruption Perception Index |
| CPSM | Center for Participatory Social Management |
| CRC | Convention on the Rights of the Child |
| CTF | Commission of Truth and Friendship |
| *Darul Islam* | 'Abode of Islam'; Islamic separatist movement |
| DAU | Dana Alokasi Umum (General Allocation Fund) |
| *dealiranisasi* | weakening of *aliran* |
| *demokratisasi* | democratization |
| Dian Desa | 'Light of the Village'; Indonesian NGO for rural technology support |
| DPA | Dewan Pertimbangan Agung (Supreme Advisory Council) |
| DPD | Dewan Perwakilan Daerah (Regional Representative Council) |
| DPOD | Dewan Pertimbangan Otonomi Daerah (Regional Autonomy Advisory Council) |
| DPP | Dewan Pimpinan Pusat (Central Executive Board) |
| DPR | Dewan Perwakilan Rakyat (House of Representatives) |
| DPRD | Dewan Perwakilan Rakyat Daerah (House of Regional Representatives) |
| *dwifungsi* | 'dual function' (military and socio-economic) of the armed forces |
| FATF | Financial Action Task Force |
| Fitra | Forum Indonesia untuk Transparansi Anggaran (Indonesian Forum for Budgetary Transparency) |
| FKAWJ | Forum Komunikasi Ahlus Sunnah Wal Jamaah (Communication Forum of the |

|                            | Followers of the Sunna and the Community of the Prophet) |
|----------------------------|----------------------------------------------------------|
| Forum-LSM-DIY              | Forum Lembaga Swadaya Masyarakat – Daerah Istimewa Yogyakarta (Yogyakarta NGO Forum) |
| FPSB                       | Forum Peduli Sumatra Barat (West Sumatra Concern Forum) |
| Fretilin                   | Frente Revolucionária de Timor-Leste Independente (Revolutionary Front for an Independent East Timor) |
| Front Pembela Islam        | Islamic Defenders Front |
| GAM                        | Gerakan Aceh Merdeka (Free Aceh Movement) |
| GDP                        | Gross Domestic Product |
| Gerakan Anti Politisi Busuk | Anti-Rotten Politicians Movement |
| GMIM                       | Gereja Masehi Injili di Minahasa (The Christian Evangelical Church in Minahasa) |
| Golkar                     | Partai Golongan Karya (Functional Group Party) |
| *gotong royong*            | mutual help |
| *hak prerogatif*           | prerogative right |
| HMI                        | Himpunan Mahasiswa Islam (Islamic Student Association) |
| HWK                        | Himpunan Wanita Karya (Women's Functional Association) |
| IBRA                       | Indonesia Bank Restructuring Agency |
| ICCPR                      | International Covenant on Civil and Political Rights |
| ICESCR                     | International Covenant on Economic, Social and Cultural Rights |
| ICG                        | International Crisis Group |
| ICJ                        | International Commission of Jurists |
| ICMI                       | Ikatan Cendekiawan Muslim se-Indonesia (Association of Indonesian Muslim Intellectuals) |
| ICTJ                       | International Center for Transitional Justice |
| ICW                        | Indonesia Corruption Watch |
| ILO                        | International Labour Organization |
| IMF                        | International Monetary Fund |
| *Indonesia Raya*           | Greater Indonesia |
| INFID                      | International NGO Forum for Indonesian Development |
| INFIGHT                    | Indonesian Front for the Defence of Human Rights |

| | |
|---|---|
| IPW | Indonesian Procurement Watch |
| *jalan tengah* | middle way |
| *kabupaten* | district |
| *kekeluargaan* | family principle |
| *kelompok kematian* | burial association |
| *kepala dinas* | head of government office |
| *kering* | dry |
| *keterbukaan* | 'openness', the limited liberalization initiated by Suharto in 1989 |
| *kiai* or *kiyayi* | Islamic scholar, head of pesantren |
| KKN | Kolusi, Korupsi dan Nepotisme (corruption, collusion and nepotism) |
| KNIL | Koninklijk Nederlandsch-Indisch Leger (Royal Netherlands Indies Army) |
| KNPI | Komite Nasional Pemuda Indonesia (National Indonesian Youth Committee) |
| Koalisi Kebangsaan | Nationhood Coalition |
| Koalisi Kerakyatan | People's Coalition |
| Koalisi Masyarakat Anti Skandal Bank Lippo | People's Coalition against the Lippo Bank scandal |
| *koalisi pelangi* | rainbow coalition |
| Komnas HAM | Komite Nasional Hak Asasi Manusia (National Human Rights Commission) |
| Kosgoro | Koperasi Serba Guna Gotong Royong (All-Purpose Cooperative of Mutual Assistance) |
| KPA | Konsorsium Pembaruan Agraria (Consortium for Agrarian Reform) |
| KPA | Komite Peralihan Aceh (Aceh Transition Committee) |
| KPI | Komisi Penyiaran Indonesia (Indonesian Broadcasting Commission) |
| KPK | Komisi Pemberantasan Korupsi (Corruption Eradication Commission) |
| KPKPN | Komisi Pemeriksa Kekayaan Penyelenggara Negara (Public Servants' Wealth Audit Commission) |
| KPPU | Komisi Pengawas Persaingan Usaha (Business Competition Supervisory Commission) |
| KPU | Komisi Pemilihan Umum (General Election Committee) |
| KPUD | Komisi Pemilihan Umum Daerah (Local Election Commission) |

| | |
|---|---|
| KUHAP | Kitab Undang-Undang Hukum Acara Pidana (Indonesian Code of Criminal Procedure) |
| Laskar Jihad | Jihad warriors |
| LeIP | Lembaga Kajian dan Advokasi untuk Independensi Peradilan (Indonesian Institute for the Independence of the Judicary) |
| LIPI | Lembaga Ilmu Pengetahuan Indonesia (Indonesian Institute of Sciences) |
| LMMDD-KT | Lembaga Musyawarah Masyarakat Dayak Daerah – Kalimantan Tengah (Dayak Deliberative Council of Central Kalimantan) |
| LP3ES | Lembaga Penelitian, Pendidikan dan Penerangan Ekonomi dan Sosial (Institute for Social and Economic Research, Education and Information) |
| LSP | Lembaga Studi Pembangunan (Institute for Development Studies) |
| MAPPI | Masyarakat Pemantau Peradilan Indonesia (Indonesian Judicial Watch Society) |
| Masyumi | Majelis Syuro Muslimin Indonesia (Consultative Council of Indonesian Muslims) |
| MDI | Majelis Dakwah Islamiyah (Council for Islamic Propagation) |
| MKGR | Musyawarah Kekeluargaan Gotong Royong (a mass organization close to Golkar) |
| MMI | Majelis Mujahidin Indonesia (Indonesian Mujahedin Council) |
| MoU | Memorandum of Understanding |
| MP | Member of Parliament |
| MPR | Majelis Permusyawaratan Rakyat (People's Consultative Assembly) |
| MRP | Majelis Rakyat Papua (Papuan's People Assembly) |
| MTI | Masyarakat Transparansi Indonesia (The Indonesian Transparency Society) |
| Muhammadiyah | Muslim modernist organization |
| *musyawarah dan mufakat* | a debating principle; debating until a compromise is reached that everybody can accept |
| NCCT | Non-Cooperative Countries and Territories |
| *negara hukum* | rule-of-law state |

| | |
|---|---|
| *negara kekeluargaan* | family state |
| NKRI | Negara Kesatuan Republik Indonesia (Unitary State of the Republic of Indonesia) |
| NU | Nahdatul Ulama ('Awakening of *ulama*'); traditionalist Muslim organization |
| OMSP | Operasi Militer Selain Perang (Military Operation other than War) |
| OPM | Organisasi Papua Merdeka (Free Papua Movement) |
| *Orde Baru* | New Order |
| *otonomi daerah* | regional autonomy |
| Pam Swakarsa | Pasukan Pengamanan Swakarsa (Self-Service Security Force) |
| PAN | Partai Amanat Nasional (National Mandate Party) |
| *Pancasila* | 'five pillars'; state philosophy |
| *pasukuan ninja* | ninja troops |
| PBB | Partai Bulan Bintang (Star and Crescent Party) |
| PBR | Partai Bintang Reformasi (Star Party of Reform) |
| PD | Partai Demokrat (Democrat Party) |
| PDI | Partai Demokrasi Indonesia (Indonesian Democratic Party) |
| PDI-P | Partai Demokrasi Indonesia – Perjuangan (Indonesian Democratic Party – Struggle) |
| PDP | Presidium Dewan Papua (Papua Presidium Council) |
| PDS | Partai Damai Sejahtera (Prosperity and Peace Party) |
| *pembangunan* | development |
| *pemekaran* | literally: 'blossoming' (the splitting off of new districts and provinces) |
| Perpu | Peraturan Pemerintah Pengganti Undang-Undang (government regulation in lieu of a law) |
| *pesantren* | Islamic boarding school |
| *pilkada* | *pilihan kepala daerah* (election of regional head) |
| PKB | Partai Kebangkitan Bangsa (National Awakening Party) |
| PKI | Partai Komunis Indonesia (Indonesian Communist Party) |

| | |
|---|---|
| PKS | Partai Keadilan Sejahtera (Justice and Welfare Party) |
| PNI | Partai Nasional Indonesia (Indonesian Nationalist Party) |
| PPATK | Pusat Pelaporan dan Analisis Transaksi Keuangan (Financial Transaction Reporting and Analysis Center) |
| PPDK | Partai Persatuan Demokrasi Kebangsaan (United Democratic Nationhood Party) |
| PPP | Partai Persatuan Pembangunan (United Development Party) |
| P3M | Perhimpunan Pesantren dan Pengembangan Masyarakat (Indonesian Society for Pesantren and Community Development) |
| PRD | Partai Rakyat Demokratik (Democratic People's Party) |
| *preman* | thug |
| *pribumi* | native or indigenous |
| PSI | Partai Sosialis Indonesia (Indonesian Socialist Party) |
| *reformasi* | reform |
| RMS | Republik Maluku Selatan (Republic of the South Moluccas) |
| *santri* | devout Muslim |
| Satkar Ulama | *ulama* work squad |
| *sekretaris daerah* | regional secretary |
| SMID | Solidaritas Mahasiswa Indonesia untuk Demokrasi (Indonesian Student Solidarity for Democracy) |
| *sharia* | Islamic law |
| TI-I | Transparency International – Indonesia |
| TNI | Tentara Nasional Indonesia (Indonesian Armed Forces) |
| TRC | Truth and Reconciliation Commission |
| UDHR | Universal Declaration of Human Rights |
| *ulama* | Muslim scholar |
| USAID | United States Agency for International Development |
| *ustadz* | religious teacher |
| UU ORMAS | UU Organisasi Kemasyarakatan (law on mass organizations) |
| UUD | Undang-Undang Dasar (constitution) |
| *walikota* | mayor |
| YIS | Yayasan Indonesia Sejahtera (Indonesian Welfare Foundation) |

| | |
|---|---|
| YLBHI | Yayasan Lembaga Bantuan Hukum Indonesia (Indonesian Legal Aid Foundation) |
| YLKI | Yayasan Lembaga Konsumen Indonesia (Indonesian Consumers Foundation) |

# Introduction

# 1 The New Order and its legacy

Reflections on democratization in Indonesia

*Marco Bünte and Andreas Ufen*

## INTRODUCTION

Indonesia has been a democratic latecomer. The global trend towards democracy that has been termed 'the third wave of democratization' (Huntington 1991) has reached Indonesia relatively late, at the end of the 1990s. This striking tide of political change began in Southern Europe in 1974, spread to the military regimes of South America in the late 1970s and early 1980s, and culminated in the democratizations in Eastern Europe in the late 1980s. The third wave of democratization reached the shores of East and Southeast Asia by the mid to late 1980s. Here, authoritarian regimes were replaced with democracies in the Philippines in 1986, in South Korea in 1987 and in Thailand in 1992. Indonesia, however, in the mid-1990s still seemed to be a safe place of authoritarian rule. Anders Uhlin in 1997 contended that 'the third wave has obviously failed to have any profound impact on Indonesia's democratic development' (Uhlin 1997: 2). At that time the country has been in a 'pre-transition phase' (*ibid.*: ch. 7); that this was *literally* true became clear shortly afterwards when the Suharto regime suddenly began to crumble in the wake of the 1997 Asian crisis and gave way to a far more liberal political regime under Suharto's successor, Bacharuddin Jusuf Habibie. Habibie embarked on a course of political reform: he promised fresh elections for spring 1999, released political prisoners, decentralized political power, allowed political parties to operate freely and liberalized the press laws. These reforms paved the way for the first free and fair parliamentary elections since 1955 on 7 June 1999, and the election of Abdurrahman Wahid as president in October 1999. Only one and a half years after the collapse of the authoritarian regime, Indonesia had become an 'electoral democracy'. Yet, as Michael Malley has observed, democratization did not end at this point but was replaced by a 'protracted transition' in which authoritarian enclaves remained in place and competing elites struggled over the main state institutions and the direction of reform (Malley 2000). Further initiatives have suffered serious setbacks because politicians could not agree on the course of reforms and extra-parliamentary opposition forces remained weak. It was not until 2002 that Indonesia witnessed a new round of political reforms providing for the direct election of the president. All in all, progress in Indonesia's democratization has been somewhat slow and results have often been ambiguous. On the one hand, the transition opened up unprecedented freedoms, giving the Indonesian population the opportunity to elect their own leaders and the liberty to organize themselves freely. The free and fair parliamentary elections in 1999 and 2004, the first direct election of the Indonesian president in 2004 and the direct elections of regional heads since 2005 are encouraging signs of this new openness. On the other hand, the spread of democracy has by no means eradicated all forms of political repression as the military still exercises a huge influence, the political elite often uses power for their own ends and, above all, corruption is endemic and often leads to frustration within the Indonesian populace.

The aim of this book is to give an overview of the difficult, multilayered and often contradictory results of the democratization process. How has Indonesia's transition proceeded and what is the quality of Indonesia's nascent democracy? In order to discuss these questions in detail, this book's focus is on regime change in Indonesia. This chapter, therefore, begins with a discussion of various regime types ranging from authoritarianism to democracy. We distinguish between different key definitions of democracy – electoral and liberal democracy – and illuminate the grey zone between these conceptions. We also present the mid-range conceptions of hybrid regimes and defective democracies which combine both democratic and authoritarian elements. The conceptual question of how democratic deepening and enhancing the quality of democracy can be conceptualized is also discussed. This chapter provides conceptual clarity and links our empirical findings in Indonesia to the study of third wave democracies. The first part of the chapter is primarily about defining democracy. It prepares the ground for the second part, which describes Indonesia's path towards democracy from the Suharto period towards the current political regime of President Susilo Bambang Yudhoyono.

## CONCEPTUALIZING DEMOCRACY

Conceptualizing democracy is not an easy task, since the meaning of the term is highly controversial and there is no common definition among scholars. Whereas studies in the 1970s concentrated on the modelling of regimes that were dominated by a social elite or specific class ('bourgeois democracy', 'social democracy'), scholars recently have agreed to use a purely political conception of the term (Diamond 1999: 7). Generally, the theoretical approaches are divided into two strands: one-dimensional procedural conceptions, and more complex substantial definitions of democracy which revolve around the three dimensions of free elections, equality and horizontal control (Lauth 2004; Merkel 2004; Croissant and Merkel 2004).

**Electoral democracy**

The focal point of minimalist and procedural definitions of democracy is elections. The idea of elections as the conceptual core of democracy goes back to Joseph Schumpeter who defined democracy as a 'political method [. . .] for arriving at political decisions in which individuals acquire the power to decide by means of a competitive struggle for the people's vote' (Schumpeter 1975: 242).

In order to navigate around the stormy sea of a normative-oriented democracy discourse, most of the scholars studying third wave democratization at first decided to use this minimalist procedural definition of democracy. For instance, Przeworski and his colleagues defined democracy as a 'system in which parties lose elections' (Przeworski 1991: 10) or as 'a regime in which government offices are filled as a consequence of contested elections' (Przeworski *et al.* 1996: 50f.). Some scholars regard this procedural conception as unsatisfactory and incomplete as it privileges elections over other dimensions of democracy and risks what Terry Lynn Karl calls the 'fallacy of electoralism' (Karl 1995). This concentration on elections as the conceptual core of a definition of democracy neglects the fact that even multiparty elections can exclude large parts of the population from contesting power. Moreover, it does not take into account whether these elections are really meaningful (Hadenius 1992). Schmitter and Karl (1991: 78), therefore, remind us that elections occur only at a special point in time and that citizens are called to choose merely between policy alternatives offered by political parties which can, especially in the early stages of democratic transition, vary widely. Elections, therefore, are only a necessary and not sufficient component of democracy.

A broader understanding of democracy, which has become the cornerstone of the transition debates, is provided by Robert Dahl. He contends that Schumpeter's conception of democracy which is focused on elections is too restricted. In his concept of polyarchy[1] Robert Dahl elaborated on the Schumpeterian minimalist definition by arguing that in a democracy not only is extensive competition necessary to enable people to form and express their political preferences in a meaningful way, but also substantial levels of freedom (Dahl 1971: 3). Dahl makes 'open contestation' and 'public participation' the centre of his conception of polyarchy, which is only viable if it encompasses not only free and fair elections, inclusive suffrage and the right to run for office but also freedom of expression, free access to alternative information and associational autonomy (Dahl 1971: 3). Freedom of information is an intrinsic feature of the democratic process because voters cannot make a choice about candidates and issues unless they have access to alternative sources of information. Citizens also cannot organize and mobilize support for different candidates and issues if they are lacking freedom of association, assembly and movement. This Dahlean conception of democracy has been very influential and has been adopted by many scholars studying third wave democratizations as it remains a procedural (not substantial) definition and does not carry the Western values. The American organization Freedom House has become the main proponent of this idea, providing data and timelines for democratic development in each country over the last three decades. According to Freedom House, a country is considered democratic when it fulfils the requirement of free elections.

## Liberal democracy

More recently, a growing number of scholars have used a broader and expanded conception under the banner of liberal democracy. They question the tendency to classify regimes as democratic simply because they have multiparty elections with some degree of competition and basic liberties. They have used a more demanding definition which revolves around the core components of free elections, equality and the rule of law.[2] This concept of liberal democracy expands beyond electoral democracy since it requires the absence of reserved domains for the military and both vertical and horizontal accountability of the rulers. Whereas vertical accountability is to be secured by elections, horizontal accountability is assured by a separation of powers and by independent state institutions like an independent judiciary, parliament, election commission and central bank (O'Donnell 1999). Some scholars expand the category of liberal democracy even further; in their conception, a liberal democracy encompasses extensive provisions for political and civic pluralism as well as individual and group freedoms, so that contending interests and values may be expressed and compete through the ongoing processes of articulation and representation. Liberal democracy is comprised of the state, controlled by elected representatives, and the military, which is subordinated to elected officials. State power is constrained with the rule of law and independent government institutions guaranteeing horizontal accountability. Individuals have substantial freedom of belief, opinion, speech, publication, assembly, demonstration and petition, and have access to various sources of information. Minorities are not subject to excessive control by the government but are able to express and represent their interests freely. Moreover, citizens are required to be politically equal under the law (Diamond 1999: 10f.). The concept of a liberal democracy, however, has been highly contested since the beginning of the 1990s as many Asian politicians and scholars have rejected this model as inappropriate for Asia. Advocates of the Asian values perspective, such as Singapore's elder statesman Lee Kuan Yew, Malaysia's then Prime Minister Mahathir Mohamad and Indonesia's former President Suharto, have rejected the Western notion of democracy with its emphasis on human rights and social entitlements over the rights of the community. Here, social obligations and the rights of the community play a much greater role and liberal democracy is not preferable. However, as Larry Diamond concludes, 'one may accept many of the cultural objections of advocates of the Asian values perspective [. . .] and still embrace the political and civil fundamentals of liberal democracy' (Diamond 1999: 15).

Conceptually, there have been several recent major innovations. Wolfgang Merkel has coined the concept of 'embedded democracy', that illustrates the inner workings of the core components of liberal democracy. Embedded democracy has five defining elements (partial regimes): a democratic electoral regime, political rights of participation, civil rights, horizontal accountability and the guarantee that the effective power to govern lies in the hands of democratically elected representatives. The partial regimes are mutually embedded, i.e. the functioning of one partial regime supports or hinders the functioning of the other. For instance, political rights and civil liberties have an influence on the electoral regime, while horizontal accountability affects both the electoral regime and civil rights (Merkel 2004).[3]

## Hybrid regimes, defective democracies, and the debates on democratic deepening

The growing prevalence of regimes located somewhere between electoral and liberal democracy, which are minimally democratic but not liberal democracies, attracted the attention of scholars studying worldwide democratization. Empirical evidence suggests that 'many of the new democracies have very little to offer outside of elections' (Croissant and Merkel 2004: 1). While many regimes in Southern and Eastern Europe today are making progress in democratic consolidation and are moving up the ladder to liberal democracies, most of the young democracies in Asia, Africa and Latin America suffer from a lacking institutionalization of basic freedoms and meaningful elections.[4] In many of the new democracies elected politicians and officials are seen as corrupt, the effective power to govern is restricted by an interventionist military, guerrilla fighters, paramilitary forces or gangs of robbers, or the separation of powers and the rule of law function poorly. While free and fair elections still mark the watershed between 'electoral democracies' and 'closed authoritarian', 'electoral authoritarian' and 'competitive authoritarian' regimes (Levitsky and Way 2002; Schedler 2006; Snyder 2006), there is a lot of uncertainty about how to conceptualize the 'midrange categories' that are located in the 'grey zone' between electoral and liberal democracy (Carothers 2002; Rüb 2003). Terry Karl first used the term 'hybrid regimes' to describe the emerging democracies of Central America:

> Gains in the electoral arena have not been accompanied by the establishment of civilian control over the military or the rule of law. Elections are often free and fair, yet important sectors remain politically and economically disenfranchised. Militaries support civilian presidents, but they resist efforts by civilians to control internal military affairs, dictate security policy, make officers subject to the judgment of civil courts, or weaken their role as the ultimate arbiters of politics. Impunity is

condemned, yet judiciaries remain weak, rights are violated, and contracts are broken.

(Karl 1995: 80)

Karl uses the term 'hybrid regime' to indicate that these regimes combine democratic and authoritarian features and, as a result, considers them to be neither democratic nor authoritarian (see also Diamond 2002; Carothers 2002). Other scholars classify these regimes as subtypes of democracy, as 'defective' democracies (Merkel 2004). In a review of the literature David Collier and Steven Levitsky found more than 550 forms or subtypes of democracy (Collier and Levitsky 1997); for instance, 'delegative democracies' lack checks and balances (O'Donnell 1996), 'illiberal democracies' (Zakaria 1997) fail to uphold the rule of law and 'clientelist democracies' are weak on programmatic party politics (Kitschelt 2000).

However conceptualized, hybrid regimes or defective democracies contain both democratic elections and authoritarian residuals. They show a considerable degree of stability and call into doubt some of the basic assumptions of transition theory (Carothers 2002). The transition paradigm sees democratization as analytically distinct stages of transition and consolidation. Transition in this sense means the interval between one regime and another (O'Donnell and Schmitter 1986: 6). Democratic transition ends 'when sufficient agreement has been reached about political procedures to produce an elected government, when a government comes to power that is a direct result of a free and popular vote, and when the executive, legislative and judicial power generated by the new democracy does not have to share power with other bodies de jure' (Linz and Stepan 1996: 3). After the end of the transition, democratic consolidation or democratic deepening begins.

Yet, after more than a decade of studies in democratic consolidation, the precise analytical meaning is still controversial. Minimalist conceptions (Przeworski 1991) compete with maximalist (Huntington 1991), simple versions (di Palma 1990) with considerably sophisticated ones (Merkel 1998). The controversial points mainly concern the amount of time needed for the consolidation of post-authoritarian democracies and on which levels this takes place. Scholars using a minimalist, procedural definition simply refer to 'avoiding democratic breakdown'[5] whereas transitologists, making use of a maximalist definition, allude to enhancing the quality of democracy even further (Schedler 1998: 95f). The latter includes democratic deepening or moving forward from electoral to liberal democracy, yet this requires making the formal structures of democracy more liberal, accountable, representative and accessible. In general, this process encompasses the institutionalization of political parties and the party system, the neutralization of veto actors and the awakening of civil society. As recent studies have shown, the consolidation of a young democracy is certainly not inevitable and the many regimes that inhabit the grey zone between electoral and liberal democracy call into doubt whether democratic consolidation is progressing. Consequently, consolidation has become a controversial concept[6] that has been partly replaced by the concept of the quality or depth of democracy. The progress of Indonesia along her path toward a fully fledged democratic state and the quality of her transition are critically important issues and shall be addressed in depth.

## INDONESIA'S PROTRACTED TRANSITION FROM NEO-PATRIMONIAL RULE

The presentation of different regime types and the debates on democratic deepening serves as a background for the following brief overview of Indonesia's political trajectory after 1965. It will illustrate in particular some of the specifics of liberalization, transition and democratic deepening. To understand politics in Indonesia today, it is still imperative to begin with an analysis of the New Order. This regime was established by the Indonesian military in 1965–66 and lasted for more than 30 years until 1998. The New Order left its mark on the national psyche and still shapes the current configuration of power. Legacies of it are the ubiquitous, far from politically neutral armed forces; a politicized Islam; Golkar, a well-organized political party, which at least in the Outer Islands builds on old networks and resources; a fractured opposition; an economy dominated by well-connected conglomerates; and a range of social, ethnic, religious and centre – periphery conflicts all over the archipelago. The current state of democracy in Indonesia is shaped by the patrimonial character of the New Order and the peculiarities of Indonesia's transition. Chehabi and Linz have stressed that 'if the sultanistic regime is replaced by a democracy, chances are this new democracy will display strong clientelist tendencies, with the democratically elected leaders using the resources of their office to build nationwide patron–client relationships'[7] (1998: 45). Weak institutions and the low quality of democracy today are to be judged against the backdrop of a neo-patrimonial regime that became increasingly sultanistic.[8]

### The past: New Order Indonesia

In neo-patrimonial systems,[9] the ruling coalition occupies the state apparatus and thereby controls a major segment of the national economy. The coalition consists of cliques whose members are bound to each other by patron–client relationships. At the apex of the clientelist network is the neo-patrimonial leader as the highest patron. In Indonesia, the patrimonial logic of Javanese kingdoms was transformed into neo-patrimonial arrangements through the interplay of clientelist and capitalist mechanisms, a modernized – though not modern – administration and military, and through courts, political parties and trade unions. The result can be a lasting, highly stable authoritarian system. Indonesia's New Order with Suharto as the highest patron was a paragon of neo-patrimonialism (Crouch 1979; Schulte Nordholt 1987; Ufen 2002). The Indonesian people were conceived of as a homogenous body, the nation-state as a huge family. These organicist ideas legitimized the forced incorporation, unification and control of trade unions, women, youth, students, civil servants and professional organizations (Bachriadi, Faryadi and Setiawan 1997; Hadiz 1997). Moreover, the ideologists based their worldview on Western modernization theory; that is, on notions of 'national security', 'political stability' and 'economic development'. Those excluded from the power circles were conceptualized as 'floating mass' (*massa mengambang*) and as a result were not mobilized but were instead depoliticized (van Langenberg 1990). These doctrines were complemented by a moderate, at times anti-Western nationalism, a pronounced anti-communism (Goodfellow 1995; Heryanto 2006) and the *dwifungsi* doctrine denoting the 'double function' of the armed forces in internal and external security as well as in socio-political (*sospol*) matters. In summation, the New Order was a neo-patrimonial, corporatist modernization regime dominated by the military. Important features of the regime were the three-party system with Golkar as the hegemon and the marked centralism in a polity that was not only ethnically and religiously heterogeneous, but also characterized by striking regional and socio-economic contrasts. Economically, the whole power construct endured with the support of politically dependent, predominantly ethnic Chinese entrepreneurs as well as by means of huge oil and gas revenues (particularly in the 1970s).

The elites were able to build a range of interdependencies strengthening the cohesiveness of the regime coalition. At all administrative levels prosecutors, officers and bureaucrats worked hand in hand. The army occupied strategic positions in the civil administration, in the regime party Golkar and in nationalized companies. All in all, the power of Suharto expanded over three decades. In the initial stage, he was forced to cooperate closely with high-ranking generals of his generation but, as time passed, he increasingly centralized decision-making in the palace. Suharto decided over the appointment of generals, ministers, parliamentarians, judges and high-ranking managers in state companies. In the meantime, his family built an entrepreneurial network worth several billion US dollars. Political power was progressively centralized and personalized and the New Order increasingly assumed the shape of a sultanistic regime (Chehabi and Linz 1998; Aspinall 2005a). The economic reforms, the integration into globalized financial and production networks and the growing complexity of the social structure resulted in power shifts between the state and civil society groups and between elite groups of the regime coalition.

## From liberalization to protracted transition

Until the 1990s, Suharto was able to maintain regime coherence. Only shortly before his downfall cracks within the ruling coalition – notably between 'hardliners' and 'soft-liners' – appeared and splits in the opposition ranks between 'moderates' and 'radicals' became ever more visible. Yet, until the beginning of 1998 Suharto had managed to keep the loyalty of his supporters. The capitalist penetration of all social sectors, the cultural 'Westernization' (*westernisasi*) and the international discourse on human rights and liberal democracy all contributed to the delegitimization of organicist ideologies (Bourchier 1996). Socio-structural and socio-cultural developments entailed a reawakening of the student movement, even giving rise to some new bonds between NGOs, students, workers and peasants. During this period, the number of strikes and demonstrations rose significantly and new organizations were established by former members of the power elites (Hadiz 1997; Lucas 1997), and even illegal trade unions and political parties emerged. In the official realm of politics some remarkable changes occurred. In 1993, a party leader – namely Megawati Sukarnoputri of PDI (Partai Demokrasi Indonesia, Indonesian Democratic Party) – was freely elected. Around the same time, Abdurrahman Wahid and Amien Rais, representing the two giant Muslim organizations Nahdatul Ulama and Muhammadiyah respectively, dared criticize the ruling elite on many occasions. Time and again, the press tested the limits of restriction and even highlighted several scandals involving the Suharto family. Among the wider public, a lively debate on human rights and *demokratisasi* ('democratization') flourished and even the army leadership felt the compulsion to explain its stance on the reform issue.[10]

However, these first cracks in the regime coalition alone were not sufficient to bring down an authoritarian system such as the New Order; two other factors played a decisive role in the liberalization process: popular pressure and external shocks. In Indonesia, these key factors were ultimately decisive for the breakthrough in May 1998. Since July 1997, the Asian financial crisis had caused innumerable collapses of companies as well as swelling the numbers of unemployed. The government lost most of its sovereignty in economic policy-making and was forced by the International Monetary Fund (IMF) to introduce a wide range of reforms. The IMF demanded a strict austerity course, improved supervision of banks, destruction of monopolies and general enforcement of deregulation measures. In this atmosphere of political insecurity and economic crisis, students began in February 1998 to demonstrate for sweeping reforms (Eklöf 1999; Aritonang 1999; Aspinall 2005a: 202ff), and set the pace for the loosely connected opposition forces. The regime coalition, not knowing how to react, could only resort to a course of 'wait and see'. However, an increasing number of fractures emerged against the backdrop of mounting pressure by international actors. From mid-May 1998 until the fall of Suharto the regime coalition slowly dissolved. Parts of it, in cooperation with protesting students and supported by calls of the middle class for reform, forced Suharto from office. In sum, the resignation of the president was effected by diverse, yet hardly unified opposition forces and finally even by factions of the military leadership and of political parties, parts of the business community and highly regarded Islamic leaders. But the old elites could not possibly be substituted by reform-minded counter-elites, for the latter were ill-prepared and disorganized:

> [. . .] when Suharto's government collapsed, principled opposition remained weak, allowing for a rapid reconsolidation of the ruling coalition which had underpinned the New Order, the subsequent blurring of the division between 'reformist' and 'status quo' forces, and numerous obstructions to democratic transition and consolidation.
>
> (Aspinall 2005a: 5)

Consequently, the liberalization was replaced by a 'protracted transition' (Malley 2000) that was characterized by piecemeal reforms, numerous setbacks and a huge gap between those now occupying, on the one hand, the state apparatus and leadership positions in political parties and, on the other hand, the still emaciated civil society (Törnquist 2000; Prasetyo, Priyono and Törnquist 2003).

## POLITICAL REFORMS IN POST-SUHARTO INDONESIA

The transition period began with the fall of Suharto. If we define transition as the phase between the breakdown of authoritarianism and the successful implementation of sufficiently free and fair elections, the period started on 21 May 1998 and ended on 20 October 1999.[11] Indonesia became an electoral democracy after the national polls and the election of the president by the People's Consultative Assembly (MPR). Then, attempts at democratic consolidation started.

### Transition to electoral democracy

Habibie, who took over as president the same day Suharto stepped down, was oriented towards preserving New Order privileges – for himself, for Golkar and for his followers in the Association of Indonesian Muslim Intellectuals (ICMI). He still had to rely on the military leadership and stood at the helm of a new conservative government but was at the same time forced to accommodate national and international demands for political reform.[12] He announced his clear intention to hold free and fair elections as soon as possible. Basic civil liberties and political rights were hence introduced and legally guaranteed, political prisoners were released, and the notorious Pancasila indoctrination was stopped. Moreover, independent trade unions and professional organizations as well as around two hundred political parties were established, and for the first time since the 1950s, newspapers and magazines were able to cover all kinds of scandals and to instigate debates on long-suppressed issues. Nevertheless, these reforms were far from consistent.

Habibie and most of his allies were not fully interested in investigating the crimes of New Order elites or in punishing recalcitrant debtors. Surprisingly for many Indonesians as well as foreign observers, the presidential family, most of their cronies and even the cruellest generals (such as Prabowo, the son-in-law of Suharto) escaped legal proceedings or at least prison sentences. At the same time, the armed forces abandoned the *dwifungsi*, but only as doctrine; the territorial organization was not significantly addressed. Due to the flawed reform process, the student movements proceeded with large-scale demonstrations throughout 1998 in order to bring down Habibie, who was still perceived as representative of the New Order regime. But in November 1998 the so-called 'Ciganjur Group',[13] comprised of main opposition leaders Megawati Sukarnoputri, Amien Rais, Abdurrahman Wahid and the Sultan of Yogyakarta, opted for moderation and resisted the students' demands for radical reforms. As Webber notes:

> The students became increasingly marginalized in the transition process, which henceforth was managed primarily through 'elite networks' and 'court politics'. [. . .] The democratic transition process in Indonesia thus corresponded closely to the model of an (in this case, implicit) pact between 'soft-liners' in regime and opposition 'moderates'.
>
> (Webber 2006: 408)

In Indonesia, the soft-liners almost single-handedly decided upon new laws on elections and the composition of parliaments, which were finally passed in November 1998 and January 1999. The opposition moderates were, until the elections, doomed to watch the process from the sidelines because these laws were debated and passed in the MPR, a parliament still largely dominated by New Order politicians. The New Order party Golkar, represented by Habibie and Akbar Tanjung and at that time at least tentatively reformed, prepared its return to power. But in spite of its well-oiled machinery, Golkar lost the national elections in June 1999 and gained only 22.5 per cent of the votes. The PDI-P under Megawati won with 33.8 per cent, the PAN under Amien Rais – who had been one of the *reformasi* heroes – achieved a disappointing 7.1 per cent, and the PKB under Abdurrahman Wahid received merely 12.6 per cent. The elections thus produced a multi-party system with no clear majorities. The subsequent struggle for the presidency, in 1999 still decided upon by the MPR, surprisingly saw the rise of Abdurrahman Wahid in spite of the weakness of his PKB fraction.

## Consolidating democracy?

The consolidation period was to begin after Abdurrahman Wahid assumed the presidency in October 1999 notwithstanding his fragile backing in parliament.[14] The above-mentioned pact of soft-liners and opposition moderates was reflected in his first cabinet, a grand coalition including all the key political forces. This 'rainbow coalition' already signified a growing cartelization of political parties (Slater 2004). Abdurrahman had a reputation for being a liberal Muslim leader with the intellectual capacity and willingness to cure the sick body politic. In fact, he began his tenure with far-reaching reforms, such as dissolving the information ministry and Bakorstanas, a part of the New Order intelligence network. He touched on a taboo and spoke in favour of legalizing the Communist Party (*Partai Komunis Indonesia*, PKI) and started to reform the armed forces by appointing an admiral as its Commander and a civilian as Minister of Defence. After a few months in office he dared to sack Wiranto, the Coordinating Minister for Political Affairs and Security and the last Commander of the Armed Forces under Suharto. With Agus Wirahadikusumah, he supported the rise of a known reformer in the army. With regard to independence movements in Papua and Aceh, he at least made clear that some of the grievances in the regions were understandable as well as legitimate and that the government in Jakarta was willing to offer special autonomy rights. Unfortunately most of the reform enthusiasm had dissipated within a few months of Wahid's ascension to the presidency. The military initially seemed to lose ground, but soon managed to recover step by step. Further, the president himself was not always that democratic. He dismissed ministers but was unable to explain his decisions. Confronted with an unruly parliament (which he once described as a 'kindergarten'), he reacted ever more stubbornly. Finally in June 2001, in a kind of *autogolpe*, he even attempted to obtain military consent for the declaration of martial law in order to stay in power.

The downfall of Abdurrahman Wahid epitomized major weaknesses of the system, that is: a still unresolved separation of powers, especially between the legislature and the president as the chief executive; the opportunity for the army leadership to influence, if not determine, the outcome of power struggles at the very centre of Indonesian politics; the bickering of politicians which resulted in a standstill of normal parliamentarian procedures for months; a further delegitimization of political parties; and the ever unclear, hardly provable, but certainly huge role of money politics evinced, for example, by 'Buloggate' and 'Baligate'.[15] The political developments during the presidencies of Habibie and Abdurrahman Wahid thus fit into the model of 'reform through transaction':

> [. . .] because the incumbent elites acquiesce in regime change, reforms through transaction generate political openings for elite competition and subsequently create a stake in the new system for both old and new elites.
> [. . .] the lingering power of the old elites and the loss of identity of the antiauthoritarian coalition, two factors that manifest themselves in the stepwise process of transition, lead to the adoption of institutional rules that are not optimal for democratization. More specifically, the new institutional rules generate repeated clashes between the executive and

legislature and leave a legacy that hinders governability and democratic consolidation.

(Munck and Leff 1999: 210)[16]

The slow fall of Abdurrahman Wahid and his controversial replacement by Megawati indicated from the very beginning her fundamental vulnerability, for she did not rise to power through popular elections but by elitist power battles. This lack of legitimacy was never fully offset by her inherited charisma or by the fact that her party, the PDI-P, had won the elections in 1999.[17] Megawati faced most of the problems which had already plagued the Wahid presidency: an economy still suffering from the devastating Asian crisis, widespread corruption, separatist conflicts, the ill-planned implementation of radical decentralization laws since 2001 and a military unwilling to accept civilian control. During Megawati's tenure conflicts in both Poso and the Moluccas came to an end but the situation in Aceh and Papua worsened, not least because she tried to maintain a united, centralized Greater Indonesia (*Indonesia Raya*) and, to this end, helped the armed forces to gain new strength. She supported the implementation of martial law in Aceh and the division of Papua into three provinces, apparently a move to weaken the independence movement. She even backed the election of Sutiyoso as governor of Jakarta even though the general was implicated in the attack on the PDI headquarters in 1996 (AJI/FORUM-ASIA/ ISAI 1997).

Nevertheless, major constitutional reforms were passed during her incumbency (Ellis 2005) and the power of the legislature has been significantly strengthened since 2002. Moreover, the military lost their reserved seats in 2004; the MPR now consists entirely of elected representatives – the members of the DPR and the members of the new regional chamber, the DPD (*Dewan Perwakilan Daerah* or Regional Representative Council). The president and vice president are elected as one ticket in a direct election. Newly established under Megawati were a Constitutional Court with powers of judicial review of legislation, a Corruption Eradication Commission, an Ombudsman's Commission, numerous auditing bodies and specialist anti-corruption courts. These reforms were a major step towards a more stable and balanced democratic regime. The relation between the executive and the legislature is now better defined and the re-emergence of a kind of 'delegative democracy',[18] like that under Abdurrahman Wahid, has become less probable. Nevertheless, some of the reform measures are still incomplete; the DPD, for instance, does not wield the usual veto power of a second chamber.

Moreover, disillusionment with political parties and power-hungry wheeler-dealers in the parliaments grew among the electorate. In 2004, voters responded by punishing established parties. The outcome was the sudden invigoration of the hitherto ailing PD (*Partai Demokrat*, Democrat Party) as well as the emergence of the Islamist PKS (*Partai Keadilan Sejahtera*, Justice and Welfare Party) as the strongest party in a few major cities, inter alia in the capital Jakarta. The first direct presidential elections in 2004 (Ananta, Arifin and Suryadinata 2005) witnessed a tendency toward personalization, enhanced by the usage of professional campaign advisors and the increasing impact of mass media. General Susilo Bambang Yudhoyono was elected because he imparted a perception of being above the bickering of political parties. When Yusuf Kalla became Golkar chairman in December 2004 and steered the party towards the new government, the president gained a sufficient majority in the national parliament. But a clear distinction between government and opposition is still lacking. The cabinet included representatives of almost all major parties, continuing the party cartel approach which already characterized the 'rainbow coalitions' of Susilo's predecessors B.J. Habibie, Abdurrahman Wahid and Megawati Sukarnoputri. So far, further military reforms are postponed and past human rights abuses are investigated only tentatively. The only palpable success is the peaceful solution of the Aceh conflict, and ten years after the fall of Suharto the state of democracy is still dubious. To sum up, the unravelling of the New Order resulted in new laws on political parties, on parliaments, on parliamentary and presidential elections, and on decentralization, amongst others. A range of new institutions were introduced and 'the rules of the game' were newly defined. But to many observers, sweeping institutional reforms were hardly accompanied by fundamental reconfigurations of power groups. Although Chinese and *pribumi* (indigenous) entrepreneurs lost parts of their business empires due to the financial crisis, almost the same tycoons – most of them tarnished by long-standing collaboration with New Order politico-bureaucrats – prevail up to this day. At both the national and local levels old networks have been dissolved but, as a rule, not yet replaced by genuinely democratic coalitions. At all levels, money and violence have become major means to allocate government offices and varied spoils linked to them. The civil society still seems to be emaciated; in this vein, Törnquist captures major characteristics of Indonesia's current form of democracy:

> For although predominantly 'pacted' or negotiated transitions at elite level, followed by top-down crafting of 'good' rights and institutions have introduced important civil and political rights as well as general elections, they have not altered the dominance of the upper classes and their practices. Equally problematic is that none of the opposing popular oriented perspectives have evolved into forceful and viable alternatives. Civic activists have often played a crucial role in the initial dismantling of dictatorship and the introduction of democracy, but thereafter they have been coopted typically into clientelist parties or confined to direct practices in civil society at the periphery of the state, government and business.
>
> (Törnquist 2006: 227)

## THE STRUCTURE OF THIS BOOK

This cursory overview gives a first impression of the mixed results of the transition to electoral democracy and the attempts at democratic deepening. In the following, this volume tries to convey a more detailed picture of the consolidation period. Inspired by Linz and Stepan (1996) and Wolfgang Merkel (1998), we address the question of democratic deepening and political reforms in four arenas or at four levels: central state institutions, political parties and the party system, veto actors, and civil society. Democratic deepening means that all relevant groups within a society increasingly regard the main political institutions as the only legitimate means in the contest for political power. A democracy is consolidated when no relevant political, military or economic player is mobilizing his or her resources against the democratic game. Structurally, no authoritarian enclaves are to remain; that is, no relevant corporate actors such as the military, religious groups or financial, business and agrarian oligarchies should mobilize against the new political system and act outside the democratic arena.

At the level of *state institutions*, Indonesia has witnessed major changes since 1998. Before, political power was radically centralized in the hands of the neo-patrimonial ruler Suharto. This radically changed with the subsequent democratization and decentralization reforms, and in 1998–99 the role of Parliament vis à vis the President was strengthened. The second wave of reforms changed the system of checks and balances with the introduction of direct presidential elections. In this vein, *Patrick Ziegenhain* describes the shifting role of the Indonesian legislature during democratization. Under New Order rule it mostly served as an instrument of the regime coalition. Today, Parliament is no longer a mere rubber-stamp and instead is one of the key power centres with the President requiring the support of major segments of the political elite represented in the House. Although the role of the legislature has changed greatly since 1998, it is still marked by a range of deficiencies. Decision-making is extraordinarily slow as MPs debate – according to traditional practice – until a compromise is reached that everybody can accept (*musyawarah dan mufakat*). Moreover, MPs get their jobs because of good connections to party elites and/or with the help of payments during the process of nominating electoral candidates; logically, they seek 'reimbursement' as soon as they begin working in the DPR. But 'money politics' also affects other dimensions of law-making: 'Allegedly ministries, state enterprise executives and other government agencies lubricate the legislative procedures of the DPR with more or less open financial donations to the legislators. Hence, allegations have abounded that particular ministers made payments, which were disguised in fraudulent legal expense accounts, to DPR members.' As a consequence, the public reputation of the DPR sank rapidly. Thus, the body does not sufficiently fulfil the usual representative, legislative, and oversight functions of Parliament.

*Petra Stockmann* describes the difficult and disputed evolution of the rule of law. She shows that there has been an intensive struggle over its implementation between reformers and status quo forces at risk of losing their privileges if reform proceeds. Using a broad definition of 'Rechtsstaat', Stockmann analyses recent constitutional changes, the introduction and work of the Constitutional Court and the implementation of international human rights instruments. Whereas the introduction of free and fair elections has been a major but easy step, the realization of the rule of law remains an uphill struggle. Stockmann concludes that although progress has been made in recent years, impunity for human rights violators still persists. Indonesia still has to go a long way to build up the functioning judicial sector necessary for the 'Rechtsstaat' to successfully protect citizens from abuses of state power.

The findings about the dysfunctional role of the judicial sector are partly confirmed by *Sofie Arjon Schütte* who investigates the battle against corruption in Indonesia. Currently, it is undermining the effectiveness of democratic institutions and may, in the end, erode their legitimacy. After estimating the extent of corruption, Schütte assesses the institutional changes in the fight against it. Despite widespread corruption-fighting rhetoric institutions still lack clout and the remnants of patrimonial rule are still deeply ingrained in the state apparatus. Patronage still constitutes the greatest obstacle. In this regard, Schütte highlights the importance of civil society initiatives that succeeded in making a few corruption cases public in the last few years.

*Marco Bünte* looks at the vertical distribution of power within Indonesia's new institutional framework. He analyses Indonesia's protracted decentralization reforms and its multiple consequences for the young democracy. He shows that the devolution of state power has been a protracted bargaining process between centralistic and local forces. With the absence of a strong rule of law, the legal framework was often abused by alliances of politicians, bureaucrats and private interests for rent-seeking activities. Moreover, he illustrates that decentralization had a number of side effects, such as the rise of corruption and money politics, the consolidation of local oligarchies and the revival of primordialism. All in all, it has led to a severe weakening of the Indonesian state, which has been used by the nationalist elite to slow down (in some fields even subvert) the decentralization process. Although decentralization has been intended to bring democracy to lower levels of government, the use of intimidation, discrimination and political violence show that formal political spaces opened up by democratization and decentralization have been captured by local elites.

*Marcus Mietzner* adds to this discussion by an analysis of the quality of local elections. He explores the impact of direct elections at the provincial, district and sub-district levels on power configurations. New laws on local elections introduced in October 2004 stipulated that from June 2005 onwards, governors, district heads and mayors were to be elected directly. According to Mietzner, these reforms reshaped local politics in that they provided a new mechanism of vertical accountability. The elections proved to be highly competitive with an incumbency turnover rate of 40 per cent. Even though almost all competitors belonged to old established elites, the electorate favoured relatively 'clean' politicians. Candidates from the military generally did not fare well; voters preferred skilful technocrats with proven track records. Moreover, the much feared sectarianism and politicization of primordial loyalties did not take place. In sum, he demonstrates that direct polls have introduced a new tool of vertical accountability and, therefore, enhanced the quality of Indonesia's young democracy. But he also hints at major weaknesses of political parties. To secure nomination, candidates did not have to show a strong commitment to programmatic objectives but instead needed to offer money so that local party branches could fill their war chests. Candidates, mostly career bureaucrats, wealthy businesspeople as well as party politicians, and members of parliament belonging to oligarchic elites, used political parties to compete for office; that is, to access to vast financial resources.

This fits into the analysis by *Andreas Ufen* who investigates the role of political parties at the *intermediate level*. He shows that parties nowadays in some respects contribute to a deepening of democracy. This judgement, however, has to be put into perspective. The contribution is indicated by a relatively low polarization of the party system and a moderate volatility of voting. The constellation of political forces is quite stable and continuities between the party system of the 1950s and the current one are evident. There are no influential anti-system parties and even the Islamist parties keep a low profile with regard to the politicization of religion. The elections at the national and local levels were generally conducted freely and fairly without significant disturbances. Although the party system is fragmented it also means that no one party – especially not the once hegemonic Golkar party – is able to control the political process. Yet, all these remarkable developments are to be seen against the background of conspicuous weaknesses of parties indicated by a number of features: the rise of presidential or presidentialized parties with weakened political machines; the stimulation of populism and the surging impact of mass media and modern campaign techniques; the authoritarianism and personalism within parties with powerful 'advisors' and executives which punish unruly members, marginalize internal opposition and increase factionalization; the dominance of 'money politics' with bought candidacies, MPs acting as brokers for private companies, businessmen taking over party chairmanships and billionaire financiers determining policies behind the scenes; poor political platforms; decreasing party loyalties; the cartel-like cooperation of parties as indicated by rainbow coalitions, an unorganized opposition, the *musyawarah dan mufakat* mechanism and the collusion in tolerating corruption; and, finally, the emergence of new, powerful local elites, inter alia invigorated by the *pilkada*.

*Dirk Tomsa* confirms many of these findings. By focusing on the former New Order regime party Golkar, he is able to disentangle major dynamics of party politics and elite reconfiguration after the fall of Suharto. Tomsa highlights patronage-driven factionalism and 'money politics' and the under-mining of formal institutions by powerful leaders. Thus, parties are poorly institutionalized; the only exceptions being the Justice and Welfare Party PKS and Golkar. Whereas the PKS's success rests upon an elaborate ideol-ogy, Golkar relies on an impressive organizational apparatus, particularly on the Outer Islands where the party commands control over vast patronage networks. The party still benefits from its once hegemonic position during Indonesia's New Order, so much so that even today party institutionalization is uneven. Nevertheless, there is still enough space for genuine competition as demonstrated by the presidential convention and the national party con-gress. During the past few years even Golkar fell victim to processes of de-institutionalization. Formal regulations are often not mandatory and are manipulated at will by party elites. Furthermore, internal frictions in the central board and over-centralization of decision-making threaten organiza-tional cohesion.

At the *level of veto actors*, both partners in the New Order regime coalition – the military and the conglomerates – came under intense pressure to reform. *Jun Honna* explores the changing political role of the Indonesian military. He demonstrates that it has adapted to the new political landscape and uses the security discourse to legitimize its future involvement in politics. Officers have preserved considerable powers and are able to strongly influence major policy decision. Although military leaders accept the need for civilians to manage politics, they still define themselves as patriotic 'guardians of the nation' and the Constitution, and persistently resist civilian control. Honna points to a range of diluted reforms: the sociopolitical section of the armed forces (TNI) was eliminated, but at the same time its political role was over-taken by the territorial commands; the military is no longer one of the pillars of Golkar, nevertheless officers continue to collaborate with political party elites; military businesses have long since been scheduled to come under civil-ian control, but the reform policy is continually obstructed; Police and TNI are separated by law, but in reality the distinction is often obscured. Today, regional military commands act quite autonomously. All these are part of the *dwifungsi* legacy of the TNI. Due to the lack of state capacity the TNI's NKRI (Unitary State of the Republic of Indonesia) discourse is partly con-vincing for the public. But in contrast to its self-claimed guardianship role, the military has not effectively controlled the violence in May 1998, in East Timor in 1999, and the regional conflicts in Aceh, Maluku, Ambon and Papua; it instead incited some of these violent outbursts. Honna even sus-pects that the military has manipulated communal strife in its own favour, evidenced by the increasing number of territorial units.

*Christian Chua* looks at another important veto actor: the Chinese con-glomerates. Under Suharto they were the politically vulnerable cronies and 'pariah' capitalists. Chua shows that in the aftermath of the Asian crisis and the fall of Suharto the expected restructuring of big business was botched. Bank recapitalization, debt settlement and asset sales in favour of most conglomerates undermined the reform process from the very beginning. After initial insecurity with respect to their fate under the new form of government, big business quickly recovered and dictated the terms of rehabilitation. Entrepreneurs turned out to be highly flexible in the new environment: whereas under the New Order they had to bribe the upper echelons in the neo-patrimonial system, they now tampered with parliamentarians during the law-making process and started to approach bureaucrats and politicians at all levels. *Otonomi daerah* was, thus, transformed into a mechanism where 'diffuse patronage networks replicated the old systems of patronage in mini-aturised form'. According to Chua, some surprising judicial decisions appear to have been bought, for example, the anti-monopoly commission KPPU that regularly ruled in favour of prosecuted business interests. He sees a major shift in the balance of power between political and economic elites: the latter 'will eventually gain the upper hand over the political sphere'. To him, demo-cratic consolidation was essentially a 'consolidation of capitalist power' and real institutional structures were not significantly altered.

At the *level of mass support and civil society*, two articles in this volume address the contribution of civil society to democratic deepening and reveal its inherent weakness and ambiguity in Indonesia. The third article looks at civil society and anti-regime forces in the war-torn provinces of Aceh and Papua. *Mikaela Nyman* depicts the characteristics of Indonesian civil society from a social movement perspective. According to Nyman, it is especially the deep penetration of the New Order state into society through repression and ideology that explains the inherent weakness of civil groups under the demo-cratic framework. Before civil society can act as agent for change it has to overcome internal rivalry and primordialism. It is also often too fragmented into diverse issue groups to act as catalyst for change. The labour movement has fallen short of expectation, whilst the women's movement has also not had a significant influence in recent years. Yet, given Indonesia's repressive past, civil society has made remarkable progress. This could be seen in its contribution to the fight against corruption (see also Schütte's chapter). Although its organizations have not built a coherent reformist movement, the unprecedented freedom of press and association have caused civil society to thrive, fuelling hope that it may provide a viable alternative for further democratization.

*Bob S. Hadiwinata* sheds light on the highly ambiguous character of some civil society organizations. Based on the observations of different groups involved in ethnic and religious conflicts, he makes it clear that a vibrant 'un-civil society' is detrimental to the consolidation of democracy. Taking the Muslim extremist movement Laskar Jihad and the extremely ethno-nationalist organization LMMDD-KT (Dayak Deliberative Council of Central Kalimantan) as case studies, Hadiwinata illustrates the counterpro-ductive impact of these groups on democracy. They were able to spread ethnic and religious hatred in ethnically and religiously sensitive areas, which triggered political violence. The militancy of Laskar Jihad served as a strong signal to Indonesian Christians to acknowledge Muslim hegemony. Similarly, the lack of remorse shown by the Dayak elite in the aftermath of the Sampit massacre conveyed the message to other minorities in the region that they must accept Dayak supremacy. These parochial features within a 'bad civil society' have the potential to erode the trust between the ethnic and religious groups on the archipelago and thus undermine the efforts of democratic consolidation.

*Felix Heiduk* adds to this discussion by looking at the conflict-ridden provinces of Aceh and Papua. He argues that the democratization of the political system in 1999 did not bring lasting peace to these areas and that the ongoing conflict prevented civilian institutions from taking roots. Heiduk shows that democratization did not reach the ground and the population consequently became increasingly alienated from the state. In both areas of conflict repression, state-sponsored violence and continued human rights violations by the military contributed to a sense of grievance and frustration within the people. This triggered further unrest, leading to a vicious circle of continuous violence and repression. The Special Autonomy Laws were never thoroughly implemented and the ongoing presence of the military served as a sign that Jakarta was breaking its promises. While very positive developments could be witnessed in post-tsunami Aceh, the division of Papua into three provinces intensified the frictions between the Papuan population and the central government.

## CONCLUSION

The emerging picture of the state of Indonesia's young democracy is very complex, and the collection of essays in this volume presents a mixture of reform successes and failures. While progress has undoubtedly been made, the characterization of Indonesia's current political system is still contested. The democracy has been classified as 'predatory' (Robison 2002), 'patrimonial' (Webber 2006), one without effective government (McLeod 2005) and as simultaneously exhibiting political reforms and lacking substantive democratic quality (Aspinall 2005b). If we take Dahl's concept of polyarchy as a conceptual yardstick – comprising the components of free and fair elections, inclusive suffrage and citizenship, freedom of expression and information, and associational autonomy – Indonesia can be described as a democracy. Since 1998 civil liberties and political rights have been constitutionally enshrined and enforced, as far as economic constraints and a weak security apparatus allow. Press freedom, for example, is widely guaranteed and independent political parties, trade unions and professional organizations have been formed. In 1999 and 2004, sufficiently free and fair national elections were held. Turnout at all elections exceeded 80 per cent of eligible votes and political parties have not seriously contested their outcome. The introduction of direct elections of local government heads added another tool of accountability and has thus enhanced the quality of Indonesia's young democracy. The reforms of the military still wield some ambiguous results: it remains a powerful but far from omnipotent player after 1998. Efforts to bring the military under civilian control and return it to the barracks have enjoyed some, but by no means complete, success. On the one hand, the *dwifungsi* (dual function) doctrine and military representation in parliaments has been abolished but, on the other, the TNI has not yet abolished its territorial structure or restricted its business activities. Thus, it has managed to preserve some privileges of the New Order period and has managed to find a new role under the guidance of the preservation of the unitary state. Whether Indonesia can be categorized as a tutelary democracy is contested. The critical question would be whether the military could prevail over a (directly-elected) president and majority in the Parliament on an issue where the two sides have intensely held and conflicting interests.

The most important failure of reform and obstacle to the consolidation of a liberal democratic framework is the inability to ensure the rule of law. Although a Constitutional Court has been newly established, Indonesia is still lacking important components of a 'Rechtsstaat'. The judiciary is undermined by corruption, which is itself a remnant of the neo-patrimonial nature of the Suharto regime (Webber 2006: 409). Consequently, the process of democratic deepening is still in its infancy and already full of shortcomings, missed opportunities and setbacks. The breakdown of authoritarianism has entailed the establishment of an array of organizations which do not fit in with the overly optimistic models that revolve around restructuring civil society under conditions of political liberalization. Because of authoritarian remnants and the insecurities resulting from the collapse of the New Order, one might argue that a 'low quality democracy' (see also Mietzner in this volume) has unfolded. Human rights are acknowledged but in many cases not legally enforced, and past human rights violations are seldom dealt with. An effective monopoly of force did not exist during the first transition years and currently in many parts of the archipelago the security situation is still fragile. The military has secured some enclaves and from time to time has exerted excessive influence on state policies. Moreover, civil society has only a weak impact on government policies and religion has been further politicized.

## NOTES

1 Polyarchy, literally 'government of the many', is considered to be the basic characterization of existing democracies. It is, on the one hand, remote from the ideal form of democracy but, on the other hand, it has no defects to the extent that the democratic character might be denied. The ideal form of a democracy is reserved for those political systems which are almost completely responsible to all its citizens.
2 On the relationship between the rule of law and democracy, see O'Donnell 2004 and Merkel 2004.

3 O'Donnell calls these dimensions democracy, liberalism and republicanism (O'Donnell 1999:33).

4 For an overview over the current trends in democratization, see Croissant and Merkel 2004; Freedom House 2007; and BTI 2006.

5 The minimalist definition goes back to Juan Linz who defined consolidation as a state of affairs 'in which none of the major political actors, parties or organized interests, forces or institutions, consider that there is any alternative to democratic processes to gain power [. . .]. No political institution or group has a claim to veto the action of democratically elected decision makers. [. . .] to put it simply, democracy must be seen as the "only game in town" ' (Linz 1990: 156).

6 It is controversial because it carries a strong teleological flavour. Yet, many scholars have accepted the utility of the consolidation concept and the type of consolidation presented by Linz.

7 On the difficulties of transition after neo-patrimonial rule, see Bratton and van der Walle (1994).

8 See the definition by Chehabi and Linz (1998: 7): 'It is based on personal rulership, but loyalty to the ruler is motivated not by his embodying or articulating an ideology, nor by a unique personal mission, nor by any charismatic qualities, but by a mixture of fear and rewards to his collaborators. [. . .] The binding norms and relations of bureaucratic administration are constantly subverted by arbitrary personal decisions of the ruler, which he does not feel constrained to justify in ideological terms. [. . .] The staff of such a ruler is constituted [. . .] by people chosen directly by the ruler.'

9 On patrimonialism and sultanism, see Weber 1972; on neo-patrimonialism in general, see Eisenstadt 1973.

10 At the same time, since the late 1980s, the whole society as well as the state apparatus were Islamized (Hefner 2000; Porter 2002; Effendy 2003). That means, the multi-religious state philosophy Pancasila was preserved as lowest common denominator, but Islamic leaders, associations and ideas became increasingly important. The result was the establishment of a very influential organization of Islamic intellectuals (ICMI) in 1990, the passing of controversial laws on sharia courts and education, the establishment of an Islamic bank and insurance company, and the growing presence of widely known orthodox Muslims in universities, the administration, Golkar and the cabinet. Even in the army, *santri* got the opportunity to achieve highest ranks.

11 This is, once again, the transition to electoral democracy. Others define transition as the period between the dissolution of the authoritarian regime and the institution of a 'consolidated democracy' (see Webber 2006). For Aspinall (2005b), the 2004 polls marked the end of Indonesia's tumultuous political transition.

12 For the first phase after Suharto, see Emmerson 1999; Budiman, Hatley and Kingsbury 1999; Forrester 1999; Lloyd and Smith 2001; Kingsbury and Budiman 2001.

13 The four were pressed by students to form a presidium. They declined to do so, but instead signed the 'Ciganjur Declaration' on 10 November 1998 demanding free elections until May 1999, an end to ABRI's *dwifungsi* until 2004, an inquiry into the wealth of Suharto and the dissolution of the notorious Pam Swakarsa (Self-Service Security Force).

14 On the Wahid era, see Kawamura 2000; Törnquist 2000; Kingsbury and Budiman 2001.

15 These were the two scandals involving some top politicians like Abdurrahman Wahid, Akbar Tanjung from Golkar, Habibie and others.

16 In this vein, Webber (2006: 408) noted that 'opposition moderation was functional

for the democratic transition, but dysfunctional for the quality of the new democracy that emerged from it'.

17 Megawati, although once perceived as reformist, followed in the footsteps of her father when she reversed a few of the reforms initiated by her predecessor. While Abdurrahman Wahid was usually characterized as 'erratic', Megawati gained a questionable reputation as an apathetic, passive president. She was in some ways an old-style Javanese leader like her father more than 40 years before, but without his abilities to mobilize the Indonesian 'rakyat' (people) and invent fancy syncretist ideologies.

18 'Delegative democracies rest on the premise that whoever wins election to the presidency is thereby entitled to govern as he or she sees fit, constrained only by the hard facts of existing power relations and by a constitutionally limited term of office' (O'Donnell 1996: 98). Accountability to institutions like courts and legislatures '[. . .] appears as a mere impediment to the full authority that the president has been delegated to exercise' (O'Donnell 1996: 99). See also: Slater 2004.

## BIBLIOGRAPHY

AJI, FORUM-ASIA and ISAI (1997) *Jakarta Crackdown*, Jakarta: ISAI.

Ananta, A., Arifin, E.N. and Suryadinata, L. (2005) *Emerging Democracy in Indonesia*, Singapore: Institute of Southeast Asian Studies.

Aritonang, D. (1999) *Runtuhnya Rezim daripada Soeharto – Rekaman Perjuangan Mahasiswa Indonesia 1998*, Bandung: Pustaka Hidayah.

Aspinall, E. (2005a) *Opposing Suharto. Compromise, Resistance, and Regime Change in Indonesia*, Stanford: Stanford University Press.

—— (2005b) 'Elections and the Normalization of Politics in Indonesia', *South East Asia Research*, 13 (2): 117–56.

Aspinall, E. and Fealy, G. (eds) (2003) *Local Power and Politics in Indonesia. Decentralisation & Democratisation*, Singapore: Institute of Southeast Asian Studies.

Bachriadi, D., Faryadi, E. and Setiawan, B. (eds) (1997) *Reformasi Agraria – Perubahan Politik, Sengketa, dan Agenda Pembaruan Agraria di Indonesia*, Jakarta: Universitas Indonesia and KPA.

Bendel, P., Croissant, A. and Rüb, F.W. (eds) (2003) *Zwischen Demokratie und Diktatur. Zur Konzeption und Empirie demokratischer Grauzonen*, Opladen: Leske&Budrich.

Bertelsmann Transformation Index (BTI) (2006) Online. Available at HTTP: <http://www.bertelsmann-transformation-index.de/fileadmin/pdf/BTI_2006_Ranking_detailliert.pdf> (accessed 16 June 2007).

Bourchier, D. (1996) *Lineages of Organicist Political Thought in Indonesia*, Diss., Melbourne: Monash University.

—— (2000) 'Habibie's Interregnum: Reformasi, Elections, Regionalism and the Struggle for Power', in C. Manning and P. van Diermen (eds) *Indonesia in transition: social aspects of reformasi and crisis*, Singapore: Institute of Southeast Asian Studies.

Bratton, M. and van der Walle, N. (1994) 'Neopatrimonial Regimes and Political Transitions in Africa', in *World Politics*, 46 (4): 453–89.

Budiman, A., Hatley, B. and Kingsbury, D. (eds) (1999) *Reformasi: Crisis and Change in Indonesia*, Clayton, Australia: Monash Asia Institute.

Bünte, M. (2003) *Regionale Autonomie in Indonesien – Wege zur erfolgreichen Dezentralisierung*, Hamburg: Institut für Asienkunde.

Carothers, T. (2002) 'The End of the Transition Paradigm', *Journal of Democracy*, 13 (1): 5–21.

Chehabi, H. E. and Linz, J.J. (1998) 'A Theory of Sultanism,' in H.E. Chehabi and J.J. Linz (eds), *Sultanistic Regimes*, Baltimore: The Johns Hopkins University Press.

Collier, D. and Levitsky, S. (1997) 'Democracy with Adjectives: Conceptual Innovation in Comparative Research,' *World Politics*, 49 (3): 430–51.

Colombijn, F. and Lindblad, J.T. (2002) (eds) *Roots of violence in Indonesia. Contemporary violence in historical perspective*, Leiden: KITLV Press.

Croissant, A. (2004) 'Introduction: Democratization in the early Twenty-First Century', *Democratization*, 11 (5): 1–9.

Croissant, A. and Merkel, W. (2004) 'Conclusion: Good and Defective Democracies', *Democratization*, 11 (5): 199–213.

Crouch, H. (1979) 'Patrimonialism and Military Rule in Indonesia', *World Politics*, July: 571–87.

Dahl, R. (1971) *Polyarchy. Participation and Opposition*, New York and London: Yale University Press.

Diamond, L. (1999) *Developing Democracy Toward Consolidation*, Baltimore and London: Johns Hopkins University Press.

——— (2002) 'Elections Without Democracy. Thinking About Hybrid Regimes', *Journal of Democracy*, 13 (2): 21–35.

di Palma, G. (1990) *To Craft Democracies. An Essay on Democratic Transitions*, Berkeley/Los Angeles/Oxford: University of California Press.

Effendy, B. (2003) *Islam and the state in Indonesia*, Singapore: Institute of Southeast Asian Studies.

Eisenstadt, S.N. (1973) *Traditional Patrimonialism and Modern Neo-Patrimonialism*, London: Sage Publications.

Eklöf, S. (1999) *Indonesian Politics in Crisis – The Long Fall of Suharto, 1996–98*, Copenhagen: NIAS.

Ellis, A. (2005) *One year after the elections: Is democracy in Indonesia on course?*, Jakarta: IDEA.

Emmerson, D.K. (ed.) (1999) *Indonesia beyond Suharto: Polity, Economy, Society, Transition*, Armonk, New York: M.E. Sharpe.

Engberg, J. and Ersson, S. (2003) 'Illiberal democracy in the "Third World": an empirical enquiry', in J. Haynes (ed.) *Democracy and Political Change in the 'Third World'*, London: Routledge.

Erb, M., Priyambudi S. and Faucher, C. (eds) (2005) *Regionalism in Post-Suharto Indonesia*, London: Routledge.

Forrester, G. (ed.) (1999) *Post-Soeharto Indonesia: Renewal or Chaos?*, Singapore: Institute of Southeast Asian Studies.

Freedom House (2007) *Freedom in the World 2007*, New York: Freedom House.

Goodfellow, R. (1995) *Api Dalam Sekam: The New Order and the Ideology of Anti-Communism*, Working Paper No. 95, Melbourne: Monash University Press.

Hadenius, A. (1992) *Democracy and Development*, Cambridge: Cambridge University Press.

Hadiz, V. (1997) *Workers and the State in New Order Indonesia*, London: Routledge.

Hefner, R.W. (2000) *Civil Islam, Muslims and Democratization in Indonesia*, New Jersey: Princeton University Press.

Heryanto, A. (2006) *State Terrorism and Political Identity in Indonesia. Fatally Belonging*, London: Routledge.

Hill, H. (1996) *The Indonesian Economy since 1966: Southeast Asia's emerging Giant*, Cambridge: Cambridge University Press.

Huntington, S. (1991) *The Third Wave. Democratization in the late 20th Century*, Norman, London: University of Oklahoma Press.

Karl, T.L. (1995) 'The Hybrid Regimes of Central America', *Journal of Democracy*, 6 (3): 72–86.

Kawamura, K. (2000) 'Political Reform in the Post-Soeharto Era', in Y. Sato (ed.) *Indonesia Entering a New Era. Abdurrahman Wahid Government and Its Challenge*, Chiba: Institute of Developing Economies.

King, D.Y. (1982) 'Indonesia's New Order as a Bureaucratic Polity, a Neopatrimonial Regime or a Bureaucratic Authoritarian Regime: What Difference Does It Make?', in B. Anderson and A. Kahin (eds) *Interpreting Indonesian Politics: Thirteen Contributions to the Debate*, Ithaca, New York: Cornell University Press.

Kingsbury, D. and Budiman, A. (eds) (2001) *Indonesia – The Uncertain Transition*, Adelaide: Crawford House Publishing.

Kitschelt, H. (2000) 'Linkages between citizens and Politicians in Democratic Polities', *Comparative Political Studies*, 33 (67), 845–79.

Lauth, H.J.(2004) *Demokratie und Demokratiemessung*, Opladen: VS Verlag.

Levitsky, S. and Way, L. (2002) 'The Rise of Competitive Authoritarianism', *Journal of Democracy*, 13 (2), 51–65.

Linz, J.J. (1990) 'Transitions to Democracy', *The Washington Quarterly*, 13 (3), 143–64.

—— (2000) *Totalitarian and Authoritarian Regimes*, Boulder, Colorado: Lynne Rienner.

Linz, J.J. and Stepan, A. (1996) *Problems of Democratic Transition and Consolidation*, Baltimore, MD: Johns Hopkins University Press.

Lloyd, G. and Smith, S. (eds) (2001) *Indonesia Today: Challenges of History*, Singapore: Institute of Southeast Asian Studies.

Lucas, A. (1997) 'Land Disputes, the Bureaucracy and Local Resistance in Indonesia', in J. Schiller and B. Martin-Schiller (eds) *Imagining Indonesia: Cultural Politics and Political Culture*, Athens: Ohio University Center for International Studies.

Malley, M. (2000) 'Beyond Democratic Elections: Indonesia Embarks on a Protracted Transition', *Democratization*, 7 (3): 153–80.

—— (2003) 'New Rules, Old Structures and the Limits of Democratic Decentralization', in E. Aspinall and G. Fealey (eds) *Local Power and Politics in Indonesia. Decentralization and Democratization*, Singapore: Institute of Southeast Asian Studies.

Manning, C. and van Diermen, P. (eds) (2000) *Indonesia in transition: social aspects of reformasi and crisis*, Singapore: Institute of Southeast Asian Studies.

McLeod, R. (2005) The Struggle to Regain Effective Government under Democracy in Indonesia, *Bulletin of Indonesian Economic Studies*, 41 (3): 367–87.

Merkel, W. (1998) 'The Consolidation of Post-Autocratic Democracies: A Multi-Level Model', *Democratization*, 5 (3): 33–67.

—— (1999) *Systemtransformation*, Opladen: Leske&Budrich.

—— (2004) 'Embedded and Defective Democracies', *Democratization*, 11 (5): 33–55.

Merkel, W. and Croissant, A. (2000) 'Formale und informale Institutionen in defekten Demokratien', *Politische Vierteljahresschrift (PVS)*, 41 (1): 3–30.

Merkel, W., Puhle, H.-J., Croissant, A., Eicher, C. and Thierry, P. (2003) *Defekte Demokratie. Band 1: Theorie*, Opladen: Leske&Budrich.

Mietzner, M. (2000) 'The 1999 General Session: Wahid, Megawati and the Fight for the Presidency', in C. Manning and P. van Diermen (eds) *Indonesia in transition: social aspects of reformasi and crisis*, Singapore: Institute of Southeast Asian Studies.

Munck, G.L. and C.S. Leff (1999) 'Modes of Transition and Democratization. South America and Eastern Europe in Comparative Perspective', in L. Anderson (ed.) *Transitions to Democracy*, New York: Columbia University Press.

National Democratic Institute (2001) *The Fundamental Changes that Nobody Noticed: The MPR Annual Session, November 2001*. Online. Available HTTP: <http://www.accessdemocracy.org/usr_search.asp?SearchType=adv&DocURL= doc&DocType=0&lang_all=on&RC=35&TS=0&Author=0&Publisher=1&Date =0&keywords> (accessed 17 August 2002).

O'Donnell, G. (1996) 'Delegative Democracy', in L. Diamond and M.F. Plattner (eds) *The Global Resurgence of Democracy*, Baltimore and London: Johns Hopkins University Press.

—— (1999) 'Horizontal Accountability in New Democracies', in A. Schedler, L. Diamond and M.F. Plattner (eds) *The Self-Restraining State. Power and Accountability in New Democracies*, Boulder: Lynne Rienner.

—— (2004) 'Why the Rule of Law Matters', *Journal of Democracy*, 15 (4): 32–46.

O'Donnell, G. and P. Schmitter (1986) *Transitions from Authoritarian Rule: Tentative Conclusions about Uncertain Democracies*, Baltimore: Johns Hopkins University Press.

O'Rourke, K. (2002) *Reformasi: The Struggle for Power in Post-Soeharto Indonesia*, Crows Nest: Allen & Unwin.

Porter, D. (2002) *Managing Politics and Islam in Indonesia*, London and New York: RoutledgeCurzon.

Prasetyo, S.A., Priyono, A.E. and Törnquist, O. (eds) (2003) *Indonesia's Post-Suharto Democracy Movement*, Jakarta: Demos.

Przeworski, A. (1991) *Democracy and the Market: Political and Economic Reforms in Eastern Europe and Latin America*, Cambridge: Cambridge University Press.

Przeworski, A. et al. (1996) 'What makes democracies endure?', *Journal of Democracy*, 7 (1): 39–55.

Rinakit, S. (2005) *The Indonesian Military after the New Order*, Singapore: Institute of Southeast Asian Studies.

Robison, R. (2002) 'What sort of democracy? Predatory and neo-liberal agendas in Indonesia', in: C. Kinnvall and K. Jönnson (eds) *Globalization and Democratization in Asia: The Construction of Identity*, London: Routledge.

Rose, R. and Doh C. Shin (2001) 'Democratization Backwards: The Problem of Third-Wave Democracies', *British Journal of Political Science*, 31 (2): 331–54.

Rüb, F.W. (2003) 'Hybride Regime – Politikwissenschaftliches Chamäleon oder neuer Regimetypus? Begriffliche und konzeptionelle Überlegungen zum neuen Pessimismus in der Transitologie', in P. Bendel, P., A. Croissant and F.W. Rüb (eds) *Zwischen Demokratie und Diktatur. Zur Konzeption und Empirie demokratischer Grauzonen*, Opladen: Leske&Budrich.

Sato, Y. (2000) 'Birth of a New Government: Background, Features and Tasks', in Y. Sato (ed.) *Indonesia Entering a New Era. Abdurrahman Wahid Government and Its Challenge*, Chiba: Institute of Developing Economies.

Schedler, A. (1998) 'What is democratic consolidation?', *Journal of Democracy*, 9 (2): 91–107.

—— (2001) 'Taking Uncertainty Seriously: The Blurred Boundaries of Democratic Transition and Consolidation,' *Democratization*, 8 (4): 1–22.

—— (ed.) (2006) *Electoral Authoritarianism: The Dynamics of Unfree Competition*, Boulder, London: Lynne Rienner.

Schedler, A., Diamond, L. and Plattner, M.F. (eds) (1999) *The Self-Restraining State. Power and Accountability in New Democracies*, Boulder, Colorado: Lynne Rienner.

Schmitter, P. and Karl, T.L. (1991) 'What democracy is . . . and is not', *Journal of Democracy*, 2 (3): 75–88.

Schulte Nordholt, N.G. (1987) 'Neo-Patrimonial State in Indonesia', in M. Heper (ed.) *The State and Public Bureaucracies – A Comparative Perspective*, New York, Westport, Connecticut, London: Greenwood Press.

Schumpeter, J. (1975) *Capitalism, Socialism and Democracy*, New York: Harper and Row.

Sen, A. (1999) 'Democracy as a Universal Value', *Journal of Democracy*, 10 (3): 3–17.

Shevtsova, L. (2001) 'Russia's Hybrid Regime', *Journal of Democracy* 12 (4): 65–70.

Slater, D. (2004) 'Indonesia's Accountability Trap: Party Cartels and Presidential Power after Democratic Transition', *Indonesia*, 78: 61–92.

Snyder, R. (2006) 'Beyond Electoral Authoritarianism: The Spectrum of Non-Democratic Regimes', in A. Schedler (ed.) *Electoral Authoritarianism: The Dynamics of Unfree Competition*, Boulder: Lynne Rienner, pp. 219–33.

Suryadinata, L. (2002) *Elections and Politics in Indonesia*, Singapore: Institute of Southeast Asian Studies.

Törnquist, O. (2000) 'Dynamics of Indonesian democratisation', *Third World Quarterly*, 21 (3): 383–423.

—— (2006) 'Assessing Democracy from Below: A Framework and Indonesian Pilot Study', *Democratization*, 13 (2): 227–55.

Ufen, A. (2002) *Herrschaftsfiguration und Demokratisierung in Indonesien (1965–2000)*, Hamburg: Institut für Asienkunde.

Uhlin, A. (1997) *Indonesia and the Third Wave of Democratization: The Indonesian Pro-Democracy Movement in a Changing World*, New York: St. Martins.

van Dijk, C. (2001) *A country in despair. Indonesia between 1997 and 2000*, Leiden: KITLV Press.

van Langenberg, M. (1990) 'The New Order State: Language, Ideology, Hegemony', in A. Budiman (ed.) *The State and Civil Society in Indonesia*, Clayton, Victoria: Monash University, Centre for Southeast Asia Studies.

Webber, D. (2006) 'Consolidated Patrimonial Democracy? Democratization in Post-Suharto Indonesia', *Democratization*, 13 (3): 396–420.

Weber, M. (1972) *Wirtschaft und Gesellschaft*, Tübingen: Mohr.

Wessel, I. and Wimhöfer, G. (eds) (2001) *Violence in Indonesia*, Hamburg: Abera.

Wiarda, H.W. (2001) ' "Transitology" and the Need for New Theory', *East European Politics and Societies*, 15 (3): 485–501.

Winters, J.A. (1996) *Power in Motion: Capital Mobility and the Indonesian State*, Ithaca: Cornell University Press.

Zakaria, F. (1997) 'The Rise of Illiberal Democracy', *Foreign Affairs*, 76: 22–43.

# Part I
# The restructuring of core state institutions

# 2 The Indonesian legislature and its impact on democratic consolidation

*Patrick Ziegenhain*

## INTRODUCTION

Since the start of the reform era in 1998, the Indonesian legislature (Dewan Perwakilan Rakyat, DPR) has gradually become one of the key actors of political decision-making in the archipelago. However, the debate in the DPR on fuel prices in March 2005 illustrated its persistent shortcomings. At that time, the Indonesian government led by President Susilo Bambang Yudhoyono announced a hike in domestic fuel prices by an average of 29 per cent. Many factions in the DPR criticized the government's policy, expressing the popular demand to stop the fuel price hike. A brawl among legislators ended the second day of the plenary session, 'leaving the public disgusted by the immaturity of their representatives' (*The Jakarta Post Online*, 17 March 2005). Those who disagreed with the government's fuel policy, particularly from the PDI-P opposition, started bombarding the DPR leaders with objections and complained that the plenary session leaders were not taking into account the objections expressed by their faction.

The supporters of the government proposal responded with loud retorts of their own in the general direction of those who opposed. After DPR chairman Agung Laksono (Golkar) unilaterally put an end to the debate, some PDI-P faction members rushed to the raised podium to protest the chairman's decision. Seeing the DPR chairman physically threatened, a number of Golkar legislators scrambled up on the platform and jostled and argued with the PDI-P members (Wadrianto 2005). Other legislators followed suit and the melee was on, complete with shoving and a few punches by dozens of other legislators eager to join in or diffuse the fray in front of the chairman's platform. Surrounding the speaker's dais, 'their actions and taunts were more akin to professional wrestlers than learned gentlemen entrusted with the affairs of state' (*The Jakarta Post Online*, 18 March 2005). The violence lasted for several minutes with some people knocked over, but in the end nobody was seriously injured. That the whole incident was caught on TV cameras and broadcasted hourly on television only made matters worse.

This scenario occurring in the DPR did not befit a legislature's ideal role but rather depicted the prevailing weaknesses of Indonesian legislators several years after the regime change in 1998. The Indonesians' trust in their democratic institutions could not have been helped by such behaviour. However, the legitimacy of state institutions is a crucial point for the acceptance of democratic order, particularly in countries that have recently witnessed a democratic transition process such as Indonesia. After the end of the authoritarian Orde Baru in 1998, the power of the once-dominating executive branch of government has been reduced significantly in favour of the national legislature.

The democratization process in Indonesia evolved as a pacted transition, during which moderate opposition reformers made an unwritten compromise with the former elites. The latter, such as the former quasi-government party Golkar were not excluded from the new political system but in fact became powerful players. The Indonesian legislature, in which the transformed Golkar faction was and is a major force, thus played an ambiguous role in the transition process. On one hand, the broad inclusion of the various hetero-geneous groups in the decision-making processes of the legislature brought about a relatively smooth and peaceful transition. On the other, critics have complained about the sluggish pace of reform and the continuation of undemocratic political traditions.

As the new democracy in Indonesia is not yet firmly established, further efforts to deepen democracy have to be carried out by the different actors and institutions. It is not only dependent on the performance of the presi-dency, the military, the media, religious groups and civil society, but also on the Indonesian legislature.

Two free and fair elections in 1999 and 2004 led to the creation of a democratic legislature. However, democratically elected parliaments alone – even when they play a decisive role in the political system – do not necessarily guarantee democracy. Nevertheless, they are one important factor in measur-ing the democratic quality of a given political system. In this case, it is helpful to analyse the fulfilment of the main functions of parliaments such as repre-sentation, legislation and oversight. Additionally, it is necessary to assess the professionalism of the elected legislators, which is indispensable for efficient and effective parliamentary work. In order to analyse the contribution of the DPR to democratic consolidation in Indonesia, the article will start with an outline of theoretical assumptions on the role of legislatures in democratiza-tion processes. Then, after a short description of the political role of the DPR since 1998, the fulfilment of the aforementioned parliamentary functions will be evaluated.[1]

## DEMOCRATIC CONSOLIDATION AND THE ROLE OF LEGISLATURES

Generally, scholars define democratic consolidation, among other factors, as a regime that comprises popular legitimacy, diffusion of democratic values, neutralization of anti-system actors, civilian control over the military, the elimination of authoritarian enclaves and judicial reform (Schedler 1998: 91f.). In a mid- to long-term perspective, the alleviation of poverty, economic stabilization, independent media, and an effective education system are also aspects that contribute to the stability of the new democratic order. However, in order to establish a well-working democracy other features are necessary to improve the routinization of politics: an appropriate and transparent organization of functional interests, the creation or modification of political parties, the creation or stabilization of electoral rules, as well as the formation of an efficient and effective system of government in which the state institutions perform their constitutional tasks within a system of checks and balances. One of these state institutions, which is of particular importance for the consolidation of democracy, is the national parliament. Legislatures in developing countries are often regarded by scholars as less important in their respective political systems. Other factors that shape national politics are seen as more influential. The actions of presidents, prime ministers, business executives and military commanders often receive more focus in the analysis of political development. This has led to the premature conclusion that legislatures are sometimes powerful but in most cases they are not the decisive institution for policy output. The research on political development in developing countries is executive-centred; presidents and governments are widely seen as the key actors, whereby legislatures are often neglected. The recent debate about whether a presidential or parliamentary system of government is more suitable for the consolidation of democracy (Lijphart 1992; Linz and Valenzuela 1994; Mainwaring and Shugart 1997) did not focus on legislatures per se, but rather on the system of checks and balances between the executive and the legislative branches of government.

However, it is essential to assess the performance of legislatures since they can contribute decisively to the development of a new democracy. Especially in the consolidation period after the 'founding' elections, legislatures can be regarded as one of the foundation pillars of a new democracy and as a main indicator for the progress of democratic consolidation. The study of political institutions is 'integral to the study of democratization because institutions constitute and sustain democracies' (King 2003: 7).

This requires that parliaments be a strong factor in the political system since 'weak legislatures will neither bring accountability, nor guarantee fair representation' (Close 1995: 14), nor produce a well-balanced and effective legislation. A recently published empirical study of more than 30 post-authoritarian political systems revealed a direct correlation of parliamentary power with democratic consolidation (Fish 2006). According to Steven M. Fish, 'the strength of the national legislature may be a – or even the – institutional key to democratization' (Fish 2006: 18).

The political influence of legislatures is closely connected with the degree to which they fulfil their constitutional tasks and duties. The 'more powerful a legislature, the more comprehensive its functions will be and the more extensive will be its societal impact' (Smith and Musolf 1979: 44). Conversely, if the parliament does not or cannot fulfil most of its functions, it follows that the political system is either authoritarian or less democratic. The legitimacy of the new constitutional government system as a whole depends to a great extent on parliamentary performance. The efficient and effective functioning of the legislature contributes to public legitimacy of not only the institution itself but for the whole system of government. Connected with the parliamentary performance is political institutionalization, which is a crucial factor for the deepening of the democratization process. Political institutionalization means well-organized and well-functioning state institutions which fulfil their constitutional tasks. This includes the strengthening of the formal representative and governmental structures of a democratic political system. Concerning legislatures, this means that their constitutional and de facto powers enable them to be autonomous and to have significant impact on national political decision-making processes. In order to play such a role, they must be adequately equipped in terms of personnel and financial means. Only then can they become more coherent, independent, and decisive, and consequently more capable, efficient, effective, and binding.

Democratic deepening is thus dependent on political institutionalization. As US scholar Larry Diamond stated, 'the strength of formal democratic institutions and rules (as opposed to the informal practices of clientelism, vote buying, rule bending, and executive domination) no doubt facilitates the endurance and the consolidation of democracy' (Diamond 1999: 71).

By creating or establishing permanent structures and procedures for political conflict mediation, institutionalization enables political forces to improve their cooperation and dialogue. If the major political actors discuss and eventually solve problems with the inclusion of binding, authoritative political institutions such as legislatures, democratic political culture is enhanced. Therefore, political institutionalization is decisive for the deepening of democracy since it is crucial for the formation of a democratic political culture and, consequently, the legitimacy of the new democracy.

Of equal importance for democratic deepening is the overall regime performance to which legislatures can contribute positively or negatively. The new democratic order should produce at least a certain degree of positive policy outputs which are tangible to broader segments of society in order to strengthen its overall political legitimacy. People hope or expect that the new political system will produce sustained economic growth resulting in better individual living conditions and standards. Additionally, they demand that the new political order relieves the most urgent social problems such as minority suppression.

In the eyes of most people, the government bears primary responsibility for these issues. But parliament also contributes to the overall regime performance by improving legislation and taking into account the interests of all segments of society. On the contrary, they can also 'pass abusive laws, defend the establishment, and wilfully ignore the needs of the weak and marginalized'

(Close 1995: 6). For developing countries such as Indonesia, in which a large majority of the population lives in rather poor living conditions, the legitimacy of the legislature is also dependent on if people and their interests are adequately represented and what kind of attitude the national legislature adopts in the policy formulation of the government.

Three main functions of parliaments can be singled out in a plethora of scholarly literature[2] on this subject: the representative function, the oversight function, and the legislative function. The representative function refers to the function of parliaments as the embodiment of people's sovereignty. Therefore, parliaments should represent and express the interests and opinions of all societal segments. The following indicators thus give an impression of how the representative function of the legislature is fulfilled: What kind of people become members of the DPR? What is the mechanism of selection? To what extent do the people's representatives care about the interests of the general public? To which degree are the legislators accountable to their constituents?

The legislative function, which is the traditional and oldest right of parliaments, refers to the creation or deliberation of general and compulsory rules for all citizens. In a state, which is – actually and not only rhetorically – based on the rule of law, legislation is therefore of utmost importance. In order to evaluate the performance of the Indonesian DPR in the area of legislation it is necessary to check the number and the quality of the laws passed in the legislature in recent years. Was there sufficient expertise to deal with complex political questions and was there a certain bias during the legislation process?

The capacity to control the potential excesses of executive initiative and power is considered another basic task of legislatures. This oversight function means to watch and control the executive, or more specifically the government. Especially in new democracies disproportionate executive dominance, which is a typical legacy of authoritarian regimes, can be diminished by a critical and effective parliament. The oversight function of parliaments is of special importance in order to consolidate the young democracy. The weakness of a legislature in regard to the executive branch of government undermines horizontal accountability. Considering weak post-authoritarian judiciaries, the legislature 'is the only agency at the national level that is potentially capable of controlling the chief executive. Where the legislature lacks muscle, presidential abuses of power [. . .] frequently ensue' (Fish 2006: 12f.). For the assessment of the oversight function it is necessary to evaluate to what extent the legislature has had influence on the decision-making process of the government. Does the legislature possess and exercise certain prerogatives to counter executive ambitions in a system of checks and balances?

Additionally, a legislature needs a certain professionalism in order to work effectively and to demonstrate its ability to deal with relevant social and economic issues. If its decision-making procedures and capabilities fail to produce significant results, the legislature's reputation will suffer, especially if it only delays and obstructs reform-oriented legislation and policies. A well-functioning legislature in a system of checks and balances, however, can serve as a symbol for the consequent implementation of principles of democracy, representation, people's sovereignty and participation. Thus, the legitimacy of the parliament is determined by its values, actions and effectiveness.

## THE INDONESIAN LEGISLATURE DURING THE DEMOCRATIZATION PROCESS

The end of the authoritarian *Orde Baru* (1966–98) of President Suharto marked a crucial turning point not only for the country but for the legislature as well. In the *Orde Baru*, parliament exercised virtually no control over the government. Since most of its members received their seats as awards for their loyalty to the Suharto clan or the military leadership, the DPR legislators did not challenge the government's policies in general. During the Suharto presidency the Indonesian legislature 'never drafted its own legislation and has never rejected a bill submitted by the executive branch' (Schwarz 1994: 272).

However, in the last months of the *Orde Baru*, especially in April and May 1998, the regime's previously loyal supporters gradually distanced themselves from the authoritarian ruler. Finally, in a rapid process in May 1998, parliamentary control over the president contributed to Suharto's downfall. The declaration and letter from the DPR leadership on 18 May 1998, issuing an ultimatum for the resignation of Suharto and indirectly threatening an impeachment, was one of the key reasons for the end of Suharto's rule.

After the resignation of President Suharto in May 1998, the composition of the DPR remained nearly unchanged for more than one year. Despite their increasing popularity among the Indonesian people, hard-line reformers and opposition forces were not represented in the DPR. Therefore, the legislature had an enormous lack of legitimacy when it had to decide on important steps to move the country toward democracy. Especially during the MPR session in October 1998, missing input from pro-democracy forces, combined with military violence against protesting students, 'reinforced the impression of an elite trying desperately to hold onto power' (Schwarz 2000: 375f.). Still, some important changes were made by reform-minded legislators. Under public pressure they passed the necessary laws to ensure free and fair elections.

These were held in June 1999 and symbolized a new start for parliamentarism in Indonesia. The legislature then became a centre for power struggles among the political elites. The election of Abdurrahman Wahid as new president in October 1999 gave a great deal of power to the DPR. The new president became, in fact, dependent on the support of the legislature. The permanent trouble between the DPR and President Wahid resulted in a direct confrontation between the legislative and the executive branches of government (Ufen 2001: 109). Finally the DPR initiated an impeachment process against Wahid which resulted in the removal of the president. Between 1999 and 2002, four rounds of constitutional amendments gave more and more oversight power to the DPR.

After a period of non-cooperation during the presidency of Abdurrahman Wahid, the legislature became somewhat more cooperative during the presidency of PDI-P chairwoman Megawati Sukarnoputri, not least because her faction was the biggest in the DPR until 2004. Furthermore, to avoid a similar power struggle with the DPR, President Megawati Sukarnoputri tried to avoid direct confrontation with the legislature.

The election of President Susilo Bambang Yudhoyono as the first directly elected president in September 2004 had a direct impact on the legislature. In the first weeks after its inauguration, the DPR was divided almost evenly between two coalitions. On one side stood the Nationhood Coalition (*Koalisi Kebangsaan*), which supported Megawati Sukarnoputri in her failed bid in the presidential election, including Golkar, PDI-P, PDS and PBR. The People's Coalition (*Koalisi Kerakyatan*), which supported President Susilo Bambang Yudhoyono and included PPP, PD, PKS, PAN and other small parties grouped in the Democratic Pioneer Star (BPD) faction, had slightly less seats in the DPR. The trouble emerged when the different factions could not agree on which faction should name the chairmen of the committees and five other auxiliary bodies. The Nationhood Coalition insisted that the commission chairs be put to a vote, which may have resulted in a dominance of the opposition to President Susilo Bambang Yudhoyono in the DPR committees. The People's Coalition demanded that the posts should be proportionally distributed among all the factions as this was the tradition. For weeks, this dispute stalled all parliamentary activities and delayed all legislation. In the end, after intervention by the government, the DPR factions agreed to distribute the commission chairs proportionally.

The largest faction in the DPR, Golkar, moved away from its initial opposition to President Yudhoyono when his vice president, Yusuf Kalla, was elected as new chairman of the Golkar party in December 2004. Golkar then left the Nationhood Coalition and became a faction which more or less supported the Yudhoyono administration.

In conclusion, the role of the Indonesian legislature has changed greatly in recent years. The president no longer has the power to make his own policies, and needs the support of major parts of the political elites represented in the DPR. Parliament has become an important player in national politics. In scholarly transition theories, a strong and influential parliament amongst the state institutions is stressed as a precondition for the consolidation of democracy. Insofar, the Indonesian legislature seems to contribute positively to the deepening of democracy. But analysts and the Indonesian general public are rather sceptical and regard the performance of the DPR as poor, disappointing and inadequate.

In the following, the three major functions (representation, oversight, and legislation) will be analysed with regard to the Indonesian legislature in the post-Suharto era. In addition, some comments will be made on the professional attitude of the legislators.

## THE DPR AND ITS MAIN FUNCTIONS

### Ignorant to people's demands? The representation function

The opponents of the government's fuel hike in 2005 claimed to represent the interests of the common people. As the people's representatives they felt entitled to protest the unpopular decision. However, were the legislators really serving the interests of Indonesians or were their motivations instead focused on a combination of strategic reasons, party rivalries and populism? Media reports appraised that the PDI-P

> knows full well that the fuel subsidy reduction is essential, and during [party chairwoman Megawati Sukarnoputri's] three-year rule she introduced the same policy herself, though it was short-lived. Not only her party, but other political parties agree with the rationale behind the fuel price decision, but in public they pretend that they are wholeheartedly against it, for their own interests.
>
> (*The Jakarta Post Online*, 18 March 2005)

Such behaviour is quite common for parliamentary practice in recent years. Though such an attitude is also typical for parliaments in well-established democracies, it is particularly dubious for developing democracies since the legitimacy and the credibility of the legislature have weaker historical roots. The trust of the people in new democratic institutions such as parliament cannot be taken for granted but has to first be earned.

The public image of parliament was very low in the *Orde Baru* since its members were handpicked by Suharto with little input from the constituents. However, the reputation of the freely elected parliament was initially very high, since the makeup of the DPR was for the first time the result of a pluralistic and fair vote of the Indonesian people. While people in general did not feel they were being represented in the *Orde Baru*, the elections of 1999 gave the newly elected legislators a high degree of legitimacy and support from the people.

Soon afterwards, however, the reputation of the DPR steadily sank as parliament was not able to fulfil the people's high expectations for institutional reform and economic progress. The decreasing public trust in the legislature has less to do with the mechanism of representation via general elections but rather with the public perception that the elected legislators acted inadequately on behalf of the people's interest.

In a poll conducted by the research department of the *Kompas* daily in 2002, Indonesians were asked what they regarded as the primary interests of their legislators. The results are presented in Table 2.1, which shows that people perceive legislators as caring the most about their party's interests as well as personal, material interests. In public opinion legislators care least about the people they represent.

Hopes that a new generation of legislators would have a different attitude toward their parliamentary work than their predecessors were dashed. After the 2004 elections many 'new' people were elected to the DPR, but it seems that not much has changed. Former Legislator Mochtar Buchori (PDI-P faction from 1999 until 2004) wrote that

> a number of 'old' people from the old . . . [parliament] have indeed been eliminated, but among the younger members who are presently there because they have been re-elected, and the ones who are newcomers, there is educationally and culturally speaking, very little difference. The new House will be more or less the same as the old one, meaning that group and personal interests will come first, while public interests will come to the fore only later on, after group and personal interests are sufficiently satisfied.
>
> (Buchori 2004a)

The social profile of the Indonesian legislature deviates from the demographics of Indonesian society, exhibiting a strong over-representation of higher-educated, wealthy and male legislators. In the DPR between 1999 and 2004, the average age of the legislators was 54 years, the proportion of women was less than 10 per cent, and about one third of legislators were businessmen.[3] What is different compared to other national legislatures is the rather high number of legislators with a background in religious, mostly Islamic, organizations. The relative over-representation of legislators with university degrees and personal wealth in the Indonesian DPR is also commonplace in established Western democracies. Compared to other legislatures in Southeast Asia, the personal composition of the DPR is not so

*Table 2.1* Indonesians' estimation of the legislators' primary interests

|  | *August 2000* | *October 2001* | *January 2002* | *March 2002* | *May 2002* |
|---|---|---|---|---|---|
| Party interests | 70.8 | 55.1 | 42.5 | 60.0 | 61.6 |
| Private interests | – | 27.9 | 43.8 | 31.6 | 24.5 |
| People's interests | 22.2 | 11.7 | 6.4 | 4.6 | 11.0 |
| Don't know | 7.0 | 5.3 | 7.3 | 4.0 | 2.9 |

Adapted from Romli (2003: 143)

much dominated by upper-class people such as in Thailand or the Philippines (Rüland, Jürgenmeyer, Nelson and Ziegenhain 2005: 170–2). The social profile is thus not the main reason that the representation function is not fulfilled adequately.

The members of the Indonesian DPR are elected through a proportional election system with party lists.[4] This gives the political parties a decisive influence on the decision of who gets a parliamentary seat and who does not. To get a good position on the top of the party list it is more important to have good relations with the party leadership than with the local voters.

Despite their formal democratic structures, the Indonesian parties represented in the DPR, 'are frequently clustered around the party chair and his or her inner circle of clients' (Hermawan 2007: 205). Political parties are mostly organized

> like a personal enterprise; the patron turned the organisation's incentive resources such as posts in the party structure, the parliament and councils into private goods and distributed them to the party apparatus, which would redistribute them to selected party activists.
>
> (Hermawan 2007: 205f.)

The party structures thus resemble patronage structures and clientelist networks where political support can be traded for material awards and positions. Consequently, many Indonesian legislators get their seat in the DPR less because of their skills and political engagement but rather through promotion by their patrons. Direct financial contributions to the political party are also a good argument for getting a top position on the party list (Fealy 2001: 101) and thus a parliamentary mandate. Often, the financial investments for obtaining a parliamentary seat have to be earned during the parliamentary term through dubious financial transactions such as working as middleman ('*calo*') to help procure licenses and other financial advantages for 'friends and partners'. Various interest groups, especially from the business sector, lobby the legislators intensively to influence political decision-making processes in their interest. No wonder that there is, as a legislator admitted, a general tendency of the legislators to care more for business than for lower-class interests.[5]

The clientelistic structures and the influence of money politics in the selection of the DPR candidates have also impacted the accountability of the legislators. Since many of them owe their seat in the DPR to individual party leaders, they feel more accountable to them than to their constituents. Such attitudes do not only refer to the national legislature in Indonesia; other studies have shown the described phenomena can also be observed in regional and local parliaments throughout Indonesia (Bünte 2003).

The control of the party leadership over the rank-and-file legislators has been further broadened by the re-introduction of the recall mechanism into national law. Endorsed in November 2002, article 38(2) of the law on political parties stipulates that the leadership of a political party has the right to dismiss legislators from any legislative body in the country. Despite this procedure happening only occasionally, the menace of being expelled from the legislature pushes legislators to comply with the orders of the party's leadership.

Therefore, the representative function of the Indonesian parliament, i.e. representing and expressing the interests and opinions of the population, is not yet fulfilled as it should be. The formal mechanisms to determine the people's representatives by free and fair elections with a proportional election system is in line with democratic standards, however, the mentioned attitudes and actions of the legislators cause many Indonesians to feel that they are not represented by the right people.

## Inefficient and flawed: the legislation of the DPR

The debate on fuel prices in the DPR in March 2005 also revealed the missing expertise of the people's representatives in many important policy fields such as economic, fiscal and budget matters. In an interview, senior legislator Jakob Tobing (PDI-P) admitted that one of the main shortcomings of the DPR's parliamentary work is that the legislation is not adequate in depth and detail, referring specifically to the lack of expertise in economic matters. According to him, the DPR has a surplus of microeconomic experts (i.e. businessmen) and a lack of macroeconomic experts. As a consequence, the DPR is outmatched by the government departments in economic matters.[6] DPR vice chairman Muhaimin Iskandar (PKB) stated that the DPR's competencies in legislative and budget matters were very weak, since it had insufficient expert staff dealing with these matters.[7]

However, the performance of a legislature relies on legal and technical skill in writing and amending legislation, making useful proposals during negotiations with government officials and reviewing budgets. To this end, a working system of functional committees should be equipped with professional staff who have specialized expertise in their respective policy area.

When legislators in well-functioning parliaments in established democracies face deficits in certain specific policy fields, which is absolutely normal and expected, they usually rely on the advice of experts in their respective fields. Unfortunately, the Indonesian DPR members receive little to no support from internal or external experts. The parliamentary support and research units are limited to an absolute minimum. The databases of the DPR administration and the library in the DPR building are completely inadequately equipped. Additionally, the system of record-keeping and the access to information is absolutely insufficient (Schneier 2006: 12).

Individual legislators and factions cannot rely permanently on qualified experts in the different fields of legislation to support them. Outside experts are temporarily hired, but they have to be paid either by the legislators themselves or the factions.[8] These infrastructure problems leave legislators in difficult working conditions and hamper the performance and effective functioning of the DPR.

Since 2003, every legislator was given the financial means to hire a personal assistant. Former legislator Mochtar Buchori explained why this useful opportunity failed to reach its intended objective:

> The reason was that many legislators had abused this privilege. Instead of hiring someone who was really capable, many legislators hired instead members of their family: A son or a daughter, or a son-in-law or daughter-in-law, a brother or sister, or a good friend. Some personal assistants were hired simply for their good looks.
>
> (Buchori 2004b)

The mentioned infrastructural deficits have direct consequences for the daily work of the DPR. Budget allocations, organizational structures, and operating practices and procedures 'have so far survived almost unchanged [in] Indonesia's democratic transition, and are no longer appropriate for the assembly's change in role from a body merely approving government decisions to its new role as an independent legislature' (Feulner 2005). However, to fulfil their functions legislatures should have sufficiently knowledgeable, engaged and resourceful organizational structures in order to check and control executive and state bureaucratic actions and decisions. A parliament such as the DPR that is constitutionally powerful but institutionally weak is always in danger of being overruled by a better informed and financially better-equipped executive.

According to other experts, the quality of many laws passed by the DPR is often low. The main criticism derives from their inconsistency with other legislation and their imprecise formulation. Former DPR chairman Akbar Tanjung admitted these flaws in his report during the MPR consultative session in 2004 when he stated that, 'the quality of many [laws] remained a cause for concern' and that 'there must be improvements made to the quality of legislation in the future'. He acknowledged that many of the laws approved by the DPR were of questionable quality (Hari 2004a and 2004b). The general poor law enforcement in Indonesia can also be blamed on the lawmakers who often fail to produce precise and understandable regulations.

The lack of expertise of many legislators and the limited will to call in external advice from experts leads to another questionable phenomenon. Allegedly ministries, state enterprise executives and other government agencies lubricate the legislative procedures of the DPR with more or less open financial donations to the legislators. Hence, allegations have abounded that particular ministers made payments, which were disguised in fraudulent legal expense accounts, to DPR members (*The Jakarta Post Online*, 4 October 2001). Political observers such as Australian scholar Harold Crouch stated that 'it is well known that many members of the DPR are willing to accept money in exchange for their support for bills and other parliamentary measures' (Crouch 2003: 17).

The aforementioned deficiencies such as widespread lack of expertise among the legislators and infrastructure deficits resulting in sub-par legislation, together with the influence of money politics on legislative procedures, lead to a rather negative assessment of the DPR's legislative functioning.

This is in addition to the relatively low output of laws by the DPR. Between 1999 and 2004 only 139 laws were passed, most of them of low relevance such as the creation of new regencies and far fewer than previously targeted; by the end of 2005 only 10 of 55 bills to be completed became law. Given the need for reform laws after a long period of authoritarian rule, the legislative output of the Indonesian parliament is insufficient. Altogether, the legislative performance of the DPR is not efficient enough.

## Oversight of and power struggle with the government

The oversight function became the most developed parliamentary function in the post-Suharto era. The constitutional amendments between 1999 and 2002 strengthened the controlling power of the previously weak legislature. In the time of the presidency of Abdurrahman Wahid many observers even saw an over-stretching of the parliamentary oversight function. With the introduction of the direct election of the president in 2004, the powers of the executive and the legislative branches of government have become more balanced.

In regard to legislation, the president lost his formal veto right (art. 20, 4). However, any bill has to receive the agreement of the president before it can become law (art. 20A, 3). These constitutional provisions are 'arguably internally contradictory, or, at best, ambiguous' (Sherlock 2005: 6). Therefore, the legislation is no clear parliamentary prerogative – legislative outcomes have to be negotiated with government representatives. The problem is that the government can delay or even stall legislation that a parliamentary majority supports.

With only a few exceptions, all bills between 1998 and 2006 were drafted by the executive branch of government, i.e. the ministries. The DPR therefore usually reacts only to government proposals but takes no own initiative. The oversight function of the legislature is guaranteed in so far as modifications can be arranged together with government representatives. However, it is no secret that government agencies sometimes put the legislators under pressure to agree to a bill[9] or spur the legislative procedures of the DPR with financial support for the legislators.

In the reform era after 1998, the formal oversight rights of the legislature have increased enormously. Amongst other things, the DPR can now influence executive appointments such as the national police and army chiefs, cite state officials for hearings or initiate investigative committees for the examination of executive wrongdoings. However, many observers regard the oversight function as a mere intra-elite power struggle on positions and resources. Investigative committees are often initiated by parliamentary groups in opposition to the president in order to damage the president's public image rather than to reveal the real facts of the alleged power abuse by the executive branch of government.

Another aspect that does not contribute to public trust in the legislation process is the internal process of decision-making in the DPR, which is not very transparent and is still guided by the *musyawarah-mufakat* principle. Debating (*musyawarah*) until a compromise is reached that everybody can accept (*mufakat*) still characterizes the Indonesian way of making decisions in parliament. Voting, counting and recording the votes is a rare exception. Such a manner of decision-making is contrary to democratic accountability and makes it very difficult for the general public to identify and discern the political attitude of single legislators or factions. Additionally, critics of the consensus principle argue that this reflects the old *Orde Baru* mentality where no diverging opinions were tolerated. Reaching a consensus can often be translated into dubious back room dealings, horse-trading and other non-transparent ways of decision-making prone to corruption.

## Professionalism of DPR members

The nationwide televised brawls in the DPR's plenary session on the fuel price hikes made many people laugh and those more concerned cry about the apparent immaturity of many legislators. Although such physical altercations are not frequent, other forms of misbehaviour and irresponsibility are more common. Among the most serious are frequent absenteeism and money politics.

Parliamentary sessions of the DPR usually have poor attendance. While such a phenomenon is also quite common in plenary sessions of parliaments in established democracies, it is also usual in committee sessions of the DPR. In the Indonesian legislature, it is

> rarely the case that more than a dozen members are present at any meeting. If this were so because members were systematically rostered by their factions it might not be an issue, but the reality appears to be far more haphazard.
>
> (Sherlock 2003: 19)

According to legislators, their colleagues often have little knowledge of the issue in question and are often ill-prepared.[10] It is usual that legislators come late and leave meetings as it suits them. Under such conditions it is very difficult to maintain an effective working atmosphere. Constructive debates thus occur only rarely in committee sessions. As a result of this lack of professionalism and the often lacklustre attitude of the legislators, the parliamentary performance as a whole suffers.

Even more worrisome is the influence of money politics on DPR members.

The case of former DPR chairman Akbar Tanjung, who was convicted of the misuse of 40 billion Rupiah (4 million Euros) from the funds of the State Logistics Agency (Bulog) but was finally cleared of all charges in February 2004, is just the tip of the iceberg. Particularly when dealing with state-owned companies, public sector enterprises and government ministries, the legislators tend to demand extra money (Sherlock 2003: 20f.). In an interview with *The Jakarta Post*, the parliamentarian Sukono (PDI-P) confessed to having received money from the Ministry of Forestry and Agriculture and described his behaviour as absolutely normal among his colleagues. He said that 'we convened for deliberation on the [plantation] bill for days and nights. It is normal for me to accept cash' (*The Jakarta Post Online*, 21 September 2001).

Prior to 1998, large-scale corruption centred around the former president, his family and some cronies. In the meantime corruption has been exported to the local legislatures and also to the national legislature. Legislatures now have the power to determine government budgets, to make decisions about procurement and development funds, and to investigate complaints from the public. These powers are vital to control the executive branch, but it became obvious that many Indonesian legislators are willing to abuse their authority for private gain (Transparency International 2005: 161).

An established form of corruption is a major threat for the consolidation of democracy. The impact of political corruption 'has been strikingly apparent in the demise or decay of many democracies during the third wave' (Diamond 1999: 92). Therefore, in order to preserve or even to deepen democracy, combating corruption is a major performance challenge for democratic consolidation.

In October 2001, the DPR passed an ethical code (*Kode Etik*) in which the main standards of proper behaviour and action were listed – absenteeism and corruption were among the topics. However, the parliamentarians tend to ignore these regulations since the sanctions for violations are low and are almost never applied. As many legislators share the same moral values they tend to develop a certain *ésprit de corps* which tolerates violations.

For the general public, however, it is not understandable when the political elites represented in the legislature are not sanctioned for their misbehaviour. After initial optimism and trust after the inauguration of the freely elected legislature in 1999, the public support for the DPR declined dramatically when it did not fulfil the people's expectations. The decreasing public trust in the legislature is in direct relation to the frequent complaints about improper behaviour of the legislators. Corruption cases and reports about the laziness and missing competence of legislators are spurring public resentment against the legislature.

## CONCLUSION

The DPR cannot yet be described as a well-organized and well-functioning state institution. It has made remarkable progress compared to the powerless façade parliament of the Suharto era, but it still cannot be characterized as an efficient and effective legislature. Thus, political institutionalization is far from being completed.

The performance of the DPR must be improved as the legislature is not yet able to fulfil its functions in an adequate manner. As we have seen, the representation function is not sufficiently fulfilled because the selection of the legislators is in the hands of a small party elite that dominates the selection process of candidates. Consequently, the legislators usually feel more accountable to their respective party leadership than to their constituents. This negative development in terms of democratic theory has been further aggravated by the re-introduction of the recall mechanism. In terms of its legislative function the DPR also has remarkable weaknesses. Due to insufficient expertise amongst the legislators themselves and inadequate support from internal or external experts, the legislature is in practice not on an equal footing with the better informed and equipped executive branch of government. In addition to the relatively low output of laws, the influence of dubious executive payments on legislative procedures within the DPR leads to a rather negative assessment of the DPR's fulfilment of its legislative function. The oversight function is certainly the most developed parliamentary function. In many policy areas, the president now has to share power with the legislature. For the consolidation of democracy such provisions are pivotal. Nevertheless, the legislature's criticism on presidential decisions is often interpreted as a mere power struggle among the political elites rather than as the rightful and responsible behaviour of a constructive opposition within a system of checks and balances. Additionally, the underdeveloped professionalism of most legislators and the frequent reports on corruption and money politics within the legislature are tarnishing the image of the DPR the most.

What can be done to improve the performance of the Indonesian legislature? Among other things, the parliamentary support services must be better equipped and the procedures of the decision-making processes must be adapted to the post-authoritarian time (Sherlock 2005) in order to create a more professional working atmosphere.

The latter refers to an incremental change of the political culture within the DPR. However, such a change takes much more time than a transition of the political institutions. Institutional and internal structures are part of the country-specific political culture which is still determined by authoritarian traditions mixed with values in favour of personal material gains. For more than three decades Suharto's authoritarian regime 'stunted the skills needed for democratic debate and competition' (Emmerson 2004: 105). Therefore, the freely elected legislature in 1999 had to make a new start, but referred to old political traditions. Parliament inherited not only the building in Senayan, but adopted most of the rules of procedure of its authoritarian predecessors. The reform process did 'not change the underlying structure and culture of the political elite' (Katyasungkana 2000: 260).

Finally, people expect from the legislature and from the government system as a whole a certain degree of output which serves their interests. Government for the people – part of the famous Gettysburg formula of Abraham Lincoln – means that the decisions made by the people's representatives are in the interest of all the people and not only in that of the representatives.

When in the new democratic order the general public does not see any improvements in their personal lives, the legitimacy of the government system will not increase but, as can be seen in Indonesia currently, nostalgia with the former authoritarian regime and its alleged advantages could pave the way for an authoritarian backlash. US scholar Larry Diamond wrote that

> If the shallow, troubled, and recently established democracies of the world do not move forward, to strengthen their political institutions, improve their democratic functioning [. . .], they are likely to move backward, into deepening pathologies that will eventually plunge their political system below the threshold of electoral democracy or overturn them altogether.
>
> (Diamond 1999: 64)

Indonesia's democratization process advanced by constitutional amendments which gave the national legislature a democratically adequate, powerful role in the system of government. Two free and fair parliamentary elections in 1999 and 2004 were also very positive signs towards a democratic deepening. It is now up to the elected people's representatives to fulfil their constitutional tasks with a more professional attitude. The democratic consolidation, however, is stalled as long as the described shortcomings in the Indonesian DPR continue to prevail.

## NOTES

1 The empirical data for this paper is derived from the scholarly literature on transitions, legislatures and developments in Indonesia. Indonesian newspapers and journals which were available online were also used. Additional information was gathered by interviews with various members of the Indonesian legislature between 2001 and 2004.
2 Among many others see Bagehot 2001 and Obrecht 2004.
3 Own calculations based on data from Yayasan API (2000).
4 Until 2004, the electoral system was based on proportional representation with a closed list, so that voters could only elect parties and not persons. In the 2004 elections open party lists were introduced, but brought de facto only little change, since only very few candidates placed on a low place on the list succeeded in being elected.
5 Interview with Aberson Marle Sihaloho, PDI-P faction, 22 November 2002, in Jakarta.

6  Interview with Jakob Tobing, PDI-P faction, 4 December 2002, in Jakarta.
7  Interview with Muhaimin Iskandar, PKB faction, 15 November 2002, in Jakarta.
8  For further information see Rüland, Jürgenmeyer, Nelson and Ziegenhain (2005: 215f.), Sherlock (2003: 21ff.) and Ziegenhain (2005: 31).
9  Interview with Achmad Farial, PPP faction, 26 November 2002, in Jakarta.
10 Interviews with DPR members in Jakarta in 2001 and 2002.

**BIBLIOGRAPHY**

Bagehot, W. (2001) *The English Constitution (1865–1867)*, Oxford: Oxford University Press.
Blondel, J. (1973) *Comparative Legislatures*, Englewood Cliffs, New Jersey: Prentice-Hall.
Buchori, M. (2004a) 'Deadlock in the House: Where will it lead us to?', *The Jakarta Post Online*, 3 November.
—— (2004b) 'Challenges, opportunities and hope for the House', *The Jakarta Post Online*, 17 November.
Bünte, M. (2003) *Regionale Autonomie in Indonesien: Wege zur erfolgreichen Dezentralisierung*, Hamburg: Mitteilungen des Instituts für Asienkunde.
Close, D. (1995) 'Consolidating Democracy in Latin America – What role for legislatures', in D. Close (ed.) *Legislatures and the New Democracies in Latin America*, Boulder/London: Lynne Rienner Publishers.
Crouch, H. (2003) 'Political Update 2002: Megawati's holding options', in E. Aspinall and G. Fealy (eds) *Local Power and Politics in Indonesia: Decentralisation & democratisation*, Singapore: Institute for Southeast Asian Studies.
Diamond, L. (1994) 'Rethinking Civil Society: Toward democratic consolidation', *Journal of Democracy*, 5 (3): 4–17.
—— (1999) *Developing Democracy toward Consolidation*, Baltimore: Johns Hopkins University Press.
Diamond, L., Plattner, M.F., Chu, Y. and Tien, H. (eds) (1997) *Consolidating the Third-Wave Democracies: Trends and challenges*, Baltimore: Johns Hopkins University Press.
Emmerson, D.K. (2004) 'Indonesias's Approaching Elections: A year of voting dangerously?', *Journal of Democracy*, 15 (1): 94–108.
Fealy, G. (2001) 'Parties and Parliament: Serving whose interests?', in G. Lloyd and S. Smith (eds) *Indonesia Today: Challenges of history*, Singapore: Institute for Southeast Asian Studies.
Feulner, F. (2005) 'Right time for House Reform', *The Jakarta Post Online*, 23 March.
Fish, S.M. (2006) 'Stronger legislatures, stronger democracies', in *Journal of Democracy*, 17 (1): 5–20.
Hari, K. (2004a) 'Akbar admits law-making flaws', *The Jakarta Post Online*, 24 September.
—— (2004b) 'Welcome aboard', *The Jakarta Post Online*, 1 October.
Hermawan, Y.P. (2007) 'Political Parties and Elections in Post-Authoritarian Indonesia', in B. Hadiwinata and C. Schuck (eds) *Democracy in Indonesia: The challenge of consolidation*, Baden-Baden: Nomos.
Katyasungkana, N. (2000) 'Exchanging Power or Changing Power: The problem of creating democratic institutions', in C. Manning and P. van Diermen (eds) *Indonesia*

*in Transition: Social aspects of reformasi and crisis*, Singapore: Institute for Southeast Asian Studies.

King, D.Y. (2003) *Half-hearted Reform: Electoral institutions and the struggle for democracy in Indonesia*, Westport: Praeger Publishers.

Krumwiede, H.W. and Nolte, D. (2000) *Die Rolle der Parlamente in den Präsidialdemokratien Lateinamerikas*, Hamburg: Institut für Iberoamerika-Kunde.

Liebert, U. (1989) 'The Centrality of Parliament in the Consolidation of Democracy: A theoretical exploration, Working Paper No. 7'. Online. Available HTTP: <http://www.diba.es/icps/working_papers/docs/WP_I_7.html> (accessed 23 February 2004).

Lijphart, A. (ed.) (1992) *Parliamentary versus Presidential Government*, Oxford: Oxford University Press.

Linz, J.J. and Valenzuela, A. (eds) (1994) *The Failure of Presidential Democracy*, Baltimore/London: Johns Hopkins University Press.

Mainwaring, S. and Shugart, M.S. (eds) (1997) *Presidentialism and Democracy in Latin America*, Cambridge: Cambridge University Press.

Obrecht, M. (2004) 'Niedergang der Parlamente? Transnationale Politik im Deutschen Bundestag und der Assemblée nationale', PhD thesis, Albert Ludwigs University Freiburg.

O'Donnell, G. and Schmitter, P.C. (1986) *Transitions from Authoritarian Rule: Tentative conclusions about uncertain democracies*, Baltimore/London: Johns Hopkins University Press.

Olson, D.M. (1994) *Democratic Legislative Institutions: A comparative view*, Armonk/New York: M.E. Sharpe.

Romli, L. (2003) 'Potret Buram Partai Politik di Indonesia', in M. Irsyam and L. Romli (eds) *Menggugat Partai Politik*, Jakarta: Laboratorium Ilmu Politik, Fakultas Ilmu Sosial Politik, Universitas Indonesia.

Rüland, J., Jürgenmeyer, C., Nelson, M.H. and Ziegenhain, P. (2005) *Parliaments and Political Change in Asia*, Singapore: Institute for Southeast Asian Studies.

Schedler, A. (1998) 'What is Democratic Consolidation?', in *Journal of Democracy*, 9 (2): 91–107.

Schneier, E. (2006) 'Legislative Professionalizaion in Indonesia', paper presented at the 20th IPSA World Congress in Fukuoka, Japan, 9–13 July 2006.

Schuck, C. (2003) *Der indonesische Demokratisierungsprozess. Politischer Neubeginn und historische Kontinuität*, Baden-Baden: Nomos.

Schwarz, A. (1994) *A Nation in Waiting: Indonesia in the 1990s*, St Leonards: Allen & Unwin.

—— (2000) *A Nation in Waiting: Indonesia's search for stability*, St Leonards: Allen & Unwin.

Sherlock, S. (2003) *Struggling to Change: The Indonesian parliament in an era of reformasi. A report on the structure and operation of the Dewan Perwakilan Rakyat (DPR)*, Canberra: Centre for Democratic Institutions.

—— (2005) *The Legislative Process in the Indonesian Parliament (DPR): Issues, problems and recommendations*. Online. Available HTTP: <http://www.forum-politisi.org/downloads/S_Sherlock_Legislative_Process_in_the_DPR.doc> (accessed 12 September 2006).

Smith, J. and Musolf, L.D. (eds) (1979) *Legislature in Development: Dynamics of change in new and old states*, Durham: Duke University Press.

Transparency International (2005) *Global Corruption Report, 2005*. Online. Available

HTTP: <http://www.globalcorruptionreport.org/gcr2005/download/english/country_reports_a_j.pdf> (accessed 14 January 2006).

Ufen, A. (2001) 'Der Machtkampf zwischen Wahid und den Parlamenten', in P. Ziegenhain (ed.) *Politischer Wandel in Indonesien 1995–2000*, Essen: Südostasien Informationsstelle.

Wadrianto, G.K. (2005) 'Rapat Paripurna DPR Ricuh', *Kompas Online*, 16 March.

Yayasan API (ed.) (2000) *Panduan Parlemen Indonesia*, Jakarta: Yayasan API.

Ziegenhain, P. (2005) 'Deficits of the Indonesian Parliament and Their Impact on the Democratisation Process', in I. Wessel (ed.) *Democratisation in Indonesia after the fall of Suharto*, Berlin: Logos.

# 3 Indonesia's struggle for rule of law [1]

*Petra Stockmann*

## IN LIEU OF AN INTRODUCTION: 'RULE OF LAW' – WHAT SHOULD IT MEAN?

'In a state that is considered as a *negara hukum* (*Rechtsstaat* and the rule of law), law is everything. Law is the king. Law is the structure of the state and its content', to quote Jimly Asshiddiqie, Chief Justice of Indonesia's new Constitutional Court (*Suara Merdeka.com*, 27 December 2001).[2] Poignant words since, according to the country's constitution today, Indonesia is such a *negara hukum*, a state operating under the rule of law.[3]

Yet only recently has Indonesia again been named one of the world's most corrupt states (Transparency International 2004),[4] and human rights organizations regularly complain about continued impunity for perpetrators of grave human rights violations. Most people would agree that such a state of affairs regarding the judiciary clearly contradicts the rule of law principle. However, a more difficult task than listing the conditions in Indonesia that are contrary to the rule of law concept is to define what constitutes the same.

Sifting through piles of new Indonesian legislation for references to the term *negara hukum* (which literally means 'law state') turns up the following: In a state under the rule of law, all aspects of life concerning matters pertaining to society, nation and state, including governance, must always be based on law. This comes close to what Jimly Asshiddiqie might have had in mind when making his aforementioned remarks. One important principle of *negara hukum* is an independent judicial authority, free from the influence of other powers, in order to uphold law and justice. Another principle is the guarantee of equality before the law, where everyone has the right to recognition, guarantees, protection and just legal certainty. The rule of law comprises justice and prosperity of the people, and in a state under the rule of law, respect for law and justice is a *conditio sine qua non*.[5]

There is little disagreement that an independent judiciary, legal certainty and equality before the law constitute key principles of any rule of law concept. But it seems doubtful whether the same holds true for prosperity of the people. That is to say the meaning of the term is contested. Arriving at a widely accepted definition of the term 'rule of law' is possibly as difficult as trying to find a universally accepted meaning for its complement concept: democracy.

One attempt to supply a purposeful definition to the concept, which would enjoy broad international acceptance, was made under the auspices of the International Commission of Jurists (ICJ). Over a series of six conferences between 1955 and 1966, the ICJ brought together noted jurists from all over the world to discuss and possibly develop a common understanding of the rule of law concept. In an early declaration issued at the second congress in Delhi in 1959, the jurists gave an idea about how substantial an understanding of the concept they were aiming at:

> This International Congress of Jurists, consisting of 185 judges, practicing lawyers and teachers of law from 53 countries [. . .] recognizes that the Rule of Law is a dynamic concept [. . .] which should be employed not only to safeguard and advance the civil and political rights of the individual in a free society, but also to establish social, economic, educational and cultural conditions under which his [*sic*] legitimate aspirations and dignity may be realized [. . .].
>
> (ICJ 1966: 66)

The results of the different ICJ working committees were compiled in the booklet, *The Rule of Law and Human Rights. Principles and Definitions.* Areas covered in the publication include the operation of the rule of law with respect to a country's legislature, executive, judiciary, criminal process and legal profession, as well as economic and social development, along with a list of essential requirements for any society seeking to operate effectively under the rule of law.

The jurists' rule of law concept overlaps with various definitions of democracy. It includes and even exceeds, for example, Robert Dahl's procedural minima, to which numerous authors, especially those writing on regime change or transitions of political systems to democracy, typically refer to in lieu of a definition for democracy: freedom of association, freedom of expression, the right to vote, eligibility for public office, the right of political leaders to compete for support, free and fair elections, the existence of alternative sources of information and the existence of institutions for making government policies depend on votes and other expressions of preference (Dahl 1971: 3).[6] Thus, one could say that the international jurists' rule of law concept constitutes a concept of a democratic state operating under the rule of law.

For the principles included in their concept, the jurists referred to the human rights instruments codified in the then still rudimentary body of international law. As a non-governmental assembly, they also partly preempted in their compilation principles that would later be codified by the international community of states, for example, in the two International Covenants of 1966 on Civil and Political and on Economic, Social and Cultural Rights.

What relevance do such 50-year-old espousals have for today? Any attempt to evaluate the state of the rule of law, or better yet of democracy and the rule of law, in any given country needs a normative basis for assessment. To analyse and assess where Indonesia stands today with respect to her constitutional aim of being both a democracy and a *negara hukum* – a democratic state operating under the rule of law – the standards for assessment need to be clarified. The approach adopted by the ICJ can readily be adapted to the realities of international law today. Whereas their concept mirrored the key principles of international human rights instruments that had either already been established or were in the process of becoming part of international law at that time, we can today draw on the vastly expanded body of international human rights instruments for definition.

This author's suggestion is to define, for the purpose of assessment, a democratic state under the rule of law as a state in which the principles included in all international human rights instruments are realized. With the number of international human rights instruments currently standing at almost one hundred documents, this body of international human rights law is huge. It comprises covenants, conventions and related protocols, declarations, basic principles, standard rules and more. These relate to civil, political, economic, social, and cultural rights in general and to the rights of indigenous peoples and other special interest groups, including women, children, the elderly and people with disabilities. Standards concerning the administration of justice are covered in more than 20 documents including binding documents, such as the Rome Statute of the International Criminal Court and the Convention against Torture, as well as general standards, such as the Basic Principles on the Independence of the Judiciary and the Standard Minimum Rules for the Treatment of Prisoners. Social welfare and development are other themes covered in international human rights instruments, as are promotion and protection of human rights, and issues pertaining to war crimes and crimes against humanity. The process of standard setting is an ongoing one, with further documents being drafted and deliberated all the time.[7]

With this body of international human rights instruments as a background for assessment, this chapter will focus on three issues: The first part outlines and assesses the constitutional changes that Indonesia has seen over the past seven years, and gives an overview of how far Indonesia has proceeded with the ratification of international human rights instruments. Then, changes in the structure of the judiciary and selected issues concerning legal certainty and administration of justice will be discussed. The last part addresses the thorny issue of dealing with past and present grave human rights violations.

## CONSTITUTIONAL CHANGE

Indonesia has come a long way since the spring of 1998 when Suharto had just been granted special powers to 'protect the unity and integrity of the

Nation and [. . .] deal with social unrest and other dangers of subversion'[8] and when the Indonesian parliament had been no more than a rubberstamp.[9] Since the fall of Suharto Indonesia has seen four amendments of its original 1945 Constitution, which founding president Sukarno had characterized as an 'express constitution' deemed for temporary use only.[10] The amendments have brought about considerable changes concerning the formal structure of the state and the codification of human rights standards.[11]

### Free and fair elections – a constitutional necessity today

Indonesia's most visible break with its authoritarian past was arguably the election marathon of 2004, when Indonesians participated in their second relatively free and fair parliamentary elections after the landmark democratic elections of 1999. Direct, general, free, secret, honest and fair elections conducted by an independent election commission are a constitutional necessity today.[12] There are still members of parliament (MPs) with a military background but they have received their mandates from the electorate not, like previously, from the leadership of the Indonesian Armed Forces (TNI), and all have retired from active military service. Whether military or civilian, as of 2004 there are no longer any appointed MPs.

2004 was also the year Indonesians were called to the polls to choose, for the first time ever, their president and vice president in direct elections. After a second round of voting, retired general Susilo Bambang Yudhoyono and Yusuf Kalla became, respectively, Indonesia's first president and vice president endowed with a direct popular mandate.[13]

Today the national parliament, the DPR (*Dewan Perwakilan Rakyat*, People's Representative Council), is anything but a rubberstamp. As laws are still made jointly by the DPR and the government, lawmaking can at times become a difficult and lengthy process, especially in the cases when the president cannot rely on majority support in parliament. President Yudhoyono was faced with this problem at the very beginning of his presidency before Kalla became the leader of Golkar, the party holding the largest number of seats in the DPR. In addition MPs do not appear hesitant to make extensive use of their now constitutionally determined parliamentary rights and have given the government a hard time. The most visible instance of this was the impeachment saga concerning former president Abdurrahman Wahid.

The sovereignty of the people is fully exercised by the People's Consultative Assembly (*Majelis Permusyawaratan Rakyat*, MPR), as stated in the original 1945 constitution.[14] In theory at least, the MPR was set as the highest state institution with one of its tasks being to determine the president. Now, with different channels in place for a – hopefully – better expression of the sovereign will of the people, the role and function of the MPR have changed. Now, the MPR consists of the DPR and a new institution, the DPD (*Dewan Perwakilan Daerah*, Regional Representative Council), which replaces the MPR's regional representatives' faction of old. All members of both the

DPR and the DPD are elected. The DPD is much smaller than the DPR, with only one-third the number of members; the Regional Representative Council elected in 2004 is comprised of 128 MPs – four from each province. The DPD as such has only rather limited authority and its role is basically consultative. Amongst its powers are the authority to draft laws on questions that concern the regions and the right to take part in deliberations on the same.[15] But the DPD has no role in turning discussed draft legislation into law. As part of the MPR, DPD members have a voice on questions of constitutional amendment and any impeachment proceedings against the president and/or the vice president, functions with which the new MPR is endowed.[16]

## Steps towards more judicial independence

In Sukarno's 'express constitution', little was defined with respect to the judiciary. An interesting description of the state of the judiciary under Suharto was provided in 1998 by the last MPR of the New Order regime, dominated by members of the Golkar party and the military. It is hard to believe that the authors of the following scathing criticism are the same MPs who only a few months earlier had endowed Suharto with special powers, thereby delivering the president to the highest pinnacle of empowerment during the entire term of his authoritarian rule. The MPR makes note of how, especially within the system's 'organic' legal framework, legislation limiting the power of the president was notable for its absence. This created conditions conducive to corruption, collusion and nepotism, allowing an interpretation of the law which was 'solely in accordance with the taste of the ruler'. In the same breath, the last MPR under the Suharto regime admits that there had been 'abuse of authority, disregard for law, neglect of the feeling for justice and little legal protection and legal certainty for society', and continues

> The fact that judicial institutions are established by the Executive provides an opportunity for the power holders to intervene in the judicial process and leads to collusion and negative practices in the judicial process. Upholding the law has not conveyed a feeling of justice and legal certainty in those cases of opposition to the Government or for those parties which have strong links with the people, thus putting the people into a weak position.
>
> (MPR Decree X/1998, Annex, II C)

It took another four years until members of the by then newly elected and appointed MPR could agree on constitutional provisions for an improved judicial system. Today, Indonesia's constitution states unambiguously that the nation's judiciary is an independent power. That the MPR members were serious about change can be seen by the fact that they constitutionally determined the establishment of a new judicial institution, the Constitutional

Court. Manned by nine judges – of which three are selected by each of the three branches of government (the president, the Supreme Court and the DPR) – Indonesia's Constitutional Court has during its brief term thus far played a key role in promoting the rule of law in Indonesia (see below).

The main task of the Constitutional Court is to conduct judicial review of laws brought before the bench to ensure that their content is in accordance with the constitution.[17] But during the election marathon of 2004, much of the judges' time was taken up by appeals concerning the election results. Among others, the court had to deal with an appeal by General Wiranto, one of the candidates in the first round of the presidential race. Wiranto and his running mate Solahudin Wahid, former member of the National Human Rights Commission Komnas HAM, claimed that they had lost 5,434,660 votes due to inaccuracies in vote counting (*The Jakarta Post.com*, 30 July 2004; *Suara Merdeka.com*, 10 August 2004). The Constitutional Court ended up rejecting the complaint due to lack of evidence.

Just as the last New Order MPR had so pointedly criticized the executive's influence over the judiciary, so did its successor undertake steps to counter this state of affairs. The new MPR constitutionally determined new appointment procedures for Supreme Court judges and the establishment of a new institution for this express purpose, the Judicial Commission. The Commission, which was eventually established three years later, proposes candidates to the DPR which then decides whom to approve as the new members of the Supreme Court bench.[18]

### An 'Indonesian National Declaration of Human Rights' and the constitution's new human rights article

> In response to and reflecting people's aspiration for democratic life based on rule of law and respect for human rights and fundamental freedoms, the People's Consultative Assembly [. . .] issued Decree No. XVII/MPR/ 1998 on Human Rights which includes [. . .] the Human Rights Charter. The 1998 Human Rights Charter, which may be considered as an 'Indonesian National Declaration of Human Rights' consists of forty-four articles, taken mostly from the 1948 UDHR [Universal Declaration of Human Rights].
>
> (Soeprapto 2005)

The Human Rights Charter, issued by the last New Order MPR in 1998, provided the basis for the constitution's new Article 28. When two years later the newly elected and appointed MPR deliberated on human rights provisions for the constitution, they eventually agreed to include a linguistically abridged and, in terms of substance, slightly altered version of the Human Rights Charter. Although the Human Rights Charter and thus the new constitutional article are clearly modelled on the Universal Declaration of Human Rights (UDHR),[19] there are substantial differences between the

Indonesian and the international documents.[20] The omission of noteworthy rights and other deviations from the wording of the UDHR show traces of influence by the security forces in the penning of both the Human Rights Charter and Article 28. Further deviations mirror patriarchal thinking and a recourse to religion-based ideologies.

Indonesia's constitutional catalogue of rights includes numerous crucial rights and freedoms such as the non-derogable rights to life, to freedom of thought and conscience, to religion, to not be tortured or enslaved and to be recognized as a person before the law. Rights to freedom of information, expression, association, assembly, rights to education and work, social security, health care, a place of residence and a decent livelihood, as well as the prohibition of discrimination gained inclusion. Notable for their absence when compared with the Universal Declaration are the prohibition of arbitrary arrest, detention and exile, and the prohibition of arbitrary deprivation of an individual's citizenship. Moreover, the right to freedom of movement is not included.[21]

The Universal Declaration determines limitations of the rights and freedoms laid down therein.

> In the exercise of his rights and freedoms, everyone shall be subject only to such limitations as are determined by law solely for the purpose of securing due recognition and respect for the rights and freedoms of others and of meeting the just requirements of morality, public order and the general welfare in a democratic society.
>
> (Article 29 (2) Universal Declaration of Human Rights)

In the Indonesian constitution a corresponding clause exists, however, it differs markedly in substance from the international standard. 'General welfare' is exchanged for 'security', while 'religious values' have been added as grounds for the limitation of individual rights.[22] Furthermore, nowhere does the Indonesian constitution explicitly lay down that men and women have equal rights. In this respect, Article 28 in the constitution ends up taking Indonesia a step backwards in comparison to the Indonesian Human Rights Charter which states that, in the fulfilment of human rights, men and women are entitled to equal treatment and protection.[23] This clause had been dropped from the catalogue of rights that was with only small changes turned into the constitutional provision. What the constitution does include are the rights to freedom from discriminatory treatment and to protection against such treatment, as well as the right to special treatment and support in order to obtain equal opportunities and benefits, with the aim of achieving equality and justice.[24]

The absence of an explicit mention of equal rights for men and women stands out given Indonesia's commitment to international standards in this respect. Indonesia ratified the Convention on the Elimination of Discrimination against Women (CEDAW) as early as 1984, and around the time the human rights article was introduced into the constitution Indonesia ratified the Optional Protocol to CEDAW. Furthermore, the country's first Human Rights Action Plan, decreed by former president Habibie in 1998, explicitly called for the revision of domestic legislation so that it would be brought into line with the CEDAW.[25] The latter, amongst others, stipulates:

> State Parties condemn discrimination against women in all its forms, agree to pursue by all appropriate means and without delay a policy of eliminating discrimination against women and, to this end, undertake:
>
> a   To embody the principle of equality of men and women in their national constitutions or other appropriate legislation if not incorporated therein and to ensure, through law and other appropriate means, the practical realisation of this principle; [. . .]
>
> (Article 2, Convention on the Elimination of Discrimination against Women)

Why is it so important to have rights laid down in the constitution? After all, Indonesia has ratified the relevant international human rights instruments which have become part of Indonesian law and thus a legal basis for the protection of rights already exists. Surely, it is up to every sovereign state to decide on the scope of its constitution.

Put simply, the constitution is the basis of the work of the new Constitutional Court. If parliament and government pass a law which violates any constitutional right of any person or group, the latter can file an application for judicial review of the law in question with the Constitutional Court. This path of appeal is naturally blocked if rights are not determined in the constitution. Seeking legal redress becomes a more complicated matter in the case of two contradictory laws, such as when a clause in a certain law contradicts international standards accepted by Indonesia, which are normally ratified by a law.[26]

Important for the functioning of *Rechtsstaat* in Indonesia is thus that the constitutional human rights articles be brought into accordance with key provisions in international standards.

## Indonesia's increasing commitment to international human rights instruments

Ratifying international human rights instruments is an important step along this path, and since 1998 Indonesia has come quite some way in that respect. By the end of 2005, Indonesia had signed and ratified more international instruments than during the combined reign of the country's first two presidents. Under Sukarno, Indonesia acceded to the Geneva Convention (1958) and to the Convention on the Political Rights of Women (1958) as well as earlier to the International Labour Organizations (ILO) Conventions on

Abolition of Forced Labour (No. 29; 1950), the Right to Organize and Collective Bargaining (1956) and Equal Remuneration for Men and Women Workers (1957). During Suharto's New Order, the country acceded to the Convention on the Elimination of All Forms of Discrimination against Women (CEDAW, 1984), to the Convention on the Rights of the Child (CRC, 1990) and to the International Convention against Apartheid in Sports (1993).

During the first seven years of the post-Suharto era, most accessions took place under the Habibie presidency. By the end of 2005, Indonesia had ratified the Convention against Torture and other Cruel, Inhuman or Degrading Treatment and Punishment (1998) and the International Convention on the Elimination of all Forms of Racial Discrimination (1999), as well as the ILO Conventions on Freedom of Association and Protection of the Right to Organize (1998), Discrimination in Employment and Occupation (1999), Minimum Age for Admission to Employment (1999), Abolition of Forced Labour (1999), the Worst Forms of Child Labour (1999) and Labour Inspection in Industry and Commerce (2003). Indonesia had also signed, but by the end of 2005 had yet to ratify, the Optional Protocol to CEDAW (in 2000) the two Optional Protocols to CRC on the Involvement of Children in Armed Conflict and on the Sale of Children, Child Prostitution and Child Pornography (both in 2001), and the Convention on the Rights of Migrant Workers and the Members of their Families (2004).[27] In September 2005, Indonesia finally ratified the two important covenants: the International Covenants on Economic, Social and Cultural Rights (ICESCR) and on Civil and Political Rights (ICCPR), the latter albeit with one reservation concerning the right to self-determination.[28]

Indonesia has had two five-year Human Rights Action Plans. The first was released in 1998 by former president Habibie, the second was left by the outgoing Megawati administration as an ambitious legacy for Susilo Bambang Yudhoyono's government. Included in both plans are timetables for accession to international human rights instruments. Envisaged for ratification are the Convention on the Prevention and Punishment of the Crime of Genocide (2000/2007),[29] the Convention for the Suppression of the Traffic in Persons and the Exploitation of the Prostitution of Others (2004), the Optional Protocol of the Convention against Torture (2008), the Rome Statute of the International Criminal Court (2008) and both the Convention and Protocol Relating to the Status of Refugees (2009).[30]

## *Pancasila* still considered as 'the source of all sources of law'

Belief in the One God, just and civilized humanism, Indonesian unity, rule of the people guided by wisdom in deliberation/representation, and social justice for the whole Indonesian people are the Five Principles, or *Panca Sila*, coined by Indonesia's first president, Sukarno. The Principles later became moulded into a state ideology that was used to indoctrinate each and every

Indonesian citizen during the era of Suharto's New Order regime. *Pancasila* was also to be the *asas tunggal*, the sole foundation, for any kind of societal organization, and by as early as 1966 *Pancasila* had officially been accorded the status of 'source of all sources of law'.

Gone are the days of such indoctrination and organizations, including political parties, may today refer to concepts other than *Pancasila* as their ideological basis. What has not changed is *Pancasila's* status in the hierarchy of sources of law. In 2000, when the MPR came up with a new determination of the same, they enunciated that the nation's fundamental sources of law were *Pancasila* as laid down in the preamble and body of the constitution.[31] More explicit were legislators four years later, who began the Law on Legislation with the statement, '*Pancasila* is the source of all sources of law of the state.'[32] Previously the interpretation of these five general principles lay with the executive, if not with Suharto himself. With its establishment, the question is now if it is the Constitutional Court that possesses the authority to give a final and binding interpretation on the meaning of *Pancasila*.

## Dealing with contradictory legislation

Apart from *Pancasila*, the constitution heads the hierarchy of Indonesia's sources of law followed, in descending order, by laws,[33] government regulations and presidential regulations.[34] The institution in charge of deciding whether or not a law is constitutional is the Constitutional Court, but the Supreme Court also has the authority to conduct judicial reviews and decide whether lower-ranking legislation, such as a particular government regulation, sits in accordance with a law. Matters become difficult when two laws contain contradictory regulations – not such an unusual occurrence in Indonesia – as no specific institution is in charge of deciding on such a problem. One option can be to define the problem in a way so that it can be brought before the Constitutional Court for judicial review. However, if then the Constitutional Court's verdict does not live up to expectations, the problem at hand might involve structural issues rather than merely concern the violation of constitutional rights. In such a case, the problem cannot be solved by a decision of the Constitutional Court made on strictly legal terms. Law is sometimes characterized as solidified policies; accordingly, contradictory laws mirror contradictory policies. In such a case, the solution to a problem cannot – and should not – be expected from the Constitutional Court judges. Rather, it is the responsibility of legislators (that is, government and parliament) to find a political solution which can then solidify into improved, non-contradictory legislation that no longer violates rights. The problem concerning the division of Papua is a case in point.[35]

While contradicting laws are one legacy of New Order lawmaking that survives to the present day, circumscribing a law's content in its official explanation is another.[36] The latter problem was addressed by legislators in the previously mentioned 2004 Law on Legislation and their stance is supported by the Constitutional Court. As a consequence, no longer can the explanatory part of a law contain formulations which, in effect, modify the meaning of the clauses they endeavour to explain.[37] The Constitutional Court underlined this in a 2005 verdict where the part of a law being contested and brought for judicial review had been included in such an explanation.[38] This Constitutional Court verdict had considerable relevance for Indonesia's regional elections of 2005. Much had been at stake for the plaintiff, a retired general from North Sulawesi, due to just one sentence in the contested official explanation of the concerned law, which decided whether he could stand as candidate for governor in the upcoming elections of heads of the regional executives. The law under review holds that parties or party coalitions wanting to put forward a candidate for election need to overcome a defined electoral threshold, regardless of whether they are already a party or coalition represented in the provincial parliament or not, whereas the same law's explanation limited this right to parties in parliament. As the parties backing the plaintiff's proposed candidacy did not meet this requirement, his participation would have been ruled ineligible. But the Constitutional Court sided with the former general's argument of appeal, rejected any infringement on his right to run for public office and reminded lawmakers to abide by their own standards of lawmaking.[39]

## Loopholes in the liberal law of procedure remain

As a whole, Indonesia's current Code of Criminal Procedure (KUHAP), which replaced its harsh predecessor, the surviving Dutch colonial code, in 1981, is considered rather liberal. The KUHAP contains numerous precepts concerning the due process of law, which are in line with international standards such as those laid down in the ICCPR. The post-Suharto era has seen many of these standards iterated in Indonesia's new Law on Human Rights. However, criticism continues to be heaped on the KUHAP's lack of provisions for punitive sanctions in cases where officials do not abide by the Code. Furthermore, an exemption clause exists that provides a loophole allowing the KUHAP's liberal principles to be restricted or even subverted.[40] During the New Order, this meant that in cases of alleged subversion the notorious Anti-Subversion Law applied. While the Anti-Subversion Law was finally repealed in 1999, on the very same day legislators amended the Criminal Code, introducing several rubbery draconian paragraphs outlawing communism. So broad are these new clauses that they can serve as a new tool against unwanted opposition.[41] But one key difference to the workings of the Anti-Subversion Law is that these anti-communism paragraphs do not impinge on Indonesia's law of procedure: the KUHAP remains the legal basis for prosecution and trial in cases referring to communism.

The exemption clause of the KUHAP continues to exist. New legislation, for example the new Anti-Terrorism Law,[42] includes many regulations concerning procedure that not only violate international standards but also deviate significantly from provisions in the KUHAP. The regulations most criticized in this law include the broad definition of the crime of terrorism, leaving its interpretation open to abuse, the provision for detaining a suspect for up to six months without charge and the allowance for intelligence reports to be used as preliminary evidence in arresting and detaining a suspect. What has been feared since the introduction of the law, namely its abuse in silencing unwanted opposition, has sadly become reality (*Tapol Press Release*, 28 October 2002).[43] One human rights organization, which compiled different examples of such abuse in a 2005 publication, reported:

> Many of the complaints on implementation of the [anti-terrorism] law came from Muslim groups and defense lawyers, who claim that in mid-2003 police began rounding up Muslim activists and graduates of religious boarding schools with no evidence of wrongdoing. In September 2003, a coalition of nongovernment organizations named the Defense Team of the Victims of Antiterrorism Law (*Tim Pembela Korban Undang-undang Antiterorisme*, or Tim KUAT) announced a lawsuit against the police on behalf of 21 people arbitrarily detained by the police. Eleven of the 21 people had already been released due to insufficient evidence at the time of the suit.
>
> (Hicks and McClintock 2005: 11)

Had Indonesia's amended constitution included the prohibition of arbitrary arrest and detention as laid down in the Universal Declaration of Human Rights and elsewhere, victims of the Anti-Terrorism Law would have been in a position to apply for the law's judicial review by the Constitutional Court.[44]

## INSTITUTIONAL CHANGE

Too great an influence by Indonesia's ruling executive in the judicial realm had always been a focus of criticism concerning the functioning of the Indonesian judiciary. During the spring and summer of 2004, a long overdue step along the road towards the separation of powers was made:[45] No longer would the Ministry of Justice, the Ministry of Religious Affairs or the armed forces commander determine administrative, organizational or financial matters of any of the courts. For all four of Indonesia's judicatures – general, administrative, religious and military – this was henceforth done by the Supreme Court.[46] However, the necessary follow-up amendments of corresponding laws have so far only partly been accomplished.

### A glimmer of hope – Indonesia's new Constitutional Court

The Constitutional Court was established in August 2003. Compared to the implementation of other new constitutional precepts applying to the judicial realm – especially those concerning the aforementioned separation of powers – the Court saw the light of life rather quickly, if only due to a deadline designated in the constitution which Indonesia's legislature and executive chose to abide by. Barely meeting the deadline, the Law on the Constitutional Court was enacted four days ahead of time and the presidential decree appointing the nine judges came only two days before the deadline.[47]

But the DPR and the government took the liberty of limiting jurisdiction of the Constitutional Court's judges, determining that the Constitutional Court could only accept for judicial review laws that had been passed after October 1999.[48] Although legislators have produced a number of new laws since 1998, a bulk of New Order and earlier legislation remains in place with numerous regulations that could be challenged before the court. For example, at the beginning of the Constitutional Court's work the whole body of implementing legislation regarding the judicial realm, which still allowed the interference of the executive, was awaiting amendment.

Soon after their inauguration, the Constitutional Court judges were confronted with applications for judicial review concerning laws dating from the Suharto-era.[49] In one of its first verdicts, concerning a law dating from 1985, the court decided to use the opportunity to make a clear statement with respect to its mandate. The majority of the Constitutional Court judges were by no means willing to accept the legal limitation on their constitutional mandate. Declaring an opinion on the matter, the bench indicated that they would henceforth 'put aside' the contested prescription.[50] Here, the judges only provided a legal opinion; the contested article was not itself subject to judicial review. As the Constitutional Court may not act *suo moto* (on its own initiative), it took until an application for judicial review of the related article was brought before the judges that they issued a corresponding verdict. In April 2005, still with three dissenting opinions, the Constitutional Court ruled that the temporal limitation on its jurisdiction was unconstitutional and therefore no longer effective.[51]

## Breaking long-cherished taboos

In the short period of its existence, Indonesia's Constitutional Court has issued a number of important and often controversial verdicts. In one such ruling, the judges broke with taboos that had constituted a solid pillar of the New Order regime: anti-communism and the instituted discrimination against former real and alleged communists.

Communism is still illegal in Indonesia, as indicated by the aforementioned inclusion of anti-communism regulations into the Criminal Code. How strongly rooted a taboo communism is can be seen in the reaction to a bold move by former president Wahid, when in early 2000 he not only called for an investigation into the killings of suspected communists during 1965–66, but also for the revocation of a notorious 1966 MPR decree banning the Indonesian Communist Party (PKI) and associated organizations and outlawing the spreading of communism.[52] Within the MPR, most factions were decidedly against any such moves. According to reports, Wahid was even threatened with impeachment should he continue to pursue the issue (*tapol-Bulletin*, No. 158, p. 22).[53] Three years later, the MPR explicitly determined the continued validity of the 1966 Decree.[54]

Former PKI members remain subject to various forms of discrimination today. One related infringement of their political rights was that they were still denied the right to stand as candidates for the 2004 parliamentary elections. This was an issue the Constitutional Court had to rule on and it ruled in favour of the plaintiffs. In its legal argument, the Constitutional Court referred to an individual's constitutional right not to be discriminated against, to a citizen's passive voting right and to the principle of equality before the law and in governance. Once again, the importance of having rights constitutionally codified is seen. The judges' argument included that the contested prohibition was based on political considerations; in denying former PKI members their passive voting rights, the Constitutional Court saw 'nuances of a political sentencing'. In their legal considerations, the judges invoked the constitutional principle of rule of law and stressed, 'As a state under the rule of law (*negara hukum*) every prohibition that has a direct link with rights and freedoms of citizens has to be based on a final court verdict'.

Concerning the continued validity of the aforementioned 1966 MPR decree prohibiting communism, the judges argued that the decree was concerned with the prohibition of the PKI and the spreading of communist ideas, matters that were in no way linked with a denial of a person's passive voting rights, including those of a former communist. With reference to an individual's constitutional right to be free from discrimination, the Constitutional Court argued that regardless of the continued validity of the 1966 decree, former PKI members had to be treated like other citizens, without discrimination.[55] However, the end result for former PKI members, with respect to their ability to exercise their rights to stand for election to parliament, was that they would have to wait until the next elections, scheduled for 2009.

## DEALING WITH PAST AND PRESENT GRAVE HUMAN RIGHTS VIOLATIONS

'BIN [the State Intelligence Agency] is believed to have been involved in a conspiracy to murder Munir', Asmara Nababan, deputy chairman of the fact-finding team investigating the murder of the noted human rights lawyer, is reported as saying shortly before the handover of the team's findings to Indonesia's president in 2005 (*The Jakarta Post.com*, 23 June 2005). The poisoning of Munir had been the latest murder of an Indonesian human rights defender. Credible reports state that at least 15 human rights activists had been killed since 2000 while none of the perpetrators had yet been brought to justice.[56]

'They are no more', retired general Wiranto was quoted as saying in 2005 when questioned about the fate of 14 activists who 'disappeared' during 1997–98 (*Suara Pembaruan.com*, 15 June 2005). They are no more. They are dead. Will the perpetrators ever be brought to account?

Nobody knows how many people have been killed in the long-lasting conflicts in Aceh and Papua. In the case of Aceh, with reference to just the 18 months before the December 2004 tsunami devastated the province, security forces acknowledged the killing of more than 3,500 people of whom almost 700 were officially categorized as civilians.[57]

One important point is clear. For any sustainable resolution of these conflicts, past and present human rights violations need to be properly addressed. Indonesia's long tradition of impunity must be brought to an end. However, developments since Suharto's demise have yielded little in terms of hope that any comprehensive tackling of this dire issue is likely soon. Only a few cases of grave human rights violations have been addressed – due to strong domestic and international public pressure. The trials concerning the crimes committed in East Timor during 1999 have received the broadest international attention but their outcome does not bode well for the hope of seeing justice rightly served in other cases.

## Establishing domestic human rights courts to avoid an international tribunal

United Nations sources estimate that at least 1,300 people were killed before, during and after the referendum in East Timor in 1999 (Cohen 2003: 2). In the aftermath, the Indonesian government did all it could to avoid an international tribunal for the trial of the perpetrators as had been recommended by a UN-mandated Commission of Inquiry, among others.[58] The international community then came to an agreement that Indonesia should bring those responsible for the East Timor atrocities to trial in courts under its national jurisdiction. Against this backdrop of international pressure, Indonesia established human rights courts whose exclusive jurisdiction concerns cases of gross human rights violations.[59]

Indonesia's Law on Human Rights Courts, which functions as the legal basis for these courts, has been lauded for containing crucial provisions that are almost identical to those contained in the Rome Statute of the International Criminal Court.[60] The law's comprehensive definition of crimes against humanity is important for facilitating the prosecution and trial of individuals responsible for gross human rights violations, as are provisions concerning the responsibility of military commanders and other superiors. Nevertheless, the Indonesian legislators have been quite frank about the fact that the law came into being as a reaction to the vocal calls for an international tribunal. That legislators also provided the human rights courts with jurisdiction over crimes committed outside of Indonesia (i.e. including newly independent East Timor) was done with the intention '. . . to protect Indonesian citizens who have committed gross violations of human rights outside the territorial boundaries in the sense that they be tried under this Human Rights Courts Law'.[61]

The outcome of the resulting trials shows how well the 'protection' has worked. Of the 18 defendants brought to trial over the East Timor atrocities, all but one – whose appeal was still pending at the time of writing – have been acquitted, either in the first instance or in subsequent appeal proceedings. One supporting factor for this result was certainly a limitation of the court's jurisdiction, as implemented on presidential orders in 2001.[62] Torture, murder and extermination count among the crimes categorized as gross violations of human rights if they are carried out in a widespread or systematic manner according to both the Rome Statute and the Indonesian Human Rights Courts Law. But with the human rights court's jurisdiction limited to events occurring in the periods one month before the East Timor referendum on independence and 30 days immediately following the ballot, and furthermore limited only to three specific areas in East Timor,[63] it became difficult – if not impossible – to prove any widespread or systematic nature of the atrocities.[64]

Whether the East Timor trials would happen even with the Human Rights Courts Law in place was initially still subject to a degree of uncertainty, as the constitution prohibits legislation being applied retroactively (that is, to crimes committed before the concerned legislation had been put in place). This prohibition of retroactive effect of law is an important principle as regards legal certainty and a key right that has found various forms of international codification. It is considered a non-derogable right: a right that may not be suspended under any circumstance. However, in international human rights instruments an exemption is nevertheless granted; for example, the general retroactivity prohibition in the ICCPR has the addition that

> . . . nothing in this article shall prejudice the trial and punishment of any person for any act or omission which, at the time when it was committed, was criminal according to the general principles of law recognized by the community of nations.
>
> (Art. 15 (2), International Covenant on Civil and Political Rights)

Since August 2000, the Indonesian constitution has provided as a non-derogable right that no individual can be prosecuted on a retroactive legal basis. Furthermore, in 1999 legislators had included this right in the Human Rights Law. However, whereas the Indonesian Human Rights Law contains an exemption clause similar to the one stipulated in the ICCPR,[65] no such addition appears in the constitution. This is particularly poignant given that at the very time the MPR included the non-derogable rights into the constitution, legislators, who are part of the MPR, were in the last stage of deliberating the Human Rights Courts Law that explicitly allows that the law, in certain cases, is applied retroactively. As we have mentioned above, enabling that perpetrators of the atrocities in East Timor 1999 were prosecuted and tried under national jurisdiction was a key *raison d'être* for the Human Rights Courts Law. An unconditional prohibition of retroactive effect of law in the constitution would constitute a strong legal argument against the establishment of any human rights court for crimes committed before the laws was enacted in November 2000 (that is, it could be invoked to prevent that the perpetrators for the crimes in East Timor be tried under national law).

Leaving the exemption clause out of the constitution was no oversight, as was claimed at the time and thus must have been done deliberately. Whose interest would it best serve? The immediate answer seems to be: the generals'. But promising national proceedings had been the Indonesian government's strategy for avoiding an international tribunal and thus had the East Timor trials in Indonesia in fact been prevented, this could easily have backfired.

The trials took place and, in order to come to terms with the retroactivity prohibition, another article of the constitution was referred to.[66] The legal details are beyond the scope of this chapter, but it is sufficient to say that in the meantime the possibility to exempt from this prohibition has been supported by a Constitutional Court verdict. The plaintiff was the former governor of East Timor, Abilio Soares, one of six defendants in the East Timor trials who were convicted and the only one who had to spend time in prison. Soares' application to declare the clause in the Human Rights Courts Law that allows its retroactive application as unconstitutional was rejected by the Constitutional Court.[67] However, this did not end up mattering much to East Timor's former governor: by the time the Constitutional Court delivered its verdict, the Supreme Court had already overturned Soares' sentence and he had been acquitted.

### State ordained reconciliation between Indonesia and East Timor . . .

The verdicts of the Timor trials evoked strong criticism, as did the move by the governments of Indonesia and East Timor to establish a Commission of Truth and Friendship (CTF). It is feared that this commission will lead to a whitewashing of the past.[68] Critical points in the terms of reference include that the Commission does not aim at prosecution; that it will not recommend the establishment of any judicial body; and that it is authorized to recommend amnesties for cooperating perpetrators.[69] As it is not intented for the Commission to enable judicial proceedings against perpetrators of gross violations of human rights and as there are no limitations provided concerning amnesties, the door is wide open for the perpetrators of crimes against humanity committed in East Timor to be granted amnesty. This has been criticized as clearly going against international standards.[70]

The same conclusion was also reached by three international experts who expressed unequivocal opinions regarding the entire justice process concerning the crimes committed in East Timor in 1999. The three-member Commission of Experts[71] was appointed by UN Secretary-General Kofi Annan in February 2005 with the task of evaluating the justice process in both Indonesia and East Timor so far and giving recommendations for future proceedings. After initial difficulties – the Indonesian government was at first not prepared to grant the commissioners entry visas – the Commission of Experts was quick to complete its evaluation, handing over its report in June 2005.

Concerning the Truth and Friendship Commission, the experts stated, among others, '376. The Commission finds that there are certain provisions in the terms of reference of the Commission of Truth and Friendship which contradict international standards of denial of impunity for crimes against humanity, which require clarification, re-assessment and revision [. . .]' (Commission of Experts 2005: 88). Nor did the experts mince their words when they wrote regarding the flawed East Timor trials held in Indonesia,

> 515. Since the trials undertaken by the Ad Hoc Human Rights Court were seriously flawed and not in conformity with national and international legal standards, the Commission of Experts recommends that the Attorney-General's Office comprehensively review prosecutions before the Ad Hoc Court and reopen prosecutions as may be appropriate, on the basis of additional charges, new facts or evidence or other grounds available under Indonesian law. . . .
> 516. If appropriate, the Commission recommends that de novo trials take place and that indicted persons be re-tried in accordance with acceptable national and international standards.
>
> (Commission of Experts, 2005: 118f)

The Commission of Experts recommended that a deadline be set for East Timor and Indonesia to follow up on its recommendations. In the case of non-compliance, the commission advised establishing an international tribunal or using the International Criminal Court for the prosecution of the perpetrators of the atrocities committed in East Timor (Commission of Experts 2005: 120).[72]

### . . . and state ordained national reconciliation in Indonesia

Another commission is planned in Indonesia to address past gross violations of human rights: the Truth and Reconciliation Commission (TRC); Concerns quite similar to those put forward concerning the Indonesian–East Timorese CTF have been voiced with regard to the Indonesian TRC.

The idea for such a commission was first brought up in 1998 by the National Human Rights Commission Komnas HAM. Two years later, the MPR also called for such a commission to be established (ICTJ 2005). But the way the planned commission was referred to in the Human Rights Courts

Law caused NGOs to express fears that a door was being opened through which perpetrators could slip out.[73] Such fears were, in the end, not unfounded. The 2004 law, which provided the legal basis for the planned Truth and Reconciliation Commission, was clearly biased in favour of the perpetrators; strong criticism has, for example, been levelled against the amnesty mechanism provided. The scope for granting amnesties is excessively broad and the reception of compensation on the part of the victims is made dependent on the granting of amnesty to the corresponding perpetrator(s).[74] The International Center for Transitional Justice concluded,

> The Bill sets up a mechanism for reparations that is unfair to victims, subjecting them to unacceptable psychological pressures, and presenting reparations as an incentive to forgive the perpetrators. [. . .] The bill includes an amnesty mechanism that is unacceptable for the kind of crimes under the jurisdiction of the commission. Amnesties for the most serious crimes of international concern, such as genocide or crimes against humanity run counter State obligations under international law. Truth commissions cannot subvert justice. They better serve their objectives by incorporating forms of cooperation with the judicial authorities to fight impunity, which requires a concerted effort to strengthen the capabilities and ensure the fairness of the judiciary.
>
> (González 2005: 20)

It remains to be seen whether the Commission of Experts' criticism on the amnesty mechanism of the CTF will have any repercussions on the regulations for the Indonesian Truth and Reconciliation Commission.[75]

## CONCLUSION

Indonesia is a *negara hukum*, states the country's constitution. However, the fact that impunity for perpetrators of serious crimes persists in Indonesia denies this constitutional theory one important aspect for its practical reality and similarly testifies to the hybrid nature of the post-Suharto regimes. Impunity is not permissible in a democratic state operating under the rule of law. No individual stands above the law, no matter how heavily armed, how powerful, how rich. The way the government of Susilo Bambang Yudhoyono decides to tackle this problem will be a litmus test for the state of *Rechtsstaat* in Indonesia.

Two issues are currently at the forefront of international attention in this respect: the gross violations of human rights committed in East Timor and the killing of the human rights defender, Munir. But these are not the only crimes for which those responsible still need to be brought to justice: for other grave human rights violations, especially in Aceh and Papua, victims and their relatives demand and are entitled to the same.

In Indonesia today, it remains a dangerous undertaking to work for the implementation of the constitutionally-determined *negara hukum*, for the rule of law and the respect for and protection of human rights. The poisoning of Munir is the latest and most blatant example of how endangered human rights defenders in Indonesia still are. But the same goes for courageous prosecutors and judges: the killing of Judge Syaifuddin Kartasasmita by contract killers comes to mind. Kartasasmita had dared to pass sentence over Suharto's son Tommy Mandala Putra, and speculations still abound the mysterious sudden death of the late Attorney-General Baharuddin Lopa, who was regarded as a person of high integrity.[76]

There is a struggle over the rule of law in Indonesia. In both the state- and non-state sectors there are forces for change and forces fighting change, people who work to promote democracy, rule of law and human rights protection and people who stand to profit from retaining the authoritarian structure of New Order times. The international community should grant the former all the necessary support. Their ongoing and often brave work commands respect and needs backing up. One important step in this respect is that the international community be as clear on the problem of impunity as the Commission of Experts has been. That people commit gross violations of human rights and walk free simply cannot be tolerated.

As an example for positive developments concerning the rule of law in Indonesia, the work of the Constitutional Court has been mentioned. But Indonesia's Constitutional Court needs legislators to do their share of work in support of *Rechtsstaat* as well. While constitutional amendments have brought considerable improvements, they do not yet suffice. Especially given the increasing power of the security sector and in light of the abuse of power by its members, it is paramount that constitutional restrictions on their power be put in place.

All this does not say anything about implementation. Precondition for proper implementation of laws are a functioning administration, functioning law enforcement and a functioning judicial sector, and it needs the ongoing courage and political will to act accordingly. Indonesia has a long way to go yet.

## LEGAL DOCUMENTS

Human Rights Action Plan 1998–2003 included in Presidential Decree 129/1998: Keputusan Presiden Republik Indonesia Nomor 129 Tahun 1998 tentang Rencana Aksi Nasional Hak-Hak Asasi Manusia Indonesia. Online. Available HTTP: <http://www.ham.go.id/> (accessed 29 September 2004).

Human Rights Action Plan 2004–2009 included in Presidential Decree 40/2004: Keputusan Presiden Republik Indonesia Nomor 40 Tahun 2004 tentang Rencana Aksi Nasional Hak Asasi Manusia Indonesia Tahun 2004–2009. Online. Available HTTP: <http://www.ham.go.id/> (accessed 1 September 2004).

KUHAP: Kitab Undang-Undang Hukum Acara Pidana (Code of Criminal Procedure), Bandung, 1982 (Binacipta).

Law 39/1999: Undang-Undang Republik Indonesia Nomor 39 Tahun 1999 tentang Hak Asasi Manusia.

Law 26/2000: Undang-Undang Republik Indonesia Nomor 26 Tahun 2000 tentang Pengadilan Hak Asasi Manusia.

Law 24/2003: Undang-Undang Republik Indonesia Nomor 24 Tahun 2003 tentang Mahkamah Konstitusi.

Law 4/2004: Undang-Undang Republik Indonesia Nomor 4 Tahun 2004 tentang Kekuasaan Kehakiman.

Law 10/2004: Undang-Undang Republik Indonesia Nomor 10 Tahun 2004 tentang Pembentukan Peraturan Perundang-Undangan. Online. Available HTTP: <http://www.gtzsfdm.or.id/documents/laws_n_regs/laws/2004/UU_10_2004%20Pembentukan%20Peraturan%20PerUU.pdf> (accessed 22 December 2005).

Law 16/2004: Undang-Undang Republik Indonesia Nomor 16 Tahun 2004 tentang Kejaksaan Republik Indonesia. Online. Available HTTP: <http://www.kejaksaan.go.id/UU_KEJAKSAAN.htm> (accessed 28 September 2004).

Law 27/2004: Undang-Undang Republik Indonesia Nomor 27 Tahun 2004 tentang Komisi Kebenaran dan Rekonsiliasi, received from hukumonline.

MPR Decree V/1998: Ketetapan MPR Nomor V/MPR/1998 tentang Pemberian Tugas dan Wewenang Khusus kepada Presiden/Mandataris MPR RI dalam Rangka Penyuksesan dan Pengamanan Pembangunan Nasional sebagai Pengamalan Pancasila.

MPR Decree X/1998: Ketetapan MPR RI Nomor X/MPR/1998 tentang Pokok-Pokok Reformasi Pembangunan Dalam Rangka Penyelamatan dan Normalisasi Kehidupan Nasional Sebagai Haluan Negara.

MPR Decree XVII/1998: Ketetapan MPR RI Nomor XVII/MPR/1998 tentang Hak Asasi Manusia.

MPR Decree III/2000: Ketetapan MPR RI Nomor III/MPR/2000 tentang Sumber Hukum dan Tata Urutan Peraturan Perundang-undangan, in: Putusan MPR RI. Sidang Tahunan MPR RI 7–18 Agustus 2000, Sekretariat Jendral MPR RI, Jakarta.

Presidential Decree 53/2001: Keputusan Presiden Nomor 53 Tahun 2001 tentang Pembentukan Pengadilan Hak Asasi Manusia Ad Hoc pada Pengadilan Negeri Jakarta Pusat.

Presidential Decree 96/2001: Keputusan Presiden Republik Indonesia Nomor 96 Tahun 2001 tentang Perubahan atas Keputusan Presiden Nomor 53 Tahun 2001 tentang Pembentukan Pengadilan Hak Asasi Manusia Ad Hoc pada Pengadilan Negeri Jakarta Pusat.

Terms of Reference CTF: Kerangka Acuan Komisi Kebenaran dan Persahabatan Yang dibentuk oleh Republik Indonesia dan Republik Demokratik Timor-Leste, Source: Direktorat Informasi dan Media Departemen Luar Negeri – Republik Indonesia, from the homepage of the Embassy of the Republic of Indonesia in Tokyo.

UUD 1945: Undang-Undang Dasar 1945, original 1945 Constitution. Online. Available HTTP: <http://www.lin.go.id/detail.asp?idartcl=1311026XZA0002&by=HukReg> (accessed 12 March 2004).

UUD NRI 1945: Undang-Undang Dasar Negara Republik Indonesia Tahun 1945, Indonesian 1945 Constitution after its Fourth Amendment. Online. Available HTTP: <http://www.mpr.go.id/h/index.php?fz=6> (accessed 1 June 2003).

Unless otherwise mentioned, legislation has been downloaded from <http://www.ri.go.id/produk_uu/datar_isi-2.htm> and <http://www.mpr.go.id>.

## NOTES

1 I am grateful to my colleague Alex Flor from Watch Indonesia! for helpful critical comments.
2 Terms in brackets in the original.
3 Art. 1 (3) of the amended constitution, henceforth referred to as UUD NRI 1945.
4 Clear words on the pervasiveness of corruption with regard to the judiciary were used by UN Special Rapporteur Cumaraswamy: 'The Special Rapporteur considers that it is essential to place the allegations of judicial corruption in the context of the administration of justice system as a whole. Corruption is not limited to the judiciary, instead it spreads as cancer in the entire system, the judiciary, police, prosecutors and Office of the Attorney-General.' Report of the Special Rapporteur on the Independence of Judges and Lawyers Dato' Param Cumaraswamy, submitted in accordance with Commission on Human Rights Resolution 2002–43. Report on the Mission to Indonesia 15–24 July 2002, E/CN.4/2003/65/Add.2
5 Cf. General Explanations of Law 10/2004; Law 4/2004; Law 16/2004; Explanation Art. 6 (2) Law 39/1999; Considerans of Law 16/2004; no literal translations.
6 For details on this and the following: Stockmann, 2004c: 10ff.
7 For a list of international human rights instruments see <http://www.ohchr.org/english/law/index.htm>.
8 Art. 1 MPR Decree V/1998.
9 As laid down in Decree of the Provisional MPR (MPR *Sementara* or MPRS) No. XX/1966; see also Southwood and Flanagan, 1983: 222. For background on the legal and judicial system under Suharto, see Lev 1978; Lindsey 1997, 1999; Thoolen 1987.
10 '[. . .] the constitution we are now drafting is a Provisional Constitution. If I may say, this is an Express [hurriedly prepared] Constitution. Later, if we have already a state in a normal atmosphere we certainly will invite the *Majelis Permusyawaratan Rakyat* (MPR, or the People's Consultative Assembly) to draft a more complete and perfect constitution.' M. Yamin (1971) *Naskah Persiapan Undang-Undang Dasar 1945*, Vol. I, Jakarta, p. 410, quoted in Lubis, 1993: 81. The 1945 Constitution is, according to Lindsey, '[. . .] the shortest Constitution in the world, notable more for what it does not state than for what it does' (Lindsey 1999a: 17).
11 Here, I only provide a very general overview; I have covered developments in greater detail in Stockmann 2004a, 2004c, 2005.
12 Cf. the new Art. 22 E on general elections in the constitution.
13 Cf. Art. 6 A UUD NRI 1945. In 2005, another type of election was high on the political agenda: As another novelty, Indonesians have the opportunity to directly elect the heads of local governments (i.e. governors, regents, and village heads). Direct elections are, however, not determined in the constitution. The latter only requires the Executives to be democratically elected; cf. Art. 18 (4) UUD NRI 1945.
14 Cf. second part of the Art. 1 (2) of the original 1945 Constitution, henceforth referred to as UUD 1945.
15 More precisely on: regional autonomy, centre–regions relations, partition, establishment or fusion of regions, financial balancing between centre and regions as well as management of natural and other economic resources. The DPD is also authorized to supervise implementation of the concerned laws.

16 Cf. Art. 2, 3 UUD NRI 1945 for the MPR; Art. 22 C, D for the DPD.

17 Cf. for the above Art. 24, 24 C UUD NRI 1945. Other tasks of the Constitutional Court are to decide on cases concerning authority vested in state institutions under the constitution, to decide on the banning of a political party and to rule on cases of disputes concerning the election results. Furthermore, the court has a role in impeachment proceedings: It needs to approve of the DPR's impeachment proposal before the latter can be submitted to the MPR.

18 For this and other tasks of the Commission, see Art. 24 B UUD NRI 1945.

19 The Human Rights Charter explicitly also names the UDHR as its basis: 'B. Basis [. . .] 2. The Indonesian nation [*sic*] as a member of the United Nations has the responsibility to respect the Universal Declaration of Human Rights and several other international human rights instruments.' Cf. MPR Decree XVII/1998, Annex I B.

20 For a detailed analysis of the Human Rights Charter and the constitutional article against the background of the UDHR, see Stockmann, 2004c: 216–288.

21 Cf. Art. 28-J UUD NRI 1945.

22 Cf. Art. 29 (2) UDHR; Art. 28 J (2) UUD NRI 1945.

23 Cf. Art. 39 Human Rights Charter, included in the MPR Decree XVII/1998.

24 Cf. Art. 28 I (2) and 28 H (2) UUD NRI 1945 respectively.

25 Cf. Human Rights Action Plan 1998–2003, IV- IV B 2.

26 Elsewhere I have shown that other domestic legislation shows discrepancies with CEDAW (Stockmann 2004c: 281).

27 For the status of ratification see <http://www.ohchr.org/english/law/index.htm> and <http://www.ilo.org/ilolex/english/convdispl.htm>.

28 The legislators declared that the right to self-determination would not apply for a part of the population in a sovereign independent state and could not be understood as legalizing or supporting actions that would be divisive for or destroy, in whole or in part, the integrity and the political unity of a sovereign and independent state. See Press Release No. 66/PR/IX/2005, Direktorat Informasi dan Media, Departemen Luar Negeri Republik Indonesia, 30 September 2005.

29 Years given refer to the envisaged ratification in the first Human Rights Action Plan and the date for preparing ratification as determined in the second Human Rights Action Plan. The first plan covered the years 1998 to 2003, the second from 2004 to 2009.

30 Cf. Human Rights Action Plan 2004–2009, III B. The above-mentioned human rights instrument that Indonesia has so far only signed are also on the agenda for ratification within the coming years.

31 Cf. Art. 1 (3) MPR Decree III/2000.

32 Cf. Art. 2 Law 10/2004.

33 Also *Perpus* (*Peraturan Pemerintah Pengganti Undang-Undang*, government regulations in lieu of a law) which range at the same level as laws.

34 The latter were formerly called presidential decrees.

35 For an analysis of the verdict, see Stockmann 2004b.

36 Sometimes clauses are also circumscribed or even subverted by other clauses in the same law.

37 Cf. Law 10/2004, Annex Chapter I E.

38 Cf. *Putusan Perkara Nomor 005/PUU-III/2005*, available at <http://www.mahkamahkonstitusi.go.id>.

39 This was, of course, not the wording the court chose.

40 On the KUHAP see, for example, Hart 1987.

41 Cf. the new Art. 107 of the Criminal Code.

42 Different rules of procedure exempting from the KUHAP also apply for prosecution and trials before the newly established human rights courts.

43 For details on the anti-terrorism legislation see *Tapol Press Release*, 28 October 2002; Lindsey 2002.
44 More danger looms from attempts of the State Intelligence Agency BIN to increase its role in criminal proceedings. BIN's ideas initially became public when a Draft Law on State Intelligence transpired in 2003: BIN envisaged for itself the authority to detain suspects for up to 90 days for the purpose of intelligence investigation, with the option to extend this period three times. In total this detention period for investigation (i.e. without charge) would equal the one-year detention period that had been included in the Anti-Subversion Law. BIN furthermore wanted to be authorized to conduct investigations and to take a whole range of measures during these intelligence investigations. Amongst others, BIN would want to see the suspension of the defendant's rights to counsel, his or her right to refuse to give evidence and to get into contact with persons outside the prison or place of detention. For details of the Draft and criticism see, for example, *Berita hukumonline*, 01 March 2003, 04 March 2003; *The Jakarta Post.com*, 05 March 2003.
45 Already in 1999, in a brief amendment law to the Law on Judicial Authority (Law 35/1999), it had been stipulated that the judicial institutions were to be placed under the authority of the Supreme Court.
46 An element of continuity in this process of the change might be worth noting: Not only all employees of the civilian courts, but also all employees of the concerned departments at the Ministries of Justice and Religion become employees of the Supreme Court. And those holding 'structural positions' – again also at the respective ministries – are stipulated to continue in their positions. Under the military judicature, only the civilian employees become employees of the Supreme Court while the supervision of military employees is to be conducted according to the regulations for military personnel (Art. 43–45 Law 4/2004). No provisions for the possibility of any kind of lustration processes are included here.
47 Cf. Art. 24 C UUD NRI 1945 on the Constitutional Court; Art. III, Transitional Regulations, UUD NRI 1945 for the deadline. The Law on the Constitutional Court is Law 24/2003. For details on the Constitutional Court and its work, see Stockmann 2006.
48 Cf. Art. 50 Law 24/2003.
49 Already before his inauguration as Constitutional Judge, Chief Justice Jimly Asshiddiqie had hinted at a way to deal with the issue. He recalls what he stated on the matter during the fit and proper test that parliament conducted before determining its three candidates: 'During the fit and proper test, I was asked about many things, including my opinion on Article 50 of the Law on the Constitutional Court. I conveyed my opinion on the Constitutional Court, including on Article 50 which I consider as violating the Constitution. But in order not to disturb the process of establishing the Constitutional Court, I said let this Article be, as the Constitutional Court can later review this article or put aside the validity of the provision' (Asshiddiqie 2004: 13).
50 Cf. the verdict *Putusan Perkara Nomor* 004/PUU-I/2003 available at <http://www.mahkamahkonstitusi.go.id>.
51 The verdict is *Putusan Perkara Nomor* 066/PUU-II/2004 available at <http://www.mahkamahkonstitusi.go.id>.
52 Cf. *Kompas*, 14 April 2000 as reprinted in *Jurnal* 17 April 2000 (*Jurnal* is edited by the MPR Public Relation department).
53 For the positions of different MPR factions and comments from various sides see, for example, *Jurnal*, 28 March 2000; 17 April 2000.
54 This is laid down in MPR Decree I/MPR/2003.See, for example, *Kompas.com*, 8 August 2003.

55 The verdict is *Putusan Perkara Nomor* 011–017/PUU-I/2003 available at <http://www.mahkamahkonstitusi.go.id>.
56 Cf. Hicks and McClintock 2005: 13, with reference to several human rights organizations.
57 For more on these official figures (as well as on the problems concerning obtaining figures) and on the human rights abuses committed in Aceh over the past years, see Amnesty International 2004: 16f.
58 For an evaluation of the trials see Häusler 2004 and Cohen 2003.
59 On the development of the legal bases for trying gross human rights violations see, for example, ICG 2002.
60 As mentioned above, Indonesia is not yet a State Party to the Rome Statute. For details on the law and on the following see Häusler 2004; ICG 2001; Stockmann 2004c: 302ff.
61 Cf. Explanation Art. 5 Law 26/2000.
62 The relevant Presidential Decrees are Decree 53/2001 and Decree 96/2001.
63 Dili, Liquiça and Suai.
64 See also von Braun and Schlicher 2005; Stockmann, 2005: 46ff.
65 It reads: 'An exception to the right not to be tried on a retroactive legal basis can be made in the case of gross violations of human rights which are classified as crimes against humanity' (Elucidation Art. 4 Law 39/1999).
66 This was Art. 28 J (2): 'In carrying out rights and freedoms, every person is obliged to obey the limitations which are laid down in law with the sole purpose of guaranteeing recognition and respect of other people's rights and freedoms and to fulfil just requirements in accordance with moral considerations, religious values, security and public order within a democratic society.' See, for example, General Explanation of Law 26/2000.
67 The verdict is *Putusan Perkara Nomor* 065/PUU-II/2004 available at <http://www.mahkamahkonstitusi.go.id>.
68 For a detailed analysis and criticism of the CTF, see von Braun 2005 and ICTJ 2005a. For a comprehensive study on the very different East Timorese Commission of Reception, Truth and Reconciliation (CAVR), see Schlicher 2005.
69 Cf. Art. 13 c, e; 14 c i Terms of Reference CTF.
70 'Clearly, the possibility of amnesties for the most serious offenses, such as crimes against humanity, war crimes, and genocide, runs counter to international law and is against the principles that have been firmly espoused by the UN Secretary-General' (ICTJ 2005a: 28f). Also see von Braun 2005.
71 The members of the Commission are Justice P. N. Bhagwati (India), Dr. Shaista Shameem (Fiji) and Professor Yozo Yokota (Japan).
72 For comments on the report refer to the press releases by ICTJ
   • <http://www.ictj.org/downloads/COEreport-release.pdf>; tapol
   • <http://tapol.gn.apc.org/pressreleases.htm>; and Watch Indonesia!
   • <http://home.snafu.de/watchin/PE_COE.htm>.
73 See, for example, Flor 2000.
74 Cf. Art. 24–29 Law 27/2004, especially problematic are Art. 27, 29 (2).
75 Not all aspects concerning the problematic dealing with past and present human rights violations could be touched here. Currently on the agenda is also the issue of which courts have jurisdiction over crimes committed by TNI members as deliberations on the amendment of the Law on the Military Judicature (Law 31/1997) are under way. See, for example, *The Jakarta Post.com* 20 June 2005.
76 See Watch Indonesia! press release, 15 November 2004: 'Watch Indonesia! fordert transparente und lückenlose Aufklärung des Mordes an Munir', <http://home-.snafu.de/watchin/munir_15.11.04.htm>.

## BIBLIOGRAPHY

Amnesty International 'Indonesia – New military operations, old patterns of human rights abuses in Aceh (Nanggroe Aceh Darussalam)', AI Index: ASA 21/033/2004, 7 October 2004. Online. Available HTTP: http://web.amnesty.org/library/index/engasa210332004 (accessed 12 November 2005).

Asshiddiqie, J. (2004) 'Setahun Mahkamah Konstitusi: Refleksi Gagasan Dan Penyelenggaraan, Serta Setangkup Harapan', in *Menjaga Denyut Konstitusi. Refleksi Satu Tahun Mahkamah Konstitusi*, ed. by Refly Harun, Zainal A.M. Husein and Bisariyadi, Jakarta: Konstitusi Press.

Cohen, D. (2003) *Intended to Fail. The Trials before the Ad Hoc Human Rights Court in Jakarta*, ed. by the International Center for Transitional Justice. New York: International Center for Transitional Justice. Online. Available HTTP: <http://www.ictj.org/downloads/Indonesiafinal2MB.pdf> (accessed 22 January 2004).

Commission of Experts (2005) *Report to the Secretary-General of the Commission of Experts to Review the Prosecution of Serious Violations of Human Rights in Timor-Leste (the then East Timor) in 1999*, 26 May 2005. Online. Available HTTP: <http://www.etan.org/etanpdf/pdf3/N0542617.pdf> (accessed 29 June 2005).

Dahl, R.A. (1971) *Polyarchy. Participation and Opposition*, London: New Haven.

Flor, A. (2000) 'Sand in die Augen gestreut. Neues Menschenrechtsgesetz soll internationales Tribunal verhindern', in *Indonesien-Information*, 3/2000: 18–20. Also online. Available HTTP: <http://home.snafu.de/watchin/II_Dez_00/Sand_in_Augen.htm> (accessed 25 October 2005).

González, E. (2005) *Comment by the International Center for Transitional Justice on the Bill Establishing a Truth and Reconciliation Commission in Indonesia*, New York: International Center for Transitional Justice. Online. Available HTTP: <http://www.ictj.org/downloads/indo.trc.comment.pdf> (accessed 12 March 2006).

Hart, J. (1987) 'Aspects of Criminal Justice', in H. Thoolen (ed.) *Indonesia and the Rule of Law. Twenty Years of 'New Order' Government*, London: International Commission of Jurists and the Netherlands Institute of Human Rights.

Häusler, B. (2004) *Gerechtigkeit für die Opfer. Eine juristische Untersuchung der indonesischen Menschenrechtsverfahren zu den Verbrechen auf Osttimor im Jahr 1999* (Justice for the Victims. A Legal Opinion on the Indonesian human rights trials concerning the crimes committed in East Timor in 1999), Schriftenreihe Gerechtigkeit und Frieden (Justice and Peace Series), No. 98, Bonn: German Commission Justitia et Pax. Original German version and English translation also online. Available HTTP: <http://home.snafu.de/watchin/Hukum.htm> (accessed 19 September 2005).

Hicks, N. and McClintock, M. (2005) *Reformasi and Resistance: Human Rights Defenders and Counterterrorism in Indonesia*, Human Rights First. Online. Available HTTP: <http://www.humanrightsfirst.org/defenders/hrd_indonesia/reports/reformasi-resist-indonesia-may05.pdf> (accessed 12 January 2006).

Hirst, M. and Varney, H. (2005) *Justice Abandoned? An Assessment of the Serious Crimes Process in East Timor*, New York: International Center for Transitional Justice. Online. Available HTTP: <http://www.ictj.org/downloads/ictj.justice-abandoned.pdf> (accessed 20 January 2006).

ICG (International Crisis Group, 2001) *Indonesia: Impunity Versus Accountability for*

*Gross Human Rights Violations*, Asia Report No. 12, 2/2/2001. Online. Available HTTP: <http://www.crisisgroup.org/library/documents/report_archive/A400227_02022001.pdf> (accessed 20 August 2005).

ICJ (International Commission of Jurists, 1966) *The Rule of Law and Human Rights. Principles and Definitions (as elaborated at the Congresses and Conferences held under the auspices of the International Commission of Jurists, 1955–1966)*, Geneva: ICJ.

Lev, D.S. (1978) 'Judicial Authority and the Struggle for an Indonesian *Rechtsstaat*', *Law and Society Review* 13 (1): 37–71.

Lindsey, T. (1997) 'Paradigms, Paradoxes and Possibilities: Towards Understandings of Indonesia's Legal System', in V. Taylor (ed.) *Asian Laws Through Australian Eyes*, Sydney: Law Book Company.

—— (1999a) 'From Rule of Law to Law of the Rulers to Reformation?', in T. Lindsey (ed.) *Indonesia. Law and Society*, Sydney: Federation Press.

—— (ed.) (1999b) *Indonesia. Law and Society*, Sydney: Federation Press.

—— (2002) 'Indonesia's new Anti-Terrorism Laws: Damned if you do, damned if you don't', JURIST Guest Column, 30/10/2002. Online. Available HTTP: <http://jurist.law.pitt.edu/forum/forumnew65.php> (accessed 26 October 2005).

Lubis, T. M. (1993) *In Search of Human Rights. Legal-Political Dilemmas of Indonesia's New Order, 1966–1990*, Jakarta: Gramedia.

Schlicher, M. (2005) *Osttimor stellt sich seiner Vergangenheit. Die Arbeit der Empfangs-, Wahrheits- und Versöhnungskommission* (East Timor faces up to its Past. The Work of the Commission for Reception, Truth and Reconciliation), Aachen: Missio Human Rights. Online. Available HTTP: <http://www.missio-aachen.de/Images/25%20OsttimorE_tcm14-36798.pdf> (accessed 3 March 2006).

Soeprapto, E. (2005) *The Development of Indonesia's Policy on Human Rights and Fundamental Freedoms since 1945*, notes prepared for the Discussion Panel 'Indonesia and Its Human Rights Policy', Geneva, 5 April 2005.

Southwood, J. and Flanagan, P. (1983) *Indonesia: Law, Propaganda and Terror*, London: Zed Press.

Stockmann, P. (2004c) *Indonesian Reformasi as Reflected in Law. Change and Continuity in Post-Suharto Era Legislation on the Political System and Human Rights*, Münster: LIT.

—— (2004a) *Indonesia Six Years after the Fall of Suharto – Proceeding Democratically Back to the New Order?*, GIS Working Paper No. 1, Department of Government and International Studies, Hong Kong Baptist University, Hong Kong. Online. Available HTTP: <http://www.hkbu.edu.hk/~gis/STOCKMANN.doc> (accessed 15 February 2005).

—— (2004b) *Constitutional Court's ruling on the partition of Papua*, Watch Indonesia! Information und Analyse, 24/11/2004. Online. Available HTTP: <http://home-.snafu.de/watchin/papuapartition_24.11.04.htm> (accessed 24 August 2005).

—— (2005) 'Developments in legislation in the Megawati-era', in I. Wessel (ed.) *Democratisation in Indonesia after the fall of Suharto*, Berlin: Logos-Verlag.

—— (2006) *The new Indonesian Constitutional Court*. Published in cooperation with the Hanns Seidel Foundation, Jakarta, forthcoming.

Thoolen, H. (1987) *Indonesia and the Rule of Law. Twenty Years of 'New Order' Government*, London: International Commission of Jurists and the Netherlands Institute of Human Rights.

Transparency International (2004) *Transparency International Corruption Perceptions*

*Index 2004*. Online. Available HTTP: http://www.transparency.org/cpi/2004/cpi2004.en.html (accessed 20 June 2005).

von Braun, L. (2005) 'Trading Justice for Friendship. An Analysis of the Terms of Reference of the Commission of Truth and Friendship for Indonesia and East Timor', Watch Indonesia! Information and Analysis, 29/03/2005. Online. Available HTTP: http://home.snafu.de/watchin/CTF.htm (accessed 2 October 2005).

von Braun, L. and Schlicher, M. (2005) *Rethinking Justice for East Timor. Position Paper on the Reform of the International Justice Process in East Timor and Indonesia*, Berlin: Watch Indonesia! (published in cooperation with the German Commission Justitia et Pax, Misereor, missio, Diakonia). Online. Available HTTP: <http://home.snafu.de/watchin/Rethinking_Justice.htm> (accessed 9 March 2005).

# 4 Government policies and civil society initiatives against corruption

*Sofie Arjon Schütte*[1]

## INTRODUCTION

When in spring 1998 the people rallied on the streets of Jakarta and eventually succeeded in forcing President Suharto to resign, the acronym 'KKN' could be read on many banners. KKN stands for 'Corruption, Collusion and Nepotism', and ultimately symbolized what the protesters wanted to put an end to. Since then democratic general elections have been held twice, new legislation to combat corruption has been enacted, and new institutions have been established and abolished. The latest institution, and the one with the most powerful mandate, is the Corruption Eradication Commission (KPK), whose commissioners were appointed in late 2003. One year later it submitted its first case – the Governor of Aceh being the main suspect – to the equally new Special Court for Corruption Cases, which was constituted as a chamber of the Central Jakarta District Court. After two years, 24 cases had been brought to the anti-corruption court by the KPK. Together with President Susilo's declared commitment to make the fight against corruption a priority of his first 100 days in office, this gave hope for further momentum for reform, the movement of 1998 having lost its way due to the half-hearted commitment and policies of previous governments.

The prevention and prosecution of systemic corruption in Indonesia is crucial as otherwise it will undermine the new democratic institutions' effectiveness and ultimately their legitimacy. This chapter maintains that while there have been a number of noticeable efforts by the post-New Order legislature, executive and civil society, not enough has been done about curtailing the systemic character of corruption in Indonesia. A critical mass of rejection towards corrupt behaviour, necessary to make corruption the exception to the rule, has yet to be reached.

First, the extent of the problem that corruption poses in Indonesia will be outlined, followed by an explanation of how deeply ingrained corruption is in the state administration, affecting the everyday lives of many citizens. It will show that the New Order has left behind a state apparatus unable and/or unwilling to tackle the problem thoroughly due to persisting patronage in the civil service. The second section contains a summary overview of the post-New Order attempts to cope with the problem by enacting and amending legislation and establishing new institutions. This section will highlight the weaknesses that have affected both approach and implementation, as well as initial achievements. The third part of the chapter will summarize the role the public has been given by law with regard to cooperating with anti-corruption and law enforcement institutions. It will then demonstrate that despite the remaining high risks there are very outspoken, though not well integrated, civil society initiatives to fight corruption. The chapter will end with a review of the most recent reform efforts in Indonesia: the development of a 'National Action Plan against Corruption' as instructed by President Susilo on the world's first Anti-corruption Day on 9 December 2004.

## PROBLEM ANALYSIS: CORRUPTION IN INDONESIA

### Scope of corruption

Since Transparency International (TI) launched its first Corruption Perception Index (CPI) in 1995, Indonesia has found itself continuously ranked at the lower end of the corruption spectrum.[2] The announcement by Transparency International in October 2005 on the occasion of the release of the 10th CPI stated that Indonesia's position in the CPI had deteriorated since 1995. It is true that Indonesia scored better in 1996 (2.65) and 1997 (2.72) as compared to 2005 (2.2). However, this is due to a sudden drop in 1998 (2.0) and since then the score has improved. The reason for this drop may be the financial crisis revealing mismanagement and political turmoil at the time and a sudden increase in access to information effecting increased public awareness of the problem. Moreover, of the 13 surveys used for Indonesia in the 2005 CPI, only six actually date from 2005. Of the remaining seven surveys, some date back as far as 2003 and therefore cannot reflect the changes that have taken place under the Susilo government which only took office in late 2004. Reflecting the current situation more adequately is TI's Global Corruption Barometer 2005, which found that 81 per cent of the interviewed Indonesians thought that corruption would decrease during the next three years.[3]

There is, however, no doubt that Indonesia had, and still has, a very serious problem with corruption. Perception indices countrywide and media coverage show that corruption remains widespread throughout Indonesia's institutions. Recent polls identify the police, the courts, the military and the political parties as being perceived as the most corrupt institutions (Transparency International Indonesia 2004: 9). Indictments against members of the General Elections Commission (KPU) revealed the involvement in corruption of previously highly respected civil society activists and academics.

This chapter applies the definition of corruption used by Klitgaard, who has widened the very narrow definition of corruption as 'the misuse of public office for private benefit' to include others in positions of power (for example, NGOs, companies): 'Corruption exists when an individual illicitly puts personal interests above those of the people and ideals he or she is pledged to serve' (Klitgaard 1991: xi). A personal interest is not necessarily limited to one's own purse, but may include the interests of the family and affiliated groups, including political parties.

The wrath of the 1998 protesters concerning the 'N' (Nepotism) in KKN mostly focused on President Suharto's relatives and cronies. According to *Time Magazine* in 1999 (24 May 1999), the Suharto clan owned US$15 billion in property, jewellery, art and planes. Within Indonesia, the Suharto children had significant shareholdings in at least 564 companies. In New Order Indonesia trade barriers, import licenses, exclusive rights and monopolies were all used to foster the growth of particular companies that were close to the presidential palace. Long-time cronies Liem Sioe Liong (Sudono Salim) and The Kian Seng (Bob Hasan) profited hugely from the mutually beneficial relationship with Suharto. The business pattern fostered by the President eventually came to be known as 'crony capitalism': 'Without injections of public resources, these firms could not have expanded as rapidly as they did. Ruling parties have, in turn, depended on their clients for the money and the support necessary to retain power' (Wedemann 2002: 53). Crony capitalism constituted one aspect of the complex overall patrimonial political structure of the New Order. 'The emasculation of political parties and depolitization of the masses' after 1966 and competition among the elite, not over policies but rather 'power and the distribution of spoils' were described by Crouch (1979: 571, 576, 578) as patrimonial characteristics 'inherited from the politics of the pre-colonial past'. The traditional characteristics of Suharto's rule maintained a stability that lasted for almost 20 years after Crouch presented his analysis, before his forecast of large-scale outbreaks of mass opposition and intra-elite conflicts came to pass, culminating in the demise of the New Order. The mushrooming of political parties, the re-politicization of the masses, the increased competition among the members of the elite over different policy concepts, and the incarceration of 'Tommy' Suharto and The Kian Seng have, however, barely dented the continuing pattern of patronage relationships within the political and administrative machinery.

## Patronage and socio-cultural notions of corruption[4]

Corruption in Indonesia is systemic, meaning that it is ingrained in the state apparatus, its structures, procedures and policies – in other words, it is the rule rather than the exception. Its systemic character is maintained by patronage and the development of structures and policies that create further opportunities for collusion and personal enrichment. Patron–client relationships based on traditional notions of mutual loyalty have mutated into networks of accessories. This all causes administration inefficiency resulting from glossy reports and human resources management decisions that are based on loyalty – or gifts – rather than on the performance of a subordinate. Where the assignment of positions and promotions is based on loyalty and one's patron is someone else's client, a fertile ground for the systemic spread of corruption is prepared. Such mutual dependence and interconnection very much reduces the chances that determined action will be taken against those involved in corruption.[5] Palmier (1985: 223) concluded that 'It is difficult to deny the impression of a public service held together not by loyalty to the state, but simply by a common interest in using public offices for private gain'.

In Indonesia today, a public office is often still considered to be an investment that has to be made upfront – the amount involved depending on the expected amortization. Positions are commonly categorized as being *basah* (wet) where they afford opportunities (through monopolies and discretion) of obtaining additional income, while positions are described as *kering* (dry) where no such opportunities are available beyond the regular salary (Cremer 1990: 219–20).[6] The provision of service to the public remains a secondary consideration. As Schwarz (1999: 135) pointedly wrote: 'Indeed, the very term, civil servant, is something of a misnomer in Indonesia: in this quasi-feudal culture, it would be more accurate to say that government employees are the "owners" of the nation and the general public their servants.' Besides the amortization of the initial investment in the purchase of his office, the civil servant has to satisfy the numerous demands from his or her extended family and friends that come with the new position.

It is extremely difficult to define the border between socially acknowledged obligations to family and colleagues and criminal acts of corruption, nepotism and collusion. What is illegal on paper may socially still be considered legitimate. Sustained public protests, however, show that this border is frequently overstepped in Indonesia. Laws and regulations that criminalize corruption and establish penalties are part of a (legal) framework that would not have been possible to establish without social consensus. 'The fact that (almost) all players are involved in corruption does not allow the conclusion that the players consider the status quo as the desirable state of society', Dietz (1998: 54) deduces after applying game theory to corrupt interactions.

Corruption is considered a public evil in Indonesia and is pilloried as such – including by those involved in corruption themselves. A study by the Partnership for Governance Reform in 2001 as part of which 650 civil servants, 1,250 households and 400 company executives (altogether 2,300 persons) were interviewed about corruption, confirmed that about 70 per cent of the respondents considered corruption a serious vice that needed to be combated (Partnership 2001: xi). Asked about their behaviour in different hypothetical situations where bribery frequently occurs, the majority said they would actually pay bribes themselves. The survey found that the bribing of a judge was considered less acceptable (22.2 per cent), and the willingness to bribe a judge (26.8 per cent) was considerably lower than the willingness to bribe the village head to ensure necessary documents were issued faster. A total of 61.9 per cent of the respondents said bribing a village head was normal and 75.1 per cent said they would pay up (Partnership 2001: 31–2).

These findings show that people's opinions and potential behaviour (based on experience or a hypothetical situation) are at odds. Although corruption is considered a public evil, the demanding of unofficial payments in particular situations is considered normal. The willingness to actually pay up is even higher: Although a bribe might not be considered acceptable, money is nevertheless handed over due to the fear of being disadvantaged, such as having to wait unduly for an official document or losing in a court case.

So while today's Indonesia might be described as a democracy when it comes to elections, freedom of the press and a multi-party system, it is the systemic corruption in the institutions of state, such as the judiciary, the law enforcement agencies and the public administration, that still bears the chief hallmark of a patrimonial structure: patronage.

## THE INSTITUTIONAL LANDSCAPE TO FIGHT CORRUPTION

The New Order has left behind a state apparatus of about 4.6 million officials that appears unable to reform itself from within. Neither external nor internal financial oversight bodies have made much difference in the past. The Inspectorates General, introduced during the New Order into every department and non-departmental government agency, as well as local governments, have to report the results of their oversight activities in respect of both routine and special projects to the institution's agency, but this has had little effect to date. The Development Finance Controller (BPKP) was established by Suharto in 1983 as an internal control agency responsible to the president, as compared to the Supreme Audit Agency (BPK), which under the constitution reports to parliament. The credibility of the reports produced by both institutions is regularly undermined by the off-budget funds run by the institutions they audit to cover operational costs (ADB 2004: 47, 50). Another problem is the lack of follow-up on the findings of the auditors by the law enforcement institutions which, as already mentioned, are among the institutions considered to have a problem with corruption themselves. As a consequence, post-New Order efforts to battle corruption have largely focused on the investigative and punitive aspects, not least the catching of some 'big fish', as demanded by the public.

### Legislative efforts [7]

During the governments prior to the Susilo administration, state initiatives to counter corruption came mostly from the legislature but have so far not been fully put into place. In the middle of the financial crisis after Suharto had stepped down, the People's Consultative Assembly (MPR) issued Decree

TAP XI/MPR/1998 on a clean State Administration free from Corruption, Collusion and Nepotism during an extraordinary session in November 1998. Based on this decree, the House of Representatives (DPR) enacted the following laws:

### Law 28/1999 on a Corruption-free State Administration

This law sets out the principles of state administration, the rights and obligations of state officials, and provides for the auditing of the wealth of public officials and representatives by a special commission to be established by law. This Public Officials Audit Commission (*Komisi Pemeriksa Kekayaan Penyelenggara Negara*, KPKPN) was integrated into the Corruption Eradication Commission's prevention department in July 2004.

### Law 31/1999 on the Eradication of Corruption

This law replaces the New Order anti-corruption Law 3/1971 and provides for the establishment of a Joint Investigating Team made up of representatives from the police and prosecution service under the auspices of the Attorney General, and an independent anti-corruption commission. The ancillary regulation establishing the Joint Investigating Team was later struck down by the Supreme Court, before the team could prosecute its first case.

### Law 20/2001 on the amendment of Law 31/1999

This law amends and complements Law 31/1999. It partly tightens up the burden of proof, changes the sanctions in some cases and widens the scope of admissible evidence.

As the situation showed few signs of improvement after the enactment of these laws, the MPR in November 2001 issued another decree, TAP MPR VIII/MPR/2001, on Policy Direction Recommendations for the Eradication of Corruption, Collusion and Nepotism. This decree recommended a comprehensive follow-up:

- the speeding up of court proceedings;
- increasing public involvement in eradicating corruption;
- a review of all laws and regulations for indications of covering-up corrupt practices or creating opportunities for corruption;
- a review of all laws/regulations on corruption eradication to ensure consistency;
- the deliberation and enactment of laws and ancillary regulations on:
  - the anti-corruption commission
  - the protection of witnesses and victims

- – organized crime
- – access to/freedom of information
- – governmental ethics
- – money laundering
- – the ombudsman commission.

Since then, Law 30/2002 on the Corruption Eradication Commission (KPK), Law 15/2002 and Law 25/2003 on Money Laundering have been enacted and been put into effect.[8] The Financial Transaction Reporting and Analysis Centre (PPATK) was established with the power to execute government policy for the prevention and eradication of money laundering while simultaneously building an anti-money laundering regime in Indonesia. The PPATK started operating in October 2003 and eventually got Indonesia off the Financial Action Task Force's (FATF) list of non-cooperating countries and territories (NCCT) in February 2005. The other institutions established based on the MPR's decree, and their records to date, will be looked at in more detail. They are listed in chronological order, and this also reflects their increasing powers and impact so far.

## The Joint Investigation Team (2000–01)

The Joint Investigation Team under the auspices of the Attorney General was set up by Law 31/1999 on the Eradication of Corruption, and Government Regulation 19/2000. Its members were appointed by Attorney General Marzuki Darusman, and consisted of police officers, public prosecutors and academics. The team started work in June 2000 and one year later, after it had completed its investigation into the so-called 'three judges case', Regulation 19/2000 was struck down by the Supreme Court, which held that it contravened the powers provided for by Law 31/1999 and the Criminal Code. The team was then wound up. The three suspects in the infamous 'three judges case' were later acquitted of all charges based on the reasoning that the acts had happened before the enactment of Law 31/1999. Thus, there were no legal grounds for imposing penalties (*nulla poena sine lege*) (Assegaf 2002: 138–9).[9]

The whistleblower in this case, Endin Wahyudin, who had first bribed and then reported the judges, was sentenced to three years in jail for bribery and defamation. One of the members of the Joint Investigating Team, Hamid Chalid, a lecturer in the Faculty of Law at the University of Indonesia, later gave a critical account of the obstacles the team faced, and its eventual dissolution (Chalid 2001). He distinguished between internal and external problems: Internal problems included the lack of funding and offices for the first half year, a lack of terms of reference and the lack of an integrated case information system among law enforcement agencies in Indonesia. Meanwhile, a lack of legal clarity impaired investigations and was used by the judiciary to protect its members. For instance, the superiors of a suspect had to give their permission before an investigation could be started. As with previous institutions (under the New Order) that were established to combat corruption, the team had inadequate powers considering its mandate. It was supposed to overcome the lack of coordination and communication between law enforcement agencies and at the same time eradicate corruption in the justice sector. As a result, the team quickly ran up against conflicts of interest: The powers to investigate and prosecute remained with the target institutions. In his account, Chalid expressed his concern that the yet-to-be-established Corruption Eradication Commission would suffer a similar fate. Therefore, the team, together with civil society organizations, drafted a model bill for the setting up of a special court to hear corruption cases.[10] Later, the establishment of an anti-corruption court was provided for by the same law that set up the Corruption Eradication Commission. The team's experience and ultimate failure set a precedent of the counter-forces to be expected.

### The National Ombudsman (2000–today)

By Presidential Decree Number 44 President Wahid established a National Ombudsman Commission in March 2000. The President sought to apply a preventive approach to corruption following the example of the middleman (*ombudsman*) in Sweden. In general, it is the task of an Ombudsman to receive complaints from the public on the misconduct of civil servants and poor administration and to make recommendations to the respective institutions after investigation of the complaint. Since the National Ombudsman Commission was not allocated any budgetary funding at all at the beginning, it initially relied greatly on support from donors, such as the Asia Foundation and the Partnership for Governance Reform in Indonesia. After recommendations made by the Ombudsmen were not followed up by the relevant institutions in the law enforcement and justice sectors, the number of complaints received from the public sharply declined. Although it still exists and is receiving budgetary funding, the National Ombudsman Commission is widely considered as having little impact. A bill submitted to Parliament in 2002 to strengthen its legal basis has not been deliberated to date. More promising are local initiatives, such as the local Ombudsman Office in the Special Region of Yogyakarta, which has been endorsed by the Governor and enjoys a high degree of local ownership and support.

### The Public Officials Audit Commission (2001–04)

Law 28/1999 stipulates the auditing of state officials'[11] wealth as a measure to prevent and detect corruption. A special independent commission (KPKPN) was established to receive and audit the wealth declarations of Indonesia's high officials and to follow up on these declarations and complaints of corruption in the state administration.[12] Wealth declarations have to be submitted to the commission before and after holding office. The details of each declaration are published in the appendix to the *State Gazette*.[13]

The KPKPN started its work in early 2001 and sent out 51,000 forms for baseline registration. By mid-2002 only 27,000 reports had been returned and since the administrative penalties for non-compliance were insufficient, the commission resorted to publishing the names of those who had not yet submitted their declarations. The submissions have increased since the KPKPN was incorporated into the prevention department of the Corruption Eradication Commission in July 2004. The KPK has a wider mandate and the power to bring prosecutions itself, whereas the KPKPN had to hand over the results of its investigations to the law enforcement agencies or prosecution service once it found indications of illicit enrichment. With the KPK having integrated the wealth auditing function in July 2004, the number of submitted wealth declarations increased to 52,137 of a total of 102,229 requested reports by the end of 2005 (Komisi Pemberantasan Korupsi 2006: 55). Considering the systemic character of corruption based on social and financial pressures, as described above, the audit of wealth declarations provides a tool for bypassing the problems of patronage and hierarchy to a certain degree. Whistleblowing in an environment of systemic corruption is the exception, and where it does take place it can still backfire. Supervisors do not report their staff because they usually receive a part of the additional income generated by them. Equally low is the probability that the superior will be reported. Hence, the advantage of wealth reports is that the comparison of income, actual and declared wealth is applied 'externally' and does not depend on insider information.

The use of wealth declarations as a means to convict corrupt officials in Indonesia remains limited, however, when compared to Hong Kong. The 'Prevention of Bribery Ordinance' in Hong Kong

> [. . .] places the burden of proof on any civil servant accused of maintaining a standard of living considered beyond his means. Once the prosecutor is able to prove that the value of assets possessed by a suspect is higher than the emoluments earned from his employment in the civil service, he will be found guilty of corruption unless the contrary is proven by the defendant.
>
> (Wing Lo 2000: 24–5)

This is not yet possible in Indonesia; the KPK has to prove that assets unaccounted for are the result of corruption.

The wealth declaration is a purposive but one-sided instrument for detection and deterrence. The causes of corruption, such as the weaknesses in the civil service system, need to be dealt with other instruments of bureaucratic reform.

## The Corruption Eradication Commission (late 2003–today)

From the very beginning, the KPK had to face enormous public expectations (Partnership 2001: 25). The Law on the Corruption Eradication Commission states that corruption is an extraordinary problem that needs to be tackled by extraordinary means, and therefore gives the new commission a far-reaching mandate. The KPK's powers go far beyond those of similar institutions in the past. Besides prevention, the KPK is tasked with coordinating and supervising the work of other institutions authorized to eradicate corruption.[14] It is authorized to take over cases from the police and prosecution service and to conduct investigations and inquiries into, and prosecutions of, corruption cases that involve the law enforcement apparatus, give rise to particular public concern and/or involve losses to the taxpayer of at least one billion rupiah (approximately US$100,000). To fulfil these responsibilities the KPK has been given legal powers to investigate and prosecute, including the tapping and recording of communications, the investigation of suspects' bank accounts, and inquiring into the wealth and taxation affairs of suspects. In late December 2003, the five commissioners of the KPK were selected by Parliament and sworn in by the President. Since then, the KPK has become increasingly active and has maintained a high degree of public trust. It has faced difficulties as regards capacity-building and implementation of its mandate due to a lack of clarity in Law 30 of 2002 about, for instance, who may serve as an investigator, as well as various legal inconsistencies. Nonetheless, in November 2005 the KPK was engaged in prosecuting 14 cases, and ten cases had already been successfully tried by the Special Court for Corruption Cases which was established as a special chamber of the South Jakarta District Court, just in time for the Abdullah Puteh case in late 2004. Some observers have accused the KPK of being discriminatory in its prosecutions following its decision to indict only certain members of the General Elections Commission rather than other high-profile members about whom testimonies were available ('Benarkah KPK Diskriminatif?', *Koran Tempo*, 1 October 2005), but according to investigators these did not constitute enough evidence for a case. Step by step, the KPK is also advancing its second mandate: prevention. It has already established an internal, merit-based human resources management system and is seeking to push urgently needed civil service reform in the justice and other sectors. Furthermore, it started a public campaign in 2006 and promotes education on corruption issues to the young generation.

Even though governance experts like Schacter and Sha (2004: 42) maintain that government watchdog agencies such as the KPK are only successful where overall governance, such as the rule of law and the existence of participatory and accountable institutions, is already good – as in Australia and Chile – Indonesia might prove to be an exception. With presidential and public support, the KPK could turn out to be the trigger of reform that the people have been hoping for.

Besides those institutions whose establishment was based on the 1998 People's Consultative Assembly Decree, a number of additional special institutions have been set up to tackle particular issues, such as the Business Competition Supervision Commission (KPPU), with two branches in Makassar and Balikpapan, and the National Committee for Governance Policies at the Ministry of Finance.

What all of the above-listed institutions have experienced to some degree was, and partly still is, a lack of legal clarity which makes their positioning among existing agencies and structures difficult, a lack of human and other resources, and counteraction by those who have an interest in maintaining the status quo. In hindsight, the Joint Investigating Team was a bitter failure but also a lesson learnt on the forces that might be expected to emerge once established interests were threatened. The National Ombudsman Commission has somehow managed to survive but has so far failed to produce any meaningful reform. The Wealth Audit Commission had a difficult start with little powers to enforce its mandate but does have detection powers that might have more impact in the future, following its integration into the much more powerful Corruption Eradication Commission in 2004. The Corruption Eradication Commission has had a relatively good start and its successful prosecution of a number of high-profile corruption cases has kept up a high degree of public trust. This will need to be nurtured with the prosecution of more 'big fish' to maintain the momentum and public support required for further steps, such as the substantial reform of the civil service to tackle patronage networks.

## PUBLIC PARTICIPATION IN THE FIGHT AGAINST CORRUPTION

Public support and pressure is crucial in the fight against corruption, not least because it is often the citizens who are at the paying end. Public control is needed as the system of checks and balances is not working properly: the legislature that should exercise oversight is often part of the problem, particularly in the regions on both a provincial and district level, as described in the case study of West Sumatera below.

Moreover public pressure lends those reform-minded persons in the government the backup to follow through with investigations and changes. Journalists and watchdog organizations frequently uncover misconduct and bring it to the general public and law enforcers' attention. Despite some legislation giving the public a role and protection in the fight against corruption, the disincentives and risks in getting involved remain high.

## Legislation on public participation

Law 28/1998 and Law 31/1999 respectively provide as follows: 'Public participation in the administration of state means the right and responsibility of
the people to create a clean and corruption-free state administration'[15] and
'[t]he public can play a role and assist in the efforts to prevent and eradicate
corruption'.[16] Both of these laws and their ancillary regulations ensure the
public's right to:

- seek, acquire and furnish information on the administration and management of the state;
- receive equal and fair services from the state;
- express suggestions and opinions in a responsible manner on state
  policies and administration;
- receive legal protection in the aforementioned circumstances and as a
  complainant, witness, or expert witness according to the provision of the
  laws and regulations in effect.

The reporting or requesting of information or the expression of criticism
should be done in a 'polite, well-mannered and responsible'[17] way and take
into consideration 'religious and other social norms'.[18] The responsibility of
the public to deal with information in a 'responsible manner' is, of course,
open to interpretation and prone to abuse. Defamation suits have been
employed as a common means of suffocating accusations of corruption. In
circumstances where the theoretical right of the public to participate in the
fight against corruption constitutes a factual risk to the individual, the right,
and therefore the law, is ineffective. Hence, the right to receive an award or a
bonus of up to two per cent of recovered assets from a corruption case, as
provided for in Government Regulation 71/2000,[19] cannot be considered an
incentive to make reports to the law enforcement agencies as long as there is
no effective witness and whistleblower protection in place. The case of
whistleblower Endin Wahyudin, who found himself convicted of defamation
while the original suspects walked free, is not a unique occurrence. The
Coalition for Witness Protection (Koalisi Pelindungan Saksi 2005: Annex)
has published a list of eight other cases where complainants have been
accused of defamation. Less subtle forms of retaliation, such as direct threats
to witnesses and whistleblowers, often remain hidden as the effects of the
threats are twofold: the witness will not dare to report the crime nor the
attempts to pervert the course of justice. With regard to defamation suits,
former National Chief of Police Da'i Bachtiar has issued simple but effective
guidelines to discourage the misuse of this kind of legal action. As reported
by *The Jakarta Post* (2 June 2005), the National Police have been instructed
not to prioritize defamation complaints connected with corruption cases.
Junino Jahya, the Corruption Eradication Commission's Deputy for Complainants and Internal Affairs, has given assurances that based on these

guidelines, defamation accusations will not be processed until the court acquits the graft suspect. However, as was evident in the recent case of state auditor Khairansyah Salman, who helped the KPK secure convictions against members of the General Elections Commission, getting involved in the fight against corruption can still backfire. Whereas the KPK regulations protect Khairansyah as regards the General Elections Commission case, where the offering of a bribe to him was recorded, he cannot be protected beyond this case and was promptly summoned by the Attorney General's Office shortly after having received the 2005 Transparency International Integrity Award. He has been charged as a suspect for allegedly having received a bribe of Rp 10 million (about US$1,000) from the Ministry of Religious Affairs, whereas reportedly ten other potential suspects in the case have remained untouched so far. Khairansyah has returned the Integrity Award until such time as the legal proceedings against him have run their course (*Gatra Online*, 25 November 2005. Online. Available HTTP: <http://www.gatra.com/2005-11-25/artikel.php?id=90116> accessed 20 July 2006). This case has spotlighted another problem that affects not just the law enforcement agencies, but one which Indonesian society in general has to reach a consensus upon: the higher a suspect ranks in a corrupt network, the more difficult it is to find witnesses not involved in the crime to provide incriminating evidence. In these cases, law enforcers are dependent upon statements of accomplices and assistants, who will only take the risk of testifying if granted immunity.

Legal provisions on the overall protection of witnesses need to be enacted. Indonesian law enforcers, lawmakers, and human rights and anti-corruption activists have long been aware of the need and have submitted three different Witness Protection Bills to Parliament. In July 2006 the Law on the Protection of Witnesses and Victims was eventually passed, providing for the establishment of a commission to oversee its implementation. This commission needs yet to be set up. The best way to protect whistleblowers from defamation suits and retaliation for the time being is to keep identities secret.

## Civil society anti-corruption initiatives

Most of the prominent anti-corruption civil society organizations in Indonesia today were established within the first two years of Suharto's fall from power: Indonesia Corruption Watch (ICW) in June 1998, the Indonesian Forum for Budgetary Transparency (Fitra) in 1999 and Transparency International – Indonesian Chapter (TI-I) – in 2000, to name but a few of those headquartered in the capital. There are dozens of smaller local organizations some of them cooperating with each other under the umbrella of Gerak, which was set up in 2000 as an anti-corruption platform that currently has 22 member organizations. The initial concerns of these organizations may not have been corruption *per se*, but since corruption affects many aspects of life, many of them developed corruption-focused activities to complement their specific fields. Some more specialized organizations have evolved, such as Indonesian Procurement Watch (IPW) established in 2002, and campus organizations, such as the Judicial Watch Society (MAPPI) set up in 2000 at the Law Faculty of the University of Indonesia.

Since mid-2003, religious organizations have become increasingly involved in what has been called a 'moral crusade' against corruption. The Education Research and Development Institute (LP3) at the Muhammadiyah University in Yogyakarta has developed religious curricula that incorporate anti-corruption materials at the university level, and has encouraged inter-religious cooperation in the fight against corruption. The Indonesian Society for Pesantren and Community Development (P3M) has worked with young *kiai* in an effort to develop *fatwa* against specific aspects of corruption at the local and national levels. In 2002, Nahdlatul Ulama had issued a *fatwa* denying corruptors prayers at their funerals until their ill-gotten gains had been repaid (Burhan 2006: 120). In October 2003, Nahdlatul Ulama and Muhammadiyah joined forces and signed a Memorandum of Understanding with the Partnership for Governance Reform in Indonesia. So far, however, the attempts to address corruption issues within their own organizations and communities have been limited. Their role could be crucial considering the sheer number of their members.

An initiative that drew much public attention prior to the General Election in 2004 was the so-called Anti-Rotten Politician Movement (*Gerakan Anti Politisi Busuk*). At the Proclamation Monument in Jakarta on 29 December 2003, a coalition of civil society organizations announced the establishment of a movement against the (re)election of corrupt or otherwise tainted politicians regardless of their party affiliations. A series of similar announcements followed all over the country. Popular musicians like Franky Sahilatua and Harry Roesli produced songs for the campaign and it was widely covered in the media. The records of candidates were scrutinized not only for corruption, but also environmental credentials, human rights and sexual abuse. The names of those found to be tainted were then made public. The overall objective was to make people aware of whom they were voting for (Masduki 2006: 220). Whether this campaign really had an impact on voter behaviour is doubtful, with many of the usual suspects still being re-elected. Unfortunately, comprehensive information on the success or otherwise of the campaign is not available. What may be observed, however, is that it is becoming common practice for civil society organizations in many regions to undertake similar campaigns in the run-up to local elections.

Besides the public campaigns against corruption, non-governmental watch-dog organizations have brought cases of corruption and collusion to the attention of the public and, in some cases, to the courts. Prominent is the guilty verdict brought in by the Padang District Court against 43 councillors as it encouraged similar investigations and hearings all over Indonesia. The West Sumatra Concern Forum (*Forum Peduli Sumatra Barat*, FPSB) was born out of the efforts to rid the West Sumatra legislature and administration of money politics during the gubernatorial elections in 2000, when the governor was still elected by the Local Legislative Council. Subsequently, concerned NGO activists and other community members carefully scrutinized the budget formulation process in the Legislative Council. After a first action against the council was rejected by the Padang District Court in 2001, the West Sumatra Concern Forum was established in 2002 as an umbrella organization to monitor the formulation of the 2002 budget. In close cooperation with Andalas University and Padang State University, violations of the national legislation and discrepancies contained in the Legislative Council's draft budget were identified and communicated to the Legislative Council. The Council, however, ignored the Forum's advice that the draft budget be brought into line with the requirements of Government Regulation 110/2000. Neither did the Governor withhold his signature from the draft budget even though the Forum pointed out the deviations to him and the fact that 'he could be categorized as colluding with it [the Legislative Council]' (Isra 2006: 145). The Forum reported the West Sumatra Provincial Legislative Council on suspicion of corruption to the Provincial Prosecutor's Office. The Provincial Prosecutor's Office recommended that the Governor propose the annulment of the budget should it be passed, or that otherwise legal action would be taken under the Corruption Eradication Laws (No. 30/1999 and No. 20/2001). In the end, criminal prosecutions were brought against the councillors, and 43 were eventually found guilty of corruption by the Padang District Court in May 2004, a decision that was confirmed by the West Sumatra High Court. So far, 33 of these convictions have been upheld by the Supreme Court, with the rest yet to be decided in January 2006.[20] During the court proceedings, the Forum worked closely with the local and national media as well as student organizations to increase the pressure and shape public opinion. The Forum is currently concentrating on ensuring that the sentences are actually carried out as the West Sumatra Prosecutor's Office is insisting on holding back until such time as the Supreme Court hands down its decisions on the remaining ten councillors' appeals. Some of them who were re-elected in 2004 could still be found in office in January 2006 (*The Jakarta Post*, 27 January 2006).

The case of the West Sumatra Concern Forum has shown that community and watchdog organizations can make a difference, especially when they link up with expertise from universities. The case also illustrates that it takes persistent efforts to put perpetrators behind bars, and that guilty sentences do not necessarily result in their (immediate) implementation or in convicts experiencing public ostracism. Too little has been researched and done about the previously described gap between people's opinion and actual behaviour. A critical mass of resistance on the supply side of votes and bribes needs yet to be realized.

## THE SBY GOVERNMENT AND ITS EFFORTS
## AGAINST CORRUPTION

During the 2004 general elections and the direct presidential election, those who managed to convey credible anti-corruption messages as part of their campaigns garnered impressive public support, with the biggest beneficiaries being the Partai Keadilan Sejahtera[21] and incumbent President Susilo Bambang Yudhoyono. Two months after his inauguration, on the first International Anti-corruption Day on 9 December 2004, President Susilo issued a Presidential Decree on the Accelerated Eradication of Corruption. Many saw this as initial proof that he would keep his campaign promises to improve overall governance and take the war against corruption to a new level. A new departure is the mandate given to the National Development Planning Board (*Bappenas*) to coordinate with ministers, agencies' heads and the public in the development of a 2004–09 National Anti-corruption Action Plan.

The Action Plan was endorsed in late February 2005, but it is considered a *living document*, meaning that it is open to revisions and adjustments. It is divided into four parts: the prevention and suppression of corruption in the rehabilitation and reconstruction of Aceh and North Sumatra; preventative measures, including the improvement of the public service system; suppressive measures; and the monitoring and evaluation of the implementation of the Action Plan, including public participation (National Development Planning Board 2005).

So far Indonesia's Action Plan is an initiative of the executive only. It is driven by national ownership and political will – at least from the President himself and the institutions most involved in its development: Bappenas, the Ministry of Administrative Reform and – on an independent footing – the Corruption Eradication Commission. It has not become an enterprise of the United Indonesia Cabinet, however, and only to a very limited, and not systematic, extent have local governments and civil society organizations been involved in the initial development process. This may have been due to the short time period within which the strategy was assembled (two months). Eventually, the plan was termed a *living document* to allow for the local and civil society input that was not generated before. The document has been in existence for more than a year now and many provisions and their indicators still need to be analysed to clarify what really needs to be done. The original document does not reveal whether additional resources will be made available for funding activities or whether the resources will have to be taken from the budgets already allocated to the agencies in charge. The monitoring and reporting procedures set up to date by the Ministry of Administrative Reform are very elaborate, but there are no evident sanctions in place for cases of non-compliance – in terms of implementing the substance rather than reporting failures (Ministry of Adminstrative Reform's website on the Action Plan).

In addition to the Action Plan, special inter-agency task forces have been set up to recover stolen assets from overseas and to investigate certain institutions and, since mid-2005, also Judicial and Prosecutorial Commissions. Besides the engagement of the KPK, which is independent but only has the capacity to go after a limited number of cases, the President is certainly aware of the necessity to improve the performance of the other law enforcement institutions. For the two mentioned commissions, it is too early to draw any conclusions. The other two task forces have led to few convictions so far and the forfeiture of the proceeds of crime has only, after a year, produced initial successes.

Thus after almost two years in office, the political commitment shown by the President appears to still be firm, but with few results concerning the reform of the bureaucracy and the obliteration of patronage networks. A tendency to create new task forces and commissions, instead of holding leading officials accountable for the lack of progress, has been widely commented upon. This may be due to the high political cost of dismissing Cabinet members and other high-profile state officials. Only 'token' corruptors get dealt with, normally after they have fallen from grace in their networks. To date, the public perception is that the law is still being applied in a discriminatory manner. Some observers consider President Susilo's most noteworthy achievement as being the fact that he has refrained from the common failings of his predecessors, such as cronyism and political intervention in oversight bodies. He has made the fight against corruption his personal agenda but has failed so far to ensure that it is supported and endorsed by his Cabinet (Davidsen *et al.* 2006: 2, 18–19). In this context, the complaint by Cabinet members that an 'excessive' drive against corruption hampers the operation and development of state enterprises is proof positive that the efforts are beginning to bite (*Antara News*, 23 February 2006. Online. Available HTTP: <http://www.antara.co.id/seenws/?id=28657> accessed 31 July 2006).

Last but not least, an important step was taken by the legislature in March 2006 when the House of Representatives enacted the law to ratify the United Nations Convention against Corruption (Merida Convention 2003). Despite there being no sanctions for non-compliance yet, it is an important commitment to bring Indonesian legislation in line with the standards set by the United Nations concerning prevention, criminalization, asset tracing and recovery as well as international cooperation (*The Jakarta Post*, 22 March 2006 and 10 August 2006).

## CONCLUSION

Despite the many democratic characteristics now present in Indonesia, the vestiges of (neo-)patrimonial rule are still deeply ingrained in the state apparatus, and patronage constitutes the greatest single obstacle to fighting corruption from within. As of mid-2006 none of the post-New Order governments had succeeded in ridding the state apparatus of patronage, which is crucial to curb systemic corruption in a sustainable manner.

Some specific legislation has been put in place to suppress and, to a lesser degree, prevent corruption in general. However, previous governments only half-heartedly supported the institutional frameworks needed to ensure the successful implementation of the new regulations. Legislation lacking clarity and coherence made things difficult for the newly established institutions, such as the Joint Investigating Team, the National Ombudsman Commission, the Public Officials Audit Commission, the Financial Transactions Reporting and Analysis Center, and the Corruption Eradication Commission. These institutions faced not only a lack of resources, legal clarity and cooperation, but also counteraction from those who feel their interests are threatened. In the case of the Joint Investigating Team, this even led to its dissolution.

Other essential legislation and policies have still to be put in place, such as access to information and a witness protection scheme. Cases where whistle-blowers, rather than those engaged in corruption, found themselves accused and convicted make clear not only the need for adequate legislation but also for consensus among law enforcement agencies and the public in general on how to deal with the past misdeeds of those who are now willing to speak out.

Wealth declaration is a tool that enables the identification of suspicious assets belonging to state officials without depending on insider knowledge and endangering informants. The KPKPN, and later KPK, have succeeded in slowly but surely insisting on the submission of these declarations. In fact, they could make a crucial difference if measures such as the offence of illicit enrichment, a non-conviction based confiscation regime of inexplicable wealth, and/or the removal of public officials from public service as proposed in the United Nations Convention against Corruption were put in place.

Amid high expectations, the KPK has succeeded in maintaining the public trust, although it took some time to recruit and train its personnel and the number of prosecutions to date has been small. Its latest push for bureau-cratic reform, particularly within the law enforcement agencies, is a critical step and it will be interesting for international analysts to observe, not least in terms of the sequencing of reform.

Pressure from the public has had some impact on policy-makers. In par-ticular, a number of watchdog organizations have become more professional and experienced over the last few years, and have been able to shed light on some major corruption cases as well as petty corruption in public service delivery. It is interesting to note that government agencies increasingly seek the advice and cooperation of experienced civil society organizations. The National Anti-corruption Action Plan expressly states that civil society should be involved in the monitoring and evaluation processes in respect of its implementation. In this regard, the Susilo government has already made a difference. A critical mass of resistance against corruption also on the supply side has yet to be realized, however, both when it comes to votes for crooked politicians and paying bribes.

Concluding on a gloomy note would not do justice to current efforts, however. It is a fact that corruption is still widespread in Indonesia, but it is equally true that many people openly resent it and that there are an increasing number of people and institutions striving to make a difference.

## NOTES

1 At the time of writing in July 2006 the author worked as CIM integrated advisor to the anti-corruption programme of the Partnership for Governance Reform in Indonesia.
2 The CPI has a scale from one to ten, with ten being the best (cleanest) and one being the worst (most corrupt) scores. For more information on the CPI and its methodology:     <http://www.transparency.org/policy_research/surveys_indices/global/cpi> (accessed 1 July 2006).
3 A tendency supported by a CPI score of 2.4 in 2006 (released by Transparency International in November 2006).
4 This section is based on the author's unpublished master thesis, (2003) *Korruptionsbekämpfung in Indonesien seit dem Rücktritt Soehartos in Gesetzgebung und Praxis*, University of Passau.
5 Compare Manning, N. (2000) 'Pay and Patronage in the Core Civil Service in Indonesia', PRMPS, World Bank: 33–6 as quoted in World Bank (2003) *Combating Corruption in Indonesia: Enhancing accountability for development*, Jakarta: World Bank: 103.
6 Cremer maintains that these terms are an analogy to wet-rice cultivation with more harvests than dry farming.
7 This section is based on the author's aforementioned unpublished master thesis.
8 Law 13/2006 on the Protection of Witnesses and Victims has been enacted in July 2006 and awaits implementation through government regulation.
9 See also decision of the Supreme Court: MA 03/P/HUM/2000.
10 The draft law was published in 2002 in the book *Pengadilan Khusus Korupsi* by the Indonesian Institute for the Independence of the Judiciary (LeIP), The Indonesian Transparency Society (MTI), the Law and Policy Study Centre and the Joint Investigating Team.
11 *Penyelenggara negara* are defined as members of the People's Consultative Assembly, the House of Representatives and high officials of the executive and judiciary. This includes the President, the Supreme Court, the State Auditor, the Advisory Council, and all ministers, governors, judges and civil servants with strategic functions in the state administration.
12 Art. 17 of Law 28/1999.
13 *Halaman Negara*.
14 Authorized institutions in the context of this article include: the other law enforcement agencies, the Supreme Audit Agency (BPK), the State Finance Controller (BPKP) and inspectorates at each Department and non-departmental government agencies.
15 Art. 8 (1) of Law 28/1998.
16 Art. 41 (1) of Law 31/1999.
17 Art. 2 (2), Government Regulation 71/2000.
18 Art. 2 (2), Government Regulation 68/1999.
19 Arts 7–11, Government Regulation 71/2000.
20 Three of the council leaders were sentenced to five years in prison and were fined Rp 200 million each. The remaining councillors received the same fine and four years of prison.

21 The Partai Keadilan Sejahtera (PKS) was founded prior to the 1999 elections. Its slogan 'bersih dan peduli' (clean and concerned) and its reputation of indeed being clean of the usual practices won it seven seats in the House of Representatives in 1999 and 45 seats (7.54 per cent) in 2004.

## BIBLIOGRAPHY

Asian Development Bank (ADB) (2004) *Indonesia Country Governance Assessment Report*, Manila: Asian Development Bank.

Assegaf, I. (2002) 'Legends of the Fall: An Institutional Analysis of Indonesian Law Enforcement Agencies Combating Corruption', in H. Dick and T. Lindsey (eds) *Corruption in Asia. Rethinking the Governance Paradigm*, Sydney: The Federation Press.

Burhan, A.S. (2006) 'When the Kiai Help Control Local Budgeting' in Partnership for Governance Reform (ed.) *Fighting Corruption from Aceh to Papua*, Jakarta: Partnership for Governance Reform.

Chalid, H. (2001) 'A Personal Experience in Combating Corruption in Indonesia: The Wrongful Dissolution of the Joint Investigating Team against Corruption', paper presented at the Australia–Indonesia Legal Fellowship Seminar, Asian Law Centre, University of Melbourne, 18 January 2001.

Cremer, G. (1990) 'Schein-Consulting, Titelblattgeschäfte, kick-back-Auftragsforschung als Instrument der Mittelumlenkung. Beobachtungen zum Wissenschaftssektor in Indonesien', *Internationales Asienforum*, 21 (3–4): 209–34.

Crouch, H. (1979) 'Patrimonialism and Military Role', *World Politics*, XXXI (4): 571–87.

Davidsen, S., Juwono, V. and Timberman, D.G. (2006) *Curbing Corruption in Indonesia 2004–2006*, Jakarta: The United States–Indonesia Society and Centre for Strategic and International Studies.

Dietz, M. (1998) *Korruption – eine institutionenökonomische Analyse*, Berlin: Berlin Verlag.

Indonesia Corruption Watch (2004) *Daerah, Lahan Subur Korupsi: Laporan Akhir Tahun 2004*, Jakarta: Indonesia Corruption Watch.

Isra, S. (2006) 'When the People's Representatives Loot the Public Purse' in Partnership for Governance Reform in Indonesia (ed.) *Fighting Corruption from Aceh to Papua*, Jakarta: Partnership for Governance Reform in Indonesia.

Klitgaard, R. (1991) *Controlling Corruption*, Berkeley: University of California Press.

Koalisi Perlindungan Saksi (2005) *Saksi harus dilindungi. Bahan Advokasi untuk RUU Perlindungan Saksi*, Jakarta: Koalisi Perlidnungan Saksi.

Komisi Pemberantasan Korupsi (2006) *Laporan Tahunan 2005*, Jakarta: Komisi Pemberantasan Korupsi.

Magnis-Suseno, F. (1981) *Javanische Weisheit und Ethik. Studien einer östlichen Moral*, München: Oldenburg.

Masduki, T. (2006) 'Eradicating Corruption: From Acceptance to Resistance', in Partnership for Governance Reform in Indonesia (ed.) *Fighting Corruption from Aceh to Papua*, Jakarta: Partnership for Governance Reform in Indonesia.

Ministry of Adminstrative Reform's website on the Action Plan. Online. Available HTTP: <http://kormonev.menpan.go.id/> (accessed 31 July 2006).

National Development Planning Board (2005) *National Action Plan on Corruption*

*Eradication 2004–2009*. Online. Available HTTP: <http://www.bappenas.go.id/index.php?module=ContentExpress&func=display&ceid=2249> (accessed 31 July 2006).

Palmier, L. (1985) *The Control of Bureaucratic Corruption. Case Studies in Asia*, New Delhi: Allied Publishers.

Partnership for Governance Reform in Indonesia (2001) *A Diagnostic Study of Corruption in Indonesia. Final Report*, Jakarta: Partnership for Governance Reform in Indonesia.

—— (2006) *Fighting Corruption from Aceh to Papua. 10 stories on Combating Corruption in Indonesia*, Jakarta: Partnership for Governance Reform in Indonesia.

PSPK (2002) *Budaya Korupsi Indonesia*, Jakarta: Aksara Foundation.

Schacter, M. and Sha, A. (2004) 'Combating Corruption: Look Before You Leap', *Finance and Development*, December 2004: 40–3.

Schütte, S.A. (2003) *Korruptionsbekämpfung in Indonesien seit dem Rücktritt Soehartos in Gesetzgebung und Praxis*, unpublished masters thesis, University of Passau.

Schwarz, A. (1999) *A Nation in Waiting*, St. Leonards: Allen & Unwin.

Transparency International (2005) *Global Corruption Barometer 2005*. Online. Available HTTP: <http://transparency.org/policy_research/surveys_indices/gcb/2005> (accessed 31 July 2006).

Transparency International Indonesia (2004) *Indonesian Corruption Perception Index 2004*, Jakarta: Transparency International Indonesia.

Wedeman, A. (2002) 'Development and Corruption. The East Asian Paradox', in E.T. Gomez (ed.) *Political Business in East Asia*, London: Routledge.

Wing Lo, T. (2000) 'Anti-Corruption and Housing Scandals in Hongkong', *Perspectives* 3/2000: 19–45.

World Bank (2003) *Combating Corruption in Indonesia. Enhancing Accountability for Development*, Jakarta: World Bank.

# 5 Indonesia's protracted decentralization

## Contested reforms and their unintended consequences

*Marco Bünte*

### INTRODUCTION

Since the financial crisis and subsequent fall of long-term ruler Suharto from power in May 1998, Indonesia's political system has witnessed dramatic change. The most profound impact has come from the twin processes of democratization and decentralization initiated in 1998 and 1999. Democratic reforms have dismantled the neo-patrimonial system from the top, stripping Suharto and his cronies from power. Decentralization has further eroded the institutions of centralized authoritarianism created during Suharto's long period of rule. In one of the most radical attempts ever to overhaul the centralistic polity, Indonesia embarked on an ambitious decentralization programme in 1999. In order to prevent national disintegration and foster democracy, Indonesia devolved political power and responsibilities to the several hundred elected district governments. Given the urgent need for a reorganization of central local relations after democratization, Indonesia opted for a fast implementation. Within only two years all major responsibilities of the central state were to be transferred to the urban and rural districts. These were endowed with new fiscal resources to deliver public services and generate local development, with 2.4 million civil servants to be transferred to the local level. Due to the far-reaching changes amounting to nothing less than a complete overhaul of the political system within a short time, this process has been called 'big bang decentralization' (Hoffmann and Kaiser 2002). What started with a big bang approach remained highly contested in the following years. Decentralization ran into serious troubles after the first years of implementation resulting in a reformulation of the decentralization law in 2004. Yet even the law revision did not end the political bickering among major state actors. Even nearly a decade after the beginning of democratic decentralization, there seems to be no consensus within Indonesia's state elite on how to distribute political power between the centre and the regions. Moreover, the devolution of state power has been accompanied by a series of unintended consequences such as an increase in ethnic and communal conflicts, greater competition over scarce natural resources, a surge in local corruption and greater administrative and political fragmentation. Decentralization has further aggravated the weakness of the Indonesian state. What went wrong with Indonesia's decentralization? This chapter will explore why decentralization faced such enormous difficulties and caused so many problems. It will be argued that decentralization has been a protracted process that was confronted at every stage with vested and well-connected interests at both the central and the local level. Lacking both a serious discussion at the initiation stage and strong political leadership during the phase of implementation, powerful groups at the national and local level derailed the decentralization process. While the nationalist elite and the army feared the disintegration of the nation-state and therefore attempted to preserve the unitary state, regional groupings tried to extend their power base. In the absence of a strong rule of law, the legal framework was often abused by newly formed alliances of politicians, bureaucrats and private interests for rent-seeking activities. It will be shown that the degree of decentralization was often determined by a series of political bargains within and between national and regional actors. To illustrate the political economy of democratic decentralization, the process will be elucidated on two levels. On the first, the dynamics involved in the power struggle between the central government ministries and the local governments will be depicted. It will be shown that most ministries were averse to decentralization and only reluctantly took steps to support it. This resulted in a protracted decentralization, where the formal rules of the decentralization game were heavily contested among the major political players. After decentralization had encountered first serious problems, the Megawati administration introduced a new decentralization law that curtailed the scope of local governments' autonomy. After describing the regional autonomy policy and its implementation, the focus will turn to the unintended consequences that accompanied the process. This second section will look at the consequences of the reorganization of patrimonial networks at the regional and local levels.[1] It will illustrate the severe fragmentation of the Indonesian state manifesting itself in power struggles between various state elites and the mobilization of ethnic and religious identities.

## PROTRACTED AND HIGHLY COMPETITIVE: DISMANTLING THE NEO-PATRIMONIAL REGIME AND REDESIGNING THE CENTRALISTIC STATE

Historically, the Indonesian state's centralistic administration has served the purpose of the various authoritarian governments of holding the nation-state together and controlling the ethnically heterogeneous population of the archipelago. In particular, under Suharto's New Order regime the centralistic structure was integral in consolidating the power of the neo-patrimonial regime, as it served as a means to control society and direct resources from the regions to the capital and into the hands of the ruling clique. After Suharto's downfall, decentralization began to become a major issue of the democratization agenda. The dismantling of the neo-patrimonial regime and the redesigning of the state have been highly competitive processes since they involved a readjustment of political power between diverse political players at the national and local level. As such, the decentralization process became as protracted as the democratization process itself. Decentralization met fierce resistance from the entrenched elite, itself comprised of many of the elements that had made up the Suharto elite. This was particularly true of the bureaucracy, where the patrimonial style of governance typical of the New Order continued to prevail. The decentralization of the political system ultimately resembled a slow learning process, *The Jakarta Post* describing it as 'building a ship while sailing' (21 December 2000).

## Administrative and political centralism as the backbone of the neo-patrimonial regime

Indonesia has always been characterized by extreme centralism. The centralistic administrative structure of the Indonesian state served as the backbone of the various authoritarian regimes. An enduring element of colonial rule, it was used by the authoritarian governments to bind the nation together and to ensure control over the highly diverse population of the archipelago. Consequently, the administrative structure changed relatively little between 1950 and the late 1990s. Both Sukarno's 'Guided Democracy' (1957–65) and Suharto's New Order (1966–98) were centralized, authoritarian regimes in which regionalist movements were considered a major threat to Indonesia's survival as a unitary state. The New Order in particular used the centralistic administrative structure to enforce its government policies down to the village level and to control all avenues of dissent. Uniform administrative structures throughout the whole archipelago replaced traditional village structures and long-existing forms of community participation and leadership. Whereas formal institutions were highly centralistic, informal institutions were patrimonial in character. President Suharto had the formal power to appoint the governors, while the district heads were appointed by the Ministry of Home Affairs. With the help of a direct line of command and close administrative supervision, the centre exercised a tight control over the policies of local governments. Informal relations in the neo-patrimonial regime were more pyramidal; at the apex of the pyramid stood Suharto, backed by the regime coalition of the central bureaucracy and the army. The neo-patrimonial networks spun down to the provincial, district, sub-district and village levels, with officials at each level owing allegiance to those directly above them while also having responsibility for ensuring compliance from those below. The neo-patrimonial triumvirate of Golkar, bureaucrats and military officers replicated itself at every territorial level and ensured that the policies of the regime were enforced in every corner of the archipelago. Golkar represented the regime's interest in local parliaments whilst military officers were placed in key governmental positions both at the central and the local level. In 1970,

20 out of the country's 26 governors and 60 per cent of the district chiefs were military officers – these figures decreased slightly by the end of the 1980s but remained at around 50 per cent since then (Malley 1999: 76). The regime coalition could orchestrate the elections for governors and district chiefs,[2] bring through their candidates and ensure central control over local affairs. The army with its vast network of territorial representation suppressed all forms of dissent. Civil servants were forced to join Golkar and show undivided loyalty to the regime. The regime coalition used its influence for rent-seeking and to build up new business networks, and for that purpose the regime coalition also reached out to small entrepreneurs and petty criminals in the underworld. These mafia-like networks shored up the position of local strongmen and contributed to a climate of fear and intimidation at the local level (Hadiz 2003, Sidel 2004: 64ff.). Communities had only scarce opportunities to participate in local politics as political organizations were not allowed to function below the district level and villagers were considered a 'floating mass' of politically quiescent people. In this way, the regime achieved stability and curtailed participation down to the village level. For more than 40 years the periphery has been totally subordinate to the centre with no influence over government policies and no power to control local affairs. Local politics reflected the interests of the regime coalition and the centre rather than those in the regions. In the end, the chances for the introduction of a real devolution of power were extremely limited since it was closely connected to the overall leitmotif of the Suharto regime, namely economic development and political stability (Kahin 1994: 211).

## Signalling reform: The initiation of decentralization

The fall of Suharto ushered in an era of reforms (named *reformasi*). The ultimate goal of the reform movement in its various manifestations has been the democratization of the political system. The main demands, such as reducing corruption and the military's role in politics, establishing press freedom and lifting restrictions on political parties, were national in scope. Since local level representatives have been integrated into the neo-patrimonial networks of Suharto, they also came under heavy pressure to resign from office.[3] Moreover, regional and local leaders themselves were more assertive in demanding a change of the overall administrative framework and began voicing their discontent about the perceived excesses of centralized rule and demanding greater regional control over political and economic affairs. These calls were especially loud in resource-rich provinces such as Aceh, Riau, East Kalimantan and Papua. Consequently, decentralization became an important element of the reform agenda proposed by pro-democracy activists (Sulistyanto and Erb 2005: 6ff.). Supporters of decentralization equated centralized governance with the old authoritarian regime and viewed decentralization as a necessary process by which civil engagement in public affairs could be enhanced (Törnquist 2006: 227–55).

The Habibie government (May 1998 to October 1999) responded to these developments with the promulgation of a policy of regional autonomy as part of the broader reform agenda of democratization. By November 1998, Habibie had instructed his Minister of Home Affairs to put together a team of civil servants, academics and advisors (the so-called 'Team of 7') to formulate a draft of what later became Law 22/1999.[4] There has been neither a general discussion about the goals of the decentralization nor an attempt to engage other ministries within this project. The President wanted the laws passed quickly so he could present them to the MPR (*Majelis Permusyawaratan Rakyat*) and the nation in his accountability speech scheduled for late 1999. Habibie's move can thus be interpreted as a political manoeuvre to improve his election prospects. Still associated with his former patron Suharto and the New Order, and lacking a solid support base both within his party and the reform movement, Habibie was keen to distance himself from the Suharto regime and to gain recognition as a political reformer. He also wanted to underline his credibility in the eyes of the international community, which demanded good governance and political reforms.[5] Consequently, Habibie made democratic elections and local autonomy the cornerstones of his reform agenda. In May 1999 he introduced the decentralization laws into parliament, which was still largely composed of the three 'official' parties of the New Order and of many holdovers from the Suharto era. The decentralization Laws 22/1999 and 25/1999 were passed in great haste and with a minimum of public debate. Indeed, no substantial changes were made from the government's original draft legislation (Rasyid 2003: 63). Possessing little information about the likely consequences of decentralization, political party members grabbed at every opportunity to present themselves as reform-oriented. Even though decentralization stood to threaten their interests as national-level actors and elites of highly centralized political parties, most politicians voted for the decentralization laws. Thus, Indonesian decentralization has been enacted before the clarification, and ultimately against the clear interest of most of the Suharto-era political elite. It has been used as a signal to indicate that politicians embraced the reform agenda (Smith 2007). What is even more remarkable about the early debate of regional autonomy is the lack of involvement of local actors. The discourse on decentralization in its initial stage has rather been a bureaucratic process taking place in the capital Jakarta.

## The decentralization legislation: Strengthening the districts, bypassing the provinces

Laws 22/1999 and 25/1999 created the framework for Indonesia's decentralization programme and resulted in the devolution of fiscal and political power to lower levels of government, especially the district level. The devolution deliberately bypassed the provinces and strengthened the district level below. Under Laws 22/1999 and 25/1999 the central government was to cede authority to regional governments in all fields except foreign policy, defence, security, monetary policy, the legal system and religious affairs. The central government also retained a number of specific functions, such as national planning and the supervision of technical standards. Thus, the district governments, who had previously been limited to a handful of functions, were now to take over full responsibility for important areas such as education, environment, health, labour, natural resource management and public works. Provincial and local parliaments were given the power to elect and dismiss regional and local heads of government and to determine budgets and the organizational structure of the bureaucracy. The role of the provinces was confined to such areas such as mediating disputes between districts, facilitating cross-district development and representing the central government within the region. Provincial legislatures, therefore, could elect governors but Jakarta's approval was required before a governor could be installed or removed.[6]

The rationale for strengthening the district level and bypassing the provinces remained unclear. One argument in the public arena justified this by referring to Indonesian history, arguing that provinces were created by the Dutch and had no real roots in Indonesian tradition (Ferrazzi 2000: 69). The architects of the decentralization laws also argued that shifting authority to the districts would help to bring democracy closer to the people and enhance political participation. Local communities would be encouraged to participate more in local affairs than at national or provincial level. Political participation of these communities would thus be eased while local politicians could be held accountable for their actions. There also seemed to have been a fear among the architects of the decentralization laws that giving larger units more power might have generated or fuelled separatist tendencies, particularly in resource-rich or ethnically distinct areas. According to this argument, separatist sentiments had always had a focus on the provincial level, especially when there were one or two dominant ethnic groups in the provinces. The several hundred districts were much smaller territorial units than the provinces and were thus less likely to be viewed by their inhabitants as viable independent states. Altogether, federalism remained a taboo and was not propagated in election campaigns or government propaganda (Ferrazzi 2000: 79). According to Law 22, Indonesia remained a unitary state with autonomy to be given to the several hundred districts.

Law 25/1999 developed a new fiscal framework between the centre and the regions. Yet it is rather centralist in character since the central government maintains its grip on the main sources of state revenues: income tax, value added tax, foreign aid, import duties and export taxes. The law mandates that a minimum of 25 per cent of domestic revenues be transferred to local governments through a budget grant mechanism called General Allocation Fund (*Dana Alokasi Umum*, DAU). In addition, the producing localities, their host provincial governments and other local governments within the province will receive 15 per cent of oil, 30 per cent of natural gas and 80 per cent of mining, fishing and forestry revenues. Thereby, the taxing powers of local governments are not extended and the regions remain dependent on grants from the central government. Only a limited number of regions will gain from income derived from the profit of revenues coming from natural resources in their localities. The decentralization laws can thus be seen as a *divide et impera* strategy by the central government (Schulte Nordholt 2004), aimed at allowing for political and administrative decentralization while maintaining fiscal control at the centre.

## Decentralization encounters opposition: The politics of regional autonomy during the Wahid and Megawati administrations (1999–2004)

Decentralization remained one of the most important and heavily contested policies of all subsequent democratic governments. Both laws contained major weaknesses[7] and needed a multitude of implementing regulations which were to be written under President Wahid (1999–2001) and President Megawati (2001–04). Moreover, a large number of sectoral laws had to be adjusted to the decentralized context. Decentralization thus needed a great deal of coordination from the central government. Since decentralization had not been previously discussed, regional autonomy met fierce resistance from its opponents. What started as big bang decentralization ultimately became a protracted process in which centre-based political elites with vested interests in the regions and their counterparts in the regions fought over the scope of authority to be devolved to the local level.

During the Wahid administration the laws were introduced to the public with the deadline for their implementation moved forward to January 2001. Though President Wahid demonstrated his willingness to decentralize by making Ryaas Rasyid, a staunch supporter of decentralization, the new Minister for Regional Autonomy, the implementation was a rather slow and messy process. It was slowed by frequent changes within the cabinet and a general lack of coordination among several ministries. During Wahid's tenure, there was an intense debate among politicians and bureaucrats about the merits and dangers of decentralization. Analysing the regional autonomy discourse between the central government and the regions, Gabe Ferrazzi observes that it was full of mutual expostulations and denunciations. The discourse revolved around the key theme of the perceived weakness of the regions rather than on the failings of the central government to implement regional autonomy. Central government accusations that the regions were not capable or mature were common features of the discussions. The 'father-child' and 'mature centre, immature region' analogies were pervasive (Ferrazzi 2000: 69). One of the most important players in this process was the Ministry of Home Affairs, which had been the backbone of the centralistic system and was controlled by powerful civilian bureaucrats and ex-military personal. Many central ministries and senior bureaucrats who stood to lose power if decentralization proceeded also fiercely resisted regional autonomy. For them, decentralization meant a loss of privilege and a reduction of rent-seeking and patronage possibilities. Some central government ministries only hesitantly devolved authorities to the local level and only reluctantly gave out follow-up regulations, whilst several ministries seriously doubted the regions' implementation capacities. Both the Minister of Forestry and the Minister of Mines and Energy issued statements that the regions were not ready for regional autonomy and that the whole process ought to be postponed (*The Jakarta Post*, 3 May 2000). One year later, the Minister of Mines and Energy again stated that the mining industry would remain under Jakarta's control for at least five years ('Chaos rebuffed', *FEER*, 18 January 2001). The regions on their part accused the central government of reluctance to relinquish control and implement regional autonomy. In the regions the lack of central government guidelines created uncertainty and tensions with some local governments issuing regulations based on their own interpretation of the decentralization laws. Legal conflicts between the central government and the regional governments increased considerably during the implementation phase in 2001. Neither the central nor the local governments adhered to the decentralization rules set up in Law 22/1999 (Bünte 2003). For instance, in May 2001 President Wahid issued a decree that made statistics and land affairs responsibilities of the centre, although Law 22 had made land affairs a mandatory responsibility of the districts. Moreover, in order to acquire additional funds, regional administrations issued a multitude of new local regulations and fees, some of which clearly contradicted Law 22. The local governments of Lampung (South Sumatra) and Cilegon (Banten) issued regulations that made the management of local ports an authority of the local government, although Law 22 transferred this duty to the provinces (*Tempo*, 20 August 2001). The province of Riau issued a regulation to obtain a 70 per cent share in the Coastal Plain Pekanbaru Oil block. The province of West Sumatra declared the cement company PT Cement, which the central government wanted to privatize, an asset of the provincial government and demanded compensation from the central government. In most of these cases various regional elites mobilized support among their followers to seek new income and open new rent-seeking possibilities (Sakai 2000). A large number of districts produced local regulations that were considered harmful to the business climate[8] or the environment.[9] According to calculations from the Ministry of Interior there were some 3,000 regional laws and regulations that require corroboration and perhaps even revision because they might be in contravention of higher laws or the public interest (Schulte Nordholt 2004).[10] Mostly, local parliaments used a portion of the income derived from taxes and fees as compensation for the important services they were providing.

As Wahid's influence on policy-making waned during the end of his short presidency, calls for a revision of regional autonomy became stronger. In particular, Vice President Megawati highlighted the problems caused by regional autonomy and repeatedly warned of the threat of national disintegration. In fact, regional autonomy contributed to a severe weakening of the Indonesian state and caused a multitude of problems which may be summarized as follows (Bünte 2003; Alfonso and Hauter 2006; USAID 2006; Worldbank 2003; Turrer and Podger 2003):

- The position and role (function) of the provinces and governors as central government's representatives in the region remained unclear. The law had abolished the hierarchy between the different levels of government. Moreover, the distribution of functions between different levels of government has been contested between the provinces and the districts. Some governors complained about district leaders (*bupati/walikota*), ignoring their orders or even failing to appear to information meetings. As the central government tried to strengthen the role of the governors with subsequent regulations, the districts continued showing intransigence with respect to the supervisory role of the governor. Since the supervision of higher levels was not working, serious conflicts erupted about the allocation of natural resources. Some of the districts objected to sharing their natural resources with adjacent territories which resulted in serious conflicts about the use of natural resources (e.g. fishing grounds, forest reserves, mining, drinking water).
- New taxes and regulations reinforced trade restrictions.
- In general, financial management and accountability were weak, and corruption seemed to be decentralized. Elections of governors and bupatis by provincial and district parliaments were generally accompanied by money politics, while budgets for development and construction were inflated by the addition of fictional budget items for the personal benefit of the councillors (e.g. shopping trips to Singapore, recreation in Bali).
- Throughout the country, there was a growing confusion at the local level of how to implement regional autonomy. There have been contradictions between various sectoral laws and regulations (for instance in the mining and forestry sector), which led to a general confusion at the local level. The lack of administrative expertise contributed to the general lack of capacity to fully implement the new decentralization framework. This was further exacerbated by the lack of programmes organized by the central government to support capacity building in the regions.

The calls for a revision of the decentralization laws gained momentum when Megawati Sukarnoputri became President in July 2001. Megawati was widely known to favour a strong central government and to be deeply suspicious of regional autonomy. Many central government ministries joined the chorus for a revision of the law and complained about what they called the 'excesses' of regional autonomy. In public statements central government officials claimed that legal redrafting was necessary to resolve the many contradictions and inconsistencies that existed in Law 22/1999 and its implementing regulations. They argued that Law 22 had been excessively oriented towards defining the rights of the district governments without adequately specifying their corresponding responsibilities. In addition, they called for a system of checks and balances to support accountability more effectively and increase coordination among the various levels of government (*Kompas*, 5 February 2002). By early 2002, the Megawati government had begun drafting a set of revisions. A team in the interior ministry presented a draft revision of the law[11] which provided for stronger supervision of the centre over the local governments and a stronger centralization. One of the main proposed changes was the re-establishment of the government hierarchy from central government down through provinces, districts and municipalities, sub-districts and villages. The draft met fierce opposition from the association of district governments, APKASI (*Asosiasi Pemerintah Kabupaten Seluruh Indonesia*), which lobbied to halt the revision of the law (*The Jakarta Post*, 11 February 2002). After both Wahid's PKB and Golkar joined the opposition against a law revision, the Ministry of Home Affairs withdrew the draft law. Yet Megawati did not refrain from the planned revision and continued rigorously to pursue it. Hence a lively national dialogue evolved on how the regional autonomy process should be reformed. In August 2003, for instance, APKASI agreed that the law needed to be revised, but only if the revisions would strengthen and empower the regional governments and would not lead to recentralization. APKASI suggested that the revised law should more clearly set out how power is to be distributed among the various levels of government; how authority would be shared between the district heads and the local assemblies (DPRD). It advocated a process in which district heads could be chosen through direct elections (*Kompas*, 27 August 2003). On the other hand, the Indonesian Association of Provincial Governments (*Asosiasi Pemerintahan Propinsi Seluruh Indonesia*, APPSI) stressed the importance of enhancing the role of the provinces (*Kompas*, 25 September 2003). In December 2003, the DPR formed a special task force to coordinate a revision of the decentralization framework. The task force submitted the revised laws to the DPR on 10 May 2004 and set a target for the laws to be ratified by the end of September, shortly before the Megawati administration ended. Although this left just four months for the legal review process, the revised laws – Law 32/2004 on Regional Governance and Law 33/2004 on Fiscal Balancing between the Central Government and the Regional Governments – were ratified by the DPR on 29 September and signed by President Megawati on 15 October 2004, just five days before she left office.

## The new Regional Autonomy Law 32/2004

After less than four years of decentralization, the decentralization framework has been superseded by Law 32/2004. This law stands in stark contrast to Law 22/1999 both in spirit and in letter; it aims at giving the central government the tools to intervene in local affairs and making regional governments act more responsibly. The stated purpose of the law is to increase the efficiency and effectiveness of the regional administrations in order to enhance the welfare of the people (Preamble b, Law 32/2004).[12] Significantly, the elucidation emphasizes that regional autonomy must guarantee harmonious relations between one region and another in order to raise the welfare of the people and avoid disparities. Regional autonomy must also guarantee harmonious relations between the regions and the central government (Law 32/2004, Elucidation, Art. 1). It provides a list of obligatory and discretionary functions for provinces and districts with further details to be worked out in future government regulations (Arts 13 & 14).[13] In line with Law 22/1999, the national government retains power over foreign relations, monetary and fiscal affairs, defence, internal security and religious affairs. However, it still remains vague regarding the concrete distribution of authorities, which might again trigger conflicts between the central and the regional and local governments. The new law also provides for the strengthening of the role of the governor in 'guidance and supervision' of district governments (Elucidation to Law 32/2004).[14] The concept of the non-existence of hierarchy between provincial and district governments has also been abandoned in favour of a more explicit measure of hierarchy. Despite the weighty role of the governor, his or her position as (elected) head of the autonomous region and agent of the central government in the regions creates further potential for confusion. Altogether, the main innovation of the new law is the introduction of direct elections for the heads of regional governments (governors/district heads). This step was considered necessary in view of widespread allegations that members of local assemblies and political parties were abusing their power by selling their votes to the highest bidder. The direct election of regional government heads should thus change the structure of accountability at the local level. Law 32/2004 provides for an accountability framework where the regional government head accounts for his duties to the DPRD, the central government and the people through a mechanism of regular reporting (Arts 56–112). Local parliaments cannot remove heads, while the central government can unilaterally suspend them for corruption or if they 'threaten security'. In sum, the new decentralization framework can be interpreted as an attempt by the central government to direct authorities back to the centre in an effort to further regain control over local governments. It attempts to force regional governments to abide by the rules and is part of the overall agenda of regaining effective government in Indonesia (McLeod 2005). The law revision has consolidated regional autonomy as a principle of democratic state organization. However, in the absence of a strong rule of law and the weakness in implementation it remains to be seen whether the unintended effects of regional autonomy could be corrected.

## 'Not with a bang but a whimper': Protracted decentralization after law revision 2004

The new decentralization law was an attempt by the central government to address the weakness in the decentralization framework and remedy the problems caused by regional autonomy. Yet, this objective has not been fully achieved. After the revision of the law, the central government remained for the most part inactive. Several years later, the most important government regulation regarding the power sharing between the centre and the regions is still pending. Although the law mandated it to be issued in October 2006 at the latest, the regulation has yet to be promulgated at the time of writing (summer 2007). Central, provincial and local governments could not reach a consensus on how to distribute power between the various tiers of government. In particular, investment licences and land affairs were contested between the central, provincial and local governments (*The Jakarta Post*, 18 June 2007). With the central government remaining inactive in implementation, legal uncertainty is persistant. Despite the revision of the autonomy law the boundaries of authority between districts, provinces and the central government are still blurred.

With the pace of decentralization slowing down in recent years, the amount of power devolved to the local level is a point of contention. In many sectors, the process of spinning off power to the regions has been slowed or even subverted, both intentionally and unintentionally by the central government. In particular, those fields that offered huge rent-seeking possibilities for the centre have been averse to decentralization. For instance, in the forestry sector the central government has issued a series of regulations reclaiming many of the decentralized forestry administration functions. Consequently, some researchers argue that the era of decentralization in the forestry sector has effectively ended (Dermawan *et al.* 2006). Progress has been slow in other respects as well. Even in May 2006, there were more than 1,000 local government regulations waiting to be reviewed by the Ministry of Home Affairs to determine whether they are consistent with higher laws. To stop the rise of 'illegal' taxation, the Finance Ministry has issued a ban on local governments imposing new local taxes (*The Jakarta Post*, 1 May 2006).

## UNINTENDED EFFECTS: THE POLITICAL ECONOMY OF DECENTRALIZATION

The twin processes of democratization and decentralization had a number of side effects. Democratization and decentralization, and the subsequent reorganization of patrimonial networks, were accompanied by a severe weakening of the Indonesian state through administrative fragmentation and ethnic mobilization. It not only led to a consolidation of the New Order elites but also to a decentralization of corruption.

## The consolidation of local oligarchies: Money politics and the dilemma of a 'Janus-faced' civil society

One aim of the decentralization process has been to bring democracy to lower levels of government. As Suharto stepped down, the regional and local representatives of his regime also came under heavy pressure to resign. Suharto's regime coalition – knitted together through a vast network of patrimonial ties – finally weakened and destabilized, yet it did not disappear. Although the military came under heavy pressure to withdraw from politics, it remained an important player in the post-Suharto phase. The ruling party Golkar also was severely weakened, especially in Java, where Megawati's PDI-P and Wahid's PKB could fill the void and build up their core constituencies (Honna 2006). In eastern Indonesia Golkar remained much stronger. Despite the weakening of the authoritarian structures, democratization and decentralization could not crack open the dominance of the elites of the New Order. Instead, the politico-administrative elite managed to adapt to the new rules and adjust to the democratic framework (Malley 2003: 115; Hadiz 2003: 20). Cut off from the patrons in Jakarta, local bureaucrats and party bosses sought new ways to maintain control over the strategic positions within the local administrations and over economic resources. In particular at the provincial level, governors with strong ties to the fallen regime were able to defend their position. In 2002 and 2003, the Governors of Jakarta, Central Java, East Java, North Sumatra and East Kalimantan – all of whom were retired military officers – were able to secure their re-election by the respective parliaments. Exploiting their vast financial resources and the fragmentation of the party system, these governors managed to draw a majority of parliamentarians to their sides (Honna 2006). Altogether, there are three interlinked groups which compete for political power in the regional and local arena (Schulte Nordholt 2004): the first is formed by families of bureaucrats with an aristocratic background who have managed to survive the various regimes since the late colonial period (see also van Klinken 2007). The second group consists of regional bureaucrats and party bosses who used to be the local pillars of the New Order. They made and still make alliances with businessmen and local thugs in order to control the regional flows of money. The final group are newcomers that challenge the entrenched elite in attempting to form new provinces (see below).

The consolidation of the New Order elite has been accompanied by a decentralization of corruptive practices. The growing competition for local power has radically facilitated money politics and the use of intimidation and violence (Malley 2003; Hadiz 2003; Honna 2006). Across Indonesia, the political process at the local level is overshadowed by money politics. The election of the district head by local parliaments normally goes to the highest bidder. The price for the victory in these elections had already in 2001 reached 1 billion Rupiah (US$100,000). To stay in office the mayor had to pay 150–200 million Rupiah to each councillor.[15] Local councillors, for their part, engaged in corrupt practices and demanded high sums of money for the 'services' they were providing. Corruption has taken the form of local budget abuses and is difficult to control or trace back by higher levels of government, the public and the courts. The most illustrative example is the case of the provincial legislature in Padang, West Sumatra. Here, in 2001, 43 out of 55 regional councillors were sentenced for budget abuses. The case was unveiled by local community activists who pressed for the conviction of the councillors (see Schütte, this volume). In many other cases, however, corruption goes unnoticed, exposing the weakness of civil society in monitoring the process.

Local politicians were quite innovative in extracting maximum resources from local governments. Since decentralization has greatly expanded the economic resources of local governments, competition among politicians greatly increased to gain access to these resources. Local politicians often used the strategy of engineering 'civic protest' against government projects to extract money from local administrations. Since government projects – such as land use projects, village or community development projects – have been decentralized, local legislators have attempted to mobilize local residents to protest against these projects with the aim of extracting money for mediating between the protesting 'citizens' and the local administration (Honna 2006: 84). This form of 'parochial mobilisation' (Honna 2006: 85) of these 'civic protests' demonstrates the ambiguity of a ('un'-) civil society. It is often done by *preman*, local thugs or power brokers with strong connections to the underworld (Honna 2006; Hadiz 2003). The use of these elements for organizing 'mass' movements has been an important device by which local politicians have gained access to government resources, which effectively emasculated civil society in its effort to empower the 'mass' based on class or vocational identities (*ibid.*). In a nutshell, the decentralization policy has further consolidated the position of local elites, captured the institutions of local democracy to further their personal interests, or as Hadiz puts it:

> Through control over parliaments and political parties, and via business alliances and assorted instruments of political violence – a confusing array of paramilitary groups and crime/youth organizations – they are establishing newly decentralized, mutually competing, and sometimes overlapping predatory networks of patronage. In short, decentralization is making possible the emergence of more localized networks of patronage that are relatively autonomous of state authority . . .
>
> (Hadiz 2003: 15)

While local state institutions in general seem to have been captured by the entrenched elite, the direct elections of local government heads, introduced with Law 32/2004, gave fresh impetus for reforms at the local level. Most observers, therefore, welcomed the introduction of fresh local elections that have taken place since June 2005 as an important step to improve the overall accountability of local government heads. Recent studies have shown that the new electoral rules have not drastically changed the composition of the political and economic elites at the local level (Choi 2005; Rinakit 2005; Mietzner 2007). However, while entrenched elites have continued to dominate the electoral competition, voters have dramatically enhanced their bargaining power by throwing out unpopular incumbents and electing more competing figures in their stead. According to data presented by Mietzner, around 40 per cent of office holders lost their jobs and were replaced with candidates with more attractive performance records. Regional elections thus have a positive impact on Indonesia's young democracy (Mietzner 2007).[16]

### Decentralization, administrative fragmentation and the rise of primordialism

During the process of regional autonomy, sub-districts wanted to become districts. Since 1999, the number of provinces has risen from 26 to 33 and the number of districts from 292 (1998) to 483 in early 2007 (ICG 2007: 2). This administrative fragmentation is called *pemekaran* (literally 'blossoming'). The 'official' reason for this fragmentation was to bring government closer to the people or to improve government services and to distribute resources more equitably. The driving forces behind this fragmentation, however, are often money politics and aspirations for political power. Recent research in the formation of provinces has shown that regional elites often mobilize their supporters through references to history and culture (identity politics). Rent-seeking motives also come into play (Schulte Nordholt 2004; Kimura 2007; Schulte Nordholt and van Klinken 2007). The principles and procedures for establishing new districts were set out in Regulation 129/2000, according to which 19 criteria have to be taken into account to demonstrate the viability of the new unit. For instance, the Indonesian parliament, the Interior Ministry, the relevant provincial government and the district from which they wish to separate must approve. Initially a team within the ministry, the Regional Autonomy Commission, was charged with reviewing proposals and drafting legislation for the parliament's approval, but proponents quickly learned that they could speed up the process by going to the parliament's commission, whose evaluation often counts more. Corruption plays a major role, and a genuine evaluation of the criteria laid out in the regulation often loses out to money paid over and under the table to parties involved in the process. The revised Law 32/2004 reaffirms central control by increasing the formal requirements for this seemingly unlimited administrative fragmentation. According to the new law, the number of districts and/or municipalities required for erecting new districts is increased. It also sets new time limits to prevent the acceleration of *pemekaran*. New provinces may split up after ten years, new districts after seven years and sub-districts after five years. Nevertheless, the administrative fragmentation has continued and is producing a drain on the central government's budget without concomitant improvement in services. In a speech in parliament President Yudhoyono called for a halt to *pemekaran*. He instructed the cabinet to restore the role of the DPOD and remarked that since the beginning of decentralization seven new provinces and 141 new districts and municipalities had been created (ICG 2007: 2).

In some places regional autonomy and administrative fragmentation has been accompanied by the rise of primordial and communal conflict. In general, we have witnessed an enhanced significance of the local, which has been articulated in the calls for *putra daerah*, the filling of local positions with native sons.[17] In some places these measures which favour locals and exclude minorities have increased ethnic competition and triggered violent communal conflict. Many new districts were drawn along ethnic or communal lines. On the one hand, this was a healthy process, since in some places the political participation and representation of formerly ill-represented and neglected groups has been enhanced. For instance, in the Province of West Sumatra the Mentawai Archipelago detached itself from the mainland district of Padang Pariaman in October 1999. This fostered the representation of Mentawaians, who saw themselves as significantly different (in cultural and religious terms) to mainland Minangkabau. On the other hand, in some places this process turned out to be extremely problematic since it often changed the communal balances between different ethnic and religious groups. Schulte Nordholt alludes to the point that all major communal conflicts (Poso in Central Sulawesi, Ambon in Maluku, and Sampit in Kalimantan) started as district-level conflicts. Whenever violence erupts along communal lines, radical Islamic groups have been quick to exploit it (Schulte Nordholt 2004). The violence has diminished somewhat in recent years, leaving behind a fragile peace instead. The violent episodes have put in motion a set of ethnic power-sharing arrangements to prevent the recurrence of violence. Many observers were concerned that the introduction of direct local elections would trigger a new round of ethnic conflict. It was feared that candidates in regions with heterogeneous populations could be tempted to mobilize their core constituencies by fuelling racial prejudices and sentiments against rival social groups. In most cases, such primordialist outbidding did not occur. Instead, applicants in heterogeneous areas tried to form cross-cultural tickets, addressing the moderate attitude of the electorate and hoping to gain additional voices from alternative camps (Mietzner 2007).

Apart from ethnic conflict, the past five years have witnessed the emergence of local religious bylaws based on the sharia in some district regulations (Perda Sharĩa). Currently, about 53 districts have implemented or are in the process of implementing religious bylaws (Anwar 2006). Each district implementing the religious bylaws has different concerns but in general they address seven issues: the obligation to implement the sharia, decency in dressing and moral conduct, the obligation to read the Qur'an, male and female interaction, gambling, the drinking of liquor, and alms giving. Regional leaders have seemingly capitalized on the autonomy policy for their own political interests. They mostly use the morality argument, citing the failure of secular laws in addressing socio-political issues, the spread of corruption and the ongoing economic crisis as reasons for sharia-based laws. Some regencies claim that they have had a dramatic drop in crime rates and that their regional income has increased significantly since the laws were implemented. On the other hand, moderate and progressive Muslim leaders warn of the implications that these bylaws may have for the process of democratization in Indonesia. They argue that there are three main societal groups which suffer due to the implementation: the poor, women and minority groups. Some critics say that there are aspects of the religious bylaws that have created problems not only with regard to Indonesian culture and tradition but also to the constitution. A bylaw in Tangerang, for instance, prohibits women to go out at night. This local regulation has stirred up controversy amongst many Indonesian women who have to work until late in the night. Some Muslim scholars openly state that certain bylaws discriminate against women. In Padang, West Sumatra, a Perda on Islamic dress is said to impinge on people's freedom as the Perda is applied not only to Muslims but also to non-Muslims. The Bishop Conference in Indonesia reported that several Christian students complained that they had to wear Islamic dress to school even though theirs is a public school which is supposed to be faith-neutral (Assyaukanie 2007: 2; Anwar 2006).

## CONCLUSION

After three decades of centralism, Indonesia embarked on a major decentralization programme that promised to be nothing less than a complete overhaul of the political system. However, what has been referred to as 'big bang decentralization' in the end resembled a protracted process in which politicians and bureaucrats with vested interests struggled over the direction of reform. The devolution of state power has confronted vested interests at both the central and the local level. Lacking a serious discussion at its initial stage and a strong leadership during the phase of implementation, powerful groups at the national and local level derailed the whole process. While the nationalist elite and the army feared the disintegration of the state, and therefore attempted to preserve the unitary state, regional groups tried to extend their power. In the absence of a strong rule of law the legal framework was often abused by newly formed alliances of politicians, bureaucrats and private interests for rent-seeking activities. Confronted with many decentralization-related problems, nationalist politicians halted the autonomy process and called for a revision of the decentralization law. In an effort to gain further control of the restive local governments, the new law directs authorities back to the central government which is given more power to intervene in local affairs.

Despite these changes, however, it could not remedy the many unintended consequences of the decentralization process. The weakening of the Indonesian state originated from the reorganization of patrimonial networks at the regional and local level, the concomitant power play between competing forces, and the mobilization of ethnic and religious identities. With the consolidation of the regional and local elites, these conflicts have slowed in recent years.

Despite the rapid and far-reaching reforms, many characteristics of the centralistic authoritarian state remain intact today. Indonesia's democracy is still haunted by patrimonial features manifest in rampant and endemic corruption, a weak *Rechtsstaat* (rule of law) and a limited state capacity (Webber 2006). The military is still a powerful force and religious and ethnic violence still persist. These legacies of the centralistic authoritarian past manifest themselves to a far greater extent at the local level. Here, the political power of the entrenched elite is far more unbalanced and direct. Retired military officers, local bureaucrats and business men still form the local backbone of the Indonesian state. Continuities can also be found in central–local relations since Indonesia remains a unitary state and much of the political decisions continue to be made in Jakarta. Although the devolution of authority has triggered tremendous changes in local politics, reaching from issues of local governance to revenue generation and budget preparation to the participation of local civil society organizations, the local political arena is still characterized by the dominance of entrenched elites and the use of intimidation, discrimination and political violence (Hadiz 2003; Malley 2003; Schulte Nordholt 2004). Hence, much of the formal political spaces opened up by democratization and decentralization seem to have been captured by local elites. It seems as if the original objective of the decentralization process – to spread democracy from Jakarta to the regions – has failed.

However, in toto, the decentralization process has yielded mixed results. The professional optimists see decentralization in general on the right track. They, however, see it only as a means to increase service delivery and to make government more work more effectively. This view, however, neglects the political dynamics behind the decentralization process (Colongan 2003; Hofmann and Kaiser 2002, USAID 2006). The pessimists, therefore, point to the increased violence, decentralized corruption and vested interests that have been mobilized in the power play at the local level (Hadiz 2003; Honna 2006; Schulte Nordholt 2004; Malley 2003). The truth lies somewhere between these two extremes.

## NOTES

1 Regional in this context means sub-national or provincial, while local refers to the district level and the levels below.
2 The appointment of the head of the region was a combination of election by the local assembly (DPRD) and appointment of the next higher level. The elections were highly scripted. There were, however, signs of refusal and protest, for instance in the elections for the governors in Riau in 1985 and Central Kalimantan in 1993. The outcome of this orchestrated process was that local leaders were co-opted by the central government and integrated into a clear administrative hierarchy from

the centre down to the regions and the local level (Malley 1999:85ff; Mietzner, this volume).

3 In Java alone, more than 100 district heads had to resign due to local reformasi movements.

4 With the initiation of a new decentralization round he also realized the recommendations of the special session of the MPR Republik Indonesia, TAP MPR No. XV/MPR/1998 (regarding the Implementation of Regional Autonomy; a Just Regulation, Division and Utilization of National Resources and the Balancing of Center-Regional Finances within the framework of the Unitary Republic of Indonesia). Law 25 was prepared by a Team in the Ministry of Finance.

5 He was supported in this by the international development organizations (ADB, GTZ, USAID, World Bank), which from the beginning supported the decentralization programme with vast sums of money and technical advice. They also exerted pressure to keep the decentralization course during implementation (Bünte 2003; Turner and Podger 2003: 15).

6 For a critical examination of these laws, see Bell (2001).

7 Law 22 was not precise about determining the authorities of provinces and districts. The law does not give a concrete definition what is to be decentralized. It calls for a government regulation to define what is not to be decentralized. Yet, government regulation 25/2000 appears arbitrary in many of its assignments of functions to the regions. Moreover, the authority relationships between provinces and districts are not clearly defined (Bell 2001).

8 Some regulations constitute barriers to free trade and cause additional costs for goods and services originating from, or transported through, particular regions, thereby making them less competitive in the open market (Ray and Goodpaster 2003, von Lübke 2006).

9 Local governments issued new logging licences which contributed to a loss of wood.

10 The excitement over regional regulations reached a climax during the annual meeting of the MPR in November 2001, which recommended that the Supreme Court conduct a judicial review of all regional regulations that possibly contradict national laws.

11 Matrik Penyempurnaan Undang-Undang Nomor 22/199 tentang Pemerintah Daerah, Draf Hasil Tim Kecil, Salak 23. Agustus 2001.

12 Law 32/2004 uses the term regional administrations for both provincial and district governments.

13 The law avoids the omnibus assignment of residual functions to regional governments. Instead the obligatory functions of district governments under law 32/2004 are Development planning, Planning, Utilization and Supervision of Zoning, Public Order and Peace, Providing Public Means and Facilities, Handling of the Health Sector, Education, Social Affairs, Employment promotion, Facilitating the Development of Cooperatives, Environment, Land, Demographics and Civil Registry, Administrational Affairs, Capital Investment.

14 For the background to the changes brought about by law 32/2004 see USAID (2006: 36f).

15 According to a new government regulation, district heads had to annually submit accountability reports to local parliaments. If local councillors approve this report, local leaders can continue their terms in office, but if the councillors withhold approval the local leaders are sacked before completing their term. The new government regulation greatly influenced the political manoeuvring of many governors and district heads. They intensified their efforts to woo and co-opt the majority in their local assemblies. Here, they undertook the necessary measures to convince members of the local parliaments. This previous line seems redundant. These measures included the allocation of business contracts for government

projects to companies linked to faction leaders. This also included extracting some funds from routine budgets for distribution as operational funds for faction members (Honna 2006: 81).
16 Incumbents struggling with allegations of corruption were typically thrown out. The electorate thus has shown an immense political maturity in punishing corrupt leaders and rejecting platforms based on exclusivist primordial sentiments.
17 It is believed that only *putra daerah* are able to secure privileged access for their communities in the allocation of economic resources and government positions. This localism has revived the interest in *adat* (tradition and custom). Local elites have taken up the notion of *adat* to voice their claims or demand greater recognition of certain local traditions and *adat*-based rights over natural resources. Placing *adat* in the middle of the decentralization discussion is a powerful political act, because *adat* in public discourse is considered to originate from below.

## BIBLIOGRAPHY

Alfonso, R. and Hauter R. (2006) 'Four Years of Regional Autonomy, Successes and Problems', in N. Eschborn *et al.* (eds) *Indonesia today. Problems and Perspectives*, Jakarta: Konrad Adenauer Foundation.

Anwar, S. (2006) 'Sharīa, pluralism, and the prospects of democracy in post-Suharto Indonesia', paper presented at the EU-Indonesia-Day Conference, Brussels, December 2006.

Aspinall, E. and Fealey, G. (eds) *Local Power and Politics in Indonesia: Decentralisation and Democratisation*, Singapore: Institute of Southeast Asian Studies.

Assyaukanie, L. (2007) *The Rise of Religious Bylaws in Indonesia*, RSIS Commentaries, 22/2007, Singapore. Online. Available HTTP: <http://www.rsis.edu.sg/publications/Perspectives/ RSIS/0222007.pdf> (accessed 23 June 2007).

Bell, G. (2001) 'The New Indonesian Laws Relating to Regional Autonomy: Good Intentions, Confusing Laws', *Asian-Pacific Law and Policy Journal*, 2(1).

Bünte, M. (2003) *Regionale Autonomie in Indonesien*, Hamburg: Institut für Asienkunde.

—— (2004) 'Indonesia's Decentralisation: The Big Bang Revisited', in M. Nelson (ed.) *Thai Politics: Global and Local Perspectives. KPI Yearbook No. 2*, Bangkok: KPI. Online. Available HTTP: <http://www.gtzsfdm.or.id/documents/dec_ind/o_pa_doc/MarcoB%FCnte_Indonesia's%20Decentralisation_Nov2003.pdf> (accessed 12 February 2004).

Choi, N. (2005) 'Local Elections and Democracy in Indonesia. The Case of Riau Archipelago', Working Paper, No. 91, Singapore: Institute of Defence and Strategic Studies. Online. Available HTTP: <http://www.rsis.edu.sg/publications/WorkingPapers/WP91.pdf> (accessed 17 June 2007).

Colongan, J.A. (2003) 'What is happening on the ground? The Progress of decentralisation', in E. Aspinall and G. Fealey (eds) *Local Power and Politics in Indonesia: Decentralisation and Democratisation*, Singapore: Institute of Southeast Asian Studies.

Dermawan, A. *et al.* (2006) 'Origins and scope of Indonesia's decentralization laws', in C. Barr *et al.* (eds) *Decentralization of Forest Administration in Indonesia: Implications for Forest Sustainability, Economic Development and Community Livelihoods*, Bogor: Center for International Forestry Research, 31–57.

Eschborn, N. *et al.* (2006) (eds) *Indonesia today. Problems and Perspectives*, Jakarta: Konrad Adenauer Foundation.

Ferrazzi, G. (2000) 'Using the "F" Word: Federalism in Indonesia's decentralisation discourse', in *Publius*, 30 (2): 63–85.

Fitrani, F. *et al.* (2005) 'Unity in Diversity? The Creation of New Local Governments in a Decentralising Indonesia', *Bulletin of Indonesian Economic Studies*, 41 (11): 57–79.

Hadiz, V. (2003) 'Decentralisation and Democracy in Indonesia: A Critique of Neo-Institutionalist Perspectives', SEARC Working Paper Series, No. 47, Hong Kong Southeast Asia Research Centre, City University of Hong Kong. Online. Available HTTP: <http://cityu.edu.hk/searc/WP 47_03_Hadiz.pdf> (accessed 25 June 2007).

Honna, J. (2006) 'Local Civil-Military Relations in Indonesia during the First Phase of Democratic Transition 1999–2004, A Comparison of West Central and East Java', *Indonesia*, 82 (3): 75–96.

Hoffmann, B. and Kaiser, K. (2002) 'The Making of the Big Bang and its aftermath: A Political Economy Perspective', paper presented at the conference 'Can Decentralization Help Rebuild Indonesia?', Atlanta, Georgia, 2–3 May. Online. Available HTTP: <http://www1.worldbank.org/eap> (accessed 1 July 2003).

ICG (2007) 'Indonesia: Decentralisation and Local Power Struggles in Maluku', *ICG Asia Briefing, No. 64*, ICG: Jakarta and Brussels.

Kimura, E. (2007) 'Marginality and Opportunity in the Periphery: The Emergence of Gorontalo Province in North Sulawesi', Working Paper, Stanford: Stanford University.

Kahin, A. (1994) 'Regionalism and Decentralisation', in D. Bourchier and J. Legge (eds) *Democracy in Indonesia*, Melbourne: Monash University.

Malley, M. (1999) 'Regions: Centralisation and Resistance', in D. K. Emmerson (ed.) *Indonesia beyond Suharto. Polity, Economy, Society, Transition*, London: Armonk.

—— (2000) 'Beyond Democratic Elections: Indonesia embarks on a protracted transition', in *Democratisation*, 7 (3): 153–80.

—— (2003) 'New Rules, Old Structures and the Limits of Democratic Decentralisation', in E. Aspinall and G. Fealey (eds) *Local Power and Politics in Indonesia: Decentralisation and Democratisations*, Singapore: Institute of Southeast Asian Studies.

Mietzner, M. (2007) 'Indonesia's direct elections: Empowering the Electorate or Entrenching the New Order Oligarchy?', forthcoming in E. Aspinall and G. Fealey (2007) *The New Order and its Legacy*.

McLeod, R. (2005) 'The Struggle to regain effective government under democracy in Indonesia', *Bulletin of Indonesian Economic Studies*, 41 (3): 367–86.

Ray, D. and Goodpaster, G. (2003) 'Indonesian decentralisation. Local Autonomy, trade barriers and discrimination', in D. Kingsbury and H. Aveling (eds) *Autonomy and Disintegration*, London: Routledge.

Rasyid, R. (2003) 'Regional Autonomy and Local Politics in Indonesia', in E. Aspinall and G. Fealey (eds) *Local Power and Politics in Indonesia: Decentralisation and Democratisation*, Singapore: ISEAS.

Rinakit, S. (2005) 'Indonesian Regional Elections in Praxis', IDSS Commentaries, Singapore: Institute of Defence and Strategic Studies.

Sakai, M. (2003) 'The Privatisation of Padang Cement, Regional Identity and Regional Economic Hegemony in the New Era of Decentralisation', in E. Aspinall and G. Fealey (eds) *Local Power and Politics in Indonesia: Decentralisation and Democratisation*, Singapore: ISEAS.

Schulte Nordholt, H. (2004) 'Decentralisation in Indonesia: Less State, More Democracy?', in J. Harris, K. Stokke and O. Törnquist (eds) *Politicising Democracy. Local Politics and Democratisation in Developing Countries*, Basingstoke: Palgrave Macmillan.

Schulte Nordholt, H. and van Klinken, G. (2007) *Local Politics in Post-Suharto Indonesia*, Leiden: KITLV.

Sidel, J. (2004) 'Bossism and Democracy in the Philippines, Thailand and Indonesia: Towards an Alternative Framework for the Study of "Local Strongmen" ', in J. Harris, K. Stokke and O. Törnquist (eds) *Politicising Democracy, Local Politics and Democratisation in Developing Countries*, Basingstoke: Palgrave Macmillan.

Smith, B. (2007) 'The Origins of Regional Autonomy in Indonesia: Experts and the Marketing of Political Interests'. Online. Available HTTP: <http://www.clas.ufl.edu/users/bbsmith/IndonesiaDC.pdf> (accessed 20 June 2007).

Sulistiyanto, P. and Erb, M. (2005) 'Introduction: entangled politics in post-Suharto Indonesia', in M. Erb, P. Sulistiyanto and C. Faucher (eds) *Regionalism in Post-Suharto Indonesia*, London: Routledge, pp. 1–19.

Törnquist, O. (2006) 'Assessing Democracy from Below: A Framework on Indonesian Pilot Study, *Democratization*, 13 (2): 227–55.

Turner, M. and Podger, O. (2003) *Decentralisation in Indonesia: Redesigning the State*, Canberra: Asia Pacific Press.

USAID (2006) 'Stock Taking on Indonesia's Recent Decentralisation Reforms', Jakarta. Online. Available HTTP: <http://pdf.usaid.gov/pdf_docs/PNADH311.pdf> (accessed 15. May 2007).

van Klinken, G. (2007) 'Return of the Sultans: the communitarian turn in local politics', in J. Davidson and D. Henley (eds) *The Revival of Tradition in Indonesian Politics. The Deployment of Adat from colonialism to indigenism*, London: Routledge.

von Lübke, C. (2006) 'Leadership and Voice in Local Governance – Political Economy of District Business Regulations in Central Java, West Sumatra, Bali and NT', RICA Working Paper, Jakarta: World Bank.

Webber, D. (2006) 'A Consolidated Patrimonial Democracy? Democratisation in Post-Soeharto Indonesia', *Democratization* 13(3): 396–420.

# 6 Indonesia and the pitfalls of low-quality democracy

## A case study of the gubernatorial elections in North Sulawesi[1]

*Marcus Mietzner*

Since the fall of Suharto's New Order regime in 1998, analysts of Indonesian politics have struggled to characterize the political system that has taken its place. In the early years of the post-Suharto polity, commentators tended to describe Indonesia's government as a 'hybrid regime'; that is, one that has both democratic and authoritarian features (Diamond 2002). Howard and Roessler (2006), for their part, classified the interim administration of B.J. Habibie as a 'competitive authoritarian regime' that changed its nature through a 'liberalizing electoral outcome' in 1999. What exactly it changed into, however, was left open to further analysis. Stepan and Robertson (2004) maintained that post-1999 Indonesia had become 'electorally competitive' and thus qualified as an 'electoral democracy'. In their view, the elections of Presidents Wahid and Megawati Sukarnoputri contradicted the claims of those who asserted that Indonesia's politics were still dominated by the armed forces, which allegedly yielded sufficient residual powers to overturn any political decision made by the civilian executive. Fukuyama (2005), on the other hand, submitted that the 'perils of presidentialism' during the Wahid period forced Indonesia to revamp its electoral system completely, leading to the direct elections of the president and vice president in 2004.

Yet even these radical changes did not manage to remove residual doubts about Indonesia's democratic qualities. Richard Robison and Vedi Hadiz (2004) asserted that oligarchic groups groomed by the New Order continue to dominate the post-authoritarian state, successfully utilizing the new democratic framework to their advantage. In the same vein, Dan Slater (2004) suggested that Indonesia currently oscillates between a 'delegative' and a 'collusive democracy', meaning that it is confronted with presidents who either use undemocratic means to stay in power or rule through collective support by 'party cartels'.[2] Similarly, Douglas Webber (2006) has recently pointed to the cultural persistence of patron–client relationships networks in post-Suharto Indonesia, labelling it a 'consolidated patrimonial democracy'.

Most of these classifications focused on the state of national politics in Indonesia. In particular, comparative scholars have typically formed their judgments by analysing the composition of the MPR (*Majelis Permusya-waratan Rakayat*, People's Consultative Council) and the DPR (*Dewan*

*Perwakilan Rakyat*, People's Representative Council) as well as the central electoral system. Discussions of local politics, on the other hand, often only served as an addendum to the general analysis of developments in the capital Jakarta. Yet there are strong arguments to grant the debate on the democratic quality of local governance in Indonesia a more important role in character- izing the political system the country has evolved into since 1998. To begin with, a massive programme of decentralization has shifted some of the powers previously held by Suharto's centralist regime to the regions, most notably to Indonesia's 440-plus districts (*kabupaten*) and cities. Consequently, the role of central government in setting the political and economic agenda for the whole country declined as much as the authority of local leaders expanded.

Equally important, however, were the new laws on local elections intro- duced in October 2004. These stipulated that from June 2005 onwards, gov- ernors, district heads and mayors were to be directly elected by the people, rather than by local parliaments as under the previous system. This innov- ation, it will be argued, has not only altered the dynamics of local politics, but also warrants a reclassification of Indonesia's political system in comparative terms.

This chapter discusses the gubernatorial elections in North Sulawesi in June 2005 as a case study to illustrate general trends in Indonesia's direct local polls. In developing its arguments, the chapter will successively analyse the old and new electoral mechanisms, the process of nominating candidates, the socio-economic profiles of candidates and problems in the technical implementation of the polls. This will be followed by a discussion of general patterns that have emerged from the results of the elections. These patterns will reveal that while entrenched local elites have continued to dominate the electoral competition, voters have dramatically increased their bargaining power by throwing out unpopular incumbents and electing more competent figures in their stead. The electorate also expressed its newly won self- confidence by rejecting candidates deemed excessively corrupt, openly sectar- ian or exploiting their membership of the security forces. In its conclusion, the chapter will use the empirical and analytical data presented thus far to reassess Indonesia's place in the comparative scheme of political systems.

## LOCAL ELECTIONS: FROM THE NEW ORDER TO THE POST-AUTHORITARIAN TRANSITION

Following its rise to power in 1966, the Suharto government placed sympa- thizers of the regime in top positions of local government by applying both emergency powers and political pressure on the few parties that were still allowed to operate. After the New Order's institutional framework had largely been completed in the early 1970s, however, the election of local offi- cials was regulated by Law 5/1974. Based on this law, local parliaments had the authority to draft a short-list of candidates for the positions of governor, *bupati* (heads of *kabupaten*) and mayor. This list was subsequently submitted to the central government, which then picked its preferred nominee. However, the de facto right of appointment was not the only stipulation that neutralized the nominal powers bestowed on local legislatures. Most importantly, the composition of parliaments was such that it was virtually impossible for a candidate not backed by the regime to get nominated, let alone elected to top the short-list. The government's electoral machine, Golkar, controlled comfortable majorities in almost all local legislatures, and even the parliamentarians of the other two parties sanctioned by the regime, PPP and PDI, had to undergo intensive screening by the authorities before being allowed to take up their seats.

This effective combination of restrictive regulations and overwhelming political control ensured that in 24 years of local elections under Law 5/1974 only very few surprises occurred. In North Sulawesi, for example, the New Order government secured the governorship for a succession of military officers: H.V. Worang (1967–78), Willy Lasut (1978–79), Herman Harirustaman (1979–80), G. H. Mantik (1980–85), C.J. Rantung (1985–95) and E.E. Mangindaan (1995–2000). Among these governors, only Willy Lasut gained a reputation for disloyalty towards the central government, leading to his dismissal and even temporary arrest.

Central government intervention into the elections of local executives largely ended when the Habibie administration enacted a number of political laws in 1999, including Law 22 on Local Government. The changes meant that after the parliamentary elections of June 1999, local legislatures with multi-party representation were free to elect new governors and district heads whenever their terms expired. The new institutional set-up did not result in the rapid replacement of New Order incumbents, however. Particularly at the provincial level, governors with strong ties to the fallen regime were able to defend their grip on power although they did not belong to any of the political parties that elected them (Honna 2005). In 2002 and 2003, for example, the governors of Jakarta, Central Java, East Java, North Sumatra and East Kalimantan, who were all retired military officers appointed shortly before or after Suharto's fall, secured their re-election by their respective legislatures. Exploiting their vast financial resources and the fragmentation of the political party system, these governors managed to draw a majority of parliamentarians on their side, and many district heads accomplished the same feat (McCarthy 2004).

Even when no incumbent stood for re-election, the contested post would mostly go to well-entrenched bureaucrats rather than to leaders of parties who had participated in the 1999 elections. In this respect, North Sulawesi was a rather exceptional case. In 2000, Mangindaan lost his bid for re-election against the chairman of the provincial Golkar branch, A.J. Sondakh, amidst widespread speculation that the latter had bribed a large number of parliamentarians. Mangindaan, who was a popular figure but lacked an effective political vehicle, was so devastated by his defeat that he rejected the request of the central government to stay on as acting governor until Sondakh was sworn in (*Kompas*, 2 March 2000). Sondakh's appointment was challenged in the courts, citing his payments to legislators, but ultimately the case was dismissed.

The allegations of vote buying and corruption, which accompanied almost all local elections between 1998 and 2003, increased the pressure on the government to further deregulate the electoral system. Thus, after the direct election of the President and Vice President in 2004, the outgoing administration of Megawati Sukarnoputri issued another revision of the Law on Local Government, enacted in Law 32/2004. According to this new law, governors and district heads were to be elected directly by the people. The authority to nominate candidates, however, was limited to political parties that in 2004 had gained 15 per cent of the votes or parliamentary seats in their respective electoral areas. Independent candidates were not allowed to run.[3] Local Election Commissions (*Komisi Pemilihan Umum Daerah*, KPUD) were tasked with conducting the polls, marginalizing the national KPU that had organized the 2004 vote. Funding was to come mostly from local budgets, with unspecified contributions from the central government. The ballots were to be held after the lifting of a year-long moratorium on elections of local government heads, which had been imposed by Jakarta in 2004 in anticipation of the presidential polls and the enactment of the new law. Accordingly, a wave of 173 direct elections was scheduled for June 2005, with subsequent ballots occurring whenever the term of an incumbent expired (*Suara Merdeka*, 5 April 2005).

## ELECTIONS IN NORTH SULAWESI: PARTY CARTELS OR PARTY PARALYSIS?

North Sulawesi was one of the first Indonesian provinces to hold a direct election for the governorship. The new electoral mechanism, and its political implications, added to the long list of fundamental changes the territory had experienced since the end of the New Order. Most importantly, the largely Muslim area of Gorontalo had separated from North Sulawesi in 2001, establishing its own province. This separation left North Sulawesi as a predominantly Christian-Protestant province, with 63.7 per cent of the 2.1 million inhabitants of North Sulawesi adhering to the Christian-Protestant faith.[4] Around 900,000 among them are members of the largest church GMIM (*Gereja Masehi Injili di Minahasa*). Muslims and Catholics form influential minorities, with 28.4 and 6 per cent respectively, but have found it difficult to seek high political office. Previous governors have almost exclusively been active members of GMIM, making the church a strong political factor in the local elections. Ethnically, North Sulawesi is dominated by three main groups: the Bolaang Mongondow, the Sangihe-Talaud and the Minahasa.

The balance between these three constituencies in the provincial administration has often been identified as the key to North Sulawesi's relative political stability in the turbulent years of the post-Suharto transition. Religious and ethnic violence had killed thousands in its neighbouring provinces of Central Sulawesi, North Maluku and Maluku between 1999 and 2002, and despite North Sulawesi's relative isolation from the carnage, the issue of community relations was certain to emerge as an important topic for the province's 1.5 million voters.

Political parties in North Sulawesi began in late 2004 to select their candidates for the ballot, which was scheduled for June 2005. Based on the electoral laws, the right to nominate candidates rested with the local branches of the various parties, not with their central boards. This stipulation ignored the fact, however, that party leaders at the national level could dismiss local functionaries who were deemed disloyal to instructions from the capital. Intra-party disagreements over nominees were thus certain to lead to internal power struggles and cases of leadership dualism, and North Sulawesi became a prominent example in this regard. The party founded by President Susilo Bambang Yudhoyono, Partai Demokrat (PD, Democratic Party), was the most severely hit. Local party officials favoured the nomination of businessman and former Golkar politician Hengky Baramuli, with the chairman of the provincial PD branch, DP Togas, selected as his running mate. Some within the central board, however, insisted that the candidacy be handed to Johnny Lumintang, a retired three-star general (*Kompas*, 28 March 2005). Lumintang received particular support from Mangindaan, who was now PD's secretary-general and had declined an offer to run again for the governorship. The conflict was aggravated by an internal rift in the central board, with two antagonistic factions claiming the right to speak in the name of the party (*Kompas*, 24 March 2005). After several weeks of heavy party infighting, the dispute was only resolved when the KPUD finally decided to accept the nomination submitted by the local party branch. Hengky became PD's official candidate while the central board settled its problems at a national party congress in May 2005.[5] Susilo's brother-in-law was installed as new chairman to prevent the party from disintegrating further, and Mangindaan lost his post as secretary-general.

The ferociousness of the intra-party disputes over nominations revealed the commercial stakes that both the candidates and the nominating parties had in the elections. In the majority of nominations across Indonesia, the deciding factor was not loyalty to the party, ideological affinity or commitment to carry out the party's political agenda if elected. Instead, parties were more interested in the financial resources of the nominees and their preparedness to donate parts of their wealth to the party (Mietzner 2005). There were several reasons for this: first of all, local party branches recognized the opportunity to consolidate their finances by offering nominations to external candidates with vast monetary resources. The three rounds of national elections in 2004 had left most local party offices cash-strapped, with no effective system of state-sponsored party financing in place to refill the coffers. Thus parties tended to overlook their own cadres in the nomination and turned to independent and affluent bureaucrats, businesspeople and security officers. Second, parties often lacked credible candidates from their own ranks. There was a widespread view within the elite and the public that candidates for executive office needed to have extensive bureaucratic experience, and very few party politicians did (Forum Rektor Indonesia and Jawa Timur 2005). Party officials typically knew how to run a political organization and mobilize grassroots groups to support it, but had little expertise in management, budgeting or government administration. Third, the fact that most resource-rich bureaucrats, entrepreneurs and retired officers who sought nominations had close ties with the New Order regime did not reduce their popularity with the electorate. In fact, many voters even believed that such figures would be better positioned to provide stability, economic benefits and bureaucratic efficiency than inexperienced politicians, grassroots leaders or academics.[6]

It was therefore hardly surprising that most candidates competing for the North Sulawesi governorship had only ephemeral relationships with the parties that nominated them. As discussed above, Hengky Baramuli had formerly been active in Golkar and only discovered his sympathy for Partai Demokrat when the party offered itself as a political vehicle for the wealthy entrepreneur. In the same vein, the party of former President Megawati Sukarnoputri, PDI-P, denied its local chairman the nomination for governor and instead teamed him up as running mate with the experienced bureaucrat Sinyo Sarundajang. In the case of PDI-P, the local party branch had left the decision on the nomination to Megawati, who approached Sarundajang personally to offer him the candidacy. Partai Damai Sejahtera (PDS, Party of Prosperous Peace), a Christian party with a large following in North Sulawesi, also shied away from nominating its own leaders for the gubernatorial ballot. In an open contest for the nomination which involved a wide variety of bureaucrats, businessmen and security officers, the party finally declared Wenny Warouw as its candidate, a one-star police general. Similarly, Ferry Tinggogoy, a retired two-star military general, was nominated by a coalition of 17 small parties that had received around one percentage point each in the 2004 elections.

Golkar, on the other hand, was the only party that nominated its provincial chairman, A.J. Sondakh, to run in the elections. His position as the incumbent governor gave him enough power to enforce his claim on the nomination, but the party split as a result. Sondakh was deeply unpopular within the party, and when opinion polls showed that he was certain to lose the elections (*Media Indonesia*, 13 April 2005), Golkar's central board sent its emissary, Theo Sambuaga, to Manado in order to convince Sondakh not to seek the gubernatorial nomination. Sondakh remained stubborn, however, and continued to insist on his candidacy.[7] As a result, many local Golkar leaders in North Sulawesi who disliked Sondakh refused to endorse his candidacy and instead supported nominees put forward by rival parties, most notably Sarundajang.

The inability of political parties to present candidates from their own ranks, or maintain their organizational coherence if they did, pointed to severe deficiencies in Indonesia's post-authoritarian transition. In all democracies, but particularly in consolidating ones, political parties are essential for the creation of stable systems of popular representation and accountability. Parties aggregate the political viewpoints of particular sections of the electorate and nominate candidates to represent these viewpoints in legislative and executive decision-making processes. As Stepan and Linz (1996: 274) explain, 'a consolidated democracy requires that a range of political parties not only *represent* interests but seek by coherent programs and organizational activity to *aggregate* interests'. If, however, parties fail to nominate candidates who can represent the political and ideological positions of the former, and instead auction off the nomination to external figures without any affiliation to the party or its agenda, the link between political aggregation and popular representation is cut.

In terms of their functional capacity to maintain this crucial link, Indonesian parties have, in fact, been much weaker in the regions than in the centre. At the national level, parties have generally managed to mobilize their own cadres to represent them in elections. In the 2004 presidential polls, for example, they mostly supported candidates from their own ranks or, in the case of smaller parties, backed nominees who came closest to their politico-ideological convictions. By contrast, the direct local elections after 2005 revealed that political parties at the grassroots lacked the resources, institutional stability and programmatic coherence to act as effective vehicles of political aggregation and popular representation. Consequently, they surrendered their authority to nominate candidates for executive office in exchange for short-term financial gains. The major beneficiaries of this defect in the democratic fabric were independent bureaucrats, entrepreneurs and other affluent political operators. This phenomenon meant also, however, that Indonesia's provinces and districts were not in the claws of the 'party cartels' that, according to Slater (2004), dominated politics at the national level. If anything, local politics were controlled by oligarchic elites that used political parties as on-off political instruments to compete for executive power.

## THE NOMINEES: 'MONEY PRIMARIES' AMONG THE ELITE

Exploring the individual backgrounds of candidates is crucial for the analysis of the social and political context in which the ballots took place. It will point to personal affluence and bureaucratic connections as major conditions for joining the electoral race, and will provide further evidence for the disconnection between candidates and their nominating parties. Nationwide, the strongest group in the field of candidates was that of the career bureaucrats, who made up around 36 per cent of all nominees (Mietzner 2005: 17). The group included incumbent and former governors and vice governors, district heads and their deputies, executive secretaries (*sekretaris daerah*) as well as heads of government offices (*kepala dinas*). These key bureaucrats controlled large financial resources, had extensive networks in business and civil society, and had the advantage of high name recognition. In order to obtain additional campaign funds, senior bureaucrats would often form joint tickets with wealthy businesspeople who had little political experience but possessed the necessary cash to build up an effective apparatus of supporters. Twenty-eight per cent of all candidates belonged to this category. The combination of politically entrenched bureaucrats and rich entrepreneurs was so powerful that according to one statistic, 87 per cent of all local polls were won by such pairs (Rinakit 2005: 2).

The third group consisted of party politicians and members of parliament, who represented 22 per cent of the nominees. This category included businesspeople as well, however, who had taken up leadership positions in local party branches long before the elections in order to prepare for their candidacy. Eight per cent of the candidates were retired or active military and police officers. They were mostly lower-ranking personnel, with only very few generals competing for governorships or district head positions. Finally, the smallest group of candidates comprised of academics, grassroots activists, religious leaders and media figures, constituting only six per cent of all nominees. While some of them were hugely popular in their home areas, they often did not have the funds to pay political parties for the nomination or to cover the costs associated with creating a large electoral machine.

The national statistic on individual candidates mirrored the field of nominees in North Sulawesi with remarkable precision. To begin with, Sinyo H. Sarundajang, the eventual winner of the election, had been a career bureaucrat since the 1970s. Between 1986 and 1999 he was mayor of Bitung, North Sulawesi's second biggest city and site of its international port. He moved to Jakarta in 2000 and held important positions in the Department of Home Affairs, culminating in his appointment as Inspector-General. In 2001, he was sent as acting governor to North Maluku where he was tasked with containing widespread religious violence. In addition, he had to resolve the deep political crisis that had emerged in the province after the local legislature had failed several times to elect a governor. At the end of his assignment Sarundajang was widely credited with restoring security and political stability to the province. Based on this success he was named acting governor of Maluku in late 2002, the province in which thousands of Christians and Muslims had perished in communal conflicts since 1999. Once again, Sarundajang was lauded as a competent negotiator between the conflicting parties, handing over to the newly elected governor in 2003 under dramatically improved social and political conditions (*Kompas*, 30 October 2004). Following his decision to seek the governorship of his home province North

Sulawesi, Sarundajang's campaign team made the most of his reputation as a peacemaker. In a brochure promoting his previous achievements, the authors claimed that North Maluku's Muslims had granted Sarundajang the title of *khalifah* (a religious and political leader who has to be obeyed), and that Christians in Maluku revered him as a 'small angel'.

Despite his nomination by PDI-P, the party played only a minor role in Sarundajang's campaign. Instead, the campaign team consisted largely of retired bureaucrats as well as former military and police officers. C.J. Rantung, the governor between 1985 and 1995 and a retired major-general, has been a major sponsor of Sarundajang's candidacy. Rantung admitted that Golkar would have been Sarundajang's preferred political vehicle for the elections as the party had won by far the most votes in North Sulawesi in the 2004 legislative ballot.[8] No offer from Golkar was forthcoming, however, so Sarundajang accepted Megawati Sukarnoputri's invitation to represent her party in the polls. In spite of his official nomination by PDI-P, however, Sarundajang's strongest support came from Golkar politicians disillusioned with the leadership of incumbent governor and local Golkar chairman, A.J. Sondakh. Under Sondakh, Golkar had split into several factions, with officials marginalized by the governor establishing rival party boards in order to prevent Sondakh's nomination for a second term. After Sondakh was declared the Golkar nominee, however, most party dissidents threw their support behind Sarundajang. Hoping that Sondakh's possible defeat would lead to his downfall as Golkar chairman, they were less interested in facilitating Sarundajang's ascension to power than in regaining control over the party's influential patronage network.[9]

The isolation of PDI-P from Sarundajang's campaign was reflected in the low profile displayed by his running mate, local PDI-P leader and incumbent vice governor Freddy H. Sualang. Sarundajang's campaign managers made no secret of their dislike for Sualang, whose unpopularity as a member of the previous administration made him a liability rather than an asset. Sualang, a businessman trading agricultural goods, was believed to have been involved in several corruption scandals during the Sondakh government, thus reducing Sarundajang's chances to present his candidacy as a clear break with the previous administration. Consequently, instead of relying on the potentially damaging support by PDI-P, Sarundajang recruited wealthy Golkar politicians who bankrolled a campaign specifically tailored for him. Similar to Susilo's strategy in the presidential elections of 2004, Sarundajang's team set up a large number of campaign posts that featured Sarundajang's initials in eye-catching letters but made no reference to the nominating party.

In addition to his effective campaign tactics, Sarundajang benefited enormously from the poor reputation of the incumbent governor, A. J. Sondakh. A social scientist and university bureaucrat before entering politics in 1971, Sondakh had been widely accused of nepotistic practices. He was believed to have facilitated the election of two of his children to the local legislatures of North Sulawesi and Manado, and helped his wife to win a seat in the DPD

(*Dewan Perwakilan Daerah*, Regional Representatives' Council). On top of his obvious favouritism for family members, Sondakh had also been the target of serious corruption allegations. In one of the most prominent cases, 18.3 billion Rupiah (around 1.8 million USD) had disappeared in 2003 after the government paid the debts of a state-owned hotel before selling it to a private investor. While the Sondakh administration claimed it had used 25 billion Rupiah from the provincial budget to settle the outstanding debt, the creditor agency confirmed the receipt of only 6.7 billion (*Media Indonesia*, 13 December 2004). In December 2004, Sondakh was questioned by state prosecutors over the case, but could not explain where the rest of the money went. Against this background, many observers greeted with cynicism and ridicule the publication of Sondakh's personal wealth report, which the governor had to submit ahead of the 2005 elections. In the report, Sondakh declared assets worth only 3.4 billion Rupiah (around 350,000 USD). The local newspaper *Manado Post* found it 'amusing' that Sondakh had admitted to the ownership of just one used car worth a meagre 60 million Rupiah (around 6,300 USD) (*Manado Pos*, 3 June 2005).

The allegations of nepotism and corruption surrounding Sondakh were one of the main causes for the fragmentation of Golkar's North Sulawesi branch. The party had retained its hegemonic position in North Sulawesi politics in the early phase of the post-New Order transition, but the nomination of Sondakh for a second term exposed deep internal ruptures. Opponents of his rule felt excluded from the spoils of government, and they feared that Sondakh's unpopularity might undermine Golkar's long-term position in the province. Deeply split and disoriented, the party proved an ineffective instrument to win the gubernatorial election. With several Golkar-affiliated politicians using alternative political parties to challenge Sondakh in the polls, the party's tested powers of electoral mobilization were divided between the various contenders, spelling Sondakh's decline and eventual defeat.

Most importantly, Golkar's disunity extended to politics at the local level as well. In Manado, where mayoral elections were scheduled for July 2005, Golkar did not re-nominate the incumbent Wempie Frederik, a declared Sondakh opponent. As a result, Frederik left Golkar in order to run as PDI-P's candidate. Frederik's wife, a Golkar legislator in the North Sulawesi parliament, subsequently organized a 'Golkar grassroots movement' to support her husband, sparking attempts by Sondakh supporters to cancel her membership in parliament. This move further undermined Sondakh's campaign, however, with Frederik loyalists now openly declaring their support for Sarundajang in the gubernatorial poll. Significantly, the national leadership of Golkar also refused to get engaged in Sondakh's campaign. Aware that Sondakh was likely to lose the election to Sarundajang, party chairman Yusuf Kalla apparently was keen to keep a distance from the doomed candidate. Kalla only visited Manado during the last three days before the ballot when no further campaigning for gubernatorial candidates was allowed.

Instead, he helped Golkar's mayoral candidate in Manado launch his (eventually successful) campaign for the city elections while paying little attention to Sondakh's woes.

To make matters even worse for Sondakh, he got entangled in the internal conflicts of one of North Sulawesi's most influential families. Trying to profit from the popularity of the province's first governor, Arnold Baramuli, Sondakh nominated the daughter of the former as his running mate. The candidacy of Aryanthi Baramuli Putri, a businesswoman and member of the DPD, failed to produce the desired effects, however, as her uncle Hengky Baramuli was running for the governorship as well.

The divisions within the Baramuli family, which had a tremendous impact on the outcome of the polls, were related to an interesting mixture of religious, economic and political factors. Arnold Baramuli, Hengky's older brother, was initially a Christian, but later converted to Islam in what many of his critics saw as an obvious attempt to gain higher political office in Jakarta. Under President Habibie (1998–99), Arnold's career reached its peak when he was appointed chairman of the Supreme Advisory Council (*Dewan Pertimbangan Agung*, DPA). Hengky, on the other hand, remained a Christian and became a legislator for Golkar in the national parliament. The children of Arnold and Hengky assumed the religion of their respective fathers, creating religiously divergent lines of the Baramuli clan (*Manado Pos*, 13 June 2005). During the 2004 elections, the differences within the family were visible for the first time on the political stage. Yulisa Baramuli, Hengky's daughter, lost against Aryanthi in the race for a DPD seat (*Kompas*, 19 March 2004). Another of Hengky's children, Anita, was an unsuccessful candidate for Partai Demokrat for the national parliament. In the 2005 gubernatorial elections, Hengky, following the severe conflicts within Partai Demokrat described above, represented a coalition between PD and two smaller parties. The rival candidacies of two members of the Baramuli clan effectively ruled out the possibility of either of them winning the contest, demonstrating that the new electoral laws on direct polls had fuelled competition not only within entrenched bureaucratic elites, but even within political families.[10]

The dominance of exclusive elites over the electoral process was further consolidated by the candidacy of Ferry Tinggogoy. The retired two-star general and former member of the DPR was chairman of the provincial PKB branch, which had only a tiny following in North Sulawesi. It was due to Tinggogoy's efforts that splinter parties without representation in parliament were allowed to participate in the nomination process. Initially, the government had interpreted the electoral law to mean that only parties sitting in local legislatures had the right to name candidates, either on their own (if they held 15 per cent of the seats) or in a coalition that reached that threshold. In a lawsuit at the Constitutional Court in March 2005, however, Tinggogoy prevailed with his stance that the law also allowed parties not represented in parliament to combine their votes and nominate a joint candidate. The verdict changed the electoral landscape nationwide, and Tinggogoy was its first beneficiary. He was nominated by 17 small parties which paired him with the Muslim banker, Hamdi Paputungan, as his running mate. The ticket's chances of winning the gubernatorial race were limited from the outset, however. As a Catholic, Tinggogoy faced significant obstacles in a province with a two-third Christian-Protestant majority. In the same vein, Paputungan attracted some support from his home region, the predominantly Muslim district of Bolaang Mongondow, but this was unlikely to overcome the dominance of Christian-Protestant candidates from the Minahasa.

If the majority of gubernatorial nominations were linked to shadowy elite interests and their monetary resources, none of the candidacies was as obscure as that of Wenny Warouw. An active police brigadier-general, Warouw had secured the nomination of the Christian party, PDS, triumphing in the 'primaries' over two retired police and military generals – largely thanks to his superior campaign coffers. The party claimed that it had chosen Warouw because he would be tough on corruption but found it difficult to explain how its candidate had amassed an estimated wealth of 50 billion Rupiah (around 5.3 million USD) (*Manado Pos*, 30 May 2005). His assets allegedly included plantations in Minahasa, property and shares in Batam, an apartment in Perth, houses in Jakarta and Manado, and dozens of cars. Warouw, who worked for the National Intelligence Agency (*Badan Intelijen Nasional*, BIN) in North Sulawesi and Gorontalo, used some of his money to lure voters by handing out door prizes. Huge crowds would assemble in front of his campaign headquarters to find out who had won the 555 litres of petrol that were, among other gifts, up for grabs each day. Warouw did not succeed, however, to consolidate his core constituency of devout Protestant Christians. Many traditional PDS voters questioned why a police general represented their party in the ballot.[11] Even his running mate, the church youth leader Marhany Pua, could not remove these concerns. As Warouw continued to reject demands to specify the amount and origin of his wealth, doubts in his credibility grew and his ratings in the opinion polls dropped (Warouw finally disclosed his personal wealth two days before the elections but the stated figure of 10 billion Rupiah was widely perceived as another case of under-reporting). Frustrated with the constant decline in support, Warouw sponsored the publication of an opinion survey that showed him leading the other candidates by several percentage points. This did little to improve his standing in the elections, however, but rather suggested that while vast financial resources were a precondition for securing a nomination, they did not necessarily translate into success with the electorate.

The hegemonic dominance of affluent candidates from bureaucratic and entrepreneurial backgrounds undermined what Larry Diamond and Leonardo Morlino (2004: 24–5) called one of the 'substantive dimensions' of democracy: political equality. They asserted that 'to enjoy political equality, citizens must [. . .] have some measure of equality in income, wealth, and

Table 6.1 The candidates and their ranking

| Rank | Name | Ethnicity | Religion | Running for | Background | Party support | Result (%) |
|---|---|---|---|---|---|---|---|
| 1 | Sinyo H. Sarundajang | Minahasa | Christian | Governor | Bureaucrat; former acting governor of Maluku Utara and Maluku | PDIP (votes in the 2004 elections: 19.2 %) | 38.91 |
| | Freddy H. Sualang | Minahasa | Christian | Vice Governor | PDIP politician; former vice-governor | | |
| 2 | Ferry Tinggogoy | Minahasa | Catholic | Governor | Retired military officer | 14 small parties, including PKB | 20.88 |
| | Hamdi Paputungan | Bolaang Mongodow | Muslim | Vice Governor | Banker | | |
| 3 | A.J. Sondakh | Minahasa | Christian | Governor | Former governor | Golkar (36.1) | 16.46 |
| | Aryanthi Baramuli Putri | Sangihe-Talaud | Muslim | Vice Governor | Member of the DPD; businesswoman | | |
| 4 | Wenny Warouw | Minahasa | Christian | Governor | Police and intelligence officer | PDS (10.4) | 15.86 |
| 5 | Marhany Pua | Minahasa | Christian | Vice Governor | Church youth leader | PD (8.6), PKS (1.6), PKPI (2.7) | 7.89 |
| | Hengky Baramuli | Sangihe-Talaud | Christian | Governor | Golkar politician; businessman | | |
| | D.P. Togas | Minahasa | Muslim | Vice Governor | Bureaucrat; PD politician | | |

Sources: The information on ethnicity, religion and background of candidates was collected during interviews in Manado in June 2005; candidates' results were made public by the KPUD of North Sulawesi on 4 July 2005; party results for 2004 reflect the outcome of the 2004 general elections in the province of North Sulawesi and can be found on the CD-ROM 'Daerah Pemilihan & Hasil Pemilu Legislatif Indonesia 2004', issued by the national KPU in Jakarta.

status'. Accordingly, 'the more extreme are social and economic inequalities, the more disproportionate will be the power of those who control vast concentrations of wealth and hence their ability to make leaders respond to their wishes and interests'. Authors like Dietrich Rueschemeyer thus emphasized the need for lower-class interest groups, such as trade unions, to be mobilized and engaged in the electoral competition. In North Sulawesi, and Indonesia in general, this has not occurred. Political parties associated with trade unions performed poorly in the 1999 and 2004 elections (except if Golkar and PDI-P, which both run unions for cadre recruitment purposes, are included in this category). In the same vein, labour leaders and social equality activists have found it difficult to stand as candidates in the direct local polls.[12] The electoral laws did not allow for independent nominees, and even if they had, the enormous costs of running a campaign almost certainly would have discouraged candidates from lower-class backgrounds from joining the race. Observers estimated that the cost of campaigning for the governorship could reach 100 billion Rupiah, while nominees for the post of district head needed to prepare between 1.8 to 16 billion Rupiah (Rinakit 2005: 2).[13] The option of shifting the costs onto nominating parties was not available either because, as described earlier, the latter sought candidates sufficiently affluent to finance their own campaigns and, most importantly, contribute to the party's treasury. Consequently, Munck and Snyder (2004: 17) pointed out that such 'money primaries' have the potential to 'undercut the democratic principle that all citizens should be eligible to be both electors and candidates, and all candidates, in turn, should have the opportunity to reach voters with their message and run for office on a level playing field'.

## CONTESTATION AND DEFEAT: THE DECLINING IMPORTANCE OF INCUMBENCY

Levitsky and Way (2002: 52) submitted that competitive authoritarian regimes are different from democracies in that 'although elections are regularly held and are generally free of massive fraud, incumbents routinely abuse state resources, deny the opposition adequate media coverage, harass opposition candidates and their supporters, and in some cases manipulate electoral results'. In short, the extent to which incumbents misuse their power to stay in office can serve as a major indicator for the type of regime the elections are held in. In North Sulawesi, virtually all domestic and international poll observers certified that the gubernatorial ballot was free and fair, and that logistical problems in organizing the elections did not result in a significant distortion of their outcome. The polls were run by an independent electoral commission, which was not only autonomous from the provincial government and the legislature, but also from the central KPU in Jakarta. A variety of newspapers covered the campaign activities of all candidates and provided space for their advertisements. There were no reports of the police or the military intervening to any effect in favour of individual nominees, and the presence of witnesses from all campaign teams at the ballot boxes prevented systematic manipulation. Most importantly, the defeat of incumbent governor, A.J. Sondakh, provided the ultimate evidence for the genuine competitiveness of the North Sulawesi elections. While various authors have acknowledged that it is the *possibility* of all candidates and parties losing an election that distinguishes democratic from authoritarian patterns of contestation (Przeworski 1991: 10), the 'electoral loss of an incumbent is clear and indisputable evidence of a democratic election' (Munck and Snyder 2004: 12).

The high level of electoral contestation did not mean that the polls were free of irregularities, however. The main problem in North Sulawesi, as across Indonesia, related to the registration of voters. Unlike in the national polls of 2004, local election bureaus had very limited funds, severely restricting their ability to update voter registration lists. As a result, voters who were eligible to cast a ballot did not receive the necessary documents, while others who had no right to participate in the elections were invited to do so (*Suara Pembaruan*, 4 April 2005). In the mayoral elections of Bitung, which were held one month after the gubernatorial polls, around 200 fishermen from the Philippines were apparently allowed to vote leading to a deadlock in the electoral process. As the two leading candidates were only several hundred votes apart, the violation had a direct impact on the outcome of the elections. The incumbent mayor, who led in the vote count, rejected the demand by his competitor for a re-run of the ballot in the affected polling stations. Between July and December 2005, local courts, the legislature and the electoral commission led lengthy negotiations over the issue, resulting in a partial re-vote and the eventual victory of the challenger (*Kompas*, 4 August 2005). The Bitung case was a rare exception, however, with election violations in most other areas being of a much less consequential nature. Electoral supervisory bodies, which had been set up by local parliaments, often noted more administrative irregularities than substantive attempts of manipulation. For instance, nominees would be 'caught' campaigning outside of the approved schedule, banners would be removed for being put up at the wrong place and supporters would be reprimanded for staging (forbidden) motorcycle rallies around town (*Manado Pos*, 10 June 2005).

The insignificance of the electoral violations on the overall outcome of the polls was also confirmed by the courts, which swiftly threw out lawsuits by losing candidates. In early July, the provincial KPUD had declared Sarundajang the winner of the elections with 38.9 per cent of the votes, leaving Tinggogoy a distant second with 20.9 per cent. Sondakh finished only third, followed by Warouw and Hengky Baramuli. Tinggogoy and Warouw subsequently challenged the results in the courts, but could present no hard evidence that manipulations had occurred. Instead, they argued that around 25 per cent of the electorate had been disenfranchised, referring to those registered voters who had not shown up at the ballot box. The court quickly established that the electoral laws did not enshrine mandatory voting, and that thus the KPUD was under no legal obligation to force people to vote (*Kompas*, 28 July 2005). In fact, North Sulawesi's electoral participation of 75 per cent was above the national average of 69 per cent, and constituted a healthy figure as far as local polls in other consolidating democracies were concerned. Like in North Sulawesi, courts nationwide rejected serial claims by losing candidates that the elections had been rigged, almost invariably endorsing the results announced by the local election commissions. In one of the few cases in which a local court decided to overturn an election result, namely that of the mayoral elections in Depok (West Java), the judges were soon engulfed by corruption charges, leading the Supreme Court to take over the case and annul the verdict.

The low degree of systematic manipulations was not only a result of increased societal scrutiny and more rigorous mechanisms of electoral monitoring, however. Ironically, it was the large number of affluent and influential elite figures participating in the election that effectively ruled out electoral violations by a single player. The exclusivist nature of the nomination process had exposed a huge gap between entrenched elites and the rest of society, but it also created a level playing field among the nominated bureaucrats, entrepreneurs and other members of the political oligarchy. This meant that in most electoral territories, it was not only the incumbent who could count on loyalists in the local bureaucracy, controlled huge campaign funds and cultivated patronage relationships with media and civil society groups, but almost all nominees enjoyed the same extent of such elite privileges. In addition, the electoral laws also generally required incumbents to step down from their positions before contesting the elections, removing them from direct access to subordinates in the government apparatus.[14] In short, the structural advantages of office, wealth and influence neutralized each other in a highly competitive elite arena, with electoral manipulation no longer monopolized by a single state-backed nominee. While it is likely that individual candidates managed to exert illicit influence over the electoral process in areas where they possessed particularly strong patronage networks, their opponents were almost certain to do the same in their respective strongholds. In the end, the various elite players kept each other in check, using their privileged positions to report violations by their rivals to the media, hire lawyers to proceed with complaints and pay an extensive network of poll witnesses on the ground. In North Sulawesi, this 'equality among elites' made it impossible for Sondakh to take advantage of his incumbency, with his rivals matching all the resources the latter had assembled to maintain his grip on the governorship.

Sarundajang's victory in North Sulawesi ended a campaign that had been marked by personalities rather than debates of diverse political platforms. All candidates had tried to portray themselves as experienced conflict mediators, claiming to be well positioned to handle North Sulawesi's religious and ethnic heterogeneity. Sarundajang pointed to his stints as acting governor in North

Maluku and Maluku, where he had played a positive role in overcoming communal clashes and restoring socio-political stability. Ferry Tinggogoy reminded voters that he had served on UN missions to Bosnia-Herzegovina and Cambodia, and had mediated between the conflicting parties in the Southern Philippines (Tinggogoy: 2005). A.J. Sondakh, for his part, claimed credit for the relative stability during his term in office, but this achievement was clearly overshadowed by the ongoing investigations into his financial affairs. Wenny Warouw, finally, highlighted his status as an active police and intelligence officer to convince the electorate that he would be capable of maintaining stability between the various constituencies. Sarundajang's successes in both North Maluku and Maluku appeared to have impressed the electorate most, providing him with consistently high sympathy ratings. In post-election surveys, Sarundajang scored high in the 'ability' and 'honesty' fields, the two features voters identified as the most important factors in making their choice (Publika 2005).

The vagueness of the campaign was also reflected in the absence of concrete proposals for fixing the provincial economy. Manado had experienced considerable growth from the 1990s onwards but the rural areas had stagnated. Under Sondakh, the province's GDP had expanded only around 4 per cent per year, which was slightly below national average. Manado, on the other hand, had recorded 6 per cent annual growth. Most importantly, the market value of cloves and coconuts, North Sulawesi's main agricultural commodities, had declined sharply after 2002, leading to noisy protests from farmers and traders. The price of cloves, for example, had dropped from around 80,000 Rupiah per kilogram in 2001 to below 30,000 Rupiah in 2005 (*Suara Pembaruan*, 14 February 2005). Vice President and Golkar chairman Yusuf Kalla tried to stage a public relations coup during his visit to Manado a few days before the elections, announcing that the government had fixed the price of cloves at 30,000 Rupiah per kilogram. Clove farmers appeared dissatisfied with the decision, however, correctly pointing out that the executive had little control over market prices and that other measures were needed to support the industry (*Kompas*, 20 June 2005). The crisis of the agricultural sector contributed to an increase in un- and underemployment, which some observers estimated to stand at up to 400,000. During the campaign none of the candidates provided a comprehensive concept to overcome this problem and the economic difficulties are likely to persist after the polls.

## THE OUTCOME OF THE POLLS: TRENDS AND PATTERNS

The result of the North Sulawesi ballot pointed to newly emerging electoral patterns that could also be observed in other parts of the archipelago. In general terms, the election outcomes suggested that despite the dominance of entrenched elites in the field of candidates, voters felt sufficiently self-confident to pick nominees who were more likely than others to represent their interests. This was first and foremost reflected in the electoral defeats of poorly performing incumbents. Nationwide, 40 per cent of all office holders standing for re-election lost their jobs in the direct polls (Mietzner 2005). Like Sondakh, governors Sjachriel Darham of South Kalimantan, Asmawi Agani of Central Kalimantan and Aminuddin Ponulele of Central Sulawesi were thrown out by voters deeply dissatisfied with their leadership. In their stead, the electorate installed bureaucrats and politicians who were also part of elite patronage networks but seemed to be the least tainted by allegations of corruption, mismanagement and nepotistic favouritism. Sarundajang represented a type of low-profile bureaucrat that knew how to play elite power politics but conveyed an impression of genuine interest in providing good leadership to the public. It was largely this segment of the oligarchic elite that swept to power in the 2005 local polls, ending the terms of unpopular incumbents and denying victory to nominees with questionable performance records and motivations.[15] In the same vein, voters did not hesitate to re-elect incumbents if they had delivered improved public services during their term in office, and had not assumed a reputation for being excessively corrupt and dishonest. Rustriningsih, for example, who was one of the few female *bupatis* in Indonesia and exceptionally popular at the grassroots, gained 80 per cent of the votes in the 2005 district elections of Kebumen. In West Sumatra, the former *bupati* of Solok and recipient of a prestigious anti-corruption award, Gamawan Fauzi, won the governorship against a highly competitive field of candidates (*Kompas*, 19 March 2005).

The increased empowerment and maturity of the electorate was also demonstrated by its inclination to reject candidates who campaigned on exclusivist platforms. Prior to the polls many observers had been concerned that nominees might aim to attract voters by appealing to their partisan instincts such as identification with a certain religion, ethnic group or family clan. Particularly in areas with heterogeneous populations, it was feared that some candidates could be tempted to mobilize their various core constituencies by fuelling prejudices and sentiments towards rival social groups. In most cases, this has not materialized. It turned out that candidates in such regions tended to form cross-cultural tickets, addressing the moderate attitude of the electorate and hoping to gain additional votes from alternative constituencies. Nominees for the post of *bupati* in the multi-religious and conflict-ridden district of Poso in Central Sulawesi, for example, invariably linked up with running mates from a different faith than their own (*Detik*, 9 April 2005). In 1999, the *bupati* elections in Poso had triggered bloody clashes between Muslims and Christians, who both claimed the leadership of the district for their group. In the 2005 elections, by contrast, the nomination of multi-religious pairs ensured that favouritism towards either faith was effectively neutralized as an electoral issue. In the few cases in which nominees did try to mobilize sectarian issues to their benefit, the electorate proved unsupportive. In North Sulawesi, Sondakh had used his leadership role in GMIM, the dominant church in the province, to score points against Sarundajang, who was not a member. Dragged deeply into the campaign, the church did not issue an official endorsement of Sondakh, but allowed its officials to express their support individually (*Manado Post*, 6 June 2005 and 10 June 2005). In the end, voters seemed largely disinterested in Sondakh's congregational credentials, but rather focused on his track record as governor and decided it was time for him to retire. Similarly, an infamous Dayak leader in Central Kalimantan, who sought the governorship by fuelling resentment towards Madurese immigrants, finished last in the 2005 election with only four per cent of the votes.

This moderation of the electorate played a major role in the absence of communal violence during the course of the elections. Despite its vulnerability towards community tensions, North Sulawesi recorded no large-scale conflicts between its religious, ethnic or social groups as a result of the ballot. This was also true for the rest of Indonesia, where even areas with prior experiences of massive violence, like Kotawaringin Timur in Central Kalimantan or Ambon in Maluku, witnessed no significant election-related friction in key inter-constituency relationships. The occasional eruptions of violence in some provinces and districts, which gave the direct local polls a rather chaotic image in the national media, were largely contrived and lacked deep social roots. In most cases, crowds paid by individual candidates besieged the offices of electoral bodies, intimidating staff and demanding that the poll results be annulled (or upheld). In its most extreme forms, these protests led to the burning of government offices, like in the district of Kaur in Bengkulu (*Pikiran Rakyat*, 30 July 2005.). These violent actions invariably died down, however, after it became clear that the vast majority of voters accepted the outcome of the polls and thus saw no reason to join the protest. In addition, it also emerged that neither the government nor the courts could be pressured into overturning the results announced by the respective KPUDs. The Ministry of Home Affairs, for its part, declared that it had no authority to annul or alter election results, and judges, like the ones who threw out the case submitted by Tinggogoy and Warouw, tended to confirm the decisions made by the election commissions.

Finally, voters also disproved predictions that active and retired military officers would do exceptionally well in the polls, paving the way for the remilitarization of Indonesian politics. In North Sulawesi, retired three-star general Johny Lumintang failed to secure his nomination, while Ferry Tinggogoy stood no real chance against the hugely popular bureaucrat Sarundajang. The candidacy of Warouw, launched as an active police general, was equally unsuccessful. This trend prevailed in other provinces as well. In the run-up to the ballots, TNI Commander General Endriartono Sutarto had allowed six active officers to stand as candidates in the elections, but in the end, none of the six were elected (*Suara Pembaruan*, 16 April 2005). Relying on little else than their reputations as tough security managers, officers found it difficult to compete in areas where the security situation was not a prominent issue in the campaign. Confronted with experienced and cashed-up bureaucrats, they were unable to match the material resources and political proficiency of their rivals. Most significantly, the poor electoral performances of military officers have raised doubts over whether members of the armed forces will be able to defend their grip on some of their provincial strongholds on Java and other main islands. In early 2007, retired officers elected through the old indirect mechanism still held the governorships of Jakarta, Central and East Java, South Sulawesi and East Kalimantan (the governor of North Sumatra, also a former general, died in a plane crash in September 2005 and was replaced by a civilian). All these provinces will hold direct elections in 2007 and 2008, and if the outcomes of the polls conducted so far are anything to go by, the military is likely to lose further ground as far as its hold on key positions in local government is concerned.

## CONCLUSION: INDONESIA – HYBRID REGIME OR LOW-QUALITY DEMOCRACY?

In his famous 2002 article, Larry Diamond classified Indonesia as an 'ambiguous' or 'hybrid regime', pointing to the presence of unelected military representatives in the DPR and MPR. He contended that 'even if that provision were removed, the military would remain a major veto player', implying that it would be difficult for Indonesia to qualify as an electoral democracy in the foreseeable future. This pessimism was shared by scholars of local politics as well, albeit with different arguments. In her study on post-Suharto local politics in Yogyakarta, Nankyung Choi (2004: 298) concluded that 'as long as political institutions are seen as no more than a means for getting rich, the intended effects of democratization combined with decentralization will require a much longer time'. Rampant corruption, the weakness of political parties, the sale of parliamentary votes to affluent candidates for executive positions – all this seemed to 'show that regional governments have gained autonomy from the central government but are increasingly captive to local moneyed interests' (Malley 2003: 110). The dominance of oligarchic power networks over the political process appeared so pervasive that many observers were sceptical that the introduction of direct local elections in 2004 would lead to radical change. Marco Bünte (2003: 34), for example, argued that 'whether direct elections will reduce "money politics" is questionable, since vote-buying can also occur in direct elections, with ordinary voters, rather than only legislators, taking advantage'.

Does, then, the outcome of Indonesia's direct local polls after 2005 merit a re-assessment of the diverse regime classifications coined by various authors to define the post-Suharto polity? This chapter argues that it does. To be sure, many of the systemic faults that haunted local politics under the pre-2004 electoral system have extended into the new political framework. The direct polls were contested almost exclusively by wealthy and influential bureaucrats, entrepreneurs and other elites groomed under the New Order. Political parties were often too weak to send their own cadres into the electoral contest, preferring to make short-term financial gains by auctioning off the nomination to the highest bidder. Money remained a precondition for joining the electoral race, necessary to satisfy party officials, build campaign machineries and distribute spoils to the electorate. Irregularities in the electoral process occurred, and losing candidates tended to vent their frustration through violent protests.

Yet all these deficiencies cannot cancel out the major innovations introduced by the new electoral mechanism. For the first time it was the electorate, and not elite politicians, that picked the head of local government from a limited pool of candidates. By all accounts, voters made extensive use of their newly acquired powers, throwing out unpopular incumbents, shunning nominees with questionable reputations and rewarding technocrats with proven track records in effective local governance. The serial defeats of incumbents also provided evidence that despite their elitist character, the elections were highly competitive and that occasional attempts by office holders to manipulate the outcome of the polls were, in the vast majority of cases, unsuccessful. In fact, the rate of 40 per cent incumbency turnover even puts Indonesia ahead of consolidated democracies. In the United States, for example, the constant redrawing of electoral districts by partisan state legislatures has seen the rate of defeat of incumbents decline steadily, and less than ten per cent of the seats in the US House of Representatives are currently competitive (Diamond and Morlino 2004: 13).

The high level of electoral contestation and incumbency defeats in Indonesia makes it difficult to subsume the country under the available definitions of a hybrid regime. In the most frequently identified manifestation of a hybrid regime, namely competitive or electoral authoritarianism, defeats by incumbents are possible, but rare. As Levitsky and Way (2002: 53) explained, 'due to the persistence of meaningful democratic institutions in competitive authoritarian regimes, arenas of contestation exist through which opposition forces may periodically challenge, weaken, and occasionally even defeat autocratic incumbents'. In Indonesia's local elections, however, the defeat of an incumbent was almost as likely as his or her victory. In addition, many of the features that mark electoral contests in competitive authoritarian regimes were absent in Indonesia. Levitsky and Way (2003: 5) argued that rulers in such regimes often try to 'limit competition and suppress dissent' through subtle ways, 'such as bribery, blackmail, and the manipulation of debts, tax authorities, compliant judiciaries, and other state agencies to "legally" harass or persecute opponents'. In Indonesia, such cases were scant. If anything, many incumbents found themselves confronted with corruption investigations into their own conduct, seriously damaging their bids for re-election. The December 2004 interrogation of Sondakh by state prosecutors in North Sulawesi, for instance, turned the corruption allegations against the governor from a widely circulating rumour into an officially investigated case. Similar charges were brought against a number of other incumbents, and more often than not, voters would punish them as a result. This showed that the direct polls have introduced a new tool of vertical accountability to a polity which previously had 'been hijacked by interests that have little to gain from local governance characterized by greater accountability to local communities, transparency, and the like' (Hadiz 2003: 20). In the post-2005 environment, these 'interests' face a much higher risk of electoral defeat if they choose to ignore minimum standards of good governance.

The new dynamics of local politics have combined with changes at the national level to move Indonesia, in Diamond's 2002 scheme, from the category of 'ambiguous regimes' into the class of electoral democracies. The 2004 direct presidential elections, which also saw the defeat of an incumbent, were widely acknowledged as free and fair and the playing field for contestants was level. All seats in the 2004 parliament were electorally contested with military officers no longer represented by appointment. Arguably, the military also has lost its status as a veto power. In 2002, the civilian elite pushed through wide-ranging constitutional reforms against fierce and openly declared opposition by the armed forces. In addition, the central government was, in 2005, able to secure the adherence of the military to a peace agreement with separatist rebels in Aceh despite deep sentiments in the officer corps against such a deal. The poor showing of military candidates, both active and retired, in the direct local elections since 2005 also appears to indicate a further reduction of the military's influence on political and economic affairs. Thus, while the armed forces remain an important player in elite politics and have so far successfully fended off demands to reform their territorial power base, their ability to overturn key decisions made by the civilian government has not only declined, but largely evaporated.

Despite its classification as an electoral democracy, Indonesia continues to face serious problems and flaws in its socio-political system. The monopolistic grip of bureaucratic, economic and other elites on participation in electoral contests severely undermines the principle of political equality, which forms a substantive element of functioning democracies. Similarly disturbing is the structural inability of political parties to serve as vehicles of political aggregation and popular representation, allowing independent but wealthy elite figures to dominate the political process. Yet these shortcomings are common phenomena in post-authoritarian transitions, and even affect established liberal democracies. Diamond and Morlino pointed out that

> in their constant struggles to contain corruption, and in their ongoing frustrations in trying to contain the role of money in politics, even the world's most liberal democracies exhibit the pervasive imperfections of responsiveness that led Robert Dahl to adopt the term 'polyarchy' instead of 'democracy' for his seminal study.
>
> (Diamond and Morlino 2004: 33–4)

Thus Diamond, in his most recent works, introduced the concept of 'low-quality democracies'; that is, regimes that fulfil the minimum requirements of democratic states (and are therefore not hybrid regimes), but lack other dimensions of an 'ideal' liberal democracy. Among these dimensions are rule of law, equality, democratic responsiveness, high degrees of vertical and horizontal accountability, as well as extensive civil liberties. Indonesia, a decade after Suharto's fall, has emerged as such an electoral democracy with persistent quality problems, most notably in establishing clean governance, a professional judiciary and accountable security forces. But Indonesia, it appears, has finally left the large group of states that 'straddle ambiguously the boundary between low-quality democracy and semi-democracy' (Diamond and Morlino 2004: 13). Given the gloomy predictions at the outset of Indonesia's transition, which ranged from renewed military rule to territorial disintegration, this is a respectable outcome.

## NOTES

1 Some sections in this article, mostly those on general trends of local elections in Indonesia, will also appear in another publication of the author, 'Indonesia's Direct Elections: Empowering the electorate or entrenching the New Order oligarchy?' in G. Fealy and E. Aspinall (eds) *Indonesia: The New Order and its legacy* (forthcoming).
2 The term 'delegative democracy' was introduced by O'Donnell (1994), while the concept of party cartels in a 'collusive democracy' was first presented by Katz and Mair (1995).
3 In Aceh, independent candidates were allowed to stand under the new Law on the Governance of Aceh, which was passed in 2006. The legislation accommodated the 2005 Helsinki peace agreement between the Indonesian government and the separatist movement GAM (*Gerakan Aceh Merdeka*, Free Aceh Movement). This one-time exception only applied to the 2006 gubernatorial and district elections, however, and no other area received similar concessions.
4 These figures are based on data provided by the Statistics Bureau (*Badan Pusat Statistik*) in North Sulawesi. Its website can be accessed at <http://sulut.bps.go.id>.
5 Then PD general chairman Subur Budhisantoso claimed that his central board finally endorsed Hengky, but under the condition that Togas had to step down from the provincial chairmanship of the party if the pair lost the gubernatorial elections (author's interview with Subur Budhisantoso, former chairman of Partai Demokrat, Jakarta, 28 September 2006).
6 During the presidential elections of 2004, surveys showed that 45 per cent of the electorate thought that an active or former general was best qualified for the presidency, as opposed to 14 per cent who favoured a religious leader and 9 per cent who wanted a human rights activist as president. Only 8 per cent of respondents believed a professional politician should become president (International Foundation for Electoral Systems 2004).
7 Interview with Theo Sambuaga, deputy chairman of Golkar, Jakarta, 28 November 2006.
8 Interview with C.J. Rantung, Manado, 17 June 2005.
9 Interview with Golkar politicians active in Sarundajang's campaign, Manado, 16 June 2005.

10 A similar case occurred in Central Sulawesi, where two members of the family of governor Ponulele ran against each other in the mayoral elections of Palu, the provincial capital. Like in North Sulawesi, neither of the two nominees from the well-connected family was successful.

11 Interview with PDS members at Wenny Warouw's campaign headquarters, Manado 16 June 2005.

12 In his study on the sociological profiles of members of local parliaments across Indonesia for the 1999–04 period, Takashi Shiraishi (2003: 13) found that 'there are hardly any members with peasant, labor, and urban poor backgrounds'. In addition to their lack of funds to secure nominations, candidates from lower-class backgrounds were also disadvantaged by minimum requirements as far as their education was concerned. Both in the 1999 electoral laws, which produced the parliaments analysed by Shiraishi, and the 2004 laws on local elections required candidates to have at least a high-school degree to qualify for nomination.

13 The money was needed to establish a network of campaign offices, hire thousands of helpers, finance advertising campaigns in the media, employ public relations consultants and opinion pollsters, train and provide wages for monitors at the polling stations, as well as pay for entertainers at public events.

14 In the early phase of the direct elections, the terms of most incumbents had already expired due to the one-year moratorium imposed by the central government in 2004. After the first wave of elections, however, there was an increasing number of incumbents who stayed in power until election day, arguing that the law was not sufficiently clear on this issue. Following a lawsuit filed in 2006 against the participation of the incumbent governor of Banten in the gubernatorial polls, the Supreme Court ruled that incumbents had to step down at the time of their official nomination. The government, however, was slow to clarify the implementing regulations accordingly, and at the time of writing it seems that the matter has not been completely resolved.

15 There were important exceptions, of course. For example, the election of Ratu Atut Chosiyah as governor of Banten in 2006 was largely the result of her father's control of business organizations, party machines and thuggish martial arts groups in the province. Calling himself the 'governor-general' of Banten, Atut's father made no secret out of the fact that he viewed his daughter as his puppet in the governorship.

## BIBLIOGRAPHY

Bünte, M. (2003) 'Indonesia's Decentralization: The big bang revisited', in M. Nelson (ed.) *Thai Politics: Global and local*, KPI Yearbook 2002/2003, Bangkok: White Lotus.

Choi, N. (2004) 'Local Elections and Party Politics in Post-*Reformasi* Indonesia: A view from Yogyakarta', *Contemporary Southeast Asia*, 26: 280–301.

Diamond, L. (2002) 'Thinking About Hybrid Regimes', *Journal of Democracy*, 13: 21–35.

Diamond, L. and Morlino, L. (2004) 'The Quality of Democracy', Working Paper Number 20, Center on Democracy, Development, and the Rule of Law, Stanford Institute on International Studies.

Forum Rektor Indonesia and Jawa Timur (2005) 'Pemilih Kota Surabaya Cari Walikota Penyelesai Malasah', Press Release, 29 June.

Fukuyama, F., Dressel, B. and Boo-Seung, C. (2005) 'Facing the Perils of Presidentialism?', *Journal of Democracy*, 16: 102–16.

Hadiz, V.R. (2003) 'Decentralisation and Democracy in Indonesia: A critique of neo-institutionalist perspectives', Working Papers Series No. 47, Southeast Asia Research Centre, City University of Hong Kong.

Honna, J. (2005) 'The Post-Soeharto Local Politics in West, Central and East Java: Power elites, concession hunting and political premanism', paper presented at the 4th International Symposium of the *Jurnal Antropologi Indonesia*, Depok, West Java, University of Indonesia, 12–15 July.

Howard, M.M. and Roessler, P.G. (2006) 'Liberalizing Electoral Outcomes in Competitive Authoritarian Regimes', *American Journal of Political Science*, 50: 362–78.

International Foundation for Electoral Systems (2004) 'Results from Wave XIII Tracking Surveys', 23 June.

Levitsky, S. and Way, L.A. (2002) 'The Rise of Competitive Authoritarianism', *Journal of Democracy*, 13: 51–65.

Levitsky, S. and Way, L.A. (2003) 'Competitive Authoritarianism: Hybrid regime change in Peru and Ukraine in comparative perspective', paper prepared for the Annual Meetings of the American Political Science Association, San Francisco, 30 August–2 September.

Katz, R.S. and Mair, P. (1995) 'Changing Models of Party Organization and Party Democracy: The emergence of the cartel party', *Party Politics*, 1: 5–28.

McCarthy, J.F. (2004) 'Changing to Gray: Decentralization and the emergence of volatile socio-legal configurations in Central Kalimantan, Indonesia', Working Paper No. 101, Asia Research Centre, Murdoch University.

Malley, M. (2003) 'New Rules, Old Structures and the Limits of Democratic Decentralisation', in E. Aspinall and G. Fealy (eds) *Local Power and Politics in Indonesia: Decentralisation & democratisation*, Singapore: Institute of Southeast Asian Studies.

Mietzner, M. (2005) 'Local Democracy', *Inside Indonesia*, 85: 17–18.

Munck, G.L. and Snyder, R. (2004) 'Mapping Political Regimes: How the concepts we use and the way we measure them shape the world we see', paper presented at the Annual Meeting of the American Political Science Association, Chicago, 2–5 September.

Przeworski, A. (1991) *Democracy and the Market: Political and economic reforms in Eastern Europe and Latin America*, New York: Cambridge University Press.

Publika (2005) 'Honesty and Ability Key Factor for North Sulawesi Voters', Press Release, 22 June.

O'Donnell, G. (1994) 'Delegative Democracy', *Journal of Democracy*, 5: 55–69.

Rinakit, S. (2005) 'Indonesian Regional Elections in Praxis', IDSS Commentaries, Singapore: Institute of Defence and Strategic Studies.

Robison, R. and Hadiz, V.R. (2004) *Reorganising Power in Indonesia: The politics of oligarchy in an age of markets*, London and New York: RoutledgeCurzon.

Shiraishi, T. (2003) 'A Preliminary Study of Local Elites in Indonesia: Sociological profiles of DPRD members', paper presented at the International Symposium on Indonesia's Decentralisation Policy, Hitotsubashi University, Tokyo, Japan, January.

Slater, D. (2004) 'Indonesia's Accountability Trap: Party cartels and presidential power after democratic transition', *Indonesia*, 78: 61–92.

Stepan, A. and Linz, J. (1996) *Problems of Democratic Transition and Consolidation: Southern Europe, South America and post-communist Europe*, Baltimore: Johns Hopkins University Press.

Stepan, A. and Robertson, G.B. (2004) 'Arab, not Muslim, Exceptionalism', *Journal of Democracy*, 15: 140–6.

Tinggogoy, F. (2005) 'Merekat Pluralitas Sulawesi Utara', *Manado Pos*, 14 June.

Webber, D. (2006) 'A Consolidated Patrimonial Democracy? Democratization in post-Soeharto Indonesia', *Democratization*, 13: 396–420.

# Part II

# The intermediate level: Political parties

# 7 Political parties and democratization in Indonesia

*Andreas Ufen*

## INTRODUCTION

Political parties and their role in transition and consolidation processes attract the attention of a range of political scientists. As central political institutions, parties fulfil major functions in the sphere between state and civil society. To Lipset, parties are even at the core of his democracy definition:

> Democracy in a complex society may be defined as a political system which supplies regular constitutional opportunities for changing the governing officials, and a social mechanism which permits the largest possible part of the population to influence major decisions by choosing among contenders for political office, that is, through political parties.
>
> (Lipset 2000: 48)

However, democracy in Indonesia is still fraught with many weaknesses. Political parties have to consolidate themselves in an environment of contingency and ambiguity. The protracted transition fosters uncertainty and, thus, exacerbates party institutionalization. In such a situation a mix of over- or under-centralization, internal conflict and 'money politics' is common.

The diverse literature on political parties in Indonesia mirrors this complexity. Whereas some scholars assess parties and the party system since 1998 from a neo-Marxist perspective (Robison and Hadiz 2004; Hadiz 2004), others focus on the role of *aliran*[1] ('streams') (King 2003; Baswedan 2004; Johnson Tan 2004; Sherlock 2004 and 2005) and stress that many parties have a mass base and are embedded in specific milieus. Others point at deficiencies, such as 'cartelization' (Slater 2005) and formal institutional flaws (Sherlock 2005), or at the lacking or uneven institutionalization of parties and the party system (Johnson Tan 2006; Tomsa 2006b). Others cite new evidence from regression analysis and cast serious doubt on the conventional *aliran* approach (Mujani and Liddle 2007). In connection with a range of recent studies on local politics (Hadiz 2004a; Choi 2004; Vel 2005; Mietzner in this volume), the emergent picture is multifaceted. The role played by parties in the democratization after the fall of Suharto remains unclear.

But what do we expect from Indonesian political parties? According to Schmitter (1999: 477f) parties should recruit persons to 'participate actively in campaigns' and nominate candidates for office (electoral structuration); they should 'provide most citizens with a stable and distinctive set of ideas and goals' which 'make them feel part of the process of collective choice' (symbolic integration); they 'should be capable of forming a government and of providing an internal structure to the legislative process' (governing function); and they ideally aggregate interests and passions, channel expectations and produce programmes in a way satisfactory for most of the citizenry (aggregative function).

It is generally acknowledged that parties fulfil these functions better when they and the party system as a whole are well institutionalized. According to Mainwaring and Torcal (2006: 206f) institutionalized party systems are more stable, that is patterns of party competition manifest regularly. In more institutionalized systems, parties have strong roots in society and the voter–party linkage is closer. Political actors see parties as a legitimate, necessary part of democratic politics, and party organizations are not dependent on charismatic leaders but have acquired an independent status. Weakly institutionalized party systems generate more uncertainty of electoral outcomes and are inimical to electoral accountability. In contrast, institutionalized party systems are stable and parties accept the rules of the game and each other as legitimate.

This chapter shall first outline the evolution of political parties until 1998 in order to better understand some of the main forces shaping parties and the party system in Indonesia. The second part of the chapter will briefly describe the new landscape of party politics since May 1998 and portray the most important parties. The third and main part deals with the deficiencies of parties and the party system in post-Suharto Indonesia. Finally, the chapter shall present some conclusions by assessing party functions and institutionalization.

## THE EVOLUTION OF POLITICAL PARTIES IN INDONESIA UNTIL 1998

The first Indonesian parties were established in the 1910s and 1920s (that is, still under colonial rule). They were not yet able to fulfil their usual functions as at this stage elections and real parliaments did not exist. Following the failed Communist uprising in 1926–27, the Dutch curtailed political activities even more. Only after national independence was achieved did a flurry of political parties spring up and a national political party system could develop. The parties did not have any strong criteria for membership and were not able to build on a steady flow of revenues (Feith 1962: 122ff). Their leadership mostly comprised politicians with sceptical views on modern liberal democracy. Factional disputes within parties were often ignited by ideological issues, whereas today – as will be shown below – bickering is more about leadership styles and positions.

During the elections of 1955, the impact of 'money politics' was much less salient. Candidates for party posts and for the legislature usually did not have to pay for being nominated. Though party financing in the 1950s was in many cases tainted by corruption or questionable influences,[2] politics was not as closely interconnected with business as it is today. Moreover, parties in the 1950s relied more on extensive networks at the village level and sought active support by village elites.

The four most important parties, which altogether obtained four-fifths of the votes in the elections of 1955, grew out of and at the same time reshaped and politicized *aliran* (Feith 1957: 31ff; Feith 1962: 125ff; Ufen 2002: 50ff). The nationalist PNI (*Partai Nasional Indonesia*, Indonesian Nationalist Party; 1955: 22.3 per cent) represented those who were still set apart by an aristocratic Javanese *priyayi* culture and earned their living mainly as state employees and civil servants or were clients of them. Moreover, the PNI represented non-Muslims, syncretists, and those attracted by the Sukarnoist Marhaenism, which denotes a commitment to represent the 'little people' (as epitomized by Marhaen, supposedly a peasant Sukarno once met).[3] The PKI (*Partai Komunis Indonesia*, Indonesian Communist Party; 16.4 per cent) was probably the best-organized party with loyal followers among *abangan* peasants and workers. The orthodox *santri* comprised modernists and traditionalists. The latter under the NU (*Nahdatul Ulama*, Renaissance of Islamic Scholars; 18.4 per cent) consisted mostly of *ulama* (religious scholars) and their followers; the former under the Masyumi (*Majelis Syuro Muslimin Indonesia*, Consultative Council of Indonesian Muslims; 20.9 per cent) comprised urban intellectuals, traders and artisans on the Outer Islands. The big parties in the 1950s were deeply rooted, but elitist. They offered principal channels of access to the bureaucracy.

The first free and fair elections in 1955, and in particular the long campaigning period, strengthened identification with *aliran* and often entailed bitter conflicts even in remote villages, for instance between PNI secularists and pious followers of Masyumi. Because of the immense fragmentation and polarization of the party system, coalitions were generally fragile and short-lived.[4]

Due to institutional deficiencies (the excessive centralism, for example, which gave rise to regionalist movements from 1956 onwards), the rising power of the military, widespread corruption, the polarization between secularists and Islamists in the Constitutional Assembly (*Konstituante*)[5] and the fundamental opposition of the PKI to liberal democracy, parliamentarianism slowly lost its legitimacy. In July 1959, Sukarno reintroduced the Constitution of 1945, which gave him wide-ranging authorities as president. Political parties lost most of their clout during this Guided Democracy period (1959–65). The PSI and Masyumi were banned because of their tacit support of regionalist movements from 1956–58. Sukarno approached the PKI and oversaw a fragile coalition of loyal anti-imperialist nationalists, some Muslim elements, the military and communists. Political decisions were made in the newly established Dewan Nasional (National Council), in military headquarters and in informal palace meetings. In 1960, the parliament was finally dissolved and substituted by the so-called Gotong-Royong parliament,[6] a rubber-stamp body consisting of 283 members appointed by the president.

Sukarno's Guided Democracy collapsed in 1965–66. After a failed coup and the sudden rise of Suharto, hundreds of thousands of communists, many of them only alleged as such, were slaughtered. Mostly well-to-do *santri* elites, backed by the reactionary military, killed *abangan* with leftist leanings or just settled old scores.[7]

The elites of the New Order regime (1965/66–98) under Suharto were determined to restore stability. They started to depoliticize society, to centralize the administration and to streamline the political system.[8] Huge parts of the population were excluded from politics. Conflicts were covered by a ubiquitous discourse of integralism and social harmony. The New Order elites propagated the model of a 'family state' (*negara kekeluargaan*) led by Bapak ('Father') Suharto, and the polity was officially perceived as one without social classes and fundamental conflicts.

During the first phase from 1965 to 1975, parties were emasculated and token elections introduced. Political control was complemented by the 'simplification' of the party system in 1973 (that is, the forced fusion into three parties; see Table 7.1), and the law on political parties and Golkar in 1975. This law was based on the assumption that Indonesian voters formed a *floating mass*. To guarantee undisturbed development (*pembangunan*), the population at large had to be depoliticized and only Golkar (which was conceived as an assemblage of functional groups, not as a real political party) was allowed to establish branches in sub-districts and villages. In the ensuing period up to the late 1980s, the party system was marked by a moderate antagonism between the regime coalition, restrained political Islam represented by the PPP, and moderate Sukarnoism (a leftist secular nationalism) embodied by the PDI. It ended with the legalization and forced implementation of the *azas tunggal* regulations[9] and the concomitant professionalization and demilitarization of Golkar under chairman Sudharmono (1983–88). Opposition at that time was extraordinarily weak and unorganized.

During the period that followed, conflicts in the party system intensified and parliament became more active, at least for a few years (after the *keterbukaan* speech[10] by Suharto). After 1993, opposition groups emerged around Megawati Sukarnoputri in the PDI and – on a much lesser scale – around Sri Bintang Pamungkas in the PPP, but the pattern of pseudo-elections and rubber-stamp parliaments was never really challenged until the collapse of the Suharto regime. Golkar was always able to maintain a two-thirds majority in the national parliament (see Table 7.1), while the PPP and the PDI fulfilled the function of highly restricted opposition parties.

The main legacies of the New Order were the eradication of the PKI and

*Table 7.1* Results of parliamentary elections 1971–1997 (%)

|        | 1971* | 1977 | 1982 | 1987 | 1992 | 1997 |
|--------|-------|------|------|------|------|------|
| Golkar | 62.8  | 62.1 | 64.2 | 73.2 | 68.1 | 74.5 |
| PPP    | 27.1  | 29.3 | 28.0 | 16.0 | 17.0 | 22.4 |
| PDI    | 10.1  | 8.6  | 7.9  | 10.9 | 14.9 | 3.1  |

Golkar, Golongan Karya, Functional Groups

PPP, Partai Persatuan Pembangunan, United Development Party

PDI, Partai Demokrasi Indonesia, Indonesian Democratic Party

* Results after adding those of parties later merged: PPP (merger of NU 18.7 per cent; Parmusi, Partai Muslimin Indonesia, Indonesian Muslims Party 5.4 per cent; PSII, Partai Sarekat Islam Indonesia, Islamic Association Party Indonesia 2.4 per cent; Perti, Persatuan Tarbiyah Islamiyah, Islamic Education Union 0.7 per cent); PDI (merger of PNI 6.9 per cent; Parkindo, Partai Kristen Indonesia, Indonesian Christian Party 1.3 per cent; Partai Murba, Proletarian Party 0.1 per cent; IPKI, Ikatan Pendukung Kemerdekaan Indonesia, League of Upholders of Indonesian Independence 0.6 per cent; Partai Katolik, Catholic Party 1.1 per cent)

*Source:* Rüland 2001

of the political left in general, the demobilization and depoliticization of huge parts of the population as epitomized by the floating mass doctrine, the creation of a conservative, well-organized and lavishly funded catch-all party (Golkar), and the tendency to stifle democratic procedures within political parties and parliaments.

## PARTIES AND ELECTIONS AFTER THE FALL OF SUHARTO

The pressure to reform the polity was enormous immediately after the power transfer from Suharto to B.J. Habibie in May 1998. Crucial legislation on elections, the composition of parliaments, and political parties, among other things, was passed by the New Order MPs without the direct consent of the newly established parties. In many ways it was a transition 'from above'. The most prominent opposition leaders – Abdurrahman Wahid (PKB), Amien Rais (PAN) and Megawati Sukarnoputri (PDI-P) – were still sidelined until the election campaign in 1999.[11]

A bewildering range of new parties emerged in a short period of time. It reflected the overwhelming enthusiasm after four decades of authoritarianism and the concomitant suppression of political activities. A total of 148 parties were officially registered, and after a long screening process, 48 of these were eventually allowed to take part in the June 1999 elections. To be successful, parties needed the infrastructure and connections built up during the New Order period (Golkar, PPP and, to a certain degree, PDI-P), the credentials of being decidedly reformist (especially PDI-P and PAN), the indirect backing of religious organizations (PKB, PAN, PPP, PBB, etc.) or grassroots networks created long before (PK).

The 1999 and 2004 election results resemble in many respects those of 1955.[12] The results in 1999 indicated a victory for moderate Islam and secularism. Parties which stood for a firm stance on Islamic issues with a tendency to support a conservative Islamization of the country such as the PPP, the PBB and the PK performed badly and received altogether only 14 per cent of the votes. The PKB and the PAN, which predominantly have orthodox Muslim followers, together gained almost one-fifth of the votes, but their secular, Pancasilaist orientation precluded most debates in the parliament on the introduction of sharia laws or even an Islamic state from the very beginning. In the 1999 elections (Ananta, Arifin and Suryadinata 2004; Kompas 2004a) Golkar was able to maintain its dominant position in the Outer Islands (i.e. beyond Java). It came first in Western Sumatra, Riau, Jambi, Western Nusa Tenggara, East Nusa Tenggara, East Timor, Western Kalimantan, South Kalimantan, Northern, Central, South and Southeast Sulawesi as well as in Maluku and Irian Jaya. Altogether it won in 14 out of 27 provinces. In both of the southern provinces of Sulawesi, it gained a two-thirds majority. The PDI-P won in 11 provinces and achieved 79 per cent in Bali. The PKB came first only in its stronghold, East Java. The PPP won in Aceh with almost 30 per cent, well ahead of the PAN (nearly 18 per cent), which did well in Western Sumatra and in Yogyakarta.

In the 2004 polls (Sebastian 2004; Aspinall 2005; Hadiwinata 2006; Ananta, Arifin and Suryadinata 2005), no more than 24 parties were allowed to participate because of additional legal restrictions.[13] The Communist Party of Indonesia (PKI) was still banned. Only a social democratic or workers' party emerged, which gained just 0.56 per cent of the votes. Golkar won 21.6 per cent (1999: 22.5 per cent) and is now the strongest party in the parliament. The PDI-P suffered a shocking defeat and lost more than 15 percentage points due to disappointment with the Megawati presidency and the performance of PDI-P politicians in general. The other huge surprise besides the devastating loss of the PDI-P and the sudden rise of the Partai Demokrat was the triumph of the Islamist PKS (formerly PK), which won 7.3 per cent of the votes. The party was even able to come first in Jakarta, ahead of the PD. These results revealed widespread dissatisfaction with established parties, particularly in the capital. The PKB, the PPP and the PAN each lost slightly. Their dismal performance was only overshadowed by the trouncing of the PDI-P.

Six of the ten largest parties in the current national parliament are Islamic and four are secular (see Table 7.2[14]). The secular parties are Golkar (although with some reservations because of a mighty Islamic wing), the PDI-P, the PDS (essentially Christian) and the PD. The PDI-P, which has a large following among Christians and secularists, is still identified with Sukarno, the immensely popular and charismatic first president of Indonesia. Megawati, his daughter and the party chairwoman, still embodies this Sukarnoist tradition. The six Islamic parties are the PKB (moderate traditionalist Islam), the PPP (Islamist with modernists and traditionalists), the PKS (modernist Islamist), the PAN (moderate modernist), the PBB

*Table 7.2* Election results for 1999 and 2004 (DPR)[14]

| Party | Votes in % (1999) | Seats (1999) | Votes in % (2004) | Seats (2004)* |
|---|---|---|---|---|
| Golkar | 22.5 | 120 | 21.6 | 127 |
| PDI-P | 33.8 | 153 | 18.5 | 109 |
| PKB | 12.6 | 51 | 10.6 | 52 |
| PPP | 10.7 | 58 | 8.2 | 58 |
| PD | – | – | 7.5 | 56 |
| PK (2004: PKS) | 1.4 | 7 | 7.3 | 45 |
| PAN | 7.1 | 34 | 6.4 | 53 |
| PBB | 1.9 | 13 | 2.6 | 11 |
| PBR | – | – | 2.4 | 14 |
| PDS | – | – | 2.1 | 13 |
| Other parties | | 26 | | 12 |
| TNI** | | 38 | | – |
| Total | | 500 | | 550 |

Partai Golongan Karya (Golkar), Functional Groups Party; Partai Demokrasi Indonesia – Perjuangan (PDI-P), Indonesian Democratic Party – Struggle; Partai Kebangkitan Bangsa (PKB), National Awakening Party; Partai Persatuan Pembangunan (PPP), United Development Party; Partai Demokrat (PD), Democrat Party; Partai Keadilan (PK), Justice Party (2004: Partai Keadilan Sejahtera, PKS, Justice and Prosperity Party); Partai Amanat Nasional (PAN), National Mandate Party; Partai Bulan Bintang (PBB), Crescent and Star Party; Partai Persatuan Pembangunan Reformasi (PPP Reformasi), United Development Party Reform (2004: Partai Bintang Reformasi, PBR, Star Party of Reform); Partai Damai Sejahtera (PDS), Prosperity and Peace Party

* The allocation of seats was adjusted in accordance with a ruling of the Constitutional Court.
** The military (TNI, *Tentara Nasional* Indonesia) automatically received 38 seats from 1999–2004.

*Source*: Adapted from Ananta, Arifin and Suryadinata (2005: 14, 22)

(modernist Islamist, self-declared successor to Masyumi) and the PBR (split from the PPP). The PKB and the PAN define themselves as secular, but in reality they are moderate Islamic parties. The PKB is directly connected to the traditionalist Islamic Nahdatul Ulama (NU), which officially has around 40 million members. The PAN, in many ways the antagonist of the PKB, has strong links to the urban, modernist Islamic mass organization Muhammadiyah, which claims a membership of some 35 million.

Two parties of a new type also exist: the Partai Demokrat (Democrat Party) of President Susilo Bambang Yudhoyono, founded in 2001, and the Justice and Prosperity Party, PKS. Neither of them had any predecessors in the 1950s or the New Order. The PKS is an efficiently organized, Islamist cadre party. Breaches of party discipline concerning moral behaviour or corruption are severely punished. The cadres are mostly young, well-educated men, and the party combines Western management techniques and Islamist indoctrination in a unique way. In contrast to them, the Partai Demokrat is almost completely dependent on Susilo Bambang Yudhoyono. He used the PD as a vehicle in the first direct presidential elections in 2004.

The most important cleavage structuring the party system as a whole is the one dividing the secular and the Islamic parties. The latter are divided into moderate Islamic and Islamist parties.[15] The polarization between status quo- and pro-democracy parties immediately after the fall of Suharto has died down. Today, this cleavage is hardly reflected in the parliament at all. Golkar and the PDI-P, for instance, are barely different when it comes to their stance on policy issues, their involvement in corruption scandals and the way the party apparatus is managed.

## DEMOCRATIZATION OF POLITICAL PARTIES AFTER 1998: AN ASSESSMENT

But do political parties in Indonesia after 1998 fulfil the typically ascribed functions? Are they sufficiently institutionalized and, thus, support democratization? There are some indications that Indonesian parties, in fact, contribute to the consolidation of democracy:

- The polarization between parties and the volatility of voting is relatively low. After two national elections the constellation of political forces is quite stable and continuities between the party system of the 1950s and the current one are evident. That means party politics is so far not marked by sudden shifts like in neighbouring Thailand or the Philippines.
- In contrast to the 1950s, for example, there are no influential anti-system parties like the PKI. Even the Islamist parties keep a low profile and mostly do not actively support the introduction of sharia laws or the establishment of an Islamic state.
- A few of the big parties are still embedded in specific milieus. A clear cleavage structure is manifest. Although alignments between voters and parties are weakened in comparison to the 1950s, *aliran* are still structuring the party system as a whole to a certain extent.
- The two national elections, the direct presidential polls and the *pilkada*[16] were held peacefully and in general were characterized as free and fair. Although the initial enthusiasm with an impressive voter turnout of 94 per cent in 1999 is today somewhat diluted (84.1 per cent voter turnout in 2004 for those registered); elections, parliamentarianism and the role of political parties are broadly acknowledged by the wider public.
- No one party has assumed a hegemonic position in the new party system. Even Golkar with all its machinery, money and clientelist networks was reduced to a normal party which received only about one-fifth of the votes. Parties are coerced to form huge coalitions and to moderate previously uncompromising attitudes.
- Electors are able to give parties a warning as they did in many *pilkada*

and when they voted for the PD and the PKS in 2004. Parties are, therefore, forced to respond to public resentment.

* The influence of the military on political parties is clearly on the decline.

Yet in spite of all these noteworthy developments since 1998, the weaknesses of political parties prevail. Parties are no longer social movements with their own tight network of organizations like in the 1950s (Antlöv 2004a: 12). Thus, a weakening of *aliran* patterns is quite obvious. A report by the Asia Foundation (2003), for instance, revealed that, with reference to the parliamentary elections, there is an extremely high proportion of non-identifiers or 'swing voters' in the electorate (Asia Foundation 2003: 100).[17]

Another indicator of the *dealiranisasi* process, understood as a shift and weakening of the Geertzian *aliran*, is the dynamics of local politics. The *pilkada*, the first direct elections of regional heads (governors, district chiefs and mayors) which started in 2005, have demonstrated that the selection of candidates by political parties, the decisions of voters and the partisan coalition building in most cases were not the result of long-term loyalties in specific social milieus but of pragmatic decisions. Many coalitions were formed just for the sake of winning (Rinakit 2005; Djadijono 2006).

The *dealiranisasi* is accompanied by other problematic developments: the rise of presidential or presidentialized parties, the increasing intra-party authoritarianism, the prevalence of 'money politics', the lack of meaningful political platforms, weak loyalties to parties, the building of cartels and the upsurge of new local elites.

### The rise of presidential parties and the presidentialization of parties

The direct election of the president has facilitated the emergence of formerly insignificant parties as vehicles for presidential candidates. The direct identification with party leaders via the mass media has increased considerably. The best example is the Partai Demokrat utilized by Susilo Bambang Yudhoyono.[18] Such a presidential party would have been inconceivable under the old system of indirect elections. The PD has no real platform and still lacks a strong organizational structure, especially below the national level. At the last congress in 2005, Kristiani Herawati, the wife of Susilo and deputy leader of the party, reportedly engineered the election of her brother-in-law into the office of party chairman. The PD will possibly just manage to survive as long as Susilo stays in office (*Tempo*, 24–30 May 2005).

In addition, one can argue that some of the other parties – like the PDI-P under Megawati, Golkar under Yusuf Kalla, the PAN under Amien Rais, and the PKB under Abdurrahman Wahid – are being presidentialized because they are preparing their respective leaders (or their handpicked candidates) for the next presidential election in 2009 and are organizing the party machinery accordingly. The result is authoritarian personalism (see below).

Presidentialism weakens the power of political machines, enhances the appeal of populism and thus makes the clever usage of mass media and the employment of modern campaign techniques inevitable.

The elective presidency, especially with a two-ticket system in two rounds, furthers the blurring of ideological divides. The respective pairs of candidates for the presidency and the vice presidency represent different levels of religiosity and dissimilar geographical areas. Accordingly, in the two rounds of voting in 2004, all kinds of surprising party coalitions were formed.

## Internal processes: authoritarian personalism and factionalism

Parties are typically led by very powerful leaders who have successfully centralized decision-making. Some of them, like Megawati Sukarnoputri and Abdurrahman Wahid, enjoy almost cult status.[19] Authoritarian personalism is to some extent a heritage of the political culture of the New Order.[20] Party organization was as centralized as the whole polity and intra-party decision-making as opaque and undemocratic as the authoritarian system in general. The oppression in the 1990s gave rise to charismatic, supposedly pro-democratic political leaders such as Megawati, Abdurrahman Wahid and Amien Rais. After 1998, the personalism was further reinforced by the mass media, the presidential system and party laws benefiting central executives in Jakarta.

In most parties today, crucial decisions such as the nomination of candidates (Haris 2005: 9ff), are made by some core executive members who are usually loyal to one charismatic leader. The decision-making process is almost fully orientated from the top down to the branches. Furthermore, the statutes of most parties do not clearly regulate how party congresses and elections have to be organized (Notosusanto 2005). Sometimes these regulations are altered even at the beginning of conventions, with notorious examples being the recent congresses of Golkar and the PDI-P (*The Jakarta Post*, 2 April 2005).

The big political parties have designed the election and party laws to their advantage. They have banned individual or non-party candidatures and made it difficult for smaller parties to contest with their candidates. Regional parties are not admitted, with Aceh being the only exception. Law 31/2002 states that the Central Leadership Board (DPP) of a party must be located in Jakarta. The whole system of proportional representation strengthens the hold of central party leaderships. The newly introduced, partially open-list, proportional representation system makes it very unlikely that any one candidate will be elected according to this mechanism. As stipulated by Law 23/2003, only political parties or coalitions of political parties that obtained a minimum of three per cent of the seats in parliament or five per cent of the votes in the 2004 parliamentary elections are allowed to nominate pairs of candidates. In 2009 the minimum will be 15 per cent of the seats and 20 per cent of the votes.

Almost all parties have their power centre in Jakarta and chastise recalcitrant members. Intra-party opposition is marginalized in the PDI-P and the PKB in particular, sometimes by disregarding official party statutes. Noted PDI-P members such as Sophan Sophiaan, Indira Damayanti Sugondo, Meilono Suwondo, Arifin Panigoro and Haryanto Taslam were all sidelined as party critics or resigned as an expression of their disappointment with Megawati's leadership. One means of penalization is to recall[21] parliamentarians; that is, to terminate their mandate and replace them. The right to do so, a typical New Order brainchild, was reintroduced in 2002. Furthermore, Megawati still has the right to decide on vital matters without consulting the executive council (*hak prerogatif*). The last congress in Bali in 2005 was characterized by the sole candidacy of Megawati and limited time for debating her accountability speech. Party critics were systematically silenced ahead of and during the convention (*Kompas*, 1 April 2005; author's interview with Sukowaluyo, PDI-P, 4 October 2005).[22]

In the PKB, the Advisory Board (*Dewan Syuro*) stands above the executive council (*Dewan Tanfidz*) in many respects. The candidates for the Dewan Tanfidz even have to get the acknowledgement of the Dewan Syuro beforehand (Notosusanto 2005). Major disputes in the PKB were solved in a problematic way to say the least. A long-simmering internal conflict between 'PKB Kuningan' around Abdurrahman Wahid and Alwi Shihab and 'PKB Batu Tulis' led by Matori Abdul Jalil crippled the party for months. At the party congress in Semarang in 2005, Abdurrahman Wahid was elected chief patron of the Dewan Syuro by acclamation and not in accordance with party regulations. His nephew, Muhaimin Iskandar, was elected new party chairman – again by acclamation and without contender (*Tempo*, April 19–25 2005; *Kompas*, 20 April 2005).

At the last congress of the PAN in Semarang in April 2005, long-time chairman and *spiritus rector* of the party, Amien Rais, stepped down, officially to promote rejuvenation. But Amien will continue to serve as a 'party advisor', which means in actual fact he will decide on salient issues. He picked little-known businessman Sutrisno Bachir as new party chairman after having 'convinced' other candidates not to compete. Sutrisno is a long-time admirer of Amien and financier of the PAN.

Some of the examples above indicate that factionalism is common and often a direct result of intra-party authoritarianism. In many cases, even new parties are formed. The PBB was shaken by disputes between two of its founders, Chairman Yusril Ihza Mahendra and Hartono Mardjono, the latter later becoming chairman of the Indonesian Islamic Party (PII) (*Republika*, 24 February 2001). Around the same time, the PAN faced a similar crisis (*Kompas*, 22 January 2001). The PBR, formed by popular preacher Zainuddin MZ, is a splinter of the PPP and has been shaken by internal clashes itself. The PPP is again in danger of being divided by competing cliques. In the PDI-P, Dimyati Hartono and Eros Jarot, two Megawati critics, established a new political party, as did the rebels of the 2005 PDI-P party congress.

## The political economy of parties: 'money politics'

To Robison and Hadiz (2004: 258), politics in Indonesia nowadays is '[. . .] driven increasingly by the logic of money politics'. Indeed, parties need financial support from private entrepreneurs. Membership fees are mostly insignificant, as is public funding. Regulations on party financing exist, but violations are hardly ever punished (Hadiwinata 2006: 106). Entrepreneurs presumably dictate (or 'influence') the stance of parties on specific issues. In recent years, some businessmen have become party heads, for example Yusuf Kalla (Golkar) and Sutrisno Bachir (PAN) (*Kompas*, 22 December 2004; *Kompas*, 12 April 2005). Financiers like billionaire Aburizal Bakrie are even rewarded with ministerial positions.

It is no secret that before the 2005 introduction of direct elections at the provincial, district and municipal levels, when the respective parliaments had the sole power to determine who became governor, *bupati* or mayor respectively, most of these competitions were decided by the disbursement of huge amounts of money to the councillors (Rifai 2003). The institution of direct elections at these levels did not erase 'money politics' but transferred it. In the *pilkada* the pairs had to pay their respective parties for the candidacy and they had to shoulder the campaign costs. They spent an average of US$10 million at the provincial level and US$1.6 million at the municipality/regency level (Rinakit 2005). Another example was the race for governorship in Jakarta (*Tempo*, 5–11 September 2006). To get the nomination as official candidate, one had to spend around US$20 million, plus the campaign costs. This huge amount of money was the minimum a governor would have to earn once in office just to compensate his initial investment.[23]

That investments necessitate rent-seeking activities is a widespread phenomenon in parliaments, too. In the DPR the situation is as gloomy as at lower levels. Manifestations of corruption include the bribery of House members who planned to scrutinize entrepreneurs on their dubious activities, the activities of MPs as brokers to help private companies get government contracts, and financial rewards from public officers in 'fit and proper tests' before parliament. Furthermore, political parties were used by corruptors from the previous regime as safe havens from corruption litigation (*The Jakarta Post*, 10 December 2004).

In early October 2006, the DPR working group on law enforcement and regional administration recommended that the government should rehabilitate the names of regional heads and council members implicated in corruption cases. Indonesia Corruption Watch (ICW) states that at least 55 corruption cases involving 350 public officials and lawmakers were filed with district courts from January 2005 to June 2006, and about 1,200 regional council members were named suspects, charged and convicted of corruption from 1999 until the end of 2004 (*The Jakarta Post*, 7 October 2006 and 11 October 2006).

## The lack of meaningful platforms

Most parties have vague platforms. Out of the 48 which were officially accepted in 1999, eight were Islamic by their own definition, five were based on the Pancasila[24] and Islam, 31 solely on the Pancasila, two on the Pancasila and other teachings (social democratic or Marhaenist) and two exclusively on other teachings (the PUDI on 'religious democracy' and the PRD on 'people's social democracy') as their ideology (Suryakusuma 1999: 592 and 596). Six parties had a bull on a red background as their symbol, denoting a Marhaenist (i.e. Sukarnoist) platform, but they preferred to be seen as Pancasilaist. In 2004, out of the 24 parties contesting the parliamentary elections, 13 opted for Pancasila as their core ideology, five for Islam, two for Marhaenism and the other four small parties for a combination of Pancasila with the UUD 1945 (Constitution of 1945), for Pancasila with 'Justice and Democracy', and for Pancasila based on the family principle (*kekeluargaan*) and 'mutual help' (*gotong royong*) respectively (Djadijono 2006). Even a devoutly Christian party like the PDS does not refer to Christianity, but to the Pancasila.

Consequently, the main parties in Indonesia are essentially either Islamic or secular with reference to their ideology. But even the Islamic parties in general do not oppose the principles expressed by the Pancasila formula, which is hazily phrased and hardly adequate as a platform for political parties. The Sukarnoist parties add 'Marhaenism' to their main agenda. Most parties are, thus, engaged in a fight for the middle ground. Essentially Islamic parties like the PAN and the PKB have chosen a neutral platform in terms of religion; even an Islamist party like the PKS is not willing to play the Islamic card during elections, but rather focuses on issues such as the fight against corruption.

## Diminishing party loyalty

Weak platforms are also a result of the above-mentioned *dealiranisasi* process which indicates that the link between parties and voters is loosening and that the rootedness in milieus is decreasing. In a national survey, the Asia Foundation found that linkages between voters and parties are mostly 'emotional' and not based on meaningful knowledge of the specific platforms of parties (Asia Foundation 2003):

> The widespread lack of party preferences, other than those based on emotional identification, can largely be explained by the fact that most Indonesians are unaware of differences among the political parties. Two-thirds of the voters (66 percent) say they do not know what differences exist among the parties or that there are none.
>
> (Asia Foundation 2003: 100)

These observations of an increasing dealignment are corroborated by a number of surveys conducted in recent years.[25] The International Foundation for

Election Systems found out in a nationwide survey carried out in 2004 that 40.2 per cent of those who voted for Golkar in the 2004 parliamentary elections opted for Susilo and not for the official candidate of their own party, Wiranto, in the first round of the presidential elections. In addition, 23.7 per cent of PDI-P voters chose Susilo by ballot, and 22.7 per cent of PPP voters cast their ballot for Amien Rais and not the party's candidate, Hamzah Haz. Finally, 40 per cent of PBB electors, supposedly Islamists, supported Susilo (IFES 2004c).

## The collusive relationship between parties: the building of cartels

In a widely quoted article, Katz and Mair (1995) outlined how Western European catch-all parties have been transformed into parties constituting a cartel. Cartel parties are related to the state symbiotically; they are estranged from society and are dominated by public office-holders. Party activists have only marginal influence upon internal decision-making procedures and election campaigns are organized by professional experts.[26] These parties together form a cartel in that they fend off new competitors and share the spoils of office. Slater (2004) sees a parallel phenomenon in Indonesia. The existence of cartels is, among other things, indicated by rainbow coalitions (*koalisi pelangi*), the lack of an organized opposition in most parliaments, the evasion of open voting and the lack of willingness to crack down on corruption. When – according to Slater (2004: 75ff) – the cartel was endangered by the elusive policies of President Abdurrahman Wahid, who started to sack ministers and finally even tried to ban Golkar, the colluding political elites reacted by impeaching and ousting him.

Cartels are in some measure a result of a fragmented party system with unclear majorities.[27] Abdurrahman Wahid was forced to form a grand coalition in October 1999 because his party had received only 12.6 per cent of the votes.[28] After the overthrow of the Abdurrahman Wahid government in July 2001, Megawati herself depended on the support of a range of parties which then were rewarded with cabinet positions. Susilo Bambang Yudhoyono did not have the backing of a strong party since his PD received just 7.5 per cent of the ballot. Only when Yusuf Kalla became Golkar chairman in December 2004 and steered the party towards the Yudhoyono government did the president gain a sufficient majority in the DPR.

Difficulties of interparty coalition building often arise in presidential systems, especially when combined with multipartism. Executive/legislative deadlock can sometimes be the result (Mainwaring 1993).[29] In Indonesia, these tendencies brought the parliament to a virtual standstill in 2001 during the prolonged impeachment process against Abdurrahman Wahid and this happened again in late 2004. But these phases of immobility gave way to new coalitions formed to rescue the underlying logic of cartelization.

The sudden change of guard at the top of Golkar in late 2004 can be interpreted as a manoeuvre to secure the benefits of governing in Jakarta (that is, ministerial posts).[30] The move by party delegates to vote for the incumbent vice president, Yusuf Kalla, and sideline Akbar Tanjung testifies to the strength of directly elected politicians. Only now has a supposedly strong president with a parliamentary majority emerged. A stable pattern of 'government' versus 'opposition' has not developed yet, however. In many regional and provincial assemblies also, opposition to the cartels is organized only by a handful of councillors.[31]

The clearest indication of a cartel-like organization of political parties is the peculiar decision-making mechanism called '*musyawarah dan mufakat*' ('deliberation and consensus') which predominates in Indonesian parliaments. Consistent with the Rules of Procedure of the DPR (*Peraturan Tata Tertib* DPR-RI, 2001), most decisions in commission and plenary meetings of the legislatures are taken consensually and without voting. This causes delays and makes it extremely difficult for the public and even for political observers to trace back the initial stance of particular parties on particular political issues (Sherlock 2005). Even if parties express their views publicly from time to time, they often switch unexpectedly to contrary positions. In the national parliament, for example, the fuel subsidy cuts were initially resisted by the PPP, the PKS, the PAN and the PKB, but finally they all backed down. This tactic of first opposing and finally cooperating was repeated many times, as in the case of the planned probe into rice imports from Vietnam, with the PKS being the only exception, and with the purchase of 32 French-made armoured vehicles without public bidding. 'The Forum of Citizens Concerned about the Indonesian Legislature' (Formappi) stated, thus, that parliamentarians favoured lengthy debates, posturing to action, and speaking out against government policies, but generally supported the criticized bills after backroom deals (*The Jakarta Post*, 28 September 2006).

## The upsurge of new local bosses

The collapse of the New Order, where regional heads were appointed by the Minister of Domestic Affairs, and the administrative and political decentralization since then have strengthened local elites. The devolution of political power to the district (*kabupaten*) level and the concomitantly increased budgets have made local politics more competitive and political positions more attractive. The centralized neo-patrimonialism of the New Order with Suharto as the highest patron has given way to a decentralized neo-patrimonialism with a range of interwoven national and regional patron–client networks.

Local politics, tightly controlled by the military regime under the New Order at least until the early 1990s, is increasingly marked by 'predatory networks' (Robison and Hadiz 2004) and may evolve into outright 'bossism' (Sidel 1999). Although the central leaderships of political parties can dictate most decisions on policy issues and are able to push through their candidates for the national parliament and for their respective central executives, a tug of war between Jakarta and the regions is usual at lower levels (Choi 2004).[32]

Clientelist relationships that more often than not exist on a purely monetary basis predominate. Even before the introduction of the *pilkada*, political thuggery and 'money politics' were on the rise (Choi 2004).[33] Since then, militia activities have subsided. Political violence during election campaigns since 2004 has not been marked by widespread and systematic violence as was the case in the Philippines. Nevertheless, local strongmen have emerged. In some regions an explosive mixture of decentralization, the opening-up of new avenues to government spoils, and the re-accentuation of regional or cultural identities has evolved.

The *pilkada* have not only strengthened themselves but also weakened local and regional party leaders somewhat, for many of the candidates were chosen from civil servants or businessmen without any strong party links despite the fact that parties had the nomination right. Often, candidates were not party members initially or they belonged to party A but ran for party B. At this level, popular candidates look around for parties offering them the best opportunities, and party institutionalization at the local and regional level is much weaker than at the national level in Jakarta. Party offices, for example, are generally inactive between elections.

At the grassroots level, political parties frequently did not have adequate (i.e. well-to-do) popular candidates. The *pilkada*, thus, were an arena for well-connected bureaucrats and wealthy businessmen who both profited from candidacies auctioned off by weakened parties (Mietzner 2005 and in this volume).[34] This constellation strengthened tendencies of *dealiranisasi* and of entrenching newly emerging local oligarchies.

In sum, new local and regional political elites have emerged. To some extent they are balanced by politicians in Jakarta and are often not identical with well-established local or regional party leaders. Therefore, the empowerment of new local bosses has not reached Philippine proportions yet. Local or regional elites do not have a decisive impact on national politics in the DPR or in the central executives of political parties. Additionally, the DPD (*Dewan Perwakilan Daerah* or House of Regional Representatives) is insignificant in comparison to the DPR. Moreover, its delegates are not allowed to be members of political parties.

## CONCLUSION

As has been shown, there are a range of party and party system deficiencies, some of which have worsened over time: firstly, the rise of presidential or presidentialized parties, a prime example being the Partai Demokrat of Susilo Bambang Yudhoyono; secondly, the authoritarianism and personalism with powerful 'party advisors' and executives which punish unruly members, marginalize intra-party opposition and further factionalization; thirdly, the dominance of 'money politics' with bought candidacies, MPs acting as brokers for private companies, businessmen taking over party chairmanships, and billionaire financiers determining policies behind the scenes; fourthly, the erosion of ideologies with poor political platforms; fifthly, the decreasing party loyalties; sixthly, the cartel-like cooperation of parties as indicated by rainbow coalitions, an unorganized opposition, the *musyawarah dan mufakat* mechanism and the collusion in tolerating corruption; and seventhly, the emergence of new, powerful local elites.

Not all of these flaws and developments are specifically Indonesian. Because of the internationalization and presidentialization of politics, executives across the world have gained in importance. Moreover, the stability of traditional political loyalties is declining in general, and political leaders can appeal directly to voters via mass media.

Another decisive factor for party change is the shifting economic environment in new democracies, in particular in Indonesia after the disastrous Asian crisis from 1997 onwards. Whereas in the 1950s political rent-seeking was seemingly contained to a certain degree by political competitors, active party supporters, strong ideological commitments on the part of political leaders and in many cases the sheer lack of opportunities, nowadays a cartelized elite sees politics to a great extent as business.

If compared with other new democracies, the Indonesian party system is characterized by a fair degree of institutionalization (cf. Mainwaring and Torcal 2006). Patterns of party competition are quite regular, party roots in society are in part strong, but the legitimacy accorded to parties has weakened over time. Most parties are identified with specific worldviews and lifestyles. They have core constituencies and recruit their personnel in specific milieus. Yet party organization is weak and parties are often dominated by personalistic leaders. If we use the functionalist criteria as proposed by Schmitter (1999: 477f), we may conclude that Indonesian political parties recruit persons and nominate candidates, but in many cases they do so in a controversial way. Most of them do not 'provide most citizens with a stable and distinctive set of ideas and goals' which 'make them feel part of the process of collective choice'. Rather, they are isolated from the wider public, are increasingly alienated from the electorate, and their ideas and goals are ill-defined or almost non-existent. They are capable of forming governments, but the rainbow coalitions are somewhat diffuse in their composition and there is merely an inchoate differentiation between government and opposition. Politicians and parties perform poorly as lawmakers. To what extent they aggregate interests and passions, channel expectations and produce programmes in a way satisfactory for most of the citizenry remains open to question.

**NOTES**

1  In the 1950s and 1960s, the deep ideological roots of political parties were conceptualized by Indonesianists with the *aliran* (literally 'streams') approach. Clifford Geertz (1960) first outlined this model in his main work 'The Religion of Java'. His famous differentiation between *abangan* (syncretists stressing animistic beliefs), *santri* (followers of a purer Islam) and *priyayi* (those mostly influenced by a Hinduist aristocratic culture) had a lasting impact on further studies on Java. For the purpose of analysing political parties in the 1950s (and today) it is, however, much more practical to refer to a slightly different interpretation made by Geertz himself in 'Peddlers and Princes' (Geertz 1963), where he conceptualized the PNI, the Masyumi, the NU and the PKI as the organizational foci of *aliran*. According to Geertz, this *aliran* complex is as much a social movement as a political party.
2  The financing of the PNI with its contacts to the state bureaucracy was especially questionable. See Feith 1957: 26–7 and Rocamora 1975: 112ff.
3  *Abangan* and *priyayi* orientations soon aligned 'into a unit as opposed to the *santri*' (Geertz 1965: 128).
4  Usually, the NU and the PNI or the Masyumi and the PSI worked together in these coalitions, which always excluded the PKI.
5  After the elections of 1955, the *Konstituante* was given the task of writing a new constitution, but was eventually dissolved by Sukarno.
6  'Gotong Royong' means 'mutual help'.
7  The *aliran* are religiously and economically defined. Whereas it was difficult to assess what component was more salient in the 1950s, it is much safer to conclude that the religious issue was of secondary importance from 1964–66. The major determinant of political conflict at that time was class struggle couched in terms of religion (Rocamora 1975: 368; Wertheim 1969).
8  On the following: Ufen (2002: 271ff).
9  Social and political organizations were forced to accept the state ideology – Pancasila – as their 'sole foundation' (*azas tunggal*).
10  *Keterbukaan* ('openness') denotes the very hesitant and limited liberalization of the political discourse initiated by Suharto in 1989.
11  The nature of political parties reflects the uncertainties and ambiguities of the transition period. They are centralized but at the same time not fully elitist. The lack of transparency of the whole transition process and the incalculability of its outcomes exacerbated the institutionalization of parties.
12  See Liddle 2003, King 2003, Baswedan 2004, Antlöv 2004b, Cederroth 2004, Turmudi 2004, Johnson Tan 2005 and 2006, and Sherlock 2004 and 2005.
13  Only parties with at least ten MPs in the DPR or with more than three per cent of the votes in more than half of the province and district parliaments were allowed to participate in the 2004 elections. Moreover, they had to have branches in at least two-thirds of the provinces and in at least two-thirds of the districts in these provinces.
14  The members of the First Chamber, the House of Representatives (*Dewan Perwakilan Rakyat*, DPR), are elected with a proportional system in multi-member constituencies. The Second Chamber, the People's Congress (*Majelis Permusyawaratan Rakyat*, MPR), consists of the DPR members and 132 representatives of the provinces. The latter constitute the relatively weak DPD (*Dewan Perwakilan Daerah*, House of Regional Representatives), which was established in 2004. They are elected with a majority system in multi-member constituencies and are not allowed to be members of political parties. Moreover, there have been direct presidential elections since 2004 and direct elections of mayors, district chiefs and governors since 2005.
15  Islamist parties are defined here as those supporting the introduction of sharia law

and aiming at instituting an Islamic state. Although the PKS does not officially embrace this agenda, it is classified as Islamist because of its ideological and organizational background.

16  Short for *pilihan kepala daerah*, 'election of regional heads'.

17  See also the survey by the Indonesian Survey Institute (Lembaga Survei Indonesia, LSI, 2006).

18  The five pairs of candidates for the posts of president and vice president respectively were (the nominating party is mentioned in brackets): Susilo Bambang Yudhoyono (PD) and Yusuf Kalla; Wiranto (Golkar) and Solahuddin Wahid; Megawati Sukarnoputri (PDI-P) and Hasyim Muzadi, Hamzah Haz (PPP) and Agum Gumelar; Amien Rais (PAN) and Siswono Yudohusodo. In the second round, Susilo and Yusuf Kalla beat Megawati and Hasyim Muzadi and had a clear majority of more than 60 per cent.

19  Cf. Fealy (2001: 102ff).

20  The personalization is further boosted by the institution of direct presidential elections (cf. Mujani and Liddle 2006).

21  Article 12 of Law No. 31/2002 on political parties states that party members who are elected legislative members can be dismissed from the legislative body if they lose their membership in their respective political parties.

22  See also Gerakan Pembaruan PDI Perjuangan 2005.

23  If the candidates themselves are not wealthy, they have to be backed by investors who are usually members of so-called success teams (*tim sukses*) during campaigns (see, for instance, Vel 2005: 84).

24  The five principles (of Pancasila, the so-called state philosophy) are: belief in the one and only God; just and civilized humanity; the unity of Indonesia; democracy guided by the inner wisdom in the unanimity arising out of deliberations amongst representatives; and social justice for the whole of the people of Indonesia. The Pancasila still symbolize the acknowledgement of religious freedom.

25  On surveys until 2002: Johnson Tan 2002.

26  The latter point is well illustrated by Mietzner ('Opportunities, pitfalls of RI's new democracy', *The Jakarta Post*, 16 October 2006) in his analysis of the rising influence of opinion polls in Indonesia on shaping the behaviour of political party elites. See also Aspinall (2005: 143).

27  Conceivably, the fragmentation of the party system in Indonesia is not the result but the cause of the proportional system. The choice of this system after independence and again in 1998–99 was due to the high number of relevant political actors. The introduction of a majority system seems to be more probable if there are just two major players (Nohlen 2004: 408 and 415ff). See also Colomer (2005).

28  Coalitions are generally not based on well-defined contracts outlining government objectives and peculiar interests of political parties as members of this coalition. Cooperation among parties is fluid and strongly dependent on the outcome of power struggles in these parties.

29  See also the dictum of Diamond (1999: 98): '[. . .] fragmentation into a large number of parties is especially destabilizing under presidentialism.'

30  On the whole episode, see Tomsa (2006a: 17ff).

31  Interview with Anang Rosadi Adenansi, PKB, member of the provincial parliament of South Kalimantan, Banjarmasin, 1 September 2005. See also Slater (2004: 63).

32  'Around the country, local party branches erupted in furious conflicts as would-be candidates struggled to get winnable positions on party lists. Sometimes, the tension was between local party activists and national headquarters. More frequently, these were "horizontal" conflicts between local would-be candidates, each with their own clientele of supporters' (Aspinall 2005: 146).

33  'In North Sumatra, racketeering is largely the domain of old New Order "youth"/

crime organizations like the Pemuda Pancasila (Pancasila Youth) [. . .] and its powerful local rival, the Ikatan Pemuda Karya (IPK; Functional Youth Group). A number of members from such organizations currently occupy local parliamentary seats across the province' (Hadiz 2004: 715). See also Widodo 2003 on these new local elites. Many political parties have formed their own paramilitary forces: examples are the 'Task Forces' (Satgas) of the PDI-P, the Kabah Youth Movement (*Gerakan Pemuda Kabah*, GPK) of the PPP, the National Guard (*Gerakan Pemuda Kebangkitan Bangsa, Garda Bangsa*) of the PKB and the PAN Youth Force (*Barisan Muda* PAN). The Banser (*Barisan Ansor Serbaguna*) of the PKB probably has around 100,000 members. They '[. . .] have been behind many violent action campaigns, most notably when President Wahid was given a hard time by the media for his adulterous affairs and corruption' (Bertrand 2004: 339).

34 According to Rinakit (2005), 87 per cent of regional elections in 2005 were won by the incumbents, local bureaucrats and military personnel.

## BIBLIOGRAPHY

Ananta, A., Arifin, E.N. and Suryadinata, L. (2004) *Indonesian Electoral Behaviour. A Statistical Perspective*, Singapore: ISEAS.

Ananta, A., Arifin, E. N. and Suryadinata, L. (2005) *Emerging Democracy in Indonesia*; Singapore: ISEAS.

Anderson, B. (1996) 'Elections and Participation in Three Southeast Asian Countries', in R.H. Taylor (ed.) *The Politics of Elections in Southeast Asia*, Cambridge: Cambridge University Press.

Antlöv, H. (2004a) 'Introduction', in H. Antlöv and S. Cederroth (eds) *Elections in Indonesia: The New Order and Beyond*, London and New York: Routledge.

—— (2004b) 'National elections, local issues: the 1997 and 1999 national elections in a village on Java', in H. Antlöv and S. Cederroth (eds) *Elections in Indonesia: The New Order and Beyond*, London and New York: Routledge.

Arlegue, C. and Coronel, J.J.S. (2003) 'Philippines', in P.M. Manikas and L.L. Thornton (eds) *Political Parties in Asia: promoting reform and combating corruption in eight countries*, Washington D.C.: National Democratic Institute for International Affairs.

Asia Foundation (2003) 'Democracy in Indonesia. A Survey of the Indonesian Electorate 2003', Jakarta: Asia Foundation.

Aspinall, E. (2005) 'Elections and the normalization of politics in Indonesia', in *South East Asia Research*, 13 (2): 117–56.

Basaedan, A.R. (2004) 'Political Islam in Indonesia: Present and Future Trajectory', *Asian Survey*, 44 (5): 669–90.

Bertrand, R. (2004) ' "Behave Like Enraged Lions": Civil Militias, the Army and the Criminalisation of Politics in Indonesia', in *Global Crime*, 6 (3&4): 325–44.

Cederroth, S. (2004) 'Traditional power and party politics in North Lombok, 1965–99', in H. Antlöv and S. Cederroth (eds) *Elections in Indonesia: The New Order and Beyond*, London and New York: Routledge.

Choi, N. (2004) 'Local Elections and Party Politics in Post-Reformasi Indonesia: A View from Yogyakarta', *Contemporary Southeast Asia*, August: 280–301.

Colomer, J.M. (2005) 'It's Parties That Choose Electoral Systems (or, Duverger's Laws Upside Down)', in *Political Studies*, 53: 1–21.

Diamond, L. (1999) *Developing Democracy: Towards Consolidation*, Baltimore: Johns Hopkins University Press.

Djadijono, M. (2006) 'Ideologi Partai Politik' ('Ideology of Political Parties'), in I.J. Piliang and T.A. Legowo (eds) *Disain Baru Sistem Politik Indonesia*, Jakarta: CSIS.

Fealy, G. (2001) 'Parties and Parliament: Serving whose Interests?', in G. Lloyd and S. Smith (eds) *Indonesia Today: Challenges of History*, Singapore: ISEAS.

Feith, H. (1957) *The Indonesian Elections of 1955*, Ithaca: Cornell University Press.

—— (1962) *The Decline of Constitutional Democracy in Indonesia*, Ithaca: Cornell University Press.

Geertz, C. (1960) *The Religion of Java*, Glencoe, Illinois: Free Press.

—— (1963) *Peddlers and Princes*, Chicago: University of Chicago Press.

—— (1965) *The Social History of an Indonesian Town*, Cambridge, Massachusetts: MIT Press.

Gerakan Pembaruan PDI Perjuangan (2005) *Demokrasi Seolah-Olah. Tinjauan Kritis Kongres Ke-2 PDI Perjuangan* ('Pseudo-Democracy. A Critical Observation of the Second PDI-Perjuangan Congress'), Jakarta.

Hadiwinata, B.S. (2006) 'The 2004 Parliamentary and Presidential Elections in Indonesia', in A. Croissant and B. Martin (eds) *Between Consolidation and Crisis. Elections and Democracy in Five Nations in Southeast Asia*, Berlin: LIT.

Hadiz, V. (2004), 'Decentralization and Democracy in Indonesia: A Critique of Neo-Institutionalist Perspectives', in *Development and Change*, 35 (4): 697–718.

Haris, S. (2005) 'Proses Pencalonan Legislatif Lokal. Pola, Kecenderungan, dan Profil Caleg' ('The Process of Nominating Local Candidates. Patterns, Tendencies, and the Profile of Legislative Candidates'), in S. Haris (ed.) *Pemilu Langsung di Tengah Oligarki Partai. Proses nominasi dan seleksi calon legislatif Pemilu 2004* ('Direct Elections among Party Oligarchies. Nomination Process and Selection of Legislative Candidates in the 2004 Elections'), Jakarta: Gramedia Pustaka Utama.

IFES (International Foundation for Election Systems) (2004a) *Results from Wave XV of Tracking Surveys*, August 2004, Jakarta: IFES.

—— (2004b) *Results from Wave XVIII of Tracking Surveys*, 19 October 2004, Jakarta: IFES.

—— (2004c), *Results from Wave XV of Tracking Surveys*, Jakarta: IFES.

Johnson Tan, P. (2002) 'Anti-Party Reaction in Indonesia: Causes and Implications', *Contemporary Southeast Asia*, 24 (3): 484–508.

—— (2005) 'Parties and *Pestas*: An Analysis of Indonesian Democratization after the 2004 Elections through the Lens of Party System Institutionalization'. Online. Available HTTP: <http://people.uncw.edu/tanp/PartiesandPestas.html> (accessed 5 January 2006).

—— (2006) 'Indonesia Seven Years after Soeharto: Party System Institutionalization in a New Democracy', in *Contemporary Southeast Asia*, 28 (1): 88–114.

Katz, R.S. and Mair, P. (1995) 'Changing Models of Party Organization and Party Democracy. The emergence of the Cartel Party', in *Party Politics*, 1 (1): 5–28.

King, D.Y. (2003) *Half-Hearted Reform. Electoral Institutions and the Struggle for Democracy in Indonesia*, Westport, Connecticut: Praeger.

Kirchheimer, O. (1966) 'The Catch-all Party', in P. Mair (ed.) (1990) *The West European Party System*, Oxford: Oxford University Press.

Kompas (2004a) *Peta Politik Pemilihan Umum 1999–2004* ('Political Map of the General Elections 1999–2004'), Jakarta: Penerbit Buku Kompas.

—— (2004b) *Partai-Partai Politik Indonesia. Ideologi dan Program 2004–2009* ('Indonesian Political Parties. Ideology and Program 2004–2009'), Jakarta: Penerbit Buku Kompas.

Lembaga Survei Indonesia (LSI) (2006) *Two Years of Party Performance: A Public Evaluation*, Jakarta: Lembaga Survei Indonesia.

Liddle, R.W. (2003) 'New Patterns of Islamic Politics in Democratic Indonesia', in *Asia Program*, 110, Washington, D.C.: Woodrow Wilson International Center for Scholars.

Lipset, S. and Rokkan, S. (1967) 'Cleavage structures, party systems, and voter alignments: An introduction', in S. Lipset and S. Rokkan (eds) *Party Systems and Voter Alignments: Cross-National Perspectives*, New York: Free Press.

Lipset, S.M. (2000) 'The indispensability of parties', in *Journal of Democracy*, 11 (1): 48–55.

Mainwaring, S. (1993) 'Presidentialism, Multipartism, and Democracy. The Difficult Combination', in *Comparative Political Studies*, 26 (2): 198–228.

Mainwaring, S. and Torcal, M. (2006) 'Party System Institutionalization and Party System Theory after the Third Wave of Democratization', in R.S. Katz and W. Crotty (eds) *Handbook of Party Politics*, London, Thousand Oaks, New Delhi: Sage.

Mietzner, M. (2005) 'Local Democracy', in *Inside Indonesia*, 85: 17–18.

Mortimer, R. (1969) 'The Downfall of Indonesian Communism', in R. Miliband and J. Saville (eds) *The Socialist Register*.

Mujani, S. and Liddle, W. (2007) 'Leadership, Party and Religion: Explaining Voting Behavior in Indonesia', in *Comparative Political Studies*, 40 (7): 832–57.

Nohlen, D. (2004) *Wahlrecht und Parteiensystem*, Opladen: Leske&Budrich.

Notosusanto, S. (2005) *Analisa AD/ART Partai Politik* ('Analysis of Political Parties' Statutes'). Online. Available HTTP: <http://www.forum-politisi.org/arsip/article.php?id=113> (accessed 16 September 2006).

Poguntke, T. and Webb, P. (2005) (eds) *The Presidentialization of Politics. A Comparative Study of Modern Democracies*, Oxford: Oxford University Press.

Randall, V. and Svåsand, L. (2002) 'Introduction: The Contribution of Parties to Democracy and Democratic Consolidation', in *Democratization*, 9 (3): 1–10.

Rifai, A. (2003) *Politik Uang Dalam Pemilihan Kepala Daerah* ('Money Politics in the Election of Regional Heads'), Jakarta: Ghalia Indonesia.

Rinakit, S. (2005) *Indonesian Regional Elections in Praxis*, Singapore: IDSS Commentaries.

Robison, R. and Hadiz, V.R. (2004) *Reorganizing Power in Indonesia: The Politics of Oligarchy in an Age of Markets*, London and New York: Routledge.

Rocamora, J.E. (1975) *Nationalism in Search of Ideology: The Indonesian Nationalist Party, 1946–1965*, Quezon City: University of the Philippines.

Rüland, J. (2001) 'Indonesia', in D. Nohlen, F. Grotz and C. Hartman (eds) *Elections in Asia and the Pacific: A Data Handbook, Volume II*, Oxford: Oxford University Press.

Samuels, D.J. (2002) 'Presidentialized Parties. The Separation of Powers and Party Organization and Behavior', in *Comparative Political Studies*, 35 (4): 461–83.

Schmitter, P.C. (1999) 'Critical Reflections on the "Functions" of Political Parties and their Performance in Neo-Democracies', in W. Merkel and A. Busch (eds) *Demokratie in Ost und West. Festschrift für Klaus von Beyme*, Frankfurt am Main: Suhrkamp.

Sebastian, L.C. (2004) 'The Paradox of Indonesian Democracy', in *Contemporary Southeast Asia*, August: 256–79.

Sherlock, S. (2004) 'The 2004 Indonesian Elections: How the System Works and What the Parties Stand For (A Report on Political Parties)', in *Kajian*, March: 1–43.

——— (2005) *The Role of Political Parties in a Second Wave of Reformasi*, Jakarta: UNSFIR.

Sidel, J. (1999) *Capital, Coercion and Crime: Bossism in the Philippines*, Stanford: Stanford University Press.

Slater, D. (2004) 'Indonesia's Accountability Trap: Party Cartels and Presidential Power after Democratic Transition', in *Indonesia*, 78: 61–92.

Suryakusuma, J. (1999) (ed.) *Almanak Parpol Indonesia* ('Almanac of Indonesian Political Parties'), Jakarta: Almanak Parpol Indonesia.

Tomsa, D. (2006a) 'The Defeat of Centralized Paternalism: Factionalism, Assertive Regional Cadres, and the Long Fall of Golkar Chairman Akbar Tandjung', in *Indonesia*, 81: 1–22.

——— (2006b) 'Dominance by Default: Golkar and Uneven Party Institutionalization in Post-Suharto Indonesia', PhD dissertation, Asia Institute, University of Melbourne.

Turmudi, E. (2004), 'Patronage, *aliran* and Islamic ideologies during elections in Jombang, East Java', in H. Antlöv and S. Cederroth (eds): *Elections in Indonesia: The New Order and Beyond*, London and New York: Routledge.

Ufen, A. (2002) *Herrschaftsfiguration und Demokratisierung in Indonesien (1965–2000)*, Hamburg: German Institute for Global and Area Studies.

——— (2006) 'Political Parties in Post-Suharto Indonesia: Between *politik aliran* and "Philippinisation" ', GIGA Working Paper 37, Hamburg: German Institute for Global and Area Studies.

Vel, J. (2005) '*Pilkada* in East Sumba: An Old Rivalry in a New Democratic Setting', in *Indonesia*, 80: 81–107.

Widodo, A. (2003) 'Changing the cultural landscape of local politics in post-authoritarian Indonesia: the view from Blora, Central Java', in E. Aspinall and G. Fealy (eds) *Local Power and Politics in Indonesia: Decentralization and Democratization*, Singapore: Institute of Southeast Asia Studies.

# 8 Uneven party institutionalization, protracted transition and the remarkable resilience of Golkar

*Dirk Tomsa*

## INTRODUCTION

Despite its pivotal role in Indonesian politics, the Golkar Party has been widely overlooked in most analyses of the country's protracted transition to democracy. After finishing second in the 1999 elections, the former state party quickly consolidated its position in the post-New Order party system and eventually returned to the top of the voting tally in 2004, when it won the April election with 21.58 per cent. Just eight months after the polls, Golkar delegates elected Vice President Jusuf Kalla as their new party chairman, thereby further strengthening the party's strategic position in Indonesia's political system. For most observers, Golkar's victory did not come as a surprise. On the contrary, the party had actually been expected to win an even larger share of the vote (LSI 2003), not only because of the widespread dissatisfaction with the Megawati administration, but also because Golkar was believed to possess the most efficient organizational infrastructure of all Indonesian parties.

This chapter will analyse to what extent Golkar's ongoing strength can really be attributed to the party's allegedly superior organizational apparatus. It will be argued that while Golkar is indeed better institutionalized than most other Indonesian parties, its current strength should by no means be taken for granted in the long term as the party faces a number of challenges to its organizational integrity. This chapter will draw attention to some of these challenges including questions related to the upholding of internal coherence at the national as well as the local level, and the adjustment of vertical communication patterns to the increasingly localized political environment in Indonesia. The analysis will show that Golkar is actually not as well-institutionalized as many commentators seem to assume and that the former regime party's ongoing strength is not so much a result of its own potency, but rather a direct consequence of the weakness of the other parties.

## POLITICAL PARTIES AND DEMOCRATIC TRANSITIONS: CONTESTING OLD PARADIGMS

Political parties[1] have long been considered to be an indispensable part of modern democratic polities. As organizations acting on the intermediate level between state and society, they are bestowed with great responsibilities, not only for the legitimacy of a regime but also for its effectiveness and efficiency. Ideally, parties should fulfil a number of important functions in the political system, including the representation of societal interests, the integration of various actors into political decision-making processes, the aggregation of popular demands and preferences, and the simplification and structuring of electoral choices for the people. Furthermore, parties are crucial organizations for the formation of governments and oppositions, and the recruitment and training of political personnel (Gunther and Diamond 2001). However, these ideal-type functions are rarely fulfilled by parties outside Europe and North America. In fact, the performance of Asian, African, and Latin American parties is often rather weak, especially in those countries where democratic transition processes have failed to produce consolidated liberal democracies.

In recent years it has become increasingly obvious that despite the massive spread of the third wave of democratization (Huntington 1991), liberal democracies outside the developed Western world still remain few and far between. As more and more third wave countries have failed to conform to the long-established transition paradigm of liberalization, democratization and consolidation (Carothers 2002), new academic discourses have emerged, not only about the classification of regime types (Merkel 2004; Diamond 2002) but also about the causes and consequences of the flawed attempts to establish liberal democracies. In an interesting contribution to the debate, Eisenstadt (2000) has identified a number of countries where the transitions to democracy have been 'protracted' because of the absence of a chance to settle for a pacted transition and a lack of consensus about exactly how the political system should be changed. In countries like Mexico, Taiwan or South Korea, for example, the uncertainty about the outcome of negotiations between old regime forces and reformers resulted in a slow and protracted process of reforming numerous small sectors of the polity instead of a general overhaul of all relevant political institutions. Thus, enclaves of authoritarianism remained intact long after the old regime had been replaced by a newly elected government.

## THE INDONESIAN TRANSITION TO DEMOCRACY AND THE ROLE OF POLITICAL PARTIES

While the aforementioned countries may be regarded as archetypes of protracted transitions, Malley (2000) has argued that Indonesia is also likely to develop into a case of protracted transition. Writing in the early days of the post-Suharto era, he claimed that the oppositional forces in Indonesia had been unable to negotiate a pacted transition because they were not prepared to capitalize on the unexpected opportunities that opened up in front of them when the Suharto regime suddenly ruptured in the midst of economic turmoil and massive student protests.[2] Shortly after Suharto's resignation, interim president Habibie initiated the revision of electoral institutions and laws on parties and legislatures, yet there was little input from opposition forces as they were too preoccupied with establishing a reasonably competitive organizational infrastructure for their newly-founded parties (Malley 2000: 172).[3]

Not surprisingly then, the outcome of the negotiations between the Habibie government and the four old parliamentary fractions of Golkar, PPP, PDI and the military was little more than a 'half-hearted reform' (King 2003) and Indonesia's new political system at first remained laden with authoritarian leftovers. The successful holding of free and fair elections in June 1999 and the formation of a new government in October 1999 did little to change this impression. Pointing to structural advantages for Golkar enshrined in the reformulated election laws, the retention of the military's role in politics, the hesitation to fight corruption and the unwillingness to reappraise human rights violations by members of the old regime, Malley (2000: 177) concluded that 'Indonesia should be characterized as being on a protracted transition path rather than in a consolidation phase'. In the terminology of Diamond (2002), Indonesia was an 'ambiguous regime', somewhere in the grey zone between electoral democracy and some form of hybrid regime.

A few years on, Indonesia has held another free and fair legislative election and even its first ever direct presidential election, and it can now be safely labelled an electoral democracy. Nonetheless, Malley's (2000: 155) early prediction that 'regime change is likely to be accomplished only by prolonged and repeated struggles to reform specific institutions' has proven to be true. Indeed, Indonesia's democratization process has been characterized by constant bickering between elites over how and to what extent the political system should be changed. Between 1999 and 2002 Indonesia completed no less than four rounds of constitutional amendments, followed by a host of new laws regulating elections, the role of political parties and the composition of national and regional parliaments. Given this patchwork style of reform, Crouch (2003: 19) argued that the reforms 'still fall far short of a thorough overhaul of the political system, and [that] the 2004 general election is unlikely to produce a parliament fundamentally different to the present one'.

Whether Crouch's prediction was right or not probably depends on how we want to define 'fundamentally different'. As a matter of fact, the 2004 election results revealed both continuity and change. While, on the one hand, the top spots of the voting tally were still occupied by the same parties that had occupied these spots in 1999, the elections also produced extraordinary results for new parties like Susilo Bambang Yudhoyono's Democrats Party

(*Partai Demokrat*, PD) and the Prosperous Justice Party (*Partai Keadilan Sejahtera*, PKS).

The results were widely seen as retribution for the established parties which, in the view of many people, had contributed relatively little to promoting democracy in Indonesia. To be fair, representatives of the political parties have been instrumental in crafting the new political format of Indonesia's post-authoritarian system, but apart from this achievement the overall parliamentary track record of the parties has been rather disappointing so far (Ziegenhain 2005). Moreover, outside of parliament most parties have neglected efforts to develop an appealing programme or to strengthen their organizational infrastructure. This negligence has proven costly, as none of the established big parties were able to improve their result in 2004.

## THE IMPORTANCE OF PARTY INSTITUTIONALIZATION

Parties without an appealing programme based on ideological values and an efficient organizational infrastructure can be classified as weakly institutionalized. Conceptualized as a multidimensional process 'by which the party becomes established in terms both of integrated patterns of behaviour and of attitudes, or culture' (Randall and Svasand 2002: 12), the institutionalization of political parties, along with the institutionalization of the party system, is often regarded as an important indicator for the political stability of newly democratizing countries and their overall chances to consolidate in the long term. Democratization theorists like Mainwaring (1999) or Merkel (1998), for example, have long asserted that an institutionalized party system with a range of institutionalized parties is needed to strengthen political efficiency and effectiveness in regards to policy-making and policy implementation. If, on the other hand, parties fail to institutionalize, the process of deepening democracy becomes more difficult and the transition is likely to be protracted.

*Table 8.1* Election results 1999 and 2004 in percentages – gains and losses of the major parties

| Party | 2004 | 1999 | Gained/Lost |
|---|---|---|---|
| Partai Golkar | 21.58 | 22.44 | −0.86 |
| Partai Demokrasi Indonesia-Perjuangan (PDI-P) | 18.53 | 33.74 | −15.21 |
| Partai Kebangkitan Bangsa (PKB) | 10.57 | 12.61 | −2.04 |
| Partai Persatuan Pembangunan (PPP) | 8.15 | 10.71 | −2.56 |
| Partai Demokrat (PD) | 7.45 | – | +7.45 |
| Partai Keadilan Sejahtera (PKS) | 7.34 | 1.36 | +5.98 |
| Partai Amanat Nasional (PAN) | 6.44 | 7.12 | −0.68 |

*Source:* Adapted from Ananta, Arifin and Suryadinata (2005: 14, 22)

In Indonesia, most parties have extremely poor institutionalization records, especially in what Randall and Svasand (2002) have called the 'structural internal dimension of party institutionalization'.[4] This dimension, termed *systemness* by the authors, encompasses all aspects of organizational infrastructure and internal dynamics within a party. To what extent a party institutionalizes in this dimension is not just determined by its 'genetic model' (Panebianco 1988), but also by the routinization of well-known and widely accepted rules and procedures within the party (O'Donnell 1996; North 1990). These rules and procedures can be formal (e.g. party constitution or other official party statutes and decrees) or informal (e.g. factionalism, clientelism, seniority principle, corruption), and their impact on *systemness* can be analysed in a broad variety of aspects including internal power structures, succession regulations, decision-making processes, relations between the central leadership and regional branches, and the regularization of access to financial resources. A high degree of *systemness* naturally confers numerous advantages to a party, including an image of professionalism, direct communication channels with the electorate, easy access to human and financial resources, and independence from personalistic leaders.

In Indonesia, however, most political parties have notoriously weak organizational structures (Surbakti 2003; Johnson Tan 2002). Party apparatuses beyond Java are often poorly developed and the recruitment of professional cadres is widely neglected by most parties. Most significantly, the overwhelming dominance of powerful leaders has usually prevented the evolution of reliable formal institutions and instead facilitated the rise of patronage-driven factionalism and money politics. The prevalence of such 'parasitic' (Lauth 2000: 26) informal institutions has had a profoundly negative impact on the parties' image and consequently on their electoral performance in 2004. After the election, the problems for parties like PDI-P, PKB, PAN or PPP further intensified as discontented party members began to challenge the party leaders over the bad election results. Significantly though, only Amien Rais was willing to relinquish power,[5] whereas Megawati and Abdurrahman Wahid refused to step down from their party posts.[6] Hamzah Haz, who never had as firm a grip on PPP as Megawati, Amien and Gus Dur had on their parties, initially fended off a challenge to his leadership in 2005[7] but in 2007 eventually agreed not to run for the PPP chairmanship again. In sharp contrast to the aforementioned parties, the staunchly Islamic PKS has shown that long-term oriented efforts to develop an appealing ideology and an efficient, highly organized party apparatus can pay off at the ballot box. Today, PKS is one of the best-institutionalized parties in Indonesia and arguably it is the only party with a real potential to grow.

## UNEVEN PARTY INSTITUTIONALIZATION AND THE
## SPECIAL ROLE OF FORMER REGIME PARTIES:
## THE CASE OF GOLKAR

Apart from PKS, the only other party that is usually credited with a good institutionalization record is Golkar. In contrast to PKS, however, Golkar's relatively high degree of institutionalization is not backed up by a persuasive ideology, but is rather based almost exclusively on the party's organizational apparatus. Moreover, Golkar's institutional strength is not a recent achievement but rather a legacy of the past. For more than 25 years Golkar had enjoyed undisputed hegemony in Indonesia as the rigged party system of the authoritarian Suharto regime did not allow the development of genuine opposition parties. While the only two parties permitted to contest the quinquennial New Order elections, PPP and PDI, were strictly limited in their access to financial, material and human resources, Golkar had the full backing of the president himself as well as the regime's prime institutional pillars, namely the military, the bureaucracy and the big business community. With this extraordinary support, Golkar's organizational infrastructure was quickly developed to reach down to the most remote villages of the sprawling archipelago. Not surprisingly, the party won all six New Order elections with an average vote share of 67.5 per cent (Haris 2004).[8]

When Suharto stepped down in 1998, the party suddenly lost its almighty patron and with him the guarantee of unlimited resources and uncontested electoral victory. At the same time, however, the party managed to maintain close relations with crucial parts of the big business community, and much of the party's organizational infrastructure remained intact. Especially in the Outer Islands, where *reformasi* had far less of an impact than on Java, Golkar remained an omnipresent and very potent political force. Thus, it was hardly surprising that Golkar did not disappear into oblivion, but rather retained a dominant position in Indonesia's post-authoritarian party system.

Seen from a comparative perspective, the continued dominance of former regime parties after a democratic transition is neither unusual nor necessarily bad. Examples from countries like Taiwan, Mexico or some Eastern European countries all show that former regime parties often do not only survive democratic transitions, but at times can even make significant contributions to the democratization process. If, however, they perpetuate their institutional advantages at the expense of the fairness and competitiveness of elections, former regime parties are likely to obstruct the advancement of the democratization process. The potential perils inherent in the ongoing dominance of former regime parties have been highlighted by Randall and Svasand (2002: 9) who argue that '[e]xtreme unevenness of party institutionalization not only detracts from the competitiveness of the party system; it is also likely, though not bound, to mean that significant social sectors are excluded not only from power but from any meaningful party representation'. In such cases, a process of de-institutionalization of old regime parties may actually be necessary in order to ensure progress towards democracy.

In the case of post-Suharto Indonesia, party institutionalization is indeed uneven but not to the extent that it has had a profoundly negative impact on the competitiveness of elections.[9] Moreover, as far as the institutional advantages of Golkar are concerned, the degree of uneven party institutionalization may, in fact, shrink further in the future, at least if events during the long election year of 2004 are any indicator of things to come. Unprecedented internal frictions in the central board, numerous defections of local cadres to smaller parties and growing discontent from the grassroots against the persistence of overly centralized decision-making processes have presented the party with a multitude of new challenges. Understanding the underlying dynamics behind these challenges will not only help explain why Golkar won the 2004 election, but also why it did not win it by a larger margin.

## CHALLENGES TO INTERNAL COHERENCE: THE NATIONAL DIMENSION

A unified national leadership around a strong party leader can greatly contribute to a party's performance and its image amongst the population. In the 2004 election, for example, the bad results for parties like PDI-P, PPP, PKB and PAN could at least partly be attributed to their lack of internal coherence. As far as Golkar is concerned, the party has tried hard to keep its factional differences under control, but despite frequent appeals from party leaders to focus on consolidating the party's organizational unity, factional infighting flared up repeatedly between 1999 and 2002 and eventually escalated in 2004. As the following paragraphs will show, the intense conflict between supporters and opponents of party leader Akbar Tanjung ultimately had a devastating impact on the party's performance in the various electoral contests in 2004.

Ever since its foundation in 1964 (Reeve 1985; Boileau 1983), Golkar has been prone to factionalism and internal friction. When former president Suharto transformed the organization into the New Order's electoral vehicle, he deliberately fostered factional rivalries, especially between the military and Golkar's civilian politicians. In the twilight years of the New Order, religion (secularism versus Islam) and region (Java versus Outer Islands) emerged as new dividing lines, but as long as Suharto reigned supreme all factions remained loyal to the president.

After the fall of Suharto, however, the conflicts between warring factions within the central leadership board rapidly escalated when Akbar Tanjung rose to the chairmanship in a hotly contested leadership battle (Crouch 1999: 131–2). Although Akbar quickly moved to consolidate his power, his tactical manoeuvres often alienated rival groups within the party, especially those from Eastern Indonesia. Between 1999 and 2002, resistance from the so-called

*Iramasuka* faction[10] towards Akbar's leadership posed a serious threat to Golkar's institutional integrity as members of the group repeatedly attempted to suspend the chairman. Akbar, however, demonstrated pertinacity and political skilfulness, even after he was sentenced to three years in jail for embezzling 40 billion rupiah (US$4 million) from the State Logistic Agency (*Bulog*) into a Golkar electoral slush fund. Vowing to continue leading Golkar even from behind bars (*The Jakarta Post*, 14 October 2002), Akbar immediately appealed to a higher court and, after a prolonged judicial process, the Supreme Court eventually acquitted him in controversial fashion in February 2004 (*Kompas*, 13 February 2004).

Despite the *Iramasuka* faction's claim that their opposition against Akbar was based on the chairman's alleged marginalization of the interests of Eastern Indonesia, it became increasingly clear throughout the post-Suharto era that the root causes of the frictions within the party were shifting increasingly from previous socio-cultural and professional cleavages to more personalized issues of patronage and clientelism. Akbar Tanjung's support base, for example, was primarily located in the extensive patronage networks of the Islamic Student Association (*Himpunan Mahasiswa Islam*, HMI) and the National Indonesian Youth Committee (*Komite Nasional Pemuda Indonesia*, KNPI).[11] The anti-Akbar camp, on the other hand, embraced anyone who was critical of the chairman regardless of his or her geographical background.

Where factions come into being merely in response to a specific political issue or, as in the case of Golkar, as a result of personalism or clientelism, they tend to be weakly organized and in most cases short-lived or of intermediate duration only (Beller and Belloni 1978). The rise and fall of Akbar Tanjung certainly confirms this assumption. Although the chairman invested immense resources into the consolidation and enlargement of his power base, the lack of any meaningful ideological basis behind the development of his faction made it easy for his opponents to undermine his position once he showed the first signs of political exhaustion. These signs became increasingly obvious after the controversial end to Akbar's corruption trial. While the Golkar chairman was formally acquitted, his reputation – and that of his party – was clearly damaged. In the run-up to the April election open opposition against Akbar was rare, but discontent continued to smoulder underneath the surface.[12] Just two weeks after the election, this discontent erupted spectacularly at Golkar's presidential convention when party delegates from all over the country put the first nail into Akbar's political coffin by electing the former commander-in-chief of the armed forces retired General Wiranto as the party's presidential candidate.

Wiranto owed his victory primarily to widespread support from the district chapters,[13] but the surprising convention result also gave crucial insights into the internal dynamics in Golkar's national leadership board. Despite his alleged involvement in gross human rights violations in Jakarta and East Timor, for example, Wiranto was supported by some of the rather 'reformist' elements in the party, most notably former Attorney-General, Marzuki Darusman, and former Minister for Manpower, Fahmi Idris. What bound them together in the Wiranto camp was not so much a conviction that the former general would make a good president, but rather the firm belief that the notoriously dull career politician Akbar Tanjung would never have a realistic chance to become president.[14] Wiranto, on the other hand, was rumoured to have at least a theoretical chance as an unexpected dark horse candidate. For power-oriented, pragmatic politicians like Marzuki or Fahmi, who were eyeing a minister post in the new cabinet, this was certainly a sufficient incentive to support Wiranto rather than Akbar.

After the convention, Akbar tried not to appear as a sore loser (which in fact he was) and publicly claimed he would support Wiranto in his campaign for the presidency. However, in actual fact Akbar undermined the ensuing campaign wherever he could as he feared that in case of victory Wiranto would use Golkar's upcoming national party congress to oust Akbar from the central board. Against this background it was not entirely unexpected that there was fairly little assistance from Golkar for Wiranto's campaign. Akbar's reluctance to provide money and logistical support for the campaign soon triggered complaints from those regional party chapters that were actually serious about supporting their candidate.[15] In the end, the saboteurs from Slipi[16] achieved their goal as Wiranto failed to reach the decisive second round of the presidential election.

After the election, the internal rifts within Golkar grew deeper and the potential for reconciliation between the pro-Akbar camp and its opponents vanished rapidly. When the two remaining presidential contenders, Susilo Bambang Yudhoyono (SBY) and Megawati Sukarnoputri, started to approach Golkar leaders in order to form a coalition for the decisive second round, the row quickly escalated into open hostilities. While Akbar clearly favoured an alliance with Megawati, SBY's supporters gathered around Fahmi Idris and Marzuki Darusman. At a national leadership meeting in Jakarta, Akbar assertively pushed through his agenda even though many local Golkar chapters appeared to remain heavily in favour of SBY (*Kompas*, 16 August 2004). When Fahmi and his colleagues ignored the decision and continued their pro-SBY activities, Akbar pressured the central board to impose sanctions upon the dissidents. Eventually, Fahmi and Marzuki, along with several other high-ranking cadres, were expelled from the party (*Tempo Interaktif*, 20 September 2004).

The expulsion of Fahmi and the other members from the so-called 'Golkar Party Reform Forum' stood in stark contrast to previous reactions to factionalism and illustrated how selectively Golkar applied its own internal rules. Previously, the most severe sanctions imposed on a party member had been a reprimand for Marwah Daud Ibrahim in 2002,[17] while evident breaches of the official party line by members of the Akbar camp had never been punished. That Akbar was now determined to go all the way to actually expel his opponents was not only an indicator how selectively formal rules and regulations are being imposed in Golkar, it was also a clear sign that the party chairman was beginning to feel the heat over his own political future. Well aware that the next party congress was coming up at the end of the year, Akbar apparently felt the urge to take strong action against the dissidents in order not to risk his chances to retain the post of party chairman. By removing Fahmi from the party, Akbar effectively diminished the opposition's hopes of finding a suitable candidate for the upcoming leadership contest. Fahmi had been widely considered to be the only potential challenger with a reasonably large support base within the party.[18] Therefore, Akbar looked set to hang on to his last political straw, but in a surprising last-minute twist of events his hopes were dashed when recently elected Vice-President Yusuf Kalla joined the race just two days before the congress.

Backed by the power of office, Kalla easily won the contest. The vice-president's victory showed that in a party like Golkar, obtaining the chairmanship is much easier than retaining it. In view of his legendary lack of charisma, Akbar's legitimacy as chairman had always rested exclusively on his political achievements and his ability to ensure that his party had access to the best patronage resources available. But in 2004, Akbar obviously lost his famed political instinct, as was evident in a whole series of strategic miscalculations throughout the year. Thus, he quickly became a liability for Golkar's power-hungry party officials, and in the run-up to the 2004 congress even long-time die-hard supporters abandoned him and switched their allegiance to Yusuf Kalla. In the end, Akbar Tanjung was a lonely man whose final plea for respect was rowdily booed down by a 'rabid audience' (*The Jakarta Post*, 20 December 2004). Ironically, he had become a victim of the very forces that he himself had continuously nourished throughout his chairmanship, namely factionalism and patronage.

From the perspective of party institutionalization, the prevalence of informal rules and procedures such as factionalism and patronage means that formal institutions like the party constitution have been constricted in their potential to provide transparency and reliability. It therefore appears that Golkar is actually not as highly institutionalized in terms of *systemness* as is often assumed. As a matter of fact, informal institutions have shaped internal party dynamics to a much larger extent than formal rules and regulations which are often applied rather arbitrarily.

## CHALLENGES TO INTERNAL COHERENCE: THE LOCAL DIMENSION

No analysis of Golkar's party organization is complete without looking at the institutional dynamics beyond the national level. In fact, when observers try to explain Golkar's ongoing strength they frequently refer to the party's massive organizational apparatus in the regions. In this regard, Golkar obviously still benefits immensely from its hegemonic past. During the New Order,

Golkar's infrastructure was continuously developed until it reached even the remotest village in the sprawling archipelago. Thus, when Suharto's resignation in 1998 ushered in a new era of multi-party competition, Golkar could still rely on this enormous apparatus, whereas new parties had to build their own infrastructure from scratch. Today, Golkar's presence can be felt all over Indonesia. A few figures will underline this perception.

When the former hegemonic party registered for the 2004 general election in April 2003, it claimed to have 30 provincial branches, 374 regental branches and 3,936 sub-district offices (*The Jakarta Post*, 17 April 2003). At the end of the year, when all approved parties had to submit their lists of legislative candidates, Golkar was the only party that registered the maximum number of candidates.[19] Shortly afterwards, all parties were required to register their officially accredited election campaign officials and again, Golkar submitted the longest list.[20] By the time of the presidential convention in April 2004, the number of Golkar's provincial and regental branches had already been updated in accordance with the new administrative landscape. Provincial branches had risen to 32, while regental branches now stood at 421 (DPP Partai Golkar 2004). In December 2004, Golkar's national party congress was attended by delegates from now 33 provincial and 440 regental branches. These figures confirm the widespread impression that Golkar does indeed possess a very well-developed party infrastructure.[21]

However, pure statistics do not capture the real core of Golkar's power in the regions. In fact, local party branches and their respective offices are often little more than empty shells. As a general rule, party activities beyond election times are almost non-existent on the local level (Rozi Soebhan 2004; Fealy 2001). If at all, they take place not in officially designated party locations but in local parliament buildings, public places or in the houses of party officials. This is where political deals are struck, where business contracts are sealed and where connections between party officials and the bureaucracy are strengthened. Often, private gatherings such as weddings, birthdays or religious meetings are utilized to reaffirm existing bonds between party and non-party actors.

Party offices, on the other hand, are often deserted and only fulfil the symbolic function of reminding the public of the party's presence. Yet, it is precisely this kind of informal and basically non-partisan character of local politics that accounts for much of Golkar's strength on the local level, especially in the Outer Islands. The influence of Golkar's party officials in these regions is mostly based on informal positions of traditional power rather than formal party positions. Throughout its history, Golkar has always exploited local dignitaries, wealthy businessmen or religious leaders in informal local power structures for its own benefit and in the early days of the post-Suharto era these patterns of mutually beneficial cooperation had changed relatively little in many rural areas.

An example from South Sulawesi will be used here to illustrate how these patterns work.[22] Here, local politics and business is dominated primarily by traditionally powerful families like the Yasin Limpo family, the Halid family and the Baramuli family. Members of the Yasin Limpo family, for instance, occupy various positions in local governments as well as legislatures from the district level up to the national level. Local journalists argue that the prestige of the Yasin Limpos is based mainly on 'a lot of money, a lot of followers and a lot of loyal *preman* (thugs)'.[23] And of course, all family members support Golkar.

For the party, families like the Yasin Limpos have always acted as vote-getters at the local level as they represent the upper end of extensive patronage networks that reach down to the remotest villages in South Sulawesi. By accommodating the key figures of these networks into the party apparatus, Golkar has always secured broad support since many villagers simply followed the political recommendations of their local leaders. Immediately after the fall of Suharto this pattern had essentially remained the same, but in the run-up to the 2004 election this perception began to change. Although Golkar was arguably still the party with the best infrastructure, many local politicos no longer regarded it as the best vehicle for their personal aspirations and defected to other parties. The main reason for this volatile behaviour was a small but significant change in the election law. In contrast to the previous elections, the 2004 ballot papers not only featured party names and symbols but full candidate lists with photos. This suddenly opened up the possibility that smaller parties could recruit promising candidates who normally would have run for Golkar.[24] As parties like the Prosperous Justice Party (*Partai Keadilan Sejahtera*, PKS) or the Bugis-dominated United Democratic Nationhood Party (*Partai Persatuan Demokrasi Kebangsaan*, PPDK) successfully seized the opportunity, Golkar lost its absolute majority in South Sulawesi, dropping from 66 per cent in 1999 to 44 per cent in 2004.

This new development shows that relying on the exploitation of old-established patronage networks is a double-edged sword for Golkar. On the one hand, it is likely that the party can maintain its dominant position in areas like South Sulawesi as long as it can provide the goods and positions that are requested by local power holders. On the other hand, however, it seems impossible for Golkar to keep everyone happy as there are more ambitious local politicos than the party can actually accommodate in this new competitive party system. In contrast to the New Order when Golkar was the only party that could provide access to political office, today's multi-party system offers local politicos new opportunities if they join parties other than Golkar. Consequently, more defections are likely in the future.

The phenomenon of poorly developed loyalties towards political parties was not only discernible in the competition for high places on legislative candidate lists in the 2004 election. In fact, patronage-induced defections from one party to another could also be observed during various gubernatorial and *bupati* (district head) elections all over Indonesia, which until 2005 were conducted indirectly by the factions represented in provincial or district parliaments. During these elections, disobedience and defiance have been the rule rather than the exception in many regional elections as party delegates in provincial and district parliaments felt little obligation to obey the party's instructions to support a certain candidate. While Golkar has often benefited from this culture of volatility, there are also several cases where Golkar has suffered humiliating defeats. Even in strongholds like South Sulawesi, where Golkar still controls the overwhelming majority of district parliaments, the party had not been immune to the dangers of organizational incoherence and easily corrupted legislators.[25]

Since early 2005, a new system of direct elections of *bupatis* has been introduced. Thus, old-established vote-buying practices in parliament are now obsolete. Instead, with the introduction of direct elections on the local level (*pilkada*) the right to vote has been granted directly to the people. For Golkar, this electoral reform brings new problems as the party can no longer use its parliamentary majorities to push through its own candidates. What matters in direct elections is the personal appeal of individual candidates and not the infrastructure of powerful parties. Golkar had to acknowledge this political reality in dozens of direct *bupati* elections when its candidates lost heavily in districts where the party had actually enjoyed strong victories in the parliamentary elections. By early July 2005, a total of 161 *pilkada* had been conducted all over the archipelago and while Golkar candidates won 58 of these elections (36 per cent of all elections) many party strategists were disappointed because the official target had been set at 60 per cent.[26] What caused particular irritation amongst many Golkar officials was that only 30 of the party's victorious candidates were actually merited local cadres while most of the others were businessmen or bureaucrats who had run on a Golkar ticket but had no strong connections to the party.[27]

In many ways, the results from the *pilkada* were a continuation of the ambiguous trend that had already been discernible at the 2004 general elections. On the one hand, Golkar proved that it was still a very strong force at the local level. To win 36 per cent of the local elections showed that up to now apparently no other party has the capacity to match Golkar's massive apparatus. This apparatus, which the party inherited from the New Order, is a gigantic asset for Golkar, not so much because the countless branch offices could spread the party's policy directives (as there are hardly any), but because they obviously help to maintain contact with the people through informal means of communication. At the same time, however, the results of the first round of local elections and Golkar's failure to live up to its own expectations also show that Golkar's allegedly superior institutional infrastructure is actually built on a rather weak foundation. The heavy reliance on informal local networks frequently exposes Golkar to the risk of losing capable personnel to other parties and thereby undermines the formal institutionalization of the party. In other words, the creeping erosion of Golkar's strength at the local level could be interpreted as the first sign of a gradual process of de-institutionalization from the bottom up.

## CHALLENGES TO VERTICAL COMMUNICATION AND
## INTERNAL DEMOCRACY

Although in some areas this process of de-institutionalization has resulted in a gradual decline of Golkar's power at the local level, the party may regain some of its strength if it dares to empower its local cadres and encourages them to act more independently from the central leadership. If, for example, local sentiment is considered more thoroughly during the candidate selection processes at local elections, the party may score better results in future contests.[28] First steps in the direction of giving more autonomy to the local level were initiated by Akbar Tanjung and the central leadership board during the presidential convention and the 2004 national party congress, when the votes of party district branches eventually decided the contests for the presidential nomination and the chairmanship.

Interestingly though, the local party bosses have been rather 'ungrateful' for their upgraded rights, inflicting maximum damage to the dominant party elites in Jakarta as they sided with the anti-Akbar faction which had thrown its support behind candidates from outside the core party apparatus. The double defeat for Akbar Tanjung at the hands of Wiranto and Yusuf Kalla respectively, as well as Akbar's failure to mobilize support for Megawati during the second round of the presidential election, clearly indicates that the factional contests within the party do not only have a horizontal (national), but also a vertical (local–national) dimension. Indeed, it seems that relations between the party's central board in Jakarta and its more than four hundred district chapters are somewhat strained. Decades of iron-fisted, top-down decision-making processes have apparently left their mark on the party, and many local officials feel that the oligarchic political culture within Golkar has not yet genuinely changed.[29]

At the sidelines of the convention, for example, several delegates expressed feelings of bitterness after Akbar Tanjung had presented himself as the sole defender of Golkar.[30] Although Akbar's rhetoric was mainly aimed at his four rivals, many regional party representatives were irritated about the missing acknowledgement of their own contributions at the grassroots. Furthermore, local officials also took exception to the fact that the implementation committee for the convention had decided to give only one vote to each district chapter whereas provincial chapters were awarded three and the party's central board 18 votes. Additional resentment was caused when a leadership meeting shortly before the convention decided to give all these 18 votes en bloc to Akbar Tanjung (Tomsa 2006: 10).[31]

Yet, negative emotions cannot entirely account for the voting behaviour of the district leaders. On the contrary, the most important reasons were probably genuinely rational calculations about power, patronage and influence. For example, Wiranto was widely alleged to have spent a fortune on buying his victory. In contrast to Akbar who mainly concentrated on gaining support from the provincial chapters, Wiranto had focused his campaign on the district level, where he distributed most of his *gizi* (literally: nutrients; here money and other material contributions). A second rational factor that may help explain the convention outcome is the strategic thinking of the regional delegates. Many party members had noted that Akbar Tanjung's overall popularity was extremely low, not only because of his apparent lack of charisma, but especially because of his involvement in the *Bulog* corruption case. Akbar's negative public image led many delegates to the conclusion that chances to win the presidency for Golkar might be higher with a dark horse candidate like Wiranto.

The rebellion from the regions during the convention marked the first indicator that the rational calculations of lower-level party officials can no longer be easily controlled by the party's central board. In fact, the events during the convention showed that a gradual adjustment in the power balance and relative bargaining power between the local and national party elites is taking place (Tomsa 2006). Akbar either underestimated or ignored this trend. In contrast to Wiranto, whose strategy was to invest heavily in the district chapters, Akbar obviously believed that old-established, top-down patterns of communication and decision-making processes could still prevail. His calculation was simple; if he could get the support from a certain provincial chapter, the chairman of this particular chapter would then order all the district chairmen from his province to vote in accordance with the provincial chapter's choice.

But these New Order-style manoeuvres no longer work that easily in contemporary Indonesian party politics, at least not in Golkar. With the implementation of the convention the party has tried to portray itself as the vanguard of democratization and reform in Indonesia, and as part of this image-building process it has introduced new structures of internal decision-making that give the local chapters a much bigger role within the party than they had during the New Order. In that regard, one may argue that as far as vertical communication patterns are concerned, Golkar is proceeding towards greater institutionalization. To a certain extent, this may be true as the convention has shown that formal rules and regulations do indeed matter. However, at the same time the acceptance of formal institutions is still low amongst many Golkar politicians as could be seen in the various attempts by Akbar and his supporters to manipulate the convention rules to their own benefit.[32]

Akbar Tanjung's convention debacle was the first clear indicator that popular aspirations from the grassroots could no longer be ignored. Despite this early warning sign, however, the central board continued with its old-style power politics when it started to negotiate Golkar's stance for the second round of the presidential election. As soon as Akbar made it clear that he preferred a coalition with Megawati,[33] his statements were met with widespread scepticism at the grassroots level. Essentially, the criticism revolved around three main issues. Firstly, many cadres feared for the party's and their own personal credibility if they suddenly supported the very candidate they had fervently criticized in the legislative elections just three months earlier. Secondly, many party officials argued that it would only be natural if Golkar supported SBY because SBY's running mate Yusuf Kalla was one of their own. Thirdly, many local chapters in Golkar's strongholds in Eastern Indonesia favoured the SBY-Yusuf Kalla pairing because of their 'emotional relationship with Kalla'.[34] Indeed, many Golkar cadres in South Sulawesi were proud of the achievements of their *putra daerah* (son of the region). Moreover, Kalla represented a real chance for them to gain direct access to the government. But the voices from the grassroots were not heard at the party headquarters in Slipi. The decision to build a coalition with Megawati was made at a national leadership meeting in which district chapters had no right to vote. Amongst the provincial chapters who eventually made the decision only a very few had the courage to speak out against the will of the chairman,[35] so that the way was paved for an all-out yet eventually futile effort to mobilize votes for Megawati.

A third and final example that underlines the trend away from centralized paternalism to more decentralized party politics was the election of Yusuf Kalla as party chairman in December 2004. Long before the national congress was held, local party officials had already begun to urge Akbar Tanjung to extend the right to vote for the next chairman to all district chapters as had been informally agreed at the end of the 1998 extraordinary party congress. However, with the memory of the convention debacle fresh in mind, Akbar rejected the plea, arguing that the party's constitution did not allow for such a sweeping change of the rules. At a leadership meeting shortly before the congress he successfully pushed through the retention of the old rules which confined voting rights to the national and provincial leadership boards and a number of affiliated mass organizations.

With these regulations in place, Akbar looked like the strong favourite to win a second term as chairman, but only until Yusuf Kalla emerged as a surprise contender who swiftly claimed to have secured the support from 28 provincial chapters. The statement came as a shock for Akbar and his supporters. In a last frantic effort to stop the downward spiral, the incumbent chairman not only persuaded former arch-rival Wiranto to support him, but also astonished the delegates with the announcement that he would like to grant voting rights to all district chapters. Apparently Akbar believed that he could still turn things around if Wiranto could drum up some support at the grassroots and he himself could regain the trust of some of the provinces which used to back him. However, even this last-minute manoeuvre could not prevent the inevitable. Although the initiative was accepted by acclamation, Yusuf Kalla eventually won the contest easily, defeating Akbar by 323:156 votes (Tomsa 2006: 20).[36]

In sum, it is clear that the events surrounding the presidential convention, the presidential election and the national party congress were not isolated incidents but part of a wider pattern. Just as Indonesian politics in general is becoming increasingly localized, political developments within Golkar throughout 2004 have also been shaped significantly by a growing assertiveness of local political players who try to have an impact on the national level. As noted elsewhere:

> For older party elites in Jakarta who learned to navigate Indonesia's political system during the New Order years, this process has been difficult to comprehend, for they continued to view local players as mere subordinates to the dominant centre. But local officials no longer blindly follow instructions issued by a narrow-minded party oligarchy that is primarily interested in personal enrichment. Buoyed by the overall localization of politics, they have grown increasingly confident about their own role in the party and are now more inclined to challenge the authority of the central leadership board if it is in their own personal interests.
>
> (Tomsa 2006: 22)

In the long term, this new assertiveness from the margins may counter the overall trend towards de-institutionalization as local elites can be expected to continue their push towards the formal acknowledgement of their extended rights and responsibilities in official party regulations. At the moment, however, these developments are still in their infancy.

## CONCLUSION

This chapter aimed at determining whether Golkar's enduring dominance of Indonesian party politics can really be attributed to the quality of the party's organizational apparatus. After discussing some of the challenges the party faces it is clear that the widely held view that Golkar possesses a superior organizational infrastructure needs to be modified in certain aspects. To explain Golkar's ongoing strength by just pointing to the multitude of party branches all over the archipelago is a gross simplification of the concept of party organization or, as Randall and Svasand (2002) termed it, *systemness*.

Of course Golkar does still benefit from its massive machinery, especially in outlying regions such as Sulawesi where the party is still able to exploit old-established power structures for its own advantage. But the results of the 2004 parliamentary elections and subsequent events surrounding the presidential elections and the national party congress have also shown that the strength of the formal party organization is undermined by the influence of informal institutions. While formal regulations certainly exist in Golkar, they often have little power in itself. The presidential convention and the national party congress were outstanding examples of the weakness of formal institutions as party elites frequently changed and bended existing regulations at their own discretion.

Today, Golkar's position in contemporary Indonesian politics appears in a rather ambiguous light. Without a doubt, the party is still the strongest force in the party system. But it seems that Golkar's power is based far less on its own organizational strength than rather on the weakness of the other parties. As long as Golkar's rivals do not undertake any substantial efforts to institutionalize their own party structures, the former hegemonic party may be able to perpetuate its remaining institutional advantages and hence its strong position in Indonesian party politics. But the process of de-institutionalization has already begun, as is evident in the loss of numerous local party officials who once formed the key pillars of the party's organizational infrastructure. At the same time, new electoral rules such as the *pilkada* legislation, as well as the potential coming of age of new parties, may further contribute to a decline in Golkar's strength.

However, although there are signs that point towards a process of gradual de-institutionalization (and consequently, a gradual decline of power), it is far too early to write Golkar off yet. Up to now, the party has proven remarkably resilient and the election of the incumbent vice-president as party chairman in 2004 has certainly done no harm to the party's power ambitions. Moreover, there is only limited reason for optimism that other parties may catch up with Golkar in terms of developing an effective, nationwide infrastructure. Especially big parties like PDI-P, PPP or PKB have proven utterly ineffective in recruiting new personnel with genuine leadership qualities. Therefore, even if Golkar fails to address its current problems, its strong position in the party system is likely to continue simply for the lack of better alternatives.

## NOTES

1 Definitions of political parties reach from the simplistic to the comprehensive. In the context of this work I draw upon earlier definitions crafted by Sartori (1976: 63) and Puhle (2002: 81) and define political parties as political organizations with an official label that present candidates for elections (competitive or non-competitive) with the goal of placing these candidates for public office. In accordance with Puhle, I regard it as irrelevant whether these organizations actually call themselves 'parties' or not.
2 The circumstances of the fall of Suharto have been dealt with extensively elsewhere and will not be recapitulated here in detail. For good accounts of the events that led to Suharto's resignation see, for example, Ufen (2002), Luhulima (2001), van Dijk (2001), Schwartz (1999), Emmerson (1999), Aspinall, van Klinken and Feith (1999) or Forrester and May (1998).
3 Furthermore, the new parties were also reluctant to get involved in the law-making process because they were uncertain about what election system would actually be most beneficial for them. As Malley (2000: 171) pointed out, 'they could not gauge the impact of the change on their electoral performance. None had ever competed, and few even knew how strong their organizations would be at election time'.
4 According to Randall and Svasand (2002), party institutionalization is a process that takes place in four different dimensions including systemness, decisional autonomy, value infusion and reification. In the context of this chapter, the analysis

will be confined to systemness because it is in this dimension where Golkar is often described as the most privileged of all Indonesian parties. See Randall and Svasand (2002) for a full discussion of the other institutionalization categories.

5 However, even though Amien stepped down formally, he still ensured ongoing influence in PAN by installing a handpicked successor, businessman Soetrisno Bachir, at the helm of the party. Moreover, he also retained a rather informal yet influential position as chairman of the party's advisory council (*Suara Merdeka*, 12 April 2005; *The Jakarta Post*, 11 April 2005).

6 Megawati and Wahid were both re-elected as party leaders by acclamation, despite strong opposition from powerful segments of their respective parties (*Kompas*, 18 April 2005 and 1 April 2005).

7 In 2005 opponents of Hamzah initiated a move to bring forward PPP's next national congress from 2007 to 2005. The move was thwarted by Hamzah, thereby safeguarding his chairmanship until 2007 (*Kompas*, 25 April 2005; *The Jakarta Post*, 28 February 2005). When the congress was eventually held in early 2007, Suryadharma Ali, one of the ringleaders of the 2005 revolt, was elected as new chairman (*Kompas*, 4 February 2007).

8 In view of the fact that the largely ceremonial *pesta demokrasi* primarily served to provide a superficial legitimacy for the authoritarian regime, Liddle (1996) has aptly described the New Order elections as a 'useful fiction'.

9 Both the 1999 and the 2004 general elections have widely been described as free and fair. For 2004 see, for example, reports by the Australian Parliamentary Observer Delegation (2004) and the European Union Election Observation Mission to Indonesia (2004). For 1999, see National Democratic Institute (1999) or the various contributions in Blackburn (1999).

10 The term *Iramasuka* (literally: happy melody) is short for *IR*ian Jaya, *MA*luku, *SU*lawesi and *KA*limantan. It was coined due to the fact that most members of the group hailed from provinces in Eastern Indonesia.

11 In the 1970s Akbar had chaired both of these two organizations.

12 Critical members of the central board particularly resented Akbar's dominant role in manipulating candidate lists for the elections and his control of the implementation committee for the presidential convention (confidential interviews with members of Golkar's central board, 4 May 2004 and 19 May 2004).

13 See below for a more detailed discussion of the local dimension of Akbar's defeat.

14 In the various polls before the presidential elections Akbar's popularity index had never reached double digits. For an overview of various survey results, see Sebastian (2004: 268–9).

15 During fieldwork in Indonesia in 2004, several party campaigners in North and South Sulawesi expressed their disappointment about the reluctance of the central board to provide assistance. The DPP itself rejected claims of deliberate obstruction, but admitted that the cooperation between the party and Wiranto's own success team had been difficult (*Kompas*, 9 June 2004).

16 Slipi is the area in Jakarta where Golkar's headquarters are located.

17 When Akbar was convicted for his involvement in the *Bulog* corruption case, Marwah had repeatedly urged the chairman to step down from his positions as party chairman and DPR speaker.

18 Wiranto's name was also frequently mentioned in the press, but Akbar cunningly shattered the former general's hopes by setting up rigid eligibility requirements for prospective contestants. One of these regulations required potential candidates to have at least five years experience in a party board on either the national, provincial or district level. Since Wiranto had no organizational track record whatsoever, he was basically eliminated from the race before it even began (*Pikiran Rakyat*, 11 December 2004).

19 The KPU had ruled that a party could only register a maximum of 660 candidates

(120 per cent of the 550 seats to be contested) for the legislative election. Golkar was the only party to reach this benchmark, while PPP (628) and PDI-P (615) were the only other ones to submit more than 600 names (*Kompas*, 30 December 2003).

20 Altogether, Golkar registered 811 campaigners. Other parties had only been able to mobilize far smaller numbers, for instance PPP 572, PDI-P 571 or PKB 549. See <http://www.kpu.go.id/kampanye/lihat-dalam.php?ID=3andcat=Kampanye> (accessed 12 March 2004).

21 Interestingly, most other parties claim to have equally impressive organizational infrastructures. In 2005, all big parties except PKS claimed to have more than four hundred district branches, even the notoriously weakly-institutionalized PD.

22 The following two paragraphs are largely based on Tomsa (2005).

23 Personal communication with local journalists in Makassar, South Sulawesi, 1 July 2004.

24 Smaller parties often baited former Golkar members with the promise to make them the number 1 candidate on their legislative candidate list. In view of these offers, many lower-ranking Golkar backbenchers who could not compete with the patronage power of the Yasin Limpos, Halids and Baramulis were willing to jump ship simply because they saw their interests better accommodated by smaller parties (Tomsa 2005).

25 Between 1999 and 2004, Golkar lost four *bupati* elections in South Sulawesi. In all cases (Bulukumba, Sinjai, Mamasa and Enrekang), Golkar possessed the biggest amount of seats in the local parliament, and in Sinjai the party even had an absolute majority (*Fajar*, 22 June 2003, 20 August 2003 and 11 September 2003).

26 'Rekrut Calon Kepala Daerah Akan Dievaluasi', <*http://www.partai-golkar.or.id*>, accessed 10 July 2005.

27 'Rekrut Calon Kepala Daerah Akan Dievaluasi', <*http://www.partai-golkar.or.id*>, accessed 10 July 2005.

28 Interestingly, after the completion of this manuscript Golkar did indeed adjust its selection mechanisms and gave greater support to candidates who were deemed popular at the local rather the national level.

29 One example where the persistence of traditional top-down patterns of thinking was manifest was the nomination process of legislative candidates. After local party chapters had submitted their lists with proposed candidates, party chairman Akbar Tanjung and his allies in the central board made several controversial changes in order to ensure that members of their clientelistic networks were placed on top of the lists (interviews with several legislative candidates conducted between May and August 2004).

30 During a speech at the convention Akbar accused his competitors of lacking commitment to Golkar in the immediate aftermath of the fall of Suharto. Pointing to his role as the sole bearer of all criticism directed at Golkar after 1998, Akbar stressed that only he himself had shown the courage to defend Golkar against NGOs, student activists and other political parties (personal notes by the author).

31 Initially, Akbar had even demanded that the DPP be granted 97 votes, corresponding to the actual number of members of the extended DPP. This was clearly unacceptable to most regional chapters, who demanded that the DPP should simply have one vote. In the end, the compromise with 18 votes was agreed on (*Kompas*, 1 May 2003).

32 Interestingly, Akbar's efforts to weaken his rivals never included an attempt to change the agreed voting rights for the district chapters. Instead, he tried to forbid his rivals from campaigning outside Java and Bali. Earlier, he had pushed through the adjournment of the convention from its original date in February to April in order to allow him to settle his legal issues first (although this was, of course, not the official reason).

33 Despite the official rhetoric about stabilizing the political system, Akbar's main

reasons to coalesce with Megawati seemed to be driven by his personal power ambitions. Since the constitution prescribes a limitation of just two consecutive terms for the president, Akbar could easily calculate that he would become the coalition's next presidential candidate in 2009.

34 The term *hubungan emosional* was frequently used by local Golkar officials when they spoke about their preference for Yusuf Kalla (interviews with various local Golkar cadres between June and September 2004).

35 In the end, the provincial chapter of West Java was the only one to resist Akbar's pressure and maintained its neutral stance. Four other chapters (South Sulawesi, Papua, DI Yogyakarta and North Maluku), which had initially expressed support for SBY, eventually agreed to fully implement the meeting's decision, although they were visibly dissatisfied with the outcome of the meeting (*Kompas*, 16 August 2004).

36 After the last minute changes, voting rights had eventually been granted to the central board, all provincial and district boards, and all affiliated mass organizations including the three founding organizations (Soksi, MKGR and Kosgoro 1957), the youth and women's organizations founded by Golkar (AMPG and KPPG) and the five autonomous mass organizations AMPI, MDI, HWK, Al Hidayah and Satkar Ulama. Altogether, the number of votes eventually amounted to 484. In the final round of the contest, there were two abstentions and three invalid votes (*Tempo Interaktif*, 19 December 2004; *Suara Merdeka*, 20 December 2004).

## BIBLIOGRAPHY

Ananta, A., Arifin, E.N. and Suryadinata, L. (2005) *Emerging Democracy in Indonesia*, Singapore: Institute of Southeast Asian Studies.

Aspinall, E., van Klinken, G. and Feith, H. (eds) (1999) *The Last Days of President Suharto*, Clayton: Monash Asia Institute.

Australian Parliamentary Observer Delegation (2004) *The Parliamentary Elections in Indonesia – 5 April 2004*, Canberra: The Parliament of the Commonwealth of Australia.

Beller, D.C. and Belloni, F.P. (1978) 'Party and Faction: Modes of political competition', in F.P. Belloni and D.C. Beller (eds) *Faction Politics: Political Parties and Factionalism in Comparative Perspective*, Oxford: ABC-Clio.

Blackburn, S. (ed.) (1999) *Pemilu: the 1999 Indonesian Election*, Annual Indonesia Lecture Series No. 22, Clayton: Monash Asia Institute.

Boileau, J.M. (1983) *Golkar: Functional Group Politics in Indonesia*, Jakarta: Centre for Strategic and International Studies.

Carothers, T. (2002) 'The End of the Transition Paradigm', *Journal of Democracy*, 13 (1): 5–21.

Crouch, H. (1999) 'Wiranto and Habibie: Military-Civilian Relations since May 1998', in A. Budiman, B. Hatley and D. Kingsbury (eds) *Reformasi: Crisis and Change in Indonesia*, Clayton: Monash Asia Institute.

—— (2003) 'Political Update 2002: Megawati's Holding Operation', in E. Aspinall and G. Fealy (eds) *Local Power and Politics in Indonesia: Decentralisation and Democratisation*, Singapore: Institute of Southeast Asian Studies.

Diamond, L. (2002) 'Thinking about Hybrid Regimes', *Journal of Democracy*, 13 (2): 21–35.

DPP Partai Golkar (2004) *Keputusan Badan Pelaksana Konvensi Pemilihan Calon Presiden Partai Golkar Nomor 12/Balak Konvensi/Golkar/IV/2004, 18 April 2004,* Jakarta: DPP Partai Golkar.

Eisenstadt, T. (2000) 'Eddies in the Third Wave: Protracted Transitions and Theories of Democratization', *Democratization,* 7 (3): 3–24.

Emmerson, D.K. (ed.) (1999) *Indonesia Beyond Suharto: Polity, Economy, Society, Transition,* Armonk: M.E. Sharpe.

European Union Election Observation Mission to Indonesia 2004, *Final Report.* Online. Available HTTP: <http://www.id.eueom.org/EUEOM_FinalReport.pdf> (accessed 15 July 2005).

Fealy, G. (2001) 'Parties and Parliament: Serving Whose Interests?', in G. Lloyd and S. Smith (eds) *Indonesia Today: Challenges of History,* Singapore: Institute of Southeast Asian Studies.

Forrester, G. and May, R.J. (eds) (1998) *The Fall of Soeharto,* Bathurst: Crawford House.

Gunther, R. and Diamond L. (2001) 'Types and Functions of Parties', in L. Diamond and R. Gunther (eds) *Political Parties and Democracy,* Baltimore and London: The Johns Hopkins University Press.

Haris, S. (2004) 'General Elections under the New Order', in H. Antlöv and S. Cederroth (eds) *Elections in Indonesia: The New Order and Beyond,* London and New York: RoutledgeCurzon.

Huntington, S.P. (1991) *The Third Wave: Democratization in the Late Twentieth Century,* Norman and London: Oklahoma University Press.

Johnson Tan, P. (2002) 'Anti-Party Reaction in Indonesia: Causes and Implications', *Contemporary Southeast Asia,* 24 (3): 484–508.

King, D.Y. (2003) *Half-hearted Reform: Electoral Institutions and the Struggle for Democracy in Indonesia,* Westport: Praeger.

Lauth, H. (2000) 'Informal Institutions and Democracy', *Democratization,* 7 (4): 21–50.

Lembaga Survei Indonesia (LSI) (2003) *Kecenderungan Pemilih dan Peluang Golkar dalam Pemilu 2004,* Jakarta: LSI.

Liddle, R.W. (1996) 'A Useful Fiction', in R.H. Taylor (ed.) *The Politics of Elections in Southeast Asia,* Cambridge: Cambridge University Press.

Luhulima, J. (2001) *Hari-Hari Terpanjang: Menjelang Mundurnya Presiden Soeharto,* Jakarta: Penerbit Buku Kompas.

Mainwaring, S.P. (1999) *Rethinking Party Systems in the Third Wave of Democratization: The Case of Brazil,* Stanford: Stanford University Press.

Malley, M. (2000) 'Beyond Democratic Elections: Indonesia Embarks on a Protracted Transition', *Democratization,* 7 (3): 153–80.

Merkel, W. (1998) 'The Consolidation of Post-Autocratic Democracies: a Multi-Level Model', *Democratization,* 5 (3): 33–67.

—— (2004) 'Embedded and Defective Democracies', *Democratization,* 11 (5) 33–55.

National Democratic Institute (NDI) (1999) *Post-Election Statement No.3: Indonesia's June 7, 1999, Legislative Elections Vote Tabulation and the Electoral Process,* Washington/Jakarta: NDI.

North, D. (1990) *Institutions, Institutional Change and Economic Performance,* Cambridge: Cambridge University Press.

O'Donnell, G. (1996) 'Illusions about Consolidation', *Journal of Democracy,* 7 (2): 34–51.

Panebianco, A. (1988) *Political Parties: Organization and Power*, Cambridge: Cambridge University Press.

Puhle, H (2002), 'Still the Age of Catch-allism? Volksparteien und Parteienstaat in Crisis and Re-equilibration', in R. Gunther, J. Montero and J. Linz (eds) *Political Parties: Old Concepts and New Challenges*, Oxford: Oxford University Press.

Randall, V. and Svasand, L. (2002) 'Party Institutionalization in New Democracies', *Party Politics*, 8 (1): 5–29.

Reeve, D. (1985) *Golkar of Indonesia: An Alternative to the Party System*, Singapore: Oxford University Press.

Rozi Soebhan, S. (2004) 'Potret Partai Golkar Pasca Soeharto di Makassar, Sulawesi Selatan: Gejala Konservatisme Partai Politik?', in L. Romli et al. (eds) *Potret Partai Politik Pasca Orde Baru*, Jakarta: Pusat Penelitian – LIPI.

Sartori, G. (1976) *Parties and Party Systems: a Framework for Analysis*, Cambridge: Cambridge University Press.

Schwarz, A. (1999) *A Nation in Waiting: Indonesia's Search for Stability*, St Leonards: Allen and Unwin.

Sebastian, L.C. (2004) 'The Paradox of Indonesian Democracy', *Contemporary Southeast Asia*, 26 (2): 256–79.

Surbakti, R. (2003) 'Perkembangan Partai Politik di Indonesia', in H. Schulte-Nordholt and G. Asnan (eds) *Indonesia in Transition: Work in Progress*, Yogyakarta: Pustaka Pelajar.

Tomsa, D. (2005) 'Bloodied but Unbowed', *Inside Indonesia*, 83: 17–18.

—— (2006) 'The Defeat of Centralized Paternalism: Factionalism, Assertive Regional Cadres, and the Long Fall of Golkar Chairman Akbar Tandjung', *Indonesia*, 81: 1–22.

Ufen, A. (2002) *Herrschaftsfiguration und Demokratisierung in Indonesien 1965–2000*, Hamburg: Institut fuer Asienkunde.

van Dijk, K. (2001), *A Country in Despair: Indonesia between 1997 and 2000*, Leiden: KITLV Press.

Ziegenhain, P. (2005) 'Deficits of the Indonesian Parliament and their Impact on the Democratisation Process', in I. Wessel (ed.) *Democratisation in Indonesia after the Fall of Suharto*, Berlin: Logos.

# Part III

# Resistance of New Order stalwarts

# 9 Capitalist consolidation, consolidated capitalists

## Indonesia's conglomerates between authoritarianism and democracy

*Christian Chua*

Indonesia's New Order was a sophisticated political system based on an authoritarian, centralized and protectionist state apparatus that effectively secured the dominance of the bureaucratic elite. One of the regime's main characteristics was the emergence of predatory patronage networks which grew out of a unique system of collaboration between the state and the holders of capital, Indonesia's predominantly Chinese business sector. Through these networks Indonesia's politico-bureaucrats, who held instrumental power over the state, allowed a small group of ethnic Chinese businessmen to establish economically powerful conglomerates that came to dominate the private commercial sector. Due to their ethnic label, these capitalists were otherwise politically muted as well as socially limited, making them the bureaucracy's ideal partners who could not challenge the authority of the state elite, as would have occurred with an indigenous bourgeoisie of business leaders. There was no practical reason for these tycoons to rebel against their subordination: although they lacked direct political power and remained ultimately dependent on the bureaucrats, this mutually beneficial relationship developed, going on to serve the interests of both groups so well throughout the New Order era that the symbiosis lasted for more than three decades.

The financial crisis of 1997–98 forced an end to this accommodation. One objective of this chapter is to point out the consequences that subsequent reforms had for Chinese big business in Indonesia. How did political democratization – or *reformasi*, as it was called – come to affect capital? The collapse of the New Order regime seriously disrupted Indonesia's politico-business oligarchy's basis of authority, to the point where the Chinese conglomerates ended up on the brink of financial collapse. However, by looking at the ways in which capital reacted to the crisis, it will be demonstrated how *reformasi* only altered the style and left the structural substance of the old system widely intact. Hence the conglomerates, with their indispensable capital resources, had sufficient leeway to adjust to and succeed within a democratic, decentralized and deregulated environment. This chapter's second aim, therefore, is to analyse how these capitalists affected democratic consolidation in Indonesia and to point out how they resisted, influenced and even came to mould political reforms. The ongoing process of democratization in Indonesia today can thus be regarded as the emergence of a plutocratic regime. This chapter investigates its embryonic stage.

## CAPITAL IN CRISIS

*Reformasi* was intended to reconfigure the system in three areas: shifting power away, first, from the president and the political elites to the people and society; second, from Jakarta-based gatekeeping institutions to provincial parliaments and regional decision-makers; and third, from the major cronies and parasite capitalists to free markets with welcome contributions from international investors. It was widely expected that without the authoritarian, centralized and protectionist features of the old regime, Suharto's cronies would not be able to carry on. The conglomerates, according to Ufen (2002: 187), had much to fear from democratization, especially because of their ethnic – predominantly Chinese – composition. Here the consequences that the end of the New Order had for the conglomerates shall be evaluated. It will be shown that in 1998, the implementation of reforms seriously threatened business groups with the dismantling of the foundations of the old oligarchy.

### The end of authoritarianism

Authoritarianism was decisive in sustaining the New Order. Without hindrance from any noteworthy opposition, the ruling state elite around President Suharto was left to predatory capitalism without checks and balances. This situation changed tremendously with the advent of the formal-institutional and the civic sphere of democracy; that is, parliamentarism and the awakening of civil society.

With the fall of their leader, the politico-bureaucrats were suddenly confronted with attempts to install a new democratic framework designed to quash their former base of centralized institutional power. This suddenly became possible because the military, which had safeguarded the old system, accepted the one feasible option left available to it during and after the final days of the New Order: to subordinate itself to civilian supremacy. The alternative would have been to use violence openly to break down the student movement, which the military leadership under Wiranto deemed unwise (Schwarz 1999: 363–4). Thus the army retreated partially from the political sphere they had dominated for decades. This paved the way for some important reforms which severely weakened both the presidency and the state party Golkar, the two chief pillars of Suharto's old regime. This also strengthened the freedom of the new system, leading to the rise of new political players.

After 32 years of Suharto's rule the legislative term of presidents came to be five years with the possibility of one re-election. Significantly, none of Suharto's three successors – Habibie, Abdurrahman Wahid or Megawati – managed to remain in office for a prolonged period. Indonesia's sixth president, Susilo Bambang Yudhoyono, became the fourth head of state in only six years after Suharto's resignation. Symbolizing the reduction of power inherent in the office of president, Indonesia's head of state now shares power with many other political institutions at various levels, above all with Indonesia's House of Representatives, the DPR (*Dewan Perwakilan Rakyat*). Long serving as a rubber-stamp parliament for the president, the DPR has grown so much in power that it is now able to control Indonesia's executive body and even hold the president to account for his or her actions. The impeachment of Abdurrahman Wahid in July 2001 exemplifies the shift of power away from the executive to the legislature.

The strengthening of parliament has led to the growth in significance of individual politicians and parties, in terms of both physical numbers and of power. The number of parties jumped from only three government-funded and largely impotent organizations to more than 140 parties by the end of 1998, of which 48 were eligible to compete in the national elections of 1999 (Fealy 2001: 100). Golkar, the undisputed political instrument of the politico-bureaucrats, suddenly had to face serious competition and was forced to transform itself. Having long enjoyed its status as Suharto's largely unchallenged ruling party, affording it triumph in every Indonesian election including an indomitable 75 per cent of the national vote in 1997, Golkar had to settle into a new environment where it was merely one of many participants in the struggle for votes. This saw its support dwindle to only 22 per cent of votes cast in 1999, putting the former state party a distant second to the victorious PDI-P (Fealy 2001: 101). Most notably, two leading former opposition politicians, Abdurrahman Wahid and Megawati, assumed the posts of president and vice president following these first free elections of post-Suharto Indonesia. With parties and candidates now needing to appeal directly to the populace, the rigged electoral procedure that had previously been conducted every five years merely to give the appearance of a democratic system had been truly relegated to history. Politicians in Indonesia's new regime of parliamentarianism needed and obtained democratic legitimacy to govern, thereby ending the monopoly of unlimited authoritarian power.

This was a major setback for Indonesia's big business conglomerates. The time of guaranteed political protection, or at least favouritism, was over and a new era of great uncertainty had begun. Without their main patron – President Suharto, the architect and integral facilitator of the New Order patronage networks – they suddenly lacked the reliable political backing necessary to uphold the well-established symbiotic arrangements between capital and the state. Furthermore, they lost their licence to print money, for which during the New Order proximity to Suharto and his family was decisive. Thus the appointment of Suharto's confidante B.J. Habibie – known for his anti-Chinese sentiment – as his successor was met with consternation. At the beginning of his presidency, Habibie wanted to replace Chinese businesses and 'give the opportunity to the pribumi, who make up the largest population and build them up' (cited in Suryadinata 1999: 11). Commenting on the exodus of Chinese businessmen and their capital, Habibie noted: 'If the Chinese community doesn't come back because they don't trust their own country and society, I cannot force, nobody can force them. [. . .] But do you really think that we will then die? Their place will be taken over by others' (cited in Richburg 1998).

Even more worrisome than the new president – who was in the end himself a product and one of the main protagonists of the New Order – were the many unknown parties, politicians, and administrative elements that the reformed framework brought about. As economist Faisal Basri (interview 14 September 2004) reported, many businessmen relied heavily on Golkar to which they felt indebted because it protected them and provided them with privileges. But now the politico-bureaucrats that had penetrated the state apparatus through Golkar were forced to take a back seat and thus it became very unclear for the conglomerates to see whom they could choose as new partners. Politicians, and even presidents, were appearing and disappearing quickly. For years no distinct power centre inside the party system was able to establish itself. It was thus difficult to identify the important positions and the influential politicians, making the return on investment in bribes very unpredictable.

A similar dilemma surfaced with the emancipation of the civilian sphere from the former all-embracing state. The newly achieved liberalization of society came in stark contrast to the former corporatist regime under Suharto and its granted comforts for cooperating entrepreneurs, where the suppressive state with help of a pervasive developmentalist ideology forced all voices and actions into compliant submission. Now civil society regained two of its basic rights: the freedom of association and the freedom of expression. An increasingly critical population started to organize itself through countless NGOs – new and old – to fight for human rights, equality, transparency or other concerns. Many of them thus balanced, directly or indirectly, those in power. A few groups were explicitly geared towards controlling big business; one example is the *Koalisi Masyarakat Anti Skandal Bank Lippo* (People's Coalition Against the Lippo Bank Scandal), led by prominent figures such as Lin Che Wei and Faisal Basri, that closely monitored the Lippo Group and aimed to prevent excessive fraud (Agam Fatchurrochman, Programme Manager Partnership for Governance Reform in Indonesia, interview 2 September 2004). Indonesia Corruption Watch (ICW) is another group that effectively exposed many cases of fraud. According to Danang Widoyoko (Vice Coordinator of ICW, interview 7 September 2004), ICW's strategy against corruption was to draw public attention to any apparent shady dealings, to deprive businesses of the privacy they previously enjoyed as part of Suharto's corrupt system.

This points to the second characteristic of the achievement of a pro-active civil society, where public opinion weighs in strongly, influencing government and corporate decision-making and providing an important potential support base by which NGOs and other critics can mobilize in aid of their cause. The growing media industry also presented such organizations with an apt campaign platform: Indonesia's new press could print critical opinions without hindrance or fear of retribution, something unprecedented in the entirety of the whole country's history. Many journalists were eager to prove their indispensability to this new liberal society, regarding themselves as guardians of a weak infant democracy, where they could help constitute the fourth power needed to substitute for a non-existent system of checks and balances, as Teguh Santoso (Executive Editor *Rakyat Merdeka*, interview 14 June 2004) emphasized. Through the media, liberal *reformasi* ideas featured prominently in public discourse. To strive for an open society for all was taken on as the common goal.

Such an objective was, of course, not at all in accordance with the interests of the conglomerates; indeed, these developments were detrimental for them. In the eyes of many activists, the corrupt Chinese tycoons had already disqualified themselves through their previous behaviour and could not play a role in a people-based democracy. In several cases, anti-business sentiment became mixed up with anti-Chinese resentment, providing powerful ammunition for populist politicians or indigenous business rivals (see Harsono 2004). Chinese big business came under close media and public scrutiny. Economic historian Thee Kian Wie (interview 19 April 2004) stated confidently that with a free press, the kind of cronyism synonymous with Suharto's New Order would no longer be possible. Businessman Sofjan Wanandi (Gemala Group CEO, interview 08 June 2004) agreed and lamented that 'the conglomerates cannot expect anything from the government anymore. It [. . .] cannot just give monopolies because we now have so many watchdogs here and there that are complaining all the time'. Elsewhere he had disdainfully noted that 'the overall environment for business is far from being favourable. In the case of some, most likely Suharto's children and cronies, there is a witch-hunt taking place' (Wanandi 1999: 131). An anonymous 'consultant who works with many Chinese conglomerates in Jakarta', cited by the *Wall Street Journal* (McDermott and Witcher 1998), claimed with justification that the tycoons would 'much prefer martial law. [. . .] They at least know how to get along with the army'. Now they had to face an increasingly organized, pro-active and critical civil society.

## The end of centralism

The highly centralized and unitary New Order state ensured Jakarta's institutional and political authority over the provinces and districts. Demands for greater regional autonomy were not tolerated during the Suharto years. As the dominance of the centre faded in 1998, several regions started to demand more rights; some of them, like Aceh and East Timor, became more and more insistent in their calls for political independence. To avoid a Balkan-like fragmentation, the new-style central government had no choice but to give in to demands for greater regional self-determination. This acceptance of the developing situation was applauded by the World Bank:

> Decentralization may create a geographical focus at the local level for coordinating national, state, provincial, district, and local programs more effectively and can provide better opportunities for participation by local residents in decision making. Decentralization may lead to more creative, innovative and responsive programs by allowing local 'experimentation.' It can also increase political stability and national unity by allowing citizens to better control public programs at the local level.
>
> (World Bank 2005)

In essence, decentralization was seen as the way to increase the efficiency, immediacy and accountability of government, and to secure Indonesia's political stability and future national unity. In this respect, many responsibilities came to be handed over to more than 400 local governments and the distribution of revenues from natural resources was renegotiated in favour of the districts of origin. *Kabupaten* (districts) and *bupati* (district heads) thus received unprecedented power in relation to the many institutions and ministries based in Indonesia's capital (see Bünte 2003: 129–41). Another measure in favour of decentralization was the removal of the right of the president to virtually be able to approve every single physical investment proposal. Now authorization was only required for large-scale projects worth more than US$100 million (Rosser 2002: 183). This symbolized that the conglomerates' main vehicles for the allocation of favours that used to be based in Jakarta were considerably threatened to be vitiated by Indonesia's move from centralism to decentralization.

The expectation was that these structural adjustments would witness a parallel improvement in the way government, if not business, received and used its power. The World Bank viewed the decentralization of power as an 'ambitious program to tackle corruption in Indonesia from the ground up' by implementing its 'good governance initiative that may pave the way for a major improvement in accountability, transparency and participation at the local level in Indonesia – and it is hoped the economic and poverty reduction performance in the selected regions' (World Bank 2004). To this end, the Bank appealed to local authorities with offers of substantial funding and investments for '50 to 60 of the best local governments' to the tune of more than US$200 million per year, as long as they adhered to 'good governance' reforms and participated in anti-corruption initiatives (*Laksamana.net*,

10 April 2004). As the World Bank's chief governance advisor in Indonesia, Joel S. Hellman (interview 16 September 2004), pointed out, decentralization not only yielded new institutions, it also led to 'a vastly different range of political actors and entirely different interactions with institutions'. The traditional strategies of the conglomerates were thus no longer apposite.

Corruption had become less predictable in its outcomes. As economist Faisal Basri (interview 11 September 2004) stated, 'there is no guarantee, no certainty anymore that your business is successful, because power is more distributed and you have to deal with more than one instance'. He expected that this eventually would result in cleaner companies. Analyst and politician Sjahrir (interview 24 September 2004) concurred and asserted that the conglomerates were being forced to change their behaviour, because in a decentralized Indonesia substantial capital accumulation through corruption would not be possible anymore. Businessmen, such as Pharos boss Eddie Lembong (interview 21 October 2004), confirmed that 'the situation now is difficult. Power is scattered and not concentrated, which makes it complicated for businesspeople to deal with'. The boss of Artha Graha, Tomy Winata, declared:

> During the New Order, everything was easy for Chinese big business: There was one pot of money, contracts and opportunities, and the pot was with the Cendana; now the pot is spread to thousands of people. The political landscape has changed a lot and is more complex than before. Now the social cost of doing business in much higher.
>
> (Tomy Winata, interview 17 September 2004)

Thus, the end of centralized authoritarianism spelled the end of the New Order's centralized system of patronage, from which the conglomerates benefited immensely previously.

## The end of KKN

As long as the state–business oligarchy passed on enough of the huge profits generated during the New Order era, predatory and instrumental control of the Indonesian economy on the part of Suharto's family and his Chinese business cronies was tolerated. Many ordinary Indonesians, as well as foreign investors, were not greatly worried about the hijacked markets that still yielded sufficient revenues for them. On the contrary, Indonesia became one example of a workable economic miracle (World Bank 1993) despite corruption on a massive scale and widespread over-regulation of the economy. Indeed, it was the successful Indonesian case on which the neoliberal World Bank premised the adjustment of its stance on capitalism and the state (World Bank 1997). All the same, as soon as Indonesia's economy crashed, the former apologists resurfaced with their old neoliberal economic model, believing the superiority of which had been proven. They determined that

Indonesia should undergo a thorough process of deregulation to free up markets, supported by a secure network of institutions to implement and safeguard the designated economic reforms.

So the paradigm serving as the supporting logic for the New Order regime's economic policies underwent a dramatic shift. Economic liberalism used to be regarded with suspicion (see Rosser 2002), corroborated by former moves in this direction. Indonesia, driven by internal technocrats and external creditors on the back of a poor macro-economic performance, did undergo some market-oriented reforms in trade, investment and the financial sector between 1986 and 1988 and again from 1994 on (Soesastro 1999). However, the domain where the oligarchy's predatory interests were most thoroughly entrenched remained predominantly untouched by accompanying deregulation measures, which generally enabled the complicity between government and the corporate sector to continue, with several new monopolies seized in the process (Hadiz and Robison 2005). But desperate times call for desperate measures and Indonesia's crisis saw liberalism become the new cure-all for the crisis and against the detrimental effects of KKN – a 'debilitating luxury Indonesia could not afford' (Borsuk 1999: 140). Therefore, Indonesia's highly regulated economy needed to be transformed into one based on open and free markets with minimum intervention. Neoliberal institutions such as the IMF and the World Bank gave the much needed funding through which they enforced programmes of reform. This provided precisely the platform Indonesian reformers required to finally push for policies and measures to realize their economic visions of transparency, unthwarted competition, equal access to opportunities and a self-regulatory market not held back by unreasonable distortions (see, for example, Simanjuntak 2000). Indonesian economists and international observers alike argued that liberalization, deregulation and privatization were imperative if Indonesia were to regain international business confidence (Basri 2004: 55–6).

As a first step, the acceptance of the new rules of market capitalism had to be ensured by creating an appropriate institutional framework. During the New Order, no supervisory boards existed for the purpose of bringing members of the ruling oligarchy to account. A system of checks and balances was urgently needed to lay down the new rules necessary to keep the market free from predatory interests similar to those from the past. Being aware that 'the strengthening of prudential rules and regulations is essential to rebuild the banking industry' (Nasution 2003), and that international investors needed an accountable, reliable and predictable business environment, the new government had to act and establish effective watchdog organizations, reform the courts and implement laws that ensured the unsullied operation of markets.

Several measures to this end received prompt attention. The authority of former 'strategic gate-keeping terminals' (Robison and Hadiz 2004: 76) such as the State Logistics Agency (Bulog) and the National Development Planning Agency (Bappenas) was cut back significantly. New institutions like the Indonesian Bank Restructuring Agency (IBRA) and the Business

Competition Supervisory Commission (KPPU) were founded to scrutinize business practices ensuring no monopolies or unfair market dominance would occur (Faisal Basri, commissioner KPPU, interview 11 September 2004). Their power to act came from a new anti-monopoly law to promote market competition as a means to achieve overall economic efficiency and thereby improve the welfare of the general public (Thee 2002: 333–5). These new watchdog bodies and their legislated mission sent the signal once and for all that the conglomerates finally had to deal with a new deregulated economy based on a vision of unhindered operation of markets and a supporting regulatory framework that would make life difficult for Indonesia's incumbent capitalists. New supervisory boards with some very idealistic members were set up specifically to observe and keep an eye on big business and new rules would protect markets from distortions. The conglomerates had no immunity under this system.

The post-KKN economy could not be used as the personal playground of the former ruling oligarchy. This especially became clear with the abolition of privileges. Most special government projects, such as those in the automobile and aircraft industries, for instance, and all state-sanctioned licences for the import and sale of commodities ranging from cement to 'silly things like garlic' were revoked (Bambang Subiyanto, former Minister of Finance, interview 16 September 2004). Licences – reserved for well-connected businessmen – and credits from banks – up to 80 per cent of which used to be reserved exclusively for big corporations (Habir 1999: 186–7) – were cancelled. All existing government contracts were reviewed and those found to have been concluded through KKN became void (James and Nasution 2001: 199). Indonesia, according to former President Abdurrahman Wahid, had embarked on the road to an 'improved capitalism' in which businessmen could no longer count on close connections with the government, having instead to accept that their interests had become subordinate to the dynamics of the free market and the needs of Indonesia's people (interview 17 September 2004).

It is useful to recount Wallerstein's (1988: 103) premise about the inherent interest of capitalists in monopolies: 'Capitalists do not want competition, but monopoly' because they 'seek profits, maximal profits, in order to accumulate capital, as much capital as possible. They are thereby not merely motivated but structurally forced to seek monopoly positions.' In this sense, an economy operating as a composite of free markets impedes the attainment of abnormal profits and makes it difficult for businesses to become – or remain – very 'big'. Economist Chatib Basri noted that, with the implementation of legislation to ensure free markets, 'old-style business groups' would cease to exist (interview 12 May 2004). Reformer Sjahrir was 'quite sure that there is no way [for the conglomerates] to enjoy the sort of facilities they had in the Suharto era' (interview 24 September 2004). Instead it had become widely expected that they would have no alternative but to adapt and professionalize themselves, in order to survive in Indonesia's new-look free and cleaner economy. 'Since the environment has become liberal and you are a part of the international society, the way of doing business has to be tuned up and trimmed accordingly. We now have to let professional people run the business', Gunadi Sindhuwinata (President Director of Indomobil, interview 22 September 2004) admitted. The conglomerates that survived the 1998 crisis have had to accept, as Farid Haryanto (Lippo advisor, interview 21 June 2004) agreed, that growth is only possible through the market.

Sofjan Wanandi was not alone in his prediction that the conglomerates of the New Order era would disappear sooner or later if they stuck to their old business practices (interview 01 July 2003). Sampoerna's Angky Camaro summed up the changes: 'Now everything is open, licences are available to everyone. We all have to compete in the free market and the mentality of the New Order cannot survive' (interview 17 September 2004). If these experts were right – and in the immediate years after the crisis there were not many indicators that contradicted them – Indonesia's old-style capitalists certainly had a tough job cut out for them. A fundamental change was required if they were to carry on in deregulated markets without the help of KKN. How did the conglomerates survive in this new, even alien, environment?

## CAPITAL AFTER THE CRISIS

Indonesia's post-New Order government chose to focus on reviving the economy rather than restructuring it. To do this capital, domestic or foreign, was urgently needed. But hardly any foreign company was willing to invest in Indonesia (Simanjuntak 2000: 60–1). The new government thus had to somehow lure back those who were used to the way the Indonesian economy worked: the Chinese conglomerates. This desperate plight afflicting Indonesia and its new politicians gave the old corporations the upper hand. They were able to protect themselves from reform initiatives, even in areas of bank restructuring and debt refinancing. Ultimately, economic and political developments in the post-crisis phase were to be closely interrelated and shared one fundamental, somewhat paradoxical feature – the consolidation of the conglomerates.

A substantial amount of private capital – estimates ranged from US$80 billion ('Chinese-Indonesian expect return of overseas funds', *The Jakarta Post*, 26 October 1999) to as much as US$165 billion ('110,000 WNI keturunan belum pulang ke Indonesia', *Merdeka*, 06 June 1998) – had gone overseas with Indonesia's Chinese entrepreneurs. Megawati, as Vice President in 2000, was convinced that the 'repatriation of domestic funds placed abroad would indeed be a great breakthrough to save the country from crisis' (cited in Bhui 2004). This money could provide the fuel urgently needed to jump-start Indonesia's stalled economy and set the country firmly on the road to economic reconstruction. Well aware of their bargaining power, the tycoons set an intact operating environment in structural continuity as a precondition for their return to Indonesia. Indeed, Indonesia's traditional entrepreneurs came to find they did not have to worry too much. Major donors such as the IMF and the World Bank merely urged the Habibie government to strengthen Indonesia's institutions and focus on good governance in order to consolidate initial stabilization gains, to sustain economic recovery and to 'embrace the two sweeping forces of globalization and democratization' (World Bank 1999: i–ii). With only reforms on the surface drawn up to provide support for Indonesia's ailing economy, *reformasi* the way the international donors envisaged was going to have little more than a skin-deep effect on the conglomerates and their old ways of doing business. This strategy of focusing attention only on the symptoms of an ailing system left big business plenty of leeway to operate within the new environment.

The process of debt settlement clearly demonstrated the new-look, old-style relationship between Indonesia's new government and old business interests. Twenty-one major borrowers had defaulted on loans totalling Rp 650 trillion, which were taken over by IBRA and offset against government bonds (Bhui 2004). Instead of viewing the conglomerates as criminal defaulters obliged to repay their debts, IBRA became the main institution which nursed and cared for the ailing business groups even though the rules for the restructuring of loans were straightforward: debts had to be settled with cash or assets, the latter being sold to investors with no connection to the former owners. However, there were several ways for the conglomerates to get around the strict requirements, as became indicative of the slow pace of IBRA's actions. By the end of the year 2000, only 15 per cent of Indonesia's total private debt had been dealt with under IBRA's restructuring programme (Bird 2001: 63). In 2002, IBRA still expected to recover 42 per cent of outstanding non-performing loans from asset disposals and cash settlements, referring to how this recovery rate, in relative terms, 'could hardly be considered as disappointing' (IBRA 2002: 3). However, as its five-year mandate came to an end in February 2004, IBRA had recouped a mere 28.5 per cent of outstanding borrowing, thereby failing by far to reach even its own modest recovery targets (IBRA 2003).

Indonesia's non-performing loan recovery programme sat astride rosy prospects at the outset. By September 2000, several Master Settlement and Acquisition Agreements (MSAA) between IBRA and major debtors had been concluded, with the payment obligations put on record. However, it soon became clear that despite the MSAAs, the conglomerates could do as they wanted. Indonesia's big businesses remained largely unchallenged in their position of strength, supported by the IMF, backed by the government and aided by courts which regularly sided with them and refused to declare them bankrupt. The Lippo Group provides a case in point, as its CEO James Riady purposely ran the group's major listed company, Lippo Bank, 'into the ground in collusion with ING such that he could buy it back cheaply from IBRA' (Roland Haas, former President Director of Lippo Investments, interview 16 June 2004). As result, Riady regained ownership of the bank for 'virtually nothing' (Roland Haas, interview 10 August 2004).

The Salim Group, as another example, was supposed to repay Rp 48 trillion worth of debt, for which it first transferred 78 companies to the government. After it turned out that the market value of the assets was far lower than stated, the group had to add 30 more firms to reach the overall repayment amount of Rp 53 trillion (Sato 2004: 32–3). In 2000 Anthony Salim tried to buy back his assets from IBRA's holding company, Holdiko, in bulk for only Rp 20 trillion ('Babak baru Kwik versus konglomerat', *Kontan*, 31 July 2000). President Wahid and then-IBRA Head Cacuk agreed, thereby acknowledging the hypocrisy of asset sales, accepting a loss for the state of more than Rp 33 trillion and allowing the former owner to repurchase his companies at a discounted price. Eventually Salim failed to proceed with this plan because Coordinating Minister of Economy Kwik Kian Gie – backed by public outrage – objected ('Liem Sioe Liong harus tiru William Soeryadjaya', *Kompas*, 13 November 2000).

IBRA, having to recover as much of the debts as possible, often had no other choice but to give the companies to whomever was willing to pay for them – and these were in many cases the old owners, either disguised as offshore buyers, or through third parties or their overseas companies, as they themselves were officially banned from re-buying their firms. Due to a lack of interest and competition from outside, the debtors were able to determine the conditions of their debt settlement and the price of the assets that they wanted to buy. IBRA's staff usually had no way of examining the cases and exposing the financial tricks and concealments of the assets they were holding, the financial situation of their debtors or the identity of the bidders. In fact, as former IBRA Deputy Chairman Farid Haryanto (interview 21 June 2004) openly admitted, IBRA 'did not want to know' who was behind a deal, confirming that immediate money was more important than a long-term reorientation of the economy.

The whole process of bank recapitalization, debt settlement and asset sales turned out to provide a lifeline for the conglomerates. I Putu Gede Ary Suta, who later became the Head of IBRA, accurately observed, that it was a successful attempt to 'reconstruct an obsolete and defective structure': 'Instead of rigorously separating ownership of private banks from borrowers, there is an eagerness to return banks to their original owners – as long as they can raise capital to repay government loans' (cited in Hadiz and Robison 2005: 227). The conglomerates' indispensability to Indonesia's economic survival provided them with immunity against expropriation, thereby paving the way for their soft landing amid all the turmoil and uncertainty which at first seemed to spell the end to their dominance of the Indonesian economy.

The following section shows how capital was instrumental in consolidating the reform process, thus determining the extent and direction of *reformasi*. From a position of weakness, the conglomerates eventually managed to secure their own survival, dictating the terms of their rehabilitation in the process.

## Democratization

The holding of free elections in Indonesia in 1999 has often been portrayed as the ultimate triumph of democracy. The fact is, however, that the majority of Indonesians remained excluded from substantial participation in the political process. The struggle for political power was confined to only a small group of people. Established politicians rearranged themselves into barely distinguishable parties whose only ideology was the acquisition and retention of power and, thereby, access to state resources. Coalitions among the major parties were possible in any arbitrary combination, being motivated by nothing other than sheer political expediency. Most of the political actors also became interchangeable; very few new faces emerged to join Indonesia's political elite. Many of the leading politicians since 1998 – 'former apparatchik, military men, entrepreneurs, and assorted political hustlers, peddlers and enforcers of the old New Order', to use Hadiz's (2004: 699) description of PDI-P members – had already played a role in Suharto's corporatist regime. Now they had simply moved from the periphery to the actual centres of the state. Having made it there, it hardly suited the new protagonists – former high-profile critics of Suharto such as Abdurrahman Wahid, Amien Rais and Megawati – to dismantle the machinery of the old regime completely. Ironically, all they opted for was the reform of a state apparatus only to the extent that many of its previous crew and handlers simply shuffled their old positions amongst them. The revamped institutions then served as protective shells for both the new and new-look powerholders and their followers. Indonesia's process of political reform centred around nothing more than what was essentially a competition for the capture of the old vehicles of KKN, and not for their abolition or even a complete revamp in line with a programme of all-encompassing reform (Robison and Hadiz 2004: 223–52).

This defining feature of post-Suharto power struggles allowed the conglomerates to be more than just passive onlookers. Having observed the operations of the new government system for a while, their shock about the loss of their main protectors, the former state party Golkar, soon subsided, giving way to a confidence that Indonesia's new electoral democracy was by no means tantamount to structural change which might do them harm. Indonesia's post-crisis political system was serving to uphold the business environment fostered under the old regime and was characterized by major continuities in relation to the kinds of interests that would preside over the political process, to the significant benefit of big business.

Indeed, the new political framework gave Indonesia's old business magnates the opportunity to become involved in politics in either of two ways: in the background as key party financiers, or more actively as politicians themselves – a significant achievement of the new system. During the Suharto period no ethnic Chinese attained any high military or political positions (Chua 2002: 132). With the exception of Suharto's favourite crony and golfing buddy, Bob Hasan, in the former president's last officiating cabinet, and then only for two months, there had never been a minister of Chinese descent. Only a few Chinese had become members of parliament after 1965. Since 1998, however, several well-known ethnic Chinese with business backgrounds started to become politically active, such as PAN's Alvin Lie or PDI-P's Murdaya Poo, even if not in the limelight. The first to claim important positions of office were two of the most successful *pribumi* entrepreneurs: Yusuf Kalla, who became the country's Vice President and Chairman of Golkar; and Aburizal Bakrie, Coordinating Minister for the Economy under President Susilo Bambang Yudhoyono. With the absence of official restrictions, Chinese businessmen are certain to follow this trend (if after a time lag) as it becomes increasingly apparent how politics has obviously turned out to be an effective way to further their business interests.

Hitherto, Chinese tycoons have typically tried to pull political strings from the background. But cost-intensive electoralism has provided the setting whereby capital is a necessity without which candidacy for political office is not affordable. According to Hadiz (2004: 714), even a local election requires several billions of rupiah. Presidential campaigns budgeted between Rp 140 billion and Rp 500 billion per team just for the first round in 2004 (Agustina *et al.* 2004). Obviously, political parties are dependent on large donations from the business world. In 2004, the Megawati camp reported about Rp 66 billion in legal contributions, while the Susilo Bambang Yudhoyono and Yusuf Kalla team tallied Rp 16.4 billion (Adi, Irmawati and Danto 2004).

Money politics' (i.e. politics determined by money) spread down from the top – where ICW, Transparency International, and Auditor Watch (2004) discovered more than Rp 14.5 billion of unreported and thus illegal funds for 2004's presidential candidates – to the bottom of the parliamentary system with 'systematic approaches to members of parliament' made in the hope that they would vote in favour of certain business groups, as MP Alvin Lie (interview 07 September 2004) reported. Lie experienced first-hand the wily way in which tycoons were able to use the new institutions of Indonesia's democracy for personal gain. In one case, where the DPR had to decide about the sale of Indosat, 'material gains and favours' were offered so abundantly and constantly that even some of the initiators of the parliamentary faction against the sale finally supported the opposite position. Instead of separating money and politics, as the move towards parliamentarism had intended, Indonesia's reformed political system had made bedfellows of the two.

Besides the formal institutional side of democracy, Indonesia's business conglomerates had to deal with the new civil sphere. The emergence of a civil society that efficiently controlled and restricted the previously unchecked activities of big business, set standards under which entrenched corporate interests could no longer operate. It was impossible for business to work to contain the new openness of society; their only chance was to adjust. At the rhetorical level, a commitment to democratic ideas was no problem at all. Even controversial tycoon Tomy Winata considered himself to be 'the main engine of democracy in Indonesia' and accepted his 'responsibility to help the country to democratize' (Tomy Winata, interview 17 September 2004). Many observers, understandably, will not accept these kinds of statements at face value. However, opinions given by capitalists regarding their stance on democracy should be taken seriously: on the one hand, their statements alluded to the new hegemony of democratic discourse to which big business had to subscribe. On the other, such comments provided clues as to which kind of democracy Indonesia might be heading towards: a political system significantly defined and moulded by the interests of capital.

This was conditional on the end of official anti-Chinese policies which accompanied the abdication of Suharto's authoritarian regime. The New Order's concerted policy on Chinese ethnicity, by which the government marginalized, stigmatized and discriminated against the Chinese minority (Chua 2004b), was, for the time being at least, no longer applicable. The ironic result of the democratization process was the opening up of societal space for Chinese-Indonesian capitalists, allowing them to become more active and relevant participants in civil society. In this respect, some Chinese tycoons were able to utilize genuine democratic processes for their own purposes. For example, they staged demonstrations to protest against foreign competitors that wanted to take over their companies (Roland Haas, interview 21 September 2004). Rioting, as happened outside the headquarters of *Tempo* magazine by a mob supporting Tomy Winata, could be easily organized (McCawley 2003). The alleged puppeteer himself recognized that 'it is much easier to influence decision-making in a democratic environment specifically in Indonesia. Famished and poor people will do everything to maintain their survival' (Tomy Winata, interview 17 September 2004).

Public opinion, and the manipulation thereof, became yet another new area of mastered abuse. The Salim group, for instance, was eager to get back into the media business, repurchasing its former television broadcasting company Indosiar through proxies (Kwok 2002). According to Ahmad Taufik (*Tempo* journalist, interview 01 September 2004), tycoon Tomy Winata had had enough of trying to pressure the press not to write negatively about him, so he joined the media business himself. Besides starting up the police radio station *911*, the newspaper *Harian Jakarta* and the broadcaster *Jakarta TV*, Winata founded the magazine *Pilar*, positioning it in direct competition to his arch-enemy *Tempo*. With *Pilar*, Winata could provide favourable press about himself and fight *Tempo*'s negative words with his own print, while replacing *Tempo* sales and therefore the rival magazine's extent of influence by pushing *Pilar*'s circulation (Ahmad Taufik, interview 01 September 2004). Winata also allegedly made use of his relationships with influential individuals, such as the son of Jakob Utama, owner of newspaper *Kompas*, and with Abdul Latief, former New Order minister and then-owner of the TV station *Lativi*. Allegations of such relations were not undone by the nature of coverage on the notorious tycoon, tending to be mild at most (Ahmad Taufik, interview 01 September 2004). Another example is Lippo and its relationship manager for extraordinary public relations efforts, including taking journalists for helicopter joyrides, to Kota nightclubs or simply supplementing their incomes (Roland Haas, interview 10 August 2004).

Similar carrot-and-stick methods formed the core of basic tactics used to ensure a complacent level of journalism, reporting in favour of big business's interests. Rather than betting merely on bribes, some businessmen relied on violence and the threat of lawsuits. In angry reaction to a *Tempo* article implying that Winata was behind a deliberate fire at the market in Tanah Abang (Taufik, Rurit and Junaedy 2003), the tycoon allegedly sent a mob to attack *Tempo* headquarters. He then sued the journalist responsible, Ahmad Taufik, sub-editor Teuku Iskandar Ali and editor Bambang Harymurti for defamation and took the magazine to court on seven other charges, with *Tempo* forced to pay penalties totalling US$40 million (McCawley 2003). The decision of the courts to resort to criminal law instead of the press code, with the subsequent conviction of Bambang Harymurti (*Laksamana.net*, 16 September 2004), showed the fragility of press freedom and vulnerable situation that liberal elements in Indonesian society still had to face. Indonesia's business conglomerates, when forced onto the defensive, could still count on corruptible, incompetent judges as well as sections of the media industry. Tycoons also used many other tools at their disposal to intimidate journalists. Most effective – though rather conventional – was the threat to withdraw advertising custom. A more eccentric method, as *Far Eastern Economic Review* correspondent Jeremy Wagstaff reported (interview 11 June 2004), was to send a dead cat's head to the editor of an online news magazine which had investigated some of the Lippo Group's more shady business dealings. The journal was later acquired by Lippo boss James Riady – yet another way of keeping the media reporting favourably with respect to Chinese big business.

Thus, the 'democratization' in Indonesia did not at all anchor the kind of norms hoped for by reformers. On the contrary, parliamentarianism as well as the civil society were regarded and treated by the conglomerates as simple instruments to legitimize their dubious business practices that could henceforth be hidden behind a democratic façade. Indonesian post-Suharto democracy thus provided capital with powerful means and influence on politics and society.

### Decentralization

There is no doubt that the granting of regional autonomy helped to make unfeasible the kind of heavily centralized patronage network that characterized Suharto's New Order regime. The conglomerates' former partners as well as the once guaranteed benefits of that era have faded into the dim distance as Jakarta's powerful politico-bureaucrats got replaced by regional authorities whose say over local resources continues to grow. The New Order dimension of KKN was apparently only possible under a centralized, authoritarian regime. However, although many in business initially deemed the workings of the old system obsolete due to the new complexities of decentralization, *otonomi daerah* ended up being unable to meet the expectations of eliminating corruption and offering a more transparent and efficient decision-making process within Indonesia's regions. In contrast, new decentralized, diffuse patronage networks emerged, which, in many ways, replicated the old systems of patronage in miniaturized form. With the shift of authority to regional bodies, KKN was also transferred to the corresponding lower levels. According to many disillusioned reformers, this was 'the only real democratization that happened' (Sjahrir, Head *Partai Perhimpunan Indonesia Baru*, interview 24 September 2004). The Jakarta-based KKN was merely replaced by decentralized networks of collusion.

It had been an exercise in wishful thinking to expect that corruption could be eradicated by relying on the integrity of the new officials in charge of local or regional institutions. Although Pharos Group boss Eddie Lembong (interview 21 October 2004) had hoped the behaviour of the *bupati* would change over time, actual developments did little to sustain his optimism. Other businessmen complained that district heads of government behaved like absolute rulers over local fiefdoms, a common scenario indicative of how KKN-style power bases were thriving, thereby hindering fair and professional business practices (Angky Camaro, Sampoerna, interview 17 September 2004). Far away from Jakarta it was even more difficult to impose effective controls. One example from West Sumatra illustrates how authority had been abused until the law finally caught up with the perpetrators: almost all the members of one legislative council were jailed for abusing budget powers, while eight more councils in other districts had to face graft probes (Syofiardi 2004). Politicians of this leaning, being extremely prone to seeking extra-legal funding, were therefore ideal new-found friends for hopeful conglomerates. Indonesia's new decentralized political environment turned out to provide an even cheaper and simpler business environment for traditional big business. New projects could be hurried along at less cost than was the case in the old days as a local *bupati* official could not ask for as much of a kickback in money or shares as Suharto's high-ranking bureaucrats would previously have done (Joel S. Hellman, World Bank, interview 16 September 2004). Big business' main difficulty was identifying the right people with whom to deal, but working that out was just a matter of time. Anthony Salim (interview 13 April 2005) was sure that his group had mastered the new, confusing environment of post-Suharto Indonesia, stating, 'I think we adapted ourselves'. What had earlier loomed as a potential stumbling block – the greater unpredictability – had been overcome, as Salim remarked that his managers had figured out the right people to deal with: 'All the directors of my company must have relations with each political department. If this is distribution, of course, they have to talk to the trade department. If this is plantation, they have to talk to the local government.'

However, depending on developing contacts with existing officeholders was only the second-best option: better still was to fill the power vacuum themselves. Some businessmen chose the direct way into elected local political positions via the ballot box. Hadiz (2004: 713–14) reported that many people with a business background began to take advantage of the new paths to power, running for posts of *bupati*. The big conglomerates also realized the increased importance of the districts. Some of them, as Faisal Basri (interview 11 September 2004) claimed, preferred influencing the outcome of local elections by supporting candidates sympathetic to their cause or installing their own men as district leaders, in one case even a relative – nepotism in its literal sense.

When an alternative hierarchy of authority was yet to be established, the conglomerates had enormous freedom. Tomy Winata was practically given near-exclusive access to business opportunities in regions like Aceh and West Papua, for which he was admired as a 'real nationalist' by the President Commissioner of Bank Central Asia, Eugene Galbraith (interview 08 September 2004). The husband of former President Megawati, Taufik Kiemas, emphasized how 'the country needs more "crazy men" like Winata willing to invest in Indonesia's remote provinces' (cited in Borsuk 2003), concealing the fact that only Winata could go into such conflict areas because of his close ties with the military. In other regions, thugs and mobs were hired to terrify local politicians into submission over private interests (Lindsey 2001), again pointing to the new 'prominence of money and intimidation in Indonesia's more decentralized and democratic politics' (Hadiz 2004: 714).

Thus changes to regional autonomy did not end corruption at all, but provided – notwithstanding, at least initially, new factors of uncertainty and unpredictability – a relatively favourable environment for big business, in some cases granting conglomerates an even more advantageous position compared to the situation they had enjoyed under their former political patrons.

## Deregulation

Economic deregulation, another process initiated to liberate market share away from Suharto's New Order cronies, also turned out to have quite the opposite effect. In fact, moves towards deregulation ended up extending new growth opportunities to the old tyrants of the local commercial world. In Indonesia's case, the newly deregulated environment definitely favoured the incumbent players given their extensive capital backing. Benefiting immensely from this position of strength, the Chinese conglomerates were best equipped to start the new era of post-crisis economy from a pole position, with significant funds at their disposal. Business leader and CEO of the Salim Group, Anthony Salim (interview 13 April 2005), asserted that most business groups thrived in Indonesia's new competitive environment. He claimed that his company Bogasari, the world's largest flour producer, had become even more profitable than when it had operated with its former wheat monopoly. Indomobil and Indocement also reported better times compared to under pre-crisis conditions.

Admittedly, the conglomerates first had to overcome unfamiliar problems associated with a more transparent market system, missing old friends like the barriers for competitors to entry and other protective devices ensured under Suharto's supporting regime. One indicator that the old players had successfully managed to carry on within the new framework was the still rampant incidence of corruption. Many of the traditional practices were simply renamed. Instead of 'collusion', businessmen now talked about 'lobbying' (Eugene Galbraith, interview 08 September 2004) or 'communication' (Anthony Salim, interview 13 April 2005), thereby seeming to embrace the goodness of Western-style capitalism while leaving the old ways behind. The ironic reality was that Indonesia's new economic environment was even more infused with money politics. Confronted with previously unimaginable and initially dreaded conditions of unpredictability, Indonesia's worried capitalists discovered that their best chances for survival and eventual comeback lay in compensating for this loss of reliable certainty by securing support and even protection of their interests among the new class of politicians and officials monetarily. As a result, they ended up not only surviving and benefiting from Indonesia's economic deregulation, but attaining positions of power in which they could mould the ongoing process of change to fit their needs.

A good example of this adaptation to conditions was the way conglomerates managed to subordinate the new watchdogs that had been put in place to supervise them. *Reformasi* did not manage to structurally anchor a system of effective checks and balances. Thus, well-intended reforms soon fizzled out before having a chance to have any real impact, since this depended solely on the persons inside the new institutions, most of whom remained loyal to the old system and were unwilling to renounce the ways of KKN. The post-Suharto regime's personnel, therefore, constituted a vulnerable flank for them to infiltrate and win over. Therefore, to prevent uncontrollable interference from a potentially hostile new class of regulators taking hold, the old players invariably worked to bring into position and foster sympathetic relations with people predisposed to an acceptance of their ways, in order to influence the composition, orientation of, and arbitration by many institutions. Numerous examples illustrate how capital market institutions especially were excessively influenced by effectively quasi-proxy representatives of big business interests. The Capital Market Supervisory Board (*Bapepam*) was allegedly in the hands of the Riadys' conglomerate Lippo, as were several IBRA chairs (Roland Haas, interview 31 August 2004). Previous IBRA Deputy Chairman Farid Haryanto used to be a Lippo advisor before he worked for the agency and resumed this post after he left IBRA. Several Bank Indonesia officials were suspected by prominent observers of being on the payroll of the Riadys, including Aulia Pohan, Deputy Governor, and Miranda Goeltom, Senior Deputy Governor, whose elections to these posts were supposedly secured by bribes to members of parliament. The idea was that these officials would then help Lippo and other conglomerates to win back their former assets, and would politely sabotage otherwise unfavourable investigations into the conglomerates, as one respondent (confidential interview 11 September 2004) maintained. Others believe Tomy Winata supported Goeltom so that she would help him to gain control of Bank Permata, which Goeltom actually – though albeit unsuccessfully – tried to do, by lobbying for Winata at the state-owned asset management company PPA, IBRA's successor and the overseeing agency for the sale of Bank Permata (Raden Pardede, Vice President Director PPA, interview 17 September 2004).

In other cases too, the conglomerates did not always get what they wanted from the authorities. Their strategy for dealing with institutions that could not be easily bribed was to utilize the legal system (Indonesia Corruption Watch 2004) since Indonesia's new-look judiciary had, to their relief, by and large welcomed many of the rank-and-file of Suharto's New Order, leaving much of the thinking and culture pervading Indonesia's judicial system largely intact. Through absurd judgments that appear to have been bought, the courts, for instance, turned the anti-monopoly commission KPPU into a paper tiger by regularly ruling in favour of prosecuted business interests. In the case of Indomobil, despite evidence that the bidding carried out for Salim's former car manufacturer was extensively manipulated with the bidders colluding to keep the price low and enable Salim to recoup his assets (Faisal Basri, KPPU commissioner, interview 11 September 2004), the ruling of the anti-monopoly commission was rejected, first by district courts and finally by the Supreme Court. The Supreme Court justified its decision, ruling that the KPPU, being a non-judicial body, had presumptuously used the words 'for the sake of justice, based on the belief in one Supreme God' in its decree (Suryana 2003). Regardless of whether this miscarriage of justice by Indonesia's courts was due to 'gross incompetence or because of tremendous financial lobbying by the business parties' ('Antitrust body challenged', *The Jakarta Post*, 30 July 2002), they had done little to inspire confidence in the legal system except on the part of the old elitists, working hard to keep the system rotten and under their control.

Though former Bank Indonesia Senior Deputy Governor Anwar Nasution characterized his old employer as a 'nest of crooks' (*Laksama.net*, 10 May 2003), the description was obviously valid beyond the central bank, applying to many Indonesian institutions, financial or otherwise. So it was mainly business as usual for Indonesia's capitalists with their entrenched interests, relieved by the way in which the old culture had enjoyed a remarkable reorganization. They had adapted to a process of *reformasi* which had created, in the end, little more than a protective shell for the New Order's old tycoons, still able to buy support from corrupt officials and protection from judges on their payroll.

In reaction to the old conglomerates' resilience to supposedly reformed conditions, some indigenous businesspeople and politicians demanded the adoption of protectionist policies in favour of *pribumi* businesses. Aburizal Bakrie wanted the government to use this 'golden opportunity' to redistribute Chinese-Indonesian property (cited in Eklöf 2002: 232), while Yusuf

Kalla announced a plan to help 'small and medium enterprises', because '90 to 95 percents of the small businessmen are pribumis' (cited in Harsono 2004). Indigenous concerns and criticisms of their Chinese competitors were well-founded, given past experience. During Suharto's economic reforms of the 1980s, the big conglomerates were the main winners from deregulation and privatization (see Hadiz and Robison 2005). Public monopolies simply became private ones, further strengthening the dominance of Chinese-Indonesian business groups and catapulting many of them into the league of Western multinational enterprises. Rage over this discrimination of non-Chinese business interests typical during Suharto's time fuelled opposition to the neoliberal approach favoured by the IMF and others. *Pribumi* business groups have particularly been suspicious of laissez faire 'free-fight-capitalism', believing it to disadvantage indigenous entrepreneurs. Populism – a term synonymous with economic nationalism in Indonesia, specifically referring to protectionism in favour of *pribumi* – became an important force, weighing in heavily on several political issues. The power of populism was such to prevent noted economist and regional IMF head Sri Mulyani from taking up the post of Indonesia's Minister of Economics ('Susilo bends under pressure', *The Jakarta Post,* 20 October 2004). Instead, *pribumi* entrepreneur Aburizal Bakrie received this key portfolio. Along with Vice President Yusuf Kalla, Indonesia now had two businessmen-turned-politicians occupying very senior positions in government, both of whom supported adopting wealth redistribution programmes based on ethnicity, as was practised in Malaysia. The notion of free markets, therefore, became a highly contentious issue even within the inner circles of Indonesia's new government.

The conglomerates therefore had to balance carefully their opposition to IMF-proposed programmes for economic liberalization and deregulation, since a swing of the pendulum in the other direction could cause much more harm. It was better for the Chinese tycoons to deal with and work within an economic environment that was perceived by others as neutral and served their interests on the whole, than with one that was inherently hostile towards them – another reason for many of the big businessmen to become nominally fervent supporters of free markets.

## CONSOLIDATION

There is no doubt that Indonesia's political environment experienced dramatic change as a result of the financial crisis which struck the nation in 1997–98. The reform process seemed to be victorious as it threw off the yoke of Suharto's predatory, centralized authoritarianism and the country moved towards more political, economic and social freedom with the introduction of deregulation, decentralization and democracy. Economic liberalism, with safeguards put in place and overseen by various watchdog organizations, substituted for the domineering collusive practices of Suharto's tycoon cronies which had long controlled Indonesia's markets, weighed down by endemic oligarchical structures. Regional autonomy succeeded Jakarta's centralism, electoralism and the emergence of a civil society replaced Suharto's dictatorship. For the tycoons and their conglomerates, the intentions of all these new processes sounded death knells to their continuing dominance of Indonesia's economy as the reform programmes 'swept away the financial and political arrangements that held this system together' (Robison and Hadiz 2002: 39). However, *reformasi* failed to provide a fundamental break with the past. The actual degree of democratization achieved ended up being little more than a modification of Suharto's old system with a mere veneer of minor variations. Real institutional structures were not significantly altered – nor was there the intention to do so, as most of the new key powerholders merely wanted to transform and control the old system rather than completely revamp it in favour of some squeaky clean system incongruous with their interests. As a result, the reformation of the old regime went nowhere near deep enough to be called a true restructuring of Indonesia's institutions, or to seriously harm the interests of the surviving New Order oligarchy.

The old structures remained intact because of their links with and the general economy's dependence on the capital held by the Chinese conglomerates. Suharto was gone, but Indonesia's big businesses became indispensable to the resuscitation of the country's economy, because of the money and know-how only they possessed. In the end, ironically, the crisis ended up triggering a series of processes and mechanisms which yielded new opportunities for growth and consolidation of the conglomerates. Their capital and other resources proved to be the lifeblood of Indonesia's economy. Realizing that their country and whatever new regime would always need them, they were able to ensure enough of the old system remained in place for them to later revitalize and use to their advantage. From this advantageous position, Indonesia's conglomerates advanced to recover many assets previously lost and to recoup earlier losses, further stoking their arsenals to be able to resist any further intended do-gooder reforms.

Their collective reaction to *reformasi* is responsible for the survival and carry-over of many of the main features of the New Order to Indonesia's post-crisis political, judicial and economic system. The incumbent capitalists' much needed capital doubled as leverage in 'lobbying' efforts with the new system's politicians and officials, who were open to bribes and influence just like in the good old days under Suharto. Many politicians could not successfully run election campaigns without such welcome financial support, later acting as front men for the capitalists in removing the teeth from any proposed reform measures. Money helped ease the way ahead for the conglomerates in their dealings with officials and others in Indonesia's new civil society. The end of the centralized state brought many grey areas, providing new opportunities for conglomerates as they learnt how much cheaper it was to gain access to and influence regional decision-makers, who were easier to bribe compared to the old regime's powerful, Jakarta-based gatekeepers.

Similarly, reality showed how the new watchdogs, through infiltration and corruption, posed no serious obstacle for big business to freely seek the new profits offered in abundance by the free market.

In this way, the conglomerates' response to Indonesia's new political processes, economic deregulation and social reforms cannot be evaluated as solely reactionary. Their initial intention may have been to prevent the complete overthrow of the New Order system, but big business soon realized how they could invariably influence the various outcomes of democratization, decentralization and deregulation and reshape what thereafter remained of *reformasi* in accordance with their needs. In the end, the post-Suharto environment provided conditions that not only let them survive, but proved particularly beneficial to Indonesia's Chinese conglomerates. Initially daunting and unfamiliar, Indonesia's post-authoritarian environment gave rise to a plutocratic regime that removed the barriers previously designed to limit and control Chinese big business, and enabled capital and its holders in general to become emancipated from the hegemonic dominance of politico-bureaucrats. Behind the surface of a lingering *status-quo*, a major shift in the balance of power is taking place between Indonesia's political and economic elites, by which capital will eventually gain the upper hand over the political sphere. This is because democratic consolidation in Indonesia has essentially been, by being inextricably linked to the relevance and power of capital, foremost a consolidation of capitalist power.

## BIBLIOGRAPHY

Adi, M., Irmawati and Danto (2004) 'When money talks', *Tempo*, 30 August: 18–19.

Agustina, W., Hayati, I., Aditya, D., Danto and Dhyatmika, W. (2004) 'Crooning for campaign funds', *Tempo*, 21 June: 16–17.

Basri, M.C. (2004) 'Economic update 2003. After five years of reformasi ekonomi, what next?', in M.C. Basri and P. van der Eng (eds) *Business in Indonesia. New challenges, old problems*, Singapore: Institute of Southeast Asian Studies.

Bhui, A. (2004) 'IBRA's closure leaves Indonesia major challenge of avoiding new crisis', *AFX Asia*, 26 February. Online. Available HTTP: <www.infid.be/ibra_afx.-htm> (accessed 14 August 2007).

Bird, K. (2001) 'The economy in 2000. Still flat on its back?', in G.J. Lloyd and S.L. Smith (eds) *Indonesia today. Challenges of history*, Singapore: Institute of Southeast Asian Studies.

Borsuk, R. (1999) 'Markets. The limits of reform', in D.K. Emmerson (ed.) *Indonesia beyond Suharto. Polity, economy, society, transition*, New York and London: M.E. Sharpe.

——— (2003) 'How to stay on top', *Far Eastern Economic Review*, 23 October.

Bünte, M. (2003) *Regionale Autonomie in Indonesien. Wege zur erfolgreichen Dezentralisierung*, Hamburg: Institut für Asienkunde.

Chua, C. (2002) *Indonesiens Chinesen. Konstruktion und Instrumentalisierung einer ethnischen Minderheit*, Hamburg: Institut für Asienkunde.

—— (2004a) 'Old faces – new order', *The Jakarta Post*, 19 May: 10.

—— (2004b) 'Defining Indonesian Chineseness in New Order Indonesia', *Journal of Contemporary Asia*, 33 (4): 465–79.

Eklöf, S. (2002) 'Politics, business, and democratization in Indonesia', in E.T. Gomez (ed.) *Political business in East Asia*, London and New York: Routledge.

Fealy, G. (2001) 'Parties and parliament. Serving whose interests?', in G. Lloyd and S. Smith (eds) *Indonesia today. Challenges of history*, Singapore: Institute of Southeast Asian Studies.

Habir, A.D. (1999) 'Conglomerates. All in the family?', in D.K. Emmerson (ed.) *Indonesia beyond Suharto. Polity, economy, society, transition*, New York and London: M.E. Sharpe.

Hadiz, V.R. (2004) 'Decentralization and democracy in Indonesia. A critique of neo-institutionalist perspectives', *Development and Change*, 35 (4): 697–718.

Hadiz, V.R. and Robison, R. (2005) 'Neo-liberal reforms and illiberal consolidations. The Indonesian paradox', *The Journal of Development Studies*, 41 (2): 220–42.

Harsono, A. (2004) 'Indonesian Chinese face economic discrimination', *The American Reporter*, 13 November.

Heryanto, A. (1999) 'Rape, race, and reporting', in A. Budiman, B. Hateley and D. Kingsbury (eds) *Reformasi. Crisis and change in Indonesia*, Clayton: Monash Asia Institute.

Indonesia Corruption Watch (2004) 'Lifting the lid. "Judicial mafia" ', Jakarta: Indonesia Corruption Watch.

Indonesia Corruption Watch, Transparency International Indonesia and Auditor Watch (2004) 'Analisa atas laporan audit dana kampanye Capres dan Cawapres'. Online. Available HTTP: <http://www.antikorupsi.org/docs/analisadanakampan ye.pdf> (accessed 01 December 2004).

Indonesian Bank Restructuring Agency (IBRA) (2002) *IBRA 2002. Operational report*, Jakarta: IBRA.

—— (2003) *Monthly report. December 2003*, Jakarta: IBRA.

James, W.E. and Nasution, A. (2001) 'Economic reforms during the crisis and beyond', in F. Iqbal and W.E. James (eds) *Deregulation and development in Indonesia*, Westport: Praeger.

Kwok, Y. (2002) 'Indonesia fears Salim will win BCA', *CNN.com*, 11 January. Online. Available HTTP: <edition.cnn.com/2002/BUSINESS/asia/01/11/indonesia.bca/ ?related> (accessed 14 August 2007).

*Laksamana.net* (2004) 'A long way to go', 10 April 2004. Online. Available HTTP: <http://www.laksamana.net/vnews.cfm?ncat=25&news_id=6892>          (accessed 14 August 2007).

*Laksamana.net* (2004) 'BLBI muddies Bank Indonesia governor race', 10 May 2003. Online. Available HTTP: <http://www.laksamana.net/vnews.cfm?news_id=5312> (accessed 14 August 2007).

Lindsey, T. (2001) 'The criminal state. Premanisme and the new Indonesia', in G.J. Lloyd and S.L. Smith (eds) *Indonesia today. Challenges of history*, Singapore: Institute of Southeast Asian Studies.

McCawley, T. (2003) 'The press as both victim and villain', *Far Eastern Economic Review*, 23 October.

McDermott, D. and Witcher, S.K. (1998) 'Wealthy Chinese who fled unrest in Indonesia itch to get back to the only world they know', *The Wall Street Journal*, 22 May: 1.

Nasution, A. (2003) 'Combating money laundering and terrorist financing', *The Jakarta Post*, 15 February.

Richburg, K.B. (1998) 'Habibie pushes for visit to U.S.', *The Washington Post*, 19 July: A23.

Robison, R. and Hadiz, V.R. (2002) 'Oligarchy and capitalism. The case of Indonesia', in L. Tomba (ed.) *East Asian capitalism. Conflicts, growth and crisis*, Milan: Fondazione Giangiacomo Feltrinelli.

—— (2004) *Reorganising power in Indonesia. The politics of oligarchy in an age of markets*, London and New York: RoutledgeCurzon.

Rosser, A. (2002) *The politics of economic liberalisation in Indonesia. State, market and power*, Richmond, Surrey: Curzon.

Sato, Y. (2004) 'The decline of conglomerates in post-Soeharto Indonesia. The case of Salim group', *Taiwan Journal of Southeast Asian Studies*, 1 (1): 19–43.

Schwarz, A. (1999) *A nation in waiting. Indonesia's search for stability* (2nd edn.), New South Wales: St Leonards.

Simanjuntak, D.S. (2000) 'The Indonesian economy in 1999. Another year of delayed reform', in C. Manning and P. van Dierman (eds) *Indonesia in transition. Social aspects of reformasi and crisis*, Singapore: Institute of Southeast Asian Studies.

Soesastro, H. (1999) 'Government and deregulation in Indonesia', in C. Barlow (ed.) *Institutions and economic change in Southeast Asia. The context of development from the 1960s to the 1990s*, Cheltenham and Northampton, MA: Edward Elgar.

Suryadinata, L. (1999) *The ethnic Chinese issue and national integration in Indonesia*, Singapore: Institute of Southeast Asian Studies.

Suryana, A. (2003) 'KPPU loses legal battle in Indomobil case', *The Jakarta Post*, 17 January.

Syofiardi B.J. (2004) 'Eight more councils face graft probes', *The Jakarta Post*, 03 July.

Taufik, A., Rurit, B. and Junaedy, C. (2003) 'Ada Tomy di "Tenabang" ', *Tempo*, 09 March: 30–1.

Thee Kian Wie (2002) 'Competition policy in Indonesia and the new anti-monopoly and fair competition law', *Bulletin of Indonesian Economic Studies*, 38 (3): 331–42.

Ufen, A. (2002) *Herrschaftsfiguration und Demokratisierung in Indonesien 1965–2000*, Hamburg: Institut für Asienkunde.

Wallerstein, I. (1988) 'The bourgeois(ie) as concept and reality', *New Left Review*, I (167): 91–106.

Wanandi, S. (1999) 'The post-Soeharto business environment', in G. Forrester (ed.) *Post-Soeharto Indonesia. Renewal or chaos?*, Singapore: Institute of Southeast Asian Studies.

World Bank (1993) *The East Asian miracle. Economic growth and public policy*, New York: Oxford University Press.

—— (1997) *World development report 1997. The state in a changing world*, New York: Oxford University Press.

—— (1999) *Indonesia. From crisis to opportunity*, Jakarta: The World Bank.

—— (2004) 'Tackling corruption in Indonesia', *News & Broadcast*, 8 April. Online. Available HTTP: http://web.worldbank.org/WBSITE/EXTERNAL/NEWS/0,contentMDK:20190200~menuPK:34457~pagePK:34370~piPK:34424~the Site PK::4607,00.html> (accessed 14 February 2005).

—— (2005) 'Decentralization and subnational regional economics'. Online. Available HTTP: <http://www1.worldbank.org/publicsector/decentralization> (accessed 11 February 2005).

# 10 From *dwifungsi* to NKRI

## Regime change and political activism of the Indonesian military

*Jun Honna*

## INTRODUCTION

Assessing the political role of the military in the post-authoritarian Indonesia is an important inquiry into the country's evolution of democratic polity. Since the fall of President Suharto in May 1998, the military has been pressured by both society and the international community to withdraw from politics, professionalize its institutional orientation, subordinate to the principle of civilian control and return to the barracks. Yet, a decade after Suharto's downfall the process of military disengagement from politics is still incomplete, resulting in the formation of 'defective democracy' in which civilian and military elites share political power in the democratic system. Military leaders have preserved considerable powers under the civilian governments and they have influenced, albeit not dominated, political decisions and policies of civilian leaders during the post-Suharto era. Why it is that civilian political elites are incapable of navigating the military into the barracks? How can the military yield power under the democratic political environment? The scholarship of Indonesian politics has attempted to answer these questions by analysing the problems of military reform, civilian politics and weak civil society in the newly democratizing polity.[1]

What is rarely discussed, however, is the historical context. If the military still enjoys its political power, how does it differ from the past? This question requires us to look back and locate the present civil–military relations in the broader context of historical development since the pre-Suharto period. This chapter discusses Indonesia's military politics from this perspective and attempts to clarify how the military has played different political roles in response to the change in the political regime, while maintaining a constant self-role perception as the 'guardian of the nation'. This assessment will illustrate how the military elite has adapted its role to maximize its power in the civil–military political equilibrium of the time. Thus, bringing the military into the uncharted zone of 'civilian control' is only possible if the equilibrium is established in that favour, and it may depend largely on the regime leaders who are capable of minimizing the political space captured by the military.

Below, the characteristics of military politics in different regime periods shall be analysed. During the ten-year 'Parliamentary Democracy' period (1949–58), generals participated in politics as a political force competing with the various political parties. Under Sukarno's Guided Democracy (1959–65), the military emerged as one of the three dominant powers – together with President Sukarno and the Indonesian Communist Party (PKI). During the early stage of Suharto's authoritarian New Order regime (1966–98), the military became a single powerful political force dominating the polity. The military legitimized its political hijacking by developing the doctrine of 'dual function,' or *dwifungsi*. In the twilight of the New Order, however, the military was transformed into the guardian of Suharto's personal political agenda. After his fall from power in 1998, the country's second attempt at democracy forced the military to be one among equals and provided a new role as the veto power for defending the national unity. Clearly the mode of military engagement in politics varied over time. The shift was not because the military had changed its political activism – it had always tried to maximize political power – but was due to the regime architects of the time who determined the acceptable areas and scopes of military engagements in non-military affairs.

## THE PRE-NEW ORDER MILITARY: FREEDOM-FIGHTERS IN POLITICS

The Indonesian military was born in the independence struggle against Dutch attempts to resume colonial power following the three-year Japanese interregnum (1942–45). After Indonesia's national leaders, Sukarno and Hatta, had proclaimed independence on 17 August 1945, the nation embarked on a revolutionary war. Lacking the means to conduct conventional warfare, Indonesia's independent fighters engaged in guerrilla warfare against the Dutch, who were intent on the resumption of white colonial rule. The four-year armed struggle – which ended in 1949 with the recognition of Indonesia's sovereignty – greatly contributed to the formation of military thinking and the military's role in the newly independent nation.

In fact, the nature of guerrilla warfare hardly distinguished the boundary between military and non-military affairs (Said 1991). From its inception the Indonesian army was not simply a defence force; it also served as a multi-functional force. In the absence of viable administrative structures soldiers tended to have a hand in various economic, administrative, political and social fields of national life all over the archipelago. It was due to such a legacy that the army continued to play non-military roles even after independence, as opposed to the 'professional army' model based on the principle of non-interference in politics. Moreover, the war of independence effectively allowed the Indonesian revolutionary armed forces to portray themselves as the guardians of the nation, and this was the reason behind the post-revolutionary army's claim to its 'historical legitimacy' to engage in the political decision-making of the new nation-state.

The achievement of independence, however, did not guarantee a stable management of the new nation-state. In its attempts to reconcile different societal interests, the adopted parliamentary democracy regime did not deliver the political stability and economic progress expected of this political mechanism. While reflecting the country's ethnic, religious and regional diversities which had, to some extent, been put aside during the national independence struggle and which had been largely kept apart under Dutch and Japanese colonial rule, national politics in the post-colonial era revealed the difficulties of handling all these differences that were now brought into the formal political process. This social diversity, represented by various political parties, was usually established along ethnic, regional, religious and ideological lines. In this way, the country's first general election in 1955 helped sharpen the social conflict represented by the political parties rather than provide stability. The rise and fall of weak coalition governments also revealed the vulnerability of Indonesia's parliamentary democracy in the day-to-day running of the country.

During this period, the army participated in the parliament via its political wing, IPKI (League of Upholders of Indonesian Freedom), a party created by the then army commander, Abdul Haris Nasution.[2] The army had been intensively engaged in the suppression of uprisings and secessionist attempts. But when a stronger form of political leadership to counter these attempts was perceived to be necessary the army lobbied for President Sukarno to dissolve the parliament and create a strong authoritarian government. The army's concern about the increasing territorial fragmentation, caused by lingering Islamic (Darul Islam) separatist movements in West Java, Aceh and South Sulawesi since 1949, was encouraged by the breakout of regional rebellions (so-called PRRI/Permesta) in Sumatra and Sulawesi in 1956–58.[3] The US government covertly supported these rebellions in an attempt to block the increasing penetration of the communist influence in the archipelago (Kahin and Kahin 1995). Following the imposition of martial law in March 1957 and the subsequent army crackdown of the rebels in 1958, President Sukarno declared Indonesia's return to the 1945 Constitution which granted strong presidential power, and then established an authoritarian regime under the slogan of Guided Democracy in 1959. With this, Indonesia's experiment with parliamentary democracy was finally over.

Under Sukarno's Guided Democracy (1959–65) the political role of the military was enhanced. However, it was not to dominate the government, as explained by General A.H. Nasution in his famous 1958 speech about the desired role of the army. Instead, it was to pursue *Jalan Tengah*, or a 'Middle Way', as the military was to take a position halfway through the spectrum of 'dominating government' and subordination to 'civilian political authority'. Nasution insisted that Indonesia's army would neither follow Latin American militaries' tendency to establish military governments, nor Western professional militaries with their principle of civilian supremacy (Sundhaussen 1982). The idea actually reflected the civil–military power equilibrium at that time as the army had gained political influence after the 1957 establishment of martial law, although it was far from controlling the government. Thus Sukarno – the father of independence – sought to counterbalance military influence and consolidate Indonesian nationalism and territorial integrity with the use of constant mass mobilizations. He believed that PKI could be the driving force needed to achieve this end. On the other hand, Sukarno saw the army as a crucial force in materializing his adventuristic foreign policies, which were based on anti-Western nationalism, as evident in the military campaigns to 'liberate' West Irian in 1961–2 and its attempts to prevent the formation of Malaysia in 1963.[4] In this way, both the army and the PKI emerged as the two main political pillars, which competed against each other to gain influence in the Sukarno regime during the Guided Democracy period.

This competition between the military and the communists reached its peak in the alleged communist-led abortive coup in September 1965, in the course of which several high-ranking generals were killed. This event provided the perfect opportunity for the army to defeat the PKI and also to wrest power from President Sukarno, who was seen as being too close to the PKI and whose domestic and foreign policies were regarded as detrimental to the country and to the interests of the army as a whole. In the process of this bloody power-struggle, the army was to finally emerge as the most powerful institution in the polity.

## THE EARLY NEW ORDER MILITARY: THE REGIME BUILDER

The structures of military rule were constructed after the forced collapse of the Guided Democracy. The abortive coup in September 1965 resulted in the concentration of power in the hands of Major General Suharto (the Commander of the Army Strategic Reserve Command, or Kostrad) who had led the army troops which crushed the coup attempt. Suharto's military accused the PKI of leading the coup and encouraged students and Muslims to join in the army-orchestrated anti-PKI campaigns throughout the archipelago.[5] Pressured by the military which claimed that the political order could not be restored under the current circumstances, President Sukarno finally authorized Suharto to take all necessary measures to restore law and order in March 1966.[6] By this time, military-orchestrated violence had already eliminated the PKI and thus Sukarno's main civilian building block in his Guided Democracy regime. Now unconstrained by the PKI and without other civilian rivals at the national level, the armed forces had enjoyed wider political autonomy in the civil–military power equilibrium and become the dominant force in determining the direction of post-1965 Indonesian politics.

Following the official transfer of the presidency from Sukarno to Suharto in March 1968, Suharto consolidated military rule by emphasizing 'stability and order' as the necessary preconditions for economic recovery and development; ideas that had long been sidelined by Sukarno in his pursuit of anti-Western foreign policies and constant revolution.

Unlike the previous regime led by Sukarno who – as the leader of national independence – favoured populist mobilization of political forces to consolidate national integration and to pursue his radical domestic and foreign policies, Suharto's Indonesia made economic modernization the primary goal of the regime in order to 'save' the nation from the disastrous economic situation in the final Sukarno years. The military's political control was justified as being indispensable in order to safeguard national stability as the foundation for economic development and modernization.

This became the turning point in the history of Indonesia's civil–military relations. Generals were no longer satisfied with their mere 'participation' in politics, which was the original projection of their 'guardian' self-image, but were highly motivated to dominate the polity. Such a transformation occurred as the result of the infusion of the 'developmentalism' idea in the minds of the officer corps. Developmentalism, or modernization ideology, provided the military with a rationale that identified political stability as the precondition for development (Honna 2001). Since modernization was a decades-long national project, long-term political stability was thought to be crucial. This motivated the military to assume total control of the political process. Furthermore, such political intervention was not designed as a temporary measure but as a permanent one. These transformations of military thinking and motivation were notable in the transition from the post-independence to the Suharto regime.

It was against this background that the doctrine of *dwifungsi*, or dual function, was officially adopted by the military (ABRI) at the beginning of the New Order.[7] *Dwifungsi* claimed ABRI's 'permanent' role in the defence and socio-political fields and was seen as an embodiment of ABRI's 'historical mission' to protect national unity after the war of independence. Since *dwifungsi*'s primary goal in the New Order polity was the maintenance of national stability for economic development, several political programmes were introduced to this end, as discussed below.

Political repression and ideological surveillance were the major tools used in constructing and maintaining the New Order regime. Soon after the 1965 coup attempt the army established a security agency, the Operational Command for the Restoration of Security and Order (*Kopkamtib*) – headed by Suharto himself – which conducted a wide range of internal security measures, including the ideological screening of party candidates and government employees, elimination of communist remnants and the suppression of campus and labour activists. With this 'military within the military' as the core of ABRI's repressive apparatus, everyday politico-ideological surveillance was institutionalized in the country's social life (Tanter 1990).

Kopkamtib's activities were backed by military area commands which controlled political life in each geographic territory.[8] In remote areas of the archipelago, such as Aceh, Irian Jaya and East Timor (annexed in 1976), anti-separatist security operations became standard practice. In urban areas, military repression targeted the press, students, intellectuals, Islamic groups, and labour and legal activists, who were often labelled as being against the New Order. In the name of establishing a stable political system, Suharto relied on ABRI's repressive role with the doctrinal backup of *dwifungsi*.

Together with the repression of opposition, social participation in the formal political structure was tightly restricted. To ensure the regime's stability the influence of the existing political parties was reduced drastically with the establishment of a governmental party, Golkar (*Golongan Karya*, or Functional Group), which all public servants were forced to join and support. ABRI members were also appointed to the parliament (DPR) where they sat as members of the ABRI faction (F-ABRI) both at national and regional levels, as part of the *dwifungsi* mission to ensure political stability in the legislative sector.[9] ABRI members also penetrated non-military administrative bodies by occupying key positions from department ministers to village heads. Sending officers to non-military sectors, called *kekaryaan*, was justified as a necessary measure to ensure the smooth implementation of the government's development projects and to overcome alleged civilian incompetence in handling government tasks.[10] The programme of *dwifungsi* – namely the backing for Golkar, *kekaryaan* penetration and military representation in the parliament – tightly restricted political participation. In this way, under Suharto's New Order, which called for the country's all-out endeavour to achieve economic development, the military became the dominant player of the authoritarian regime building.

However, it should be noted that having wide consensus among top generals regarding the military's eagerness to be the regime builder did not automatically guarantee their agreement on the actual implementations of the *dwifungsi* policies. As the communist sweep was almost complete and a sense of political stability had been produced by the government-manipulated 1971 elections, there arose an increasing diversity of opinions regarding the practice of *dwifungsi*. Some elite military officers started to question the political programmes directed by Suharto and his close associates under the name of *dwifungsi*. Such rivalries between officers frequently undermined cohesion within the military, and in the early 1980s several prominent retired officers, including General (retired) A.H. Nasution (to whom the *dwifungsi* concept is often attributed), accused Suharto and ABRI of having misled the nation. They established a critical group consisting of 50 members, including retired officers and civilian intellectuals, calling themselves *Petisi* 50 (Petition of 50).

Despite the emergence of intra-military cleavages during the early period of the New Order, ABRI's subsequent development under the leadership of Murdani showed increasing cohesion within the military. From 1983 to 1988,

Murdani, as ABRI Commander, emerged as the most powerful commander ever seen in the past decades. It was Murdani's hard-line ABRI which supported Suharto's regime consolidation by the mid-1980s.

## THE LATE NEW ORDER MILITARY: A TOOL OF SUHARTO

From then on, however, the relationship between the President and ABRI began to change, as only a threat from within the military could really threaten Suharto's position. Suharto probably found that he had become too dependent on ABRI and started to widen his power base by relying less on ABRI in non-security affairs. Under Suharto's Fourth Development Cabinet (1983–88), Sudharmono, the head of the state secretariat, was given increased presidential trust. As Secretary of State he had authority over budget allocations and allocated much of it to support the business activities of indigenous Indonesians, or *pribumi*. This resulted in a decline in budget allocations to ABRI's business activities.[11] Also, as the Golkar Chairman from 1983 to 1988, Sudharmono attempted to make Golkar more independent of ABRI. This was achieved by recruiting new cadres from the ranks of businesses who might provide financial support for Golkar, which would in turn reduce ABRI's influence in Golkar's administration (Pangaribuan 1995: 58–9). ABRI leaders were hostile to Sudharmono's attempts even though they had been approved by Suharto, and it was against this backdrop that Murdani moved to block Suharto's attempt to appoint Sudharmono as the Vice President in 1988. Just before the presidential (and vice presidential) elections at the MPR, Suharto therefore eased Murdani out of his central position as ABRI Commander by giving him the less important position of Defence Minister. This 1998 event exacerbated the cleavage between Suharto and Murdani.

Suharto sought to counter this challenge to his rule by incorporating political Islam into the regime and by re-establishing a loyal military. This twofold strategy characterized political developments in the late New Order period. Suharto's strategic shift from repression to co-option of Islam was embodied by the creation of Indonesian Association of Muslim Intellectuals (ICMI) in December 1990. This Suharto-sponsored body was chaired by his civilian protégé, Professor B.J. Habibie (Minister of Research and Technology). The military leadership, led by Murdani and General Try Sutrisno, the new ABRI Commander, was very suspicious of ICMI. They suspected that Suharto was attempting to counterbalance ABRI by creating ICMI in order to secure his own political power (author's interview with General (retired) Benny Murdani, 23 September 1996 and 4 March 1997). They were also concerned that Habibie would consolidate his independent power base outside the military control and challenge ABRI in the presidential and vice presidential elections in 1993 (Hefner 2000; Ramage 1995).

Suharto's transformation of ABRI was accelerated after his presidential re-election in 1993. He tactically received Sutrisno as Vice President to show his respect to the military as an institution, but gave no significant authority to the former ABRI Commander, whose military position could now be given to a more loyal follower. Defence Minister Murdani also lost his strong political influence after the formation of the new Cabinet (1993–98) in which he did not belong. Now, it was time for the President to fully restructure the ABRI leadership for his own benefit.

A serious impediment encountered by Suharto in this effort was the generation gap. As a remnant of the revolutionary generation, Suharto seemed less capable of judging loyalist officers of the new generation – except for his military aids. Inevitably, Suharto started to accept the advice of trusted cronies in selecting officers who would occupy strategic positions. The role of his family – including Sitit Hardijanti Rukmana, the eldest daughter; Brigadier General Prabowo, the ambitious presidential son-in-law, married to Mamick (Suharto's youngest daughter); and even Habibie, whom Suharto had known since Habibie was a child – became increasingly apparent in military promotion practices. In May 1993, General Feisal Tanjung, a devout Muslim and long-time friend of Habibie, was appointed as the new ABRI Commander based on strong recommendations by Habibie and Prabowo. General Wismoyo Arismunandar, a brother-in-law of Suharto's wife, was named as the new Army Chief. He was later replaced by General Hartono, a close ally of Prabowo, in February 1995.

In contrast to the previous ABRI leadership under Murdani and Sutrisno, the Feisal–Hartono leadership appealed to Islamic aspirations and extensive cooperation with ICMI. This new trend was widely seen as the 'Islamization' or 'greening' (referring to the Islamic colour) of ABRI. In fact, those officers who showed strong personal commitment to Islam were now respected and earmarked for promotions. Such a trend was a historically remarkable shift as the New Order military had traditionally valued secular nationalist orientations in conducting its *dwifungsi* roles. A dispute soon emerged within society and in particular among retired generals, criticizing the trend as self-destructive for ABRI's manifested principle of being the 'national guardian'.

Above all, Suharto's efforts to reconstruct President–ABRI relations on a new basis, and his search for loyalist officers to this end, were increasingly mediated by Habibie and Feisal as well as by Prabowo and Hartono. The transformation of ABRI's high command in the post-Murdani period was managed through such processes and the renewed ABRI leadership was credibly amenable to the First Family. Suharto relied on these key allies to prepare for the smooth handling of both the 1997 general elections – in which he was expected to face a serious opposition movement centred on Megawati Sukarnoputri, daughter of Sukarno (Indonesia's first president), who chaired the Indonesian Democratic Party (PDI) – and the 1998 presidential election. Against this political backdrop, the new ABRI leadership tended to be dogmatically intolerant and repressive toward the widening popular criticism of the government and the growing democratic movements. ABRI soon identified Megawati as the primary target as she was the only politician with a chance of challenging Suharto in the next presidential election. Thus, ABRI engineered an internal conflict in the PDI that led to the toppling of Megawati as the party's chairperson in June 1996. This sparked a physical clash between security troops and Megawati's supporters – including NGOs, students and the grassroots – and resulted in a two-day mass riot in Jakarta on 27 July (Aspinall 2005).

The removal of Megawati from the political arena and the military crackdown of the popular movement greatly risked the social credibility of ABRI. The military was now widely distrusted by the public as a 'dead tool of the government', a criticism spoiling ABRI's self-claim of being the national guardian. Even within the military voices were emerging that acting as a tool of Suharto would only damage ABRI's corporate interest in the future. A growing number of officers began to see that the direction of the current ABRI leadership was not in line with ABRI's long-term political benefit but was merely serving Suharto's short-term private interests (Honna 2003: Chapter 2). There was also a serious concern among officers about the overly swift promotion of Prabowo and his allies, which had revealed inconsistencies in promotion practices and had left many officers demoralized. The antagonism between those linked with Prabowo and those who were not was sharpened; this resonated with the perceived freefall of ABRI's (and *dwifungsi*'s) credibility in society, resulting in the adoption of reform-minded positions of some of the anti-Prabowo officers. They were convinced that Prabowo's influence should be reduced and ABRI's response to societal demands for democratization should involve more dialogue rather than traditional repression (author's personal correspondence, see note).[12] The crackdown of the popular movement on 27 July 1996 significantly encouraged such a gap within the military.

Suharto's personalization of the military was a notable feature of the late New Order politics. By using the amenable ABRI, Suharto succeeded in the 1997 general elections in securing Golkar's electoral victory and his presidential re-election, and Habibie's vice presidency in March 1998. ABRI's subordination to this Suharto project illustrated well the erosion of the military's independent power in the political process. However, Suharto's joy would not last for long. Since mid-1997, Indonesia had been hit terribly by the Asian financial crisis that originated in Bangkok. A nationwide student movement demanding his resignation quickly escalated. In dealing with the movement, the gap within the military between the pro- and anti-Prabowo circles became prominent and, as seen below, the antagonism finally contributed to Suharto's historical resignation on 21 May 1998.

On 12 May, four student demonstrators were shot dead by 'mysterious' snipers dressed in police uniforms at a peaceful rally against Suharto at Trisakti University in Jakarta. It is widely believed that the snipers were military sharpshooters. The incident provoked mass protests which suddenly developed into large-scale, two-day riots in Jakarta. The rioters set fire to shopping centres and other commercial buildings, robbed citizens and raped many women.[13] Similar violence also erupted in Solo, Surabaya and Palembang. Eyewitness accounts revealed that the riots were orchestrated by soldiers in the army special force (*Kopassus*) who mobilized gangs to provoke the attacking and looting of Chinese enclaves. At that time, Kopassus was led by Major General Muchdi Purwopranjono, a leading ally of Prabowo, who had assumed the position after Prabowo had become Kostrad Commander. It seems probable that the terror in May was engineered by Prabowo and his supporters to advance their interests within the military hierarchy. On 18 May, Prabowo advised Suharto to dismiss his rival, General Wiranto, who had replaced Feisal Tanjung as ABRI Commander in 1998, and to declare a state of emergency.[14]

A group of high-ranking officers concerned about Prabowo's growing power believed that Wiranto was the man to support, and Wiranto weighed in against the moves of military officers aligned with Prabowo. Having confirmed the role played by Prabowo and his allies during the riots, Wiranto – who was under a clear threat of dismissal – reported his findings immediately to Suharto. The anger of Suharto and his family was directed against Prabowo.[15] Wiranto then followed the advice of his close allies who, after discussion with civilian leaders, finally concluded that Suharto's resignation would be the only way to restore stability and order in the nation. Following his meeting with Wiranto on 20 May, Suharto announced his resignation the next day. At the presidential palace, Wiranto declared that ABRI would support the new government led by Habibie (who was automatically promoted to the presidency) and would provide for Suharto's security. After exerting his leadership in handling the transfer of power from Suharto to Habibie, Wiranto successfully dealt with the new President in settling the problem of Prabowo, a close friend of Habibie:[16] two days after the inauguration of the new President, Wiranto discharged Prabowo from the post of Kostrad Commander.

In retrospect, the military played a crucial role in facilitating and managing the fall of Suharto (Mietzner 1999). As seen above, internal divisions within ABRI were particularly sharpened after the appointment of Wiranto as ABRI Commander. It was in this context that the Prabowo group adopted hard-line tactics against demands for Suharto's resignation and democratic reforms. These terror tactics by military extremists significantly stimulated anti-government movements in society. When disorder reached a peak, Wiranto offered military protection for Suharto if he would agree to step down. Suharto, mindful of the fate of other deposed dictators around the world, finally had to abandon his rule in a bid for protection from democratic forces demanding accountability and prosecution.

## THE POST-NEW ORDER MILITARY: THE GATEKEEPER OF NKRI

Suharto's long-term dictatorship was over and a democratic transition took place in Indonesia. Society was now free to participate in politics, and political competition, which was heavily restricted during the New Order era, soon became a societal norm. Given the circumstances, the post-Suharto era represented uncharted waters for military leaders in a hostile context of popular resentment of the military as an obstacle to meaningful political reform. Clearly, many expected a transition to civilian control of the military under the governments of Habibie (May 1998–October 1999), Abdurrahman Wahid (October 1999–July 2001), Megawati Sukarnoputri (July 2001–October 2004) and Susilo Bambang Yudhoyono (October 2004–) respectively. A decade into the post-Suharto period has revealed, however, that the military is still insufficiently controlled and that it retains significant political autonomy and influence. Below, the dynamics of how the post-Suharto democratic change weakened the military but also produced circumstances negative to the demilitarization of politics shall be examined.

Undoubtedly, the end of the New Order provided democratic change in Indonesia. It was the beginning of the 'de-concentration' of political power which had long been personalized by Suharto. His fall was followed by the empowerment of legislatures, reflecting the social demand for broader political participation. The role of the parliament both at the national and local levels was dramatically increased by the series of Constitutional amendments and these reduced the relative political power of the Executive branch. Civilian politicians have enjoyed a widening political authority in the empowered parliament and civilian party politics now dominates the country's formal political process, which in the past was monopolized by Suharto and the military. The collapse of the New Order thus facilitated the diffusion of state political power, empowering legislatures and strengthening party politics.

Thus, the post-New Order civil–military power equilibrium was clearly in favour of civilian political leaders – who had supported Suharto's resignation – and the subsequent political reforms (*reformasi*) aiming to democratize the polity. The wave of *reformasi* was generated by civil society – which had long been repressed by the New Order military – and was joined by civilian political elites who tactically saw the opportunity to yield more power in the formation of a new political regime. In order to capture the democratic transition they raised a flag of military withdrawal from politics; a flag which could expect support from civil society movements but could never harm the interests of civilian political elites. Facing such political pressures the military adapted itself by showing reform commitment. There were several steps of the post-New Order military reform.

First, in September 1998, the military commander Wiranto proclaimed 'ABRI's New Paradigm' which stated visions and policies supporting democratic transition. By admitting that the legitimacy of *dwifungsi* was no longer sacrosanct, nor a compelling justification for a pervasive military role in polit-ics, Wiranto and his generals claimed that the military abandoned *dwifungsi* in the New Paradigm (Crouch 1999). In fact, its reform projects brought about visible changes. ABRI eliminated its socio-political section – which had overseen everyday political interventions – from its organizational structure. The number of ABRI representatives in the parliament was reduced from 75 to 38 and military officers no longer sided automatically with Golkar. The military also refrained from interfering with political parties during electoral campaigns. These changes were promoted in order to rejuvenate the tarnished image of the military as the tool of Suharto in society.

The second phase of the military reform was the reorientation of the mili-tary's role in democracy and it involved the idea of limiting its role to the 'defence' field. In April 1999, under the Habibie government, the police was separated from the military and the role of internal security was handed over to the former.[17] With this separation ABRI – which now consisted of three services – renamed itself TNI (*Tentara Nasional* Indonesia: Indonesian National Military). These organizational and functional separations between the military and the police were formalized by politicians in the form of two MPR decrees in 2000 under the Wahid presidency.[18] Then in 2002, during the Megawati administration, the National Defence Law was formulated in order to replace the 1982 version which legalized *dwifungsi* under the New Order. The 2002 law clearly stated that TNI's role was to respond to the 'military threat' and that the 'non-military threat' had to be handled by government agencies other than TNI.[19] Finally in September 2004, the Military Law was enacted by the DPR. The law tried to reduce the political autonomy of TNI by compelling the military to coordinate with the Defence Department in settling TNI's administrative affairs and to hand over its businesses to the government within five years.[20] In this way, these reforms clearly aimed to eliminate *dwifungsi* and undermine the political activism of the military.

However, these institutional reforms did not guarantee a military with-drawal from politics or the unqualified acceptance of civilian control. Although the socio-political section was eliminated from the military, its political role was assumed by the territorial commands that penetrated down to the villages. Generals no longer sided with Golkar but they tactically col-laborated with political party elites, for example during elections of local heads (i.e. governors, regents and mayors) to promote military interests (Honna 2006). While military businesses were now under governmental inspection, lucrative fundraising activities were not under the control of the government because they usually involved illegal and underground businesses (The Editors 2003; Human Rights Watch 2006). Moreover, as seen below, the functional distinction between the police and the military was virtually obscured as the growing domestic disturbance and communal violence 'forced' TNI to play an active role in internal security affairs. TNI reinvented this reality and reasserted that it was actually impossible to demarcate 'defence' and 'security' and that security was part of defence. Until today, such a security discourse has contributed to the reservation of territorial commands of TNI and this in turn has helped sustain the political autonomy of regional military commands even after the introduction of New Paradigm and new legal arrangements.

Clearly the fall of Suharto had an impact that went well beyond changes in government form and style and shook the unity of the nation-state. Long-suppressed ethnic, religious and regional conflicts erupted throughout the archipelago, most notably in East Timor, Aceh, West Kalimantan, Papua, Central Sulawesi and Maluku, plunging some of Indonesia's peripheral regions into chaotic violence (Bertrand 2004). Demands for autonomy and independence coupled with religious and ethnic strife suggested a nation unravelling, but civilian leaders seemed ill-prepared to navigate these stormy waters of violence, reconciliation and transformation. A vital reason for this was the weak government leadership that had been institutionalized since the 1999 general elections, which resulted in the emergence of various new political parties with no single party ensuring the majority seats in the DPR.[21] The civilian-political fragmentation has forced the governments to be the coalition of several political parties with conflicting interests, as notably seen during the Wahid, Megawati and Yudhoyono presidencies. Moreover, the legacy of three decades of authoritarian rule has taken a toll on civil society and has complicated the process of recovery from the mismanagement, distortions, corruption, institutional atrophy and political oppression that marked Suharto's polity. Thus, the meltdown of the New Order regime not only exposed many long-suppressed problems in Indonesia but also bequeathed a legacy of weak civilian institutions to cope with these festering, if not intractable, problems.

While civilian leaders soon recognized that the newly independent police was incapable of solely handling the escalating political violence rooted in ethnic and religious animosities, TNI effectively mobilized the powerful discourse of 'security-as-part-of-defence' which embedded a telling nationalist claim for preserving NKRI (Indonesian national unity) and its stability. A slogan that called *NKRI adalah harga mati* (NKRI is a non-negotiable, absolute value) was proliferated by military elites, and the civilian inability to neutralize this discourse effectively enabled the military to reduce pressures to return to the barracks. It is thus convincingly suspected that the military has not only benefited from the communal violence but that it manipulated it in its own favour in the first place. In fact, the number of TNI's territorial units was increased, rather than decreased, during the post-Suharto era. As evident since the pre-New Order period, the military has shown high adaptability to secure its traditional guardianship identity and the associated political activism depending on the civil–military power equilibrium at the time.

In this way, it can be said that presidents of the post-Suharto era – Habibie, Wahid, Megawati and Yudhoyono – have enjoyed only ceremonial civilian control over the military. Today's generals basically accept the principle of 'civilian supremacy' but also reserve the right to determine to what extent the writ of civilian supremacy extends into what they consider to be exclusively military affairs. It seems that the military leadership recognizes that the era of military supremacy is over in Indonesia and there is no desire and power to return to the situation before. Cognizant of the high costs of political take-over to the institutional integrity of the military and how this has under-mined its ability to act decisively with the trust and confidence of the public, there appears to be wide acceptance among military leaders of the need for civilians to manage politics. This, however, is not to say that the generals are ready to accept any political decisions made by civilian elites, especially these concerning 'military issues' which – in their eyes – include intra-military affairs and 'defence' policies. When civilians intervene in these sanctuaries, the military leadership is highly motivated to sabotage the government and mobilize the institutional power to veto the policy and ultimately the political authority. This resistance is easily legitimized in the eyes of generals, with reference to the military's self-ascribed role as patriotic guardians of the nation and the Constitution. As arbiters of the national interest they thus see a duty to resist or subvert government policies that contradict what they define as the national interest. Here the military has developed its own interpretation that sees no inconsistency between accepting the principle of civilian supremacy and resisting civilian control of the military. This is clearly a legacy of the *dwifungsi* mindset adapted in the age of democratization.

Political reflections of such new civil–military relations can be found in the past decade. During the Habibie presidency the President experienced a total loss of authority in dealing with Wiranto's military in its conduct of a dirty war against East Timor's pro-independence citizens in 1999.[22] Wiranto and his aides saw Habibie's offer of referendum to East Timor as an act of undermining national integrity and thus a legitimate reason for sabotage. TNI's covert operations to prevent East Timor's independence eventually failed but it provided a lesson for the military elites: accepting civilian control risked NKRI.

During the Wahid government this lesson was utilized to justify the military's insubordination to the President. Wahid's attempts to assert control over the military backfired in the end. In trying to create a 'loyal' military, Wahid intervened extensively in personnel changes, removing Wiranto and his followers from strategic positions and placing more amenable officers in these positions (Anwar *et al.* 2002). Within the officer corps Wahid's man-oeuvre was seen to be crazy, arbitrary, unfair and harmful to the military's organizational cohesion (author's interviews, see note).[23] The consequent pol-iticization of promotions exacerbated military scepticism towards civilian control of the military, in effect strengthening the influence of conservative elements within the military (led by Army Chief General Endriartono Sutarto and Kostrad Commander General Ryamizard Ryacudu). 'TNI is not a politi-cal tool of President Wahid', also claimed the Deputy Army Chief (author's interview with Lt. General Kiki Syahnakri, 20 March 2001). Clumsy civilian interference reinforced existing prejudice within the ranks towards civilian political leaders, reducing the incentive to buy into the new arrangements and therefore slowing the pace of reform. In the end, both Sutarto and Ryacudu orchestrated TNI's exercise of veto power against Wahid when he commanded TNI to protect the President from the parliamentary move to impeach him for a corruption scandal. TNI – who backed up the parliamentary initiative and ignored the presidential instruction – significantly contributed to the downfall of Wahid before completing the term of office in 2001. Sutarto openly expressed TNI's guardianship role in the media: 'TNI is obliged to reject the president when it conflicts with the national interest' (Sutarto 2001).

Perhaps to avoid the 'mistakes' of Wahid, President Megawati gave a larger free-hand to the TNI. This, however, greatly contributed to the decline of pressures calling for military reform. A result of this was most evident in the handling of Aceh conflict in which the government efforts to promote peace negotiations with the separatist Free Aceh Movement (GAM) were repeatedly sabotaged and undermined by the assertive military leaders – especially the new Army Chief, Ryamizard, and his followers – who had insisted on the need to engage in the all-out war against GAM for the sake of upholding NKRI. This was another mode of veto power exercised by the army leadership. Megawati was convinced by them and in May 2003 she declared martial law in Aceh, allowing TNI to conduct war operations and hijack Aceh's daily political administration. The dirty war in Aceh – which produced a large number of victims among Acehnese citizens – only ended in December 2004 when the large-scale tsunami devastated the soil of Aceh. The natural disaster effectively contributed to the cease-fire between TNI and GAM and the newly launched Yudhoyono government (October 2004–) luckily used this opportunity to recover civilian initiatives in solving the problem of Aceh. Peace negotiations were re-opened, resulting in the Helsinki peace agreement in August 2005.

In the historical context, TNI has adapted to the new, emerging political landscape and honed its political skills in accommodating, deflecting and manipulating pressures for change in ways that have enabled it to maintain its political activism. The post-Suharto military is neither the regime-builder nor the tool of the president. However, it still continues to exercise strong influence on the political process in the democratic regime by preserving political autonomy to act as the veto power. In order to legitimize this role, the military has invented the discourse of NKRI. It argues that TNI is responsible for the maintenance of national unity which is threatened by separatist movements, ethnic conflicts and other communal violence in the archipelago; these are, to a large extent, the by-products of regime change in the post-Suharto era. It is this logic that TNI mobilizes to assert the existence of a 'gray zone' between internal security and external defence, develop the idea of 'security-as-part-of-defence' and insist on the utility of territorial commands in the age of democracy. By defending the territorial command system, TNI has preserved its local political influence which is vital to maintain its access to economic resources.

It is important to understand the current civil–military relations under the Yudhoyono administration in the context of these developments. Yudhoyono, as an ex-army general who knows the organizational culture of the TNI, has not taken any significant steps to rejuvenate military reform. The exception was his appointment of air force general Djoko Suyanto as TNI Commander; the first time in the history of Indonesian military, and is thus regarded as a step to neutralize the tradition of the army's dominance in the military. Army generals see Yudhoyono as a weak president who has no political capital to mobilize for progressive reform. They are also assured that, as a retired four-star general, Yudhoyono understands TNI's vested interests in securing the territorial commands vital to both the economic gains and job distributions of the majority of officers in the organization. In fact Yudhoyono, at the anniversary of TNI in 2005, openly encouraged TNI to play a bigger role in counter-terrorism operations that have been handled primarily by the police. Many in the police circle assessed that Yudhoyono's claim would undermine the efforts of the police to professionally deal with security issues (author's interview with an assistant to the Police Chief, February 2007). Needless to say, the demand of the international community on Indonesia to actively participate in the global war on terrorism has effectively contributed to the fortification of TNI's claim for fusing 'security–defence' functions. Yudhoyono's right-hand man in the army, General Djoko Santoso, echoed the claim by saying that the police are actually incapable of handling security and maintaining public order; only the military has the skill and capacity (author's interview with Lt. General Djoko Santoso, Deputy Army Chief, 11 June 2004).[24] The tension between TNI and the police was heightened in January 2007 when the Police Chief openly criticized the draft law on National Security which was prepared by the defence sector group in TNI and the Defence Department. The police insisted that it would never accept the draft bill, which attempted to place the police under the Interior Department, revoking the current position directly responsible to the president. The police reasonably suspect that the TNI wants to subordinate the police via the Interior Minister who is traditionally ex-military. The bill has since been deadlocked but Yudhoyono has shown no initiative to solve the problem, thus contributing to the deepening of the mutual distrust between the two institutions. Meanwhile, TNI successfully re-institutionalized its security functions by adopting 'military operations other than warfare' or OMSP (*Operasi Militer Selain Peran*) as part of TNI's new doctrine in the annual military leadership meeting in January 2007. The boundary between security and defence is effectively blurred by this attempt.

Yudhoyono is also seemingly unconcerned about eliminating military businesses, which constitute off-budget revenues for the military. Since effective democratic control of the military cannot be attained whilst the government is incapable of managing the military's finances, civil society has long demanded the liquidation of business activities conducted by military institutions. In March 2006, Yudhoyono allowed the Defence Department to establish a team – the National Team for TNI Business Transformation – to prepare for the possible takeover of TNI businesses. However, it was announced in June 2007 that only six out of 1,500 military businesses were subject for takeover. This was nothing but a veto by the military against the original initiative of Yudhoyono and he seems to have given up the idea in facing the resistance.

It now seems that after the fall of Suharto the military has finally discovered the concept which replaces *dwifungsi*. The old concept is no longer legitimate, but by claiming its role of defending NKRI in the time of democracy, TNI believes that it can exercise a veto power in the relationship with the government and that it can retain a political say in rejecting pressures for reform which are undesirable to the military, notably the elimination of territorial commands and business conducts. Then, how is it possible that a president – regardless of his or her background as a party leader or a military general – shrinks the political space territorialized by TNI's NKRI discourse, diminishes its political autonomy enjoyed by territorial commands and wipes out the legacy of guardianship doctrine which has justified political activism of generals in the name of safeguarding the national interest? Without these initiatives, any institutional–legal reforms to restrict the military's involvement in politics may end up like the one-hand clapping (not having any effect).

## CONCLUSION

As we have examined, the political position of the Indonesian military has changed over time. Prior to the New Order the military was active in daily politics as one of several political forces. During the early Suharto period it became the regime-builder and dominated the Indonesian polity based on the ideology of developmentalism and its doctrinal embodiment of *dwifungsi*. In the late Suharto regime, however, the military was transformed as the tool of Suharto's personal political interest. By allowing itself to play that role, the military virtually abandoned its role as the regime maintainer. After the collapse of Suharto, the military again returned to the participatory position in the political system. However, in a society which is far more complex and in which democratic political participation is widely accepted, it is impossible for the military to play its previous political role. Under these circumstances, the society at large demands the return of the military to the barracks but the current civil–military power balance still enables the military to sustain political activism, now expressed in the shape of veto power. This has been legitimized by the military elite who insist on the role of the military as the gatekeeper of NKRI during the fragile democratic transition. Such a legitimation may continue unless civilian leaders persuade the military that the ongoing democratic experiment in Indonesia will never fail again as it did in the 1950s.

As a logic, the military guardianship in Indonesia makes sense. However, as we have seen, history reveals the fact that the military has repeatedly been a promoter of large-scale violence in the country: the army crackdown of regional rebellions in the late 1950s; anti-communist mass killings in the mid-1960s; military occupation and subsequent repression in East Timor since the mid-1970s, which was followed by the escalation of military operations to suppress separatist movements in Aceh, Papua and East Timor in the late 1980s; army-orchestrated riots in the last days of Suharto; systematic destruction of East Timor leading to its independence in 1999; and the series of post-Suharto regional conflicts in Aceh, Maluku, Ambon, Papua and other areas, where the military has played the role of arsonist or bystander rather than fireman of the internal violence taking place until today. This fact clearly contradicts with the self-claimed guardianship of the military.

Such a tradition of political violence in Indonesia not only illustrates the historical role of the army as the agent of promoting human insecurity, but also reflects the great lack of state capacity in handling social problems in a peaceful manner, even after 62 years of independence. Indonesia's current experiment of democratic practice is expected to build up its ability of peaceful resolution of conflicting goals, both in order to construct viable state–society relations in the post-Suharto period and to diminish the space for the military to exercise its influence in domestic political affairs via its internal security role.

The prospect is, however, still narrow. The army's propaganda concerning the threat of a possible national breakup is so far very successful in convincing the current civilian political elite to see the situation in Aceh and Papua as a real threat to NKRI. Such a perception was significantly encouraged by the '9–11' terrorist attack on New York in September 2001 and the subsequent US-led international campaign for the war on terrorism, which strongly pressured Indonesia to improve its security sectors. This was quickly translated by Indonesia's conservative generals as a moment to hijack the 'global norm'. By linking the global agenda, they have invented a theory of a strengthening military role that is 'demanded' to save the country from the threat of 'terrorism' and other forms of non-traditional security challenges, hence running counter to efforts to weaken the military through reforms aimed at democratizing civil–military relations. When this trend encountered the bloody '10–12' bomb blast at home in Bali in October 2002 – which killed about 200 people – the perception of civilian elites was unconditionally switched to a mindset focused on security. This has allowed the TNI to strengthen the theory of global norm and take bigger initiatives in security policy-making with, of course, significant political implications.

Indonesia's uncertain path into the post-Suharto period now seems to be facing a political dilemma of 'security vs democracy'. To find the way to achieve both ends is difficult, but not impossible, and it requires considerable political skills in order for the civilian leaders to contain the military, which may resist or even sabotage unfavourable political decisions made by civilians in the name of 'safeguarding the nation'.


## NOTES

1 See Honna 2003, Kingsbury 2003, Rinakit 2005, Hafidz 2006, and Mietzner 2006.
2 For an account of military politics during 1950s, see McVey (1971).
3 Both PRRI (*Pemerintah Revolusioner Republik* Indonesia, Indonesian Revolutionary Government) and Permesta (*Piagam Perjuangan Permesta*, Charter of Common Struggle) threatened the central government but their forces were defeated by the military.
4 About these military campaigns, see Leifer (1983) and Mackie (1974).
5 Besides the official account, there is reasonable suspicion that Suharto himself manipulated or instigated the abortive coup both in order to create a breakthrough for the army to crush the PKI and to pave the way for the Kostrad Commander to take control of the army leadership. The argument in favour of this view is put forward by Anderson and McVey (1971). For an analysis of various interpretations regarding the coup, see Crouch (1988).
6 Sukarno's 'instruction' to Suharto was conveyed through a letter, dated 11 March, which was called Supersemar (Presidential Letter of 11 March). The letter authorized Suharto to handle the political situation. However, Supersemar is still a controversial issue because of a suspicion that Sukarno wrote the letter under duress. Regardless of the truth, Suharto banned the PKI on the day after the issue of the letter. PKI supporters became political prisoners, if they were arrested, or became the victims of military-supervised killing. The most commonly accepted estimate of the death toll was between 250,000 and 500,000. About the coup and the aftermath see, for example, Anderson and McVey (1971), Cribb (1990) and Robinson (1995).
7 Before the New Order period, the Indonesian military consisted of three services: the army, the navy and the air force. When the Suharto regime was launched in 1966, the police force was integrated into the military and the new four-service military forces were named as ABRI, an abbreviation of *Angkatan Bersenjata Republik* Indonesia (Armed Forces of the Republic of Indonesia).
8 There were ten area commands (Kodams) in the ABRI structure and they controlled their responsible territories. Under each Kodam, there are several Korems (regional commands) – except Kodam Jaya/Jakarta – and each Korem supervises Kodims (district commands) in its own territory. Kodims oversee Koramils (subdistrict commands). This territorial defence system enabled ABRI's everyday control of political affairs throughout the archipelago. About the New Order military organization, see Sundhaussen (1978).
9 During the 1970s, F-ABRI occupied 75 seats in the DPR which consisted of 460 members. When the size of the DPR was extended to 500 in 1987, ABRI's appointed seats were also increased to 100.
10 Regarding the *kekaryaan* practice, see MacDougall (1982). In 1971, for example, among higher central bureaucracy, 44 per cent of cabinet members, 41 per cent of Secretary Generals and 73 per cent of Inspector Generals were active-duty officers. Regional governments were also penetrated by military members. In 1977, 78 per cent of provincial governors were army men and more than half (155) of Indonesia's 294 *bupati* (regents) and mayors were ABRI men (Jenkins 1984: 47).

11 ABRI's business activities have a long history, going back to the 1950s. The lack of governmental budget to finance defence spending has been substituted by these activities conducted by military-owned enterprises. All territorial units have also been engaged in various legal/illegal profit-making activities in order to finance their operations. The official defence budget allegedly covers less than 30 per cent of the annual expenses. For the military's business activities, consult Robison (1986: Chapter 8) and Crouch (1988: Chapter 11).

12 Author's interviews with some reformist officers, including Major General Agus Widjojo (Political-Security Advisor to ABRI Commander), 30 September 1996; Brigadier General Agus Wirahadikusumah (Deputy Assistant for General Planning to ABRI Commander), 2 October 1996 and 24 January 1997; Vice-Marshal Graito Usodo (Expert Staff to ABRI Commander in the Field of Industrial Development), 26 November 1996.

13 More than 1,200 people were killed. About the riots see, for example, Siegel (2001).

14 For these accounts see Prabowo's interview, 'The Scapegoat?', *Asiaweek*, 3 March 2000.

15 Prabowo admitted that Mamiek, Suharto's youngest daughter, called him 'traitor' and asked him not to come to Suharto's palace anymore. Prabowo accused Wiranto of playing politics against him ('The Scapegoat?', *Asiaweek*, 3 March 2000).

16 Habibie approved Wiranto to remove Prabowo and, in return, Habibie assured Wiranto's support for the new government (Shiraishi 1999: 82–3).

17 However, since the manpower of the police is limited, the government may order the military to support the police in handling the internal security problems. This arrangement is explained as an option available for the civilian political authority, and is not a demand of the military (Mabes TNI 2001).

18 Two MPR decrees are: Ketetapan MPR No.VI/2000 Tentang Pemisahan Tentara Nasional Indonesia dan Kepolisian Negara Republik Indonesia, and Ketetapan MPR No.VII/2000 Tentang Peran Tentara Nasional Indonesia dan Peran Kepolisian Negara Republik Indonesia.

19 See Article 7 of the Defence Law in 2002 (UU No.3/2002 Tentang Pertahanan Nasional).

20 Articles 12 and 76 in the Military Law (UU No.34/2004 Tentang Tentara Nasional Indonesia).

21 The legislative elections in 1999 resulted in the historical defeat of Golkar and the victory of Megawati's PDI-P. But PDI-P merely shared 30 per cent of total seats in the 500-member DPR, followed by Golkar (24 per cent), United Development Party (PPP) (11 per cent), and two new parties: National Awakening Party (PKB) led by Wahid (10 per cent) and National Mandate Party (PAN) led by Amien Rais (6.8 per cent). Both Wahid and Amien were the leading democratic campaigners during the Suharto regime and their power bases were Muslim communities; Wahid was a charismatic leader of Nahdatul Ulama, the largest Islamic organization in Indonesia, while Amien led the second-largest group, Muhammadiyah, and was a vocal leader in ICMI.

22 About East Timor's struggle for independence and the military disturbance under the Habibie government see, for example, Tanter, Selden and Shalom (2001). Also see Robinson (2001) on the military use of militias in provoking violence in East Timor.

23 Author's interviews with General (retired) Wiranto, 20 March 2001 and 28 January 2004, and with Lt. General Djadja Suparman (Inspector-General of the TNI, who was also sidelined by Wahid), 23 January 2004.

24 Djoko was promoted to the Army Chief in January 2006.

## BIBLIOGRAPHY

Anderson, B. and McVey, R.T. (1971) *A Preliminary Analysis of the October 1, 1965, Coup in Indonesia*, Ithaca: Modern Indonesia Project, Cornell University.

Anwar, D.F. *et al.* (2002) *Gus Dur Versus Militer: Studi tentang Hubungan Sipil-Militer di Era Transisi*, Jakarta: Grasindo.

Aspinall, E. (2005) *Opposing Suharto: Compromise, Resistance, and Regime Change in Indonesia*, California: Stanford University Press.

Bertrand, J. (2004) *Nationalism and Ethnic Conflict in Indonesia*, London: Cambridge University Press.

Cribb, R. (ed.) (1990) *The Indonesian Killings, 1965–66: Studies from Java and Bali*, Victoria: Centre of Southeast Asian Studies, Monash University.

Crouch, H. (1988) *The Army and Politics in Indonesia*, revised edition, Ithaca: Cornell University Press.

—— (1999) 'Wiranto and Habibie: Civil-Military Relations since May 1998', in A. Budiman, B. Hatley and D. Kingsbury (eds) *Reformasi: Crisis and Change in Indonesia*, Clayton: Monash Asia Institute.

Editors, The (2003) 'Current Data on the Indonesian Military Elite', *Indonesia* 75 (April): 9–60.

Hafidz, T.S. (2006) *Fading Away? The Political Role of the Army in Indonesia's Transition to Democracy, 1998–2001*, IDSS Monograph No.8, Singapore: Institute of Defense and Strategic Studies.

Hefner, R. (2000) *Civil Islam: Muslims and Democratization in Indonesia*, NJ: Princeton University Press.

Honna, J. (2001) 'Military Ideology in Response to Democratic Pressure during the Late Suharto Era: Political and Institutional Contexts', in B. Anderson (ed.) *Violence and the State in Suharto's Indonesia*, Ithaca: Southeast Asia Program, Cornell University.

—— (2003) *Military Politics and Democratization in Indonesia*, London and New York: RoutledgeCurzon.

—— (2006) 'Local Civil-Military Relations during the First Phase of Democratic Transition, 1999–2004: A Comparison of West, Central and East Java', *Indonesia*, 82 (October): 75–96.

Human Rights Watch (2006) 'Too High a Price: The Human Rights Cost of the Indonesian Military's Economic Activities', *Human Rights Watch*, 18 (5).

Jenkins, D. (1984) *Suharto and His Generals: Indonesian Military Politics 1975–1983*, Ithaca: Modern Indonesian Project, Cornell University.

Kahin, A.R. and Kahin, G.M. (1995) *Subversion as Foreign Policy: The Secret Eisenhower and Dulles Debacle in Indonesia*, New York: The New Press.

Kingsbury, D. (2003) *Power Politics and the Indonesian Military*, London and New York: RoutledgeCurzon.

Leifer, M. (1983) *Indonesia's Foreign Policy*, London: George Allen & Unwin.

Mabes TNI (2001) *Implementasi Pradigma Baru TNI Dalam Berbagai Keadaan Mutakhir*, Jakarta: TNI.

MacDougall, J.A. (1982) 'Pattern of Military Control in the Indonesian Higher Central Bureaucracy', *Indonesia* 33 (April): 89–121.

Mackie, J. (1974) *Konfrontasi: The Indonesia-Malaysia Dispute 1963–1966*, Canberra: AIIA.

McVey, R.T. (1971) 'The post-Revolutionary Transformation of the Indonesian Army', *Indonesia* 11 (April): 131–76.

Mietzner, M. (1999) 'From Suharto to Habibie: the Indonesian Armed Forces and Political Islam during the Transition'. in G. Forrester (ed.) *Post-Suharto Indonesia: Renewal or Chaos?*, Singapore: Institute of Southeast Asian Studies.

—— (2006) *The Politics of Military Reform in Post-Suharto Indonesia: Elite Conflict, Nationalism, and Institutional Resistance*, Policy Studies 23, Washington DC: East-West Center Washington.

Pangaribuan, R. (1995) *The Indonesian State Secretariat 1945–1993*; trans. V. Hadiz (1995) Perth: Asia Research Centre on Social, Political and Economic Change, Murdoch University.

Ramage, D. (1995) *Politics in Indonesia: Democracy, Islam and the Ideology of Tolerance*, London: Routledge.

Rinakit, S. (2005) *The Indonesian Military After the New Order*, Singapore: Institute of Southeast Asian Studies.

Robinson, G. (1995) *The Dark Side of Paradise: Political Violence in Bali*, Ithaca: Cornell University Press.

—— (2001) 'People's War: Militias in East Timor and Indonesia', *South East Asia Research*, 9 (3): 271–318.

Robison, R. (1986) *Indonesia: The Rise of Capital*, Sydney: Allen & Unwin.

Said, S. (1991) *Genesis of Power: General Sudirman and the Indonesian Military in Politics 1945–49*, Singapore: Institute of Southeast Asian Studies.

Shiraishi, T. (1999) 'The Indonesian Military in Politics', in A. Schwarz and J. Paris (eds) *The Politics of Post-Suharto Indonesia*, New York: Council on Foreign Relations Press.

Siegel, J.T. (2001) 'Thoughts on the Violence of May 13 and 14, 1998, in Jakarta', in B. Anderson (ed.) *Violence and the State in Suharto's Indonesia*, Ithaca: Southeast Asia Program, Cornell University.

Sundhaussen, U. (1978) 'The Military: Structure, Procedures and Effects on Indonesian Society', in K.D. Jackson and L.W. Pye (eds) *Political Power and Communications in Indonesia*, California: University of California Press.

—— (1982) *The Road to Power: Indonesian Military Politics 1945–1967*, Kuala Lumpur, New York: Oxford University Press.

Sutarto, E. (2001) 'Kewajiban TNI Menaati Perintah', *Kompas*, 20 June.

Tanter, R. (1990) 'The Totalitarian Ambition: Intelligence and Security Agencies in Indonesia,' in A. Budiman (ed.) *State and Civil Society in Indonesia*, Victoria: Centre of Southeast Asian Studies, Monash University.

Tanter, R., Selden, M. and Shalom, S.R. (eds) (2001) *Bitter Flowers, Sweet Flowers: East Timor, Indonesia, and the World Community*, New York: Rowman & Littlefield.

# Part IV
# Civil and 'uncivil' society

# 11 Civil society and the challenges of the post-Suharto era

*Mikaela Nyman*

## INTRODUCTION

The broader historical, political and economic context cannot be ignored in any analysis regarding the reasons and timing for Suharto's fall, yet the role of what is commonly known as 'civil society' is increasingly emphasized.[1] In particular, the leading role of student activists in the broader movement for social and political change has been widely acknowledged, nationally and internationally. Whereas the students may have attracted the limelight and constituted one of the core groups of the pro-democracy movement, they certainly only represented one of numerous civil society groups.

Until the late 1990s much of the scholarly work on Indonesia's political development emphasized continuity, stability and the role of the middle class and the elite, while viewing popular movements as 'idealistic' and rejecting them as a viable approach for studies concerning political change (Tornquist 2000: 6). Since the late 1990s, however, Indonesian scholars have stressed the importance of non-state actors other than the political elite and the existence of civil society as a prerequisite for genuine democratization and reform (Culla 1999: 12–13; Hikam 1999: 260; Panjaitan 2001: 10).

In order to achieve political and social change, and perhaps eventually democracy, the development of a diverse civil society that addresses people's concerns is considered necessary by many democratization scholars (Rodan 1997: 156). Some highlight NGOs (non-governmental organizations) and social movements as the most important civil society actors (Uhlin 2002: 181). Civil society theorists explain their interconnectedness in terms of social movements being the 'dynamic element in processes that might realize the positive potentials of modern civil societies' (Cohen and Arato 1992: 492). This is of relevance for understanding the Indonesian context.

With the overwhelming majority of scholars favouring a state-centric approach and crediting the elite with being the driving force – or even the only force – in Indonesian politics and development, there is a need for research that recognizes other forces and mechanisms in society. Thus, the elite and the middle class are specifically not dealt with here. This does not imply ignorance about the role of the elite and middle class in Indonesian politics and society; it is merely an acknowledgement that other viable perspectives exist. Civil society forces are becoming increasingly important in the post-Suharto era, yet a strong and resourceful civil society does not emerge overnight.

Other limitations concern separatist movements, such as in West Papua and Aceh, which are not included in this study since they challenge the self-limiting radicalism of social movements and aim at breaking up the state. Similarly, the space provided does not allow for an in-depth discussion of Muslim civil society, which has become even more complex in the aftermath of the 11 September 2001 terrorist attacks and the October 2002 Bali bombings. This is clearly an area warranting further research.

This chapter aims to assess critically the role and situation of civil society in Indonesia's ongoing political, economic and social transformation towards democracy in the post-Suharto era. Some relevant historical background has been included to provide context for the current developments. It is argued that while social movements act as civil society's primary catalysts for change, there is a need for a strong civil society to take over where social movements leave off in order to consolidate values and attitudinal changes. For this to happen civil society requires an enabling environment, something which is still lacking to a great degree in Indonesia. Considering this, it is furthermore argued that civil society has done remarkably well in the past decade in terms of seizing crucial political opportunities, expanding political space and contributing to a more democratic Indonesia.

## THEORETICAL FRAMEWORKS AND CONCEPTS

The theoretical frameworks that have been used to analyse the role of civil society and the popular movements that spearhead it are social movement theory and the more recent framework of political opportunities in social movement studies. Before proceeding any further we need to define political opportunities, mass social movements and civil society, as well as discuss how the Indonesian definition and context might differ from a more general 'Western' definition.

### Political opportunities

The major criticism that can be brought against the concepts of civil society, social movements, and political opportunities is that they can be defined in very general terms that virtually render the concepts useless for research. This poses the need for some limiting definitions. McAdam *et al.* (1996: 27) have extracted four dimensions of political opportunities that are crucial for the emergence and destiny of social movements:

• The relative openness or closure of the institutionalized political system.

- The stability or instability of that broad set of elite alignments that typically undergird a polity.
- The presence or absence of elite allies.
- The state's capacity and propensity for repression.

(McAdam *et al.* 1996: 27)

In addition, the unique broader context of the political opportunities and limitations that shape social movements in various countries is emphasized (McAdam *et al.* 1996: 3). All four of these political opportunities are relevant for the Indonesian context as they help explain the behaviour of the pro-democracy movement and the ebb and flow of political space for civil society's actions.

## Civil society and the Indonesian context

Civil society is a broad concept that in its Western interpretation generally includes formal and informal voluntary organizations and networks, political parties, churches, trade unions and media, but excludes business and government institutions (Shaw 1994: 648; Cohen and Arato 1992: ix). It is worth noting that not all aspects or actors of civil society are necessarily positive or 'good', since civil society also includes extremist groups of various kinds, not all of them benign let alone democratic. It is furthermore mani-fested in voluntary organizations' attempts to build deeper social structures, including norms and policies (Scholte 2000: 277).

In this study civil society will be defined as comprising individuals, formal and non-formal organizations and networks, both religious and secular, in the public and political sphere outside state institutions. Business corpor-ations, government institutions, as well as organizations and political parties established by the government are not included. While not all factions of civil society necessarily oppose the state, civil society as a whole has the potential to challenge the state.

The concept has been narrowed down in order to have clear parameters for assessing similarities and differences between a general Western versus an Indonesian concept of civil society. It is important to note that this defin-ition does not necessarily encompass all Indonesian civil society elements, as the highly corporatized New Order polity left little political space for organ-izational activities outside government-initiated institutions and business. Political parties, for example, have until recently not been allowed to emerge out of any grassroots activity. Yet Megawati's party, PDI, certainly possessed civil society and social movement qualities, particularly in the 1990s when its vast network of supporters and sympathizers challenged the existing regime. There has also been a tendency to include business in Indonesia's civil society, yet scholars and commentators are increasingly drawing a sharp line between civil society and business. This seems to reflect attitudinal changes in the public mind; a consequence of escalating corruption, economic inequality and a resurgent business elite that includes the military and official power holders.[2]

## Mass social movements

Like civil society, social movements are neither clearly defined nor uniformly interpreted. Mass social movements are only partly institutionalized, they are social processes as well as structures, and they seldom have a formal membership, strategic programme or even an ideological consensus. Anti-systemic in nature and driven by a strong value-orientation they are often labelled 'moral crusades'. Their tendency to mobilize *against* rather than *for* a specific cause enables them to unify widely differing groups and actors for campaigns and protests. Far from being the main factor effecting social and political change, they nevertheless often spearhead change by undermining the legitimacy of political institutions, as well as cultural and social norms, and by moralizing government politics. It is worth noting that social movements generally do not aim at taking over political power (Pakulski 1991: xiv–xx, 32–8).

The research of Pakulski (1991) and Tarrow (1994) is useful since they take a broader approach to the study of mass social movements, not letting one specific approach dominate. The social movement framework, in particular the new social movement approach, is helpful as it offers new ways for assessing the contributions of the Indonesian pro-democracy movement and bridges the gaps highlighted by other scholars. Tarrow (1994, 1996) and McAdam *et al.* (1996) have also contributed significantly to the understanding of political opportunities in social movement discourse.

## THE INDONESIAN CIVIL SOCIETY CONTEXT

The three key issues in the Indonesian concept of civil society that sets it apart from the general Western perception concern the relation between state and civil society, the nexus between the military and civil society, and the role of religion.

## Civil society and the state

The relation and interaction between civil society and the state is a central factor. While some see civil society in opposition to the state, others emphasize their co-existence and interdependence. The dichotomy between state and society, which is emphasized in the West, is not necessarily acknowledged in Indonesia where a much more organic and controlled state developed during Suharto's New Order (Suryakusuma 1996: 93).

Besides outright repression, the New Order regime was skilled at using legal, cultural and ideological frameworks to circumscribe civil society. By using Pancasila as the sole national ideology (*pengasas-tunggalan*) other ideological discourses and challenges were obliterated, giving the state total control. It is worth noting that the concept of political opposition is not accommodated in Pancasila ideology. The official view does not allow for conflicting and divisive interests in society, and definitely not between society and state (Aspinall 1996: 217; Budiman 1999: 7). Essentially this is rooted in the idea of the integralistic state, which erases the state–society distinction.

Political parties were restricted and society was further depoliticized through the 1971 'floating mass' doctrine, which essentially reserved politics for the urban elite while the majority, the grassroots, were excluded from political activity (Dhakidae 2001: 15; Uhlin 1997: 42, 55). Civil servants were forced to abide by the principle of *monoloyalitas* (mono-loyalty to the state party, Golkar), which provided the government with extensive control over village leaders and civil servants. The 'floating mass' doctrine was only abandoned in 1999 (Antlöv 2003: 200).

The regime's obsession with controlling mass organizations became explicit with the 1985 law on social organizations, *UU Organisasi Kemasyarakatan* (UU ORMAS), which stipulated that the government policy of development had to be supported and that organizations had to adhere to and contribute to Pancasila or be considered subversive (Culla 1999: 14–15). All organizations had to accept state guidance and supervision. If an organization's activities were considered subversive, in other words threatening to national security and order, it could be dissolved (Wagemann 2000: 306–8). Social movements belonged to the category of non-formalized organizations (*Organisasi Tanpa Bentuk*, OTB), seen as increasingly dangerous from 1995 onwards and often victimized as allegedly communist (Honna 2001: 70–1).

The fate of organized labour and women further illustrate how civil society was curtailed. Workers were supposed to focus on work. There was little tolerance for any attempts to organize labour; independent unions did not exist. In a strategic move to further nullify labour's political potential, industrial relations were linked with Pancasila ideology in order to co-opt labour and create an obedient workforce by emphasizing the importance of family, harmony and consensus instead of confrontation. It was also used to justify military and government intervention in industrial relations (Ford 2000: 64; Hadiz 1994: 192–4; Tanter 1990: 253–5).

As for women, whose lives were already guided by religion and culture, their roles were defined by the government in the mid-1970s in a document called the *Panca Dharma Wanita*, which restricted women to five officially recognized roles. In order of priority, women were to be seen as: wives (as appendages to their husbands), mothers (giving birth to and educating a new generation), organizers of the household economy, social workers and dutiful citizens (Rahayu 1996: 33). Outspoken Indonesian feminist Julia Suryakusuma has called this social construction of the domesticated woman the ideology of 'state ibuism', which virtually reduces independent women to 'dependent wives who exist for their husbands, their families and the state' (Suryakusuma 1996: 98).

With limited political space elsewhere it was in fact the government-initiated institutions, parties and organizations that often harboured civil society elements. Drawing this discussion to its conclusion, Indonesia's repressive past in essence implies that very few civil society activists have experienced what it means to be part of a truly democratic, membership-based organization. This is at the core of the problems civil society now faces.

The state's deep penetration of society through both repression and 'ideological hegemony' is important for understanding the legitimacy and power of the New Order regime (Hikam 1995: 5–6: 159). It also explains the lack of alternative thinking and the need for 'a change in mindset', emphasized in 2002 by civil society representatives as well as political and social observers as the necessary preconditions not only for a strong civil society, but for democracy itself in Indonesia (interviews with Sobary 14 January 2002, YLBHI 14 January 2002, Soesastro 15 January 2002 and Hidayat 15 January 2002). The impact of decades of restrictions on political and social rights cannot be ignored when discussing the present situation and the future for civil society. Even the fragmentation of the pro-democracy movement can partly be attributed to 32 years of New Order manipulation and a lack of alternative learning.

> The most significant role of the New Order was not violence and horror, but to teach us to forget how to organize, how to develop civil society. Even when people have energy to protest, to oppose the regime, they don't know how to make a permanent movement. In the New Order all organizations in civil society were co-opted by the state. As a result people do not have any reference. All of us, Gus Dur, Megawati are pupils of what Budiman termed 'the New Order School' and have a big barrier to overcome with respect to how democracy operates.
>
> (Interview with Hidayat, 15 January 2002)

Clarifying civil society's role in relation to the post-Suharto state, Indonesia's foremost civil society scholar, Muhammad A. S. Hikam (1999: 3), defines civil society as not necessarily opposing the state, but displaying a 'high degree of independence versus the state', while it adheres to the laws and values of society and has 'self-generating', 'self-supporting' and 'voluntary' characteristics. His definition calls for great self-awareness and maturity for state and society alike, which has yet to evolve in Indonesia. The need for the state to guarantee the freedom of civil society is nevertheless underscored by civil society scholars and activists (interviews with Sobary 14 January 2002, YLBHI 14 January 2002, Soesastro 15 January 2002; Hikam 1999: 58).

Acknowledging civil and political rights implies a certain level of good governance, which has ranked high among the demands voiced by civil society, including reform of the presidential institution and judicial reform in order to establish a state of law (*negara hukum*) (Harkrisnowo 2001; Panjaitan 2001: 43, 53; Lubis and Santosa 1999: 343, 360). Therefore the

August 2002 parliamentary session's decision to end the military's presence in parliament and introduce direct presidential elections by 2004 was regarded as an important victory for civil society. They were two of the most important government reforms in four decades and were considered important strategic issues by the 1998 pro-democracy movement (*Kompas* 10 August 2002. Online; *The Jakarta Post*, 11 August 2002).

The military's encroachment on what is considered to be civil territory is further discussed below. As for the presidential elections, four amendments to the 1945 Constitution between 1999 and 2002 ensured that Susilo Bambang Yudhoyono became the first Indonesian president enjoying both constitutional and popular legitimacy; directly elected by, and accountable to, his people instead of the parliament. Given Indonesia's authoritarian past, the significance of these electoral and constitutional reforms should not be underestimated (Indobizlaw 2005; Singh 2003).

As Indonesia's democracy and civil society mature there is clearly a need for greater mechanisms for interaction between state and society. Yet with increasingly close cooperation there is also a risk of civil society being co-opted by the state, as witnessed in the past (Rodan 1996: 19; Aspinall 1996: 215).

The vision of civil society organizations, such as the well-known Indonesian Legal Aid Institution, of the state as a protector and guarantor of the people's right to fulfil their basic human rights and civil liberties, is not necessarily shared by the government (YLBHI 2001: 8). While Susilo Bambang Yudhoyono was still Megawati's Coordinating Minister for Political and Security Affairs he made it explicit that 'democracy and human rights should not be considered as the Indonesian nation's absolute goals' (Antara, 10 January 2004). However, 'establishing democracy and justice for all' is one of the three objectives in Yudhoyono's new development strategy for 2004–09, which envisages greater civil society engagement in policy-making, the economy and conflict resolution, as well as in a monitoring capacity (BAPPENAS 2005: 3). However, it will take time for any changes to materialize as long as the political culture remains oriented towards legislation and not towards implementation and management.

In January 2006 the President acknowledged shortcomings in governance that are key issues for civil society, namely that the battle against corruption and for an accountable, transparent, good and responsive government had not yet been won. Further executive, judicial and legislative reforms are required in order to realize this, as well as a continuing demand from the general public for a government that serves them well (*Tempointeraktif*, 6 January 2006).

## Civil society and the military

Military power and reform will only be briefly discussed, as the military is dealt with elsewhere. The military's power is based on the three doctrines of *dwifungsi* (dual function), territorial management and functional groups (Anderson *et al.* 1999: 146). *Dwifungsi* institutionalized and legitimized the military's deep involvement in society and its political role from 1958 onwards. It stipulated military and non-military roles for the army and created a network of military governments with subordinated civilian governments (Emmerson 1990: 115, 121; Jenkins 1984: 270). As Leifer (1995: 358) and Culla (1999: 8–9) point out, the ideas of *dwifungsi* and a strong, independent civil society are difficult to reconcile. There is simply no room for the idea of civilian supremacy over the military.

Essentially the military's socio-political role constitutes the core of the power struggle between the military and civil society that needs to be resolved in order for civil society to prosper. Besides a rethinking of the military's role in Indonesian politics and society, military–civil relations should be redefined, with the military submitting to civil supremacy. This also means that the civilian elite has to take greater responsibility. Military and political reforms are crucial, they are inseparable from each other and they depend on Indonesia's economic recovery (Habib 2001: 87; Panjaitan 2001: 47; Montaperto *et al.* 2000: 1; Sherlock 2003).

Some efforts towards military reform, including bringing the military (TNI) under civilian control, have been made, although the military still constitutes a considerable force and its future role is uncertain. While it is acknowledged that the military has behaved reasonably well and in accordance with the constitution during the post-Suharto era, apprehensions are mainly based on a widespread belief that military reforms have so far only been superficial. Nevertheless, TNI is no longer represented in the House of Representatives or the regional legislative councils. The nomination of the first Air Force Chief, Air Marshal Djoko Suyanto, to head the army-dominated military has also been hailed as a historic development and a fresh start for reform efforts (*The Jakarta Post* 18 January 2006a; Global Information Network 14 October 2005; Singh 2003).

In this context it is vital to note that parts of the army, particularly the Wiranto faction, were invaluable to the pro-democracy movement. While there was no formal alliance, the students would not have managed to occupy the parliamentary building without the indirect support and protection of parts of the military (Aspinall 2000: 316–19; McBeth *et al.* 1998: 17). Aspinall (2000: 317) sees Wiranto's blocking of a presidential declaration of martial law in May 1998 as the army's most important contribution.

Similarly in July 2001, when Abdurrahman Wahid was forced to resign and attempted to retain power using authoritarian tactics, such as declaring a state of emergency and dissolving the parliament, 'the army's decision to side with the parliament put it in the paradoxical position of defending democracy against Indonesia's great democratic hope' (HRW 2001: 1–2). This merely shows how political opportunities and elite conflict can work in civil society's favour.

## Civil society and religion

The anxiety over increasing primordial sentiments highlights another dimension, namely that freedom of thought and religion not only require a guarantee from the state, but also greater tolerance for pluralism in society. This is still lacking in Indonesia (Panjaitan 2001: 31; interviews with Kapal Perempuan 11 January 2002 and Soesastro 15 January 2002).[3] Yet in order to achieve greater tolerance in society, cooperation between state and civil society is crucial.

Primordial sentiments and the role of religion cause a lot of controversy in Indonesia. Religion easily becomes the state domain in a country where national and regional policies, as well as devastating ethnic conflicts, are underpinned by religious sentiments (Kleden 1999: 11). By the same token, the purely spiritual traits of religion effectively separates it from the political state domain, and may serve to provide religious groups with greater political space compared to many other civil society groups.

With at least 87 per cent of Indonesia's population adhering to Islam, the need for recognizing the political force of Islam is frequently emphasized (Porter 2002: 202; and see also Hefner 2000). Yet, it would be a mistake to think of Islam as a homogenous force. In the late 1990s, Muslim groups were mobilized both for and against the regime. Regardless of this, Muslim forces enjoyed a greater degree of freedom and cohesion than many other civil society groups, due to their dual base as a religious and a political movement (Porter 2002: 202; Aspinall 1996: 223).

Primordialism is the main reason why many Indonesian scholars and activists are reluctant to include religious organizations in their definition of civil society (interview with Soesastro 15 January 2002). Culla (1999: 210–11) stresses the importance of civil society's independence not only in its relationship with the state, the economic or political spheres, but also in the interaction between various civil society organizations. Civil society is broader than any narrow class, ethnic, or religious base; therefore it should be a vehicle for overcoming destructive primordial sentiments (Culla 1999: 147; Hikam 1996: 36).

Others regard religious organizations, such as the Islamic Muhammadiyah, as the 'embryo of civil society' because they are firmly embedded in the community and have made important contributions to community services, education and organization since well before independence (interview with Sobary 14 January 2002). Hikam (1996: 31, 33–5), while acknowledging critics who see an Islamization of Indonesian politics as 'dangerous' and 'detrimental' to democratization, nevertheless emphasizes the importance of a parallel process of empowering the Muslim community and building an Indonesian civil society. A modern, just and democratic society can only be achieved through integration, by finding a common ground for all societal forces. Yet, some scholars conclude that Muslims may not be interested in building civil society if it implies a tendency towards Western secularization and individualism (Culla 1999: 42–4).

This does not imply that Muslims will never embrace the civil society idea. Budiman (1990: 367) reiterates the fact that Indonesia's Muslims are neither a homogenous group, nor do they retain a constant perception of other ideologies over time. Organizations like Nahdlatul Ulama (NU) and the Yogyakarta Institute of Islamic Studies (IAIN) have recognized the need for strengthening civil society, particularly an Islamic civil society, and during 2003 and 2004 several conferences and workshops were held on this topic (Antara, 24 September 2003; 10 November 2004).

## The strength of civil society versus the weakness of the state

Budiman (1990: 9) cautioned at an early stage against perceiving democratization in terms of state versus civil society, since the diversity of civil society makes it impossible to conclude that democracy is a result of a strong civil society, when parts of it might support the authoritarian state. He nevertheless emphasized the need for closer cooperation.

In the post-Suharto era Budiman (2001: 39–40) argues that it is not the rise of civil society, nor its strength or weakness that is the main problem, but rather the weakness of existing government institutions. This is very much in line with the *negara hukum* debate. Along with Soesastro (1999: 259) he takes a critical look at civil society and concludes that while civil society is needed to control government, it also causes disorder. If political institutions are weak and people's participation high, this will inevitably result in political instability. Thus, a parallel process of strengthening both civil society and political institutions is required (Budiman 2001: 30–42).

This ties in with the self-limiting radicalism of social movements. Most civil society organizations accept the legitimacy of state authority and appeal to it, rather than destroy it. The importance of a link and dialogue between state and society in order to further the democratization process has been emphasized for years by Hikam, in addition to the view that a strong state can be a positive feature (Hikam 1999: 52–3, 73). Ultimately it is a question of awareness. Indonesians need to be educated in order to start demanding a government that will serve the people, not vice versa (interview with YLBHI 14 January 2002).

Yet, organizational capacity-building is much more than simply education; it entails having the human resources, the institutions and an enabling environment in place. These critical factors have to be developed over time. Nor will the empowerment of civil society materialize if it remains confined to the desks of academic scholars or to the margins of society. This is where civil society organizations have an important role to play: in conveying the message of democratization and the potential power and responsibility of the people in a democracy to the wider community.

Human rights activists caution against the familiar Jakarta syndrome, stressing that civil society also needs to be strengthened in the regions, not only at the centre. In this task the autonomy law could serve as a useful tool (interview with YLBHI 14 January 2002). Law 22/1999 laid down the framework for the regional autonomy. The decentralization was not implemented until January 2001, and in 2004 the law was revised to shift some government authority back to the centre. Antlöv (2003: 200) calls the new regulations 'a quiet revolution in the countryside', a major democratic breakthrough that redefines the relationship between villages and government, and transforms villagers from ignorant 'objects of development' into citizens with the right to decide their own future.

This discussion merely demonstrates the complexity of the Indonesian context, which is further analysed from a social movement perspective below.

## A SOCIAL MOVEMENT PERSPECTIVE OF THE PRO-DEMOCRACY MOVEMENT

Far from being unified, the diversity and fragmentation of the Indonesian democracy movement and its failure to achieve *reformasi* has been emphasized and heavily criticized since the early post-Suharto days (Budiman 1999; McBeth 2001; Törnquist *et al.* 2004: 3).

To some extent this is based on an uncertainty of how to define *reformasi*. Indonesians in general thought students' demands for Suharto's resignation was their ultimate goal and labelled their other differing demands '*reformasi*', without specifying the meaning of reform (McRae 2001: 20). In reality, however, Suharto's resignation was never the final goal, but students did not have a clear, united strategy of how to pursue the democratization struggle after Suharto's ousting. Thus, Suharto's name became a convenient tool in the *reformasi* struggle (McRae 2001: 21–2, 41; and interview with Hidayat 15 January 2002).

One strategy of social movements is to find collective action frames in the form of familiar symbols that will serve to mobilize people while disregarding questions concerning strategy and tactics (Tarrow 1994: 118–22; Pakulski 1991: 35–6). The students were undoubtedly successful in this. Since 1996 grassroots mobilization had posed a threat to the political leadership, while it had created greater awareness among people. Paraphrasing Lane (1999a: 242), the clear demands of the students at the time served to channel general mass disillusion in a coherent political direction.

Second, whereas various actors, organizations, supporters and sympathizers were unified under a general call for reform and change, they nevertheless retained their separate agendas and goals. This is very much in line with social movement theory, which argues that 'fragmented and disunited' does not necessarily imply 'weak'. One of the strengths of social movements is their inherently disparate nature, which makes them more difficult for an authoritarian state to repress. Under the general umbrella of the broader movement the various actors may still be able to achieve their specific goals (Pakulski 1991: 36, 73–4).

Third, the morality and value-laden characteristics of social movements are often highlighted, in addition to the fact that they do not compete for institutionalized political power (Pakulski 1991: 35–6). This moralization of politics fits the Indonesian situation nicely. The students, for example, have often been depicted as a 'moral force', aspiring to correct government, not necessarily overthrow it (Budiman in Aspinall 1996: 223; McRae 2001: 3; and interview with Hidayat 15 January 2002). They have also been accused of not taking the opportunity to access political power and not being radical enough to achieve true change (Mangunwijaya 1999). This tendency of not wanting to access formal political power is typical of social movements and does not imply that the movement as a whole has 'failed'. In fact, until recently little has been known about the degree of change desired by the various groups of actors in relation to the broader pro-democracy movement.

Fourth, the aspect of change itself is important and how 'success' can be measured. Even if mass social movements do not 'succeed' in terms of realizing officially proclaimed goals, they nevertheless do seriously challenge the political system and undermine the status quo. By their very activities they serve as catalysts for social and political change (Pakulski 1991: 36–7, 83). Tarrow (1994: 172) highlights the politicization of participants, the impacts on political institutions and practices, and the inevitable changes in political culture as three important, indirect, long-term effects of social movements. The effects Tarrow identifies are of importance since they ultimately concern the much needed change in mindset emphasized by Indonesian civil society representatives (interviews with Sobary 14 January 2002; Hidayat 15 January 2002; Soesastro 15 January 2002; see also Nyman 2006).

The pro-democracy movement has been characterized as 'a movement very much driven by reaction', which made it difficult for the various groups to unite and draw up a new vision for the country once Suharto had resigned (interview with Soesastro 15 January 2002). As mentioned previously, this mobilization against one enemy is a common social movement characteristic. Furthermore, movements do not compete for institutional political power and they often lack defined platforms and programmes, which partly explain the perceived fragmentation of the movement once Suharto had been removed (Pakulski 1991: 36–7; Tarrow 1994: 26).

Ultimately it is not the nature or role of social movements to be concerned with implementation and consolidation. That is why a strong, capable civil society has to take over where the 1998 pro-democracy movement left off.

## THE ROLE OF CIVIL SOCIETY AND THE CHALLENGES AHEAD

It deserves to be reiterated that never at any time was the Indonesian pro-democracy movement a homogenous force; the same applies for civil society. Yet the expectations on both the pro-democracy movement and civil society in terms of organization, focus, coherence, capacity and capability to unite and deliver have been simply enormous. It goes without saying that the expectations on Indonesia's transition to democracy are of an equal magnitude. Managing people's expectations successfully in the face of perceived shortcomings is extremely difficult. Civil society has certainly had to face its share of criticism and disappointment, internally and externally.

The labour movement, for example, has fallen short of expectations. First labour was criticized for its absence from the 1998 pro-democracy movement; then, for not fulfilling the high expectations regarding its democratic potential and its failure to emerge as a coherent, powerful actor in the post-Suharto years (Winters 2000: 141, Hadiz 2000: 25 and 1999: 124; Törnquist 2004). Labour activists explain it as a preference to focus on labour-related issues instead of broader democratization issues (interviews with ACILS 09 January 2002; Sisbikum 10 January 2002). In 1998 labour was in fact largely excluded by the students, who did not liaise with workers, peasants and urban poor because their struggles were perceived as being 'social-economic' and 'self-interested'. Workers were left outside the mainstream *reformasi* movement (Hadiz 1999:124; Hadiz 2000: 25; Lane 1999b: 3).

Törnquist points to the greater structural factors that limited labour's bargaining power, but also to labour's lack of capacity to take advantage of the political space that opened up in the post-Suharto era. Without a clear labour-regime to confront, without a broader labour movement agenda, all their organizing efforts have merely amounted to a fragmentation into numerous unions, federations and labour NGOs (Törnquist 2004: 1, 18; Tornquist *et al.* 2004: 15; Ford 2001: 110–12).

The women's movement has likewise been considered too disparate and divided to have a significant impact, although nobody denies it has had a strong political influence in recent years (Machali 2001: 2; interview with LBH APIK 11 January 200; *Kompas*, 25 March 2005). New women's organizations have emerged in the post-Suharto era, some with great ambitions to forge a common platform for women. One example is the Indonesian National Women's Coalition for Justice and Democracy (KPI), established in late 1998 (Sen 1999: 15; Katjasungkana 2001: 11). At the time, a majority of women wanted a strong coalition instead of a multitude of NGOs. Little had been heard of KPI by 2002 and activists suspected that the coalition had splintered into different issue-based NGOs again (interview with Solidaritas Perempuan 08 January 2002).

In 2004, KPI held its second congress, where one of the labour movement's most prominent activists, Dita Sari, criticized the women's movement for being spread over too many fronts, which she regarded as the inherent weakness of the movement. The criticism was dismissed by KPI's secretary general, lawyer and activist Nursyahbani Katjasungkana, who envisaged a broad future women's coalition with several platforms that could unite, if need be. KPI is an example of this, as it was established as an umbrella organization for a broad spectrum of organizations and individuals, ranging from academics and professionals, to housewives, peasants and urban poor (*Kompas*, 19 January 2004).

Nursyahbani's stance is similar to the views of some former student activists, who consider the existence of a variety of issues and platforms to be a healthy aspect of Indonesia's current democratization process, not a weakness. It is part of the new freedom of association for civil society activists to be able to choose from a multitude of issues according to their particular interests and priorities (interview with Adnanya 01 February 2002).

Indonesia's democratization remains an utterly complex process, as discussed throughout this book. It would be unfair not to acknowledge that impressive progress towards democratic reform has been accomplished in some areas, such as: transforming Indonesia into an electoral democracy; freedom of press and association; abolishing the doctrines of *monoloyalitas* and 'floating mass'; making the president accountable to the electorate; removing military representation from the House of Representatives and the regional legislative councils; decentralization of power to the regions; new labour legislation; new financial laws guaranteeing increased fiscal transparency and monitoring; civil service reform; the establishment of independent institutions such as the National Law Commission, the Constitutional Court and the Supreme Audit Agency; and involving civil society, media and international observers in various monitoring processes (MacIntyre and Resosudarmo 2003: 152–3; Antlöv 2003: 200 and 209–10; *The Jakarta Post* 2005; Transparency International 2005a: 159–61; Hamilton-Hart 2001: 69–73).

On the other hand, implementation of existing legal instruments, such as labour legislation or regional autonomy in Papua and Aceh, is still lacking and the democratization process has been fraught with problems. Demos' first democratization study found that the momentum of democratic transition, as well as the pro-democratic rights and institutions, have been hijacked by the elite, with civil society confined to the margins of the political system (Tornquist *et al.* 2004: 20). They base their findings on IDEA's widely accepted framework for assessing the quality of 85 rights and institutions deemed necessary for democracy, which in Demos' study have been turned into 36 criteria.[4]

> The first relates to how the people (*demos*) that are supposed to decide equally about public affairs actually identify themselves. The following 35 relate to the standard of (a) law and judiciary, citizenship and human rights, (b) government and public administration, representation and accountability, and (c) civil society (including instances of direct democracy and self-management)
>
> (Törnquist *et al.* 2004: 5)

Interestingly, the rights and freedoms necessary for a viable civil society scored well, compared with socio-economic rights, the rule of law, justice, corruption, representation, governance and control of the armed forces. The study recognizes civil society's potential in its call for 're-politicisation of civil society in order to alter power relations', which goes against 'the mainstream "democratic consolidation" thesis of crafting "good" institutions and, quite separately from that, de-politicising civil society, strengthening it against the state and avoiding conflicts' (Törnquist *et al.* 2004: 2–3, 10).

The relatively successful presidential and legislative elections in 2004, as well as findings from Demos' second-round study, show that while election laws exist and some basic freedoms are available, the concerns highlighted in 2004 are still valid. The new president is part of the old structure and the question remains whether the country is undergoing democratic consolidation or not, and what the future holds (Törnquist *et al.* 2005: 8; Choi 2004: 1–2; Singh 2003: 10). Demos furthermore contends that while important progress has been made in terms of freedom, rights and institutions, the democratic instruments are not viable and improvements in certain areas have at times been outnumbered by setbacks in other areas. One particular concern is that the elite, socially and politically as well connected as ever, has become part of the state and society; embedded in national and regional parliaments, as well as in business and civil society (Törnquist *et al.* 2005: 21, 38). They arrive at four conclusions regarding the problems and options for a human rights-based democracy:

i  There are critical basic freedoms, but a severe democratic deficit of other rights and institutions, including people's identification with the national and regional *demos*.
ii  There are free and fair elections, but only of unrepresentative and unresponsive parties and politicians.
iii  The dominant members of elite tend to adjust to the new game of democracy but monopolise it, bending and abusing the rules of the game as they go.
iv  The agents of change that brought democracy to Indonesia are still critical as civic activists and pressure groups but are 'floating' in the margins of the fledgling democratic system, thus being unable to make a real impact.

(Törnquist *et al.* 2005: 17–18)

Thus, despite gloomy reports regarding Indonesia's democratic performance, civil society has overall scored relatively high in surveys and research. Although it has not emerged as one coherent pro-democracy movement, the unprecedented freedom of press and association have caused civil society to thrive, fuelling hope that it may yet provide a viable alternative for furthering democratization (Global Information Network 14 October 2005; Ghoshal 2004: 15; Törnquist *et al.* 2004: 3; Sularto 2001).

Many respondents in 2002 saw the 2004 elections as a benchmark where the pros and cons of democratization would be weighed up, which would determine whether a new wave of *reformasi* could be expected, or perhaps a retreat to a familiar, more authoritarian system. Others were more pragmatic, perceiving 2009 as a realistic benchmark (interviews with Sobary 14 January 2002; Hidayat 15 January 2002; Soesastro 15 January 2002).

> In order for society to enter into democratic consolidation you need to go ten steps. By 2004 we will be, at most, two steps out of ten. In 2009, depending on what happens, maybe we have progressed another three steps. But again, who will lead this development? The champions can only come from civil society. They need to continue to put pressure on the government, therefore they have to be strengthened.
>
> (Interview with Soesastro 15 January 2002)

The outcome of the 2004 elections was important in terms of determining the political space available for civil society to consolidate and pursue further democratic reforms for the benefit of the greater community. With the legitimacy of the political system increasingly being questioned, Yudhoyono's government will have to face the challenges of civil society and determine the relationship between state and civil society, as well as the mechanisms for this relationship, more explicitly than previous governments have. This opens up political space for civil society to act.

What role is then accorded to civil society in the future democratization? Prior to the 2004 presidential elections, Fatah identified three major factors that will impact on Indonesia's democratic consolidation in the long term: the emergence of factions rejecting democracy; the challenge of increased militarism, including the lack of military reform; and the endurance of civil society in the face of the economic and social failure of a democratically elected regime and a growing popular support for a more authoritarian regime (Fatah 2004).

Social and political commentators emphasize broader civil society participation in governance and policy-making as a necessary condition for democracy. Qualifying this statement, it is not sufficient with broad participation *per se* or to be granted access to government; political will and proper mechanisms for real and meaningful consultation between state and civil society must exist. Respondents furthermore acknowledge the need for a stronger, more united civil society in order to re-establish 'the social contract' that has been eroded by the New Order and the solidarity among people that has been lost (interviews with Solidaritas Perempuan 8 January 2002; LBH APIK 11 January 2002; YLBHI 14 January 2002; Sobary 14 January 2002, Soesastro 15 January 2002). Besides greater internal unity within civil society, two external conditions that concern the enabling environment necessary for an emerging civil society are still lacking in Indonesia:

> There must be an enabling environment for civil society to develop. Number one is recognition by the state. It means that room for civil society has to be provided through the constitution, as in Thailand. In

the case of the Philippines, government has recognized that civil society can play a role as partner in development. This is ensured not through the constitution but through a series of government regulations on the national and regional levels. This is totally missing in Indonesia! The second aspect is an environment that would allow civil society to mobilize funding, which is a critical issue in developing countries.

(Interview with Soesastro, 15 January 2002)

An area where civil society has a strategic role to play is in rural development. While democratization and decentralization provide the necessary preconditions, they are not sufficient without active involvement from both government and civil society at national and regional level. This is the only way to ensure ordinary people are included in policy-making and governance (Antlöv 2003: 194). One should not underestimate the importance of this role. With a slow macroeconomic recovery, predictions about continued low growth that might lead to social upheaval, and the impact from exiting IMF, which implies less money for social reforms and rural development, there will definitely be a need for more human resources and services in rural areas than the government is able to provide.

Given the previous disenfranchisement of Indonesians, civil society is needed in a monitoring capacity, as well as for balancing the scales in favour of the people. With high-ranking offenders escaping justice, a resurgent business elite assuming more political power, and no transparent plan for political reforms, Indonesia might end up heavily dependent on the elite for the next few years. Antlöv (2003: 210) cautions that district elites and the state continue to pose the main threats to grassroots democracy in Indonesia.

For the democratization process to stay on track civil society has to overcome the barriers of the past and assist the wider community in doing so as well. Greater cooperation between civil society forces is required, in addition to more systematic cooperation between state and society in order to disseminate power from government to civil society. A future leadership untainted by New Order thinking is highly desirable. This change in mindset necessarily stretches beyond the leaders to the people and is seen as a task that can only be achieved through greater involvement of civil society (interviews with YLBHI 14 January 2002; Sobary 14 January 2002; and Soesastro 15 January 2002).

The fight against corruption may yet prove to be the one issue that unites civil society and enhances state–society cooperation. The President has stated that he will need support from all layers of society to put an end to corruption (State Secretariat 16 August 2005). The call for an end to corruption, collusion and nepotism (KKN) has been a prominent issue for the pro-democracy movement from the start. In Transparency International's Global Corruption Perceptions Index 2005 Indonesia ranks near the bottom of the scale as number 140 out of 159 countries. Religious bodies and NGOs were perceived as the least corrupt, while political parties were considered most corrupt; closely followed by the parliament/legislature, police and customs; and then by the judiciary, tax revenue and business sector (Transparency International 2005a: 159–61; 2005b: 18; 2005c).

Robust mechanisms and practices have yet to be established to provide for genuine and meaningful input from civil society in strategic areas, although some attempts to allow for greater formalized civil society input in various commissions and committees have been made. Examples of these are the National Law Commission, the Joint Investigation Team and the Anti-Corruption Commission (Hamilton-Hart 2001: 69–74). The signals from the Indonesian government are mixed. The views of officials range from expressing outright hostility to the idea of greater popular participation, or regarding civil society as a nuisance, to being rather sympathetic to greater civil society involvement (interview with Soesastro 15 January 2002). The problems in this context are twofold: first, there must be political will to make the necessary legislative and procedural changes in order to create an enabling environment. Second, civil society representatives have to overcome a lingering New Order legacy in the form of an ever-present suspicion and mistrust of the government's ulterior motives to be able to make a significant impact in Indonesia's future democratization.

## CONCLUSION

This chapter has assessed the current role, situation and future prospects of civil society in post-Suharto Indonesia. The historical lack of an enabling environment for civil society to prosper has been highlighted, as well as what remains to be done in this respect. Other vital issues concern the impact of the ebb and flow of political space and political opportunities in the mobilization of civil society – spearheaded in 1998 by the pro-democracy forces – as well as common misconceptions regarding the nature and role of social movements versus the nature and role of civil society. Despite allegations of fragmentation and shortcomings in achieving *reformasi*, the 1998 pro-democracy movement clearly acted within the perimeters of social movements: with diverse groups uniting for a short time against one enemy, without any plan for action post-Suharto and not aiming for political power. What is needed in the post-Suharto era to further democratization is a strong, resourceful civil society to take over where the social movement left off.

While there is no such thing as a 'hybrid civil society', civil society can be more or less mature in terms of its capacity, integrity, strategic alliances and the way it interacts with the state. Compared with countries with longer democratic traditions, it is evident that Indonesia's civil society is still in its infancy; experiencing the new political space in terms of freedom of press and association by being more diverse than ever before. While some see this diversity as a weakness, others regard it as an inevitable part of democratization. Before civil society can counterbalance the state in a meaningful manner, civil society will have to overcome internal rivalry, primordialism, and a fragmentation into diverse issue-based groupings, to organize itself more efficiently and develop a common platform around some key issues that could serve to unify a majority of civil society. One such core issue is corruption. Yet, it is not sufficient to build a strong civil society; an enabling environment is also required, where the state guarantees the necessary rights and freedoms for civil society, and mechanisms for constructive interaction with government are developed.

Given Indonesia's repressive recent past and the limitations on civil society organization and freedom of expression, civil society has made remarkable progress and demonstrated its capability to seize crucial political opportunities and expand its political space. There is no denying that civil society is currently fragmented; however, this is a consequence of the New Order repression. In the new climate of openness, people's interests are not limited to democratization. Developing critical thinking and awareness in a society that has experienced systematic oppression for a generation is not an easy task, yet it is one of the fundamental building blocks for a strong civil society that has the ability not only to check and balance the state, but also possesses the strength to monitor and balance itself. In order for any democratization worth its name to take place, civil society needs to be an integral part of it.

Thus, the period between the 2004 and the 2009 elections is a crucial window of opportunity for civil society to consolidate and take a more proactive stance in matters of governance and public-policy making. With Indonesia moving beyond the initial democratic transition phase, civil society needs to translate the lessons learnt in the early post-Suharto years into a language that people in the broader community will understand. It is the task of civil society to facilitate the necessary links between the government and the people and continue to put pressure on both parties to actively participate in furthering the democratization process. All stakeholders need to gain a deeper appreciation of the rights and obligations of the state and its citizens in a modern democracy – and make it work in an Indonesian context. This is the challenge for civil society beyond 2006.

## NOTES

1 Some of these findings have been published and discussed in further depth in Nyman, M. (2002) and in Nyman, M. (2006). I am grateful for the Nordic Institute of Asian Studies (NIAS) granting permission to use some of the findings and direct quotes in this chapter.
2 See Nyman (2006) for an in-depth discussion on the Indonesian civil society concept and context.
3 Primordial conflicts (based on religion, ethnicity, race, class) are often referred to as 'horizontal conflicts' and seen as destructive for national unity and stability. They are also referred to as SARA (*suku, agama, ras, antar golongan,* meaning matters

regarding ethnic, religious and racial relations) (Sumartana 1999: 253). Examples
in the post-Suharto era are the bloody clashes between Christians and Muslims in
Maluku, and between transmigrants from Madura and Dayaks in Kalimantan
(Budiman 2001: 33–4). Ethnicity has also been used by the government as a tool for
preventing working class mobilization (Hikam 1995: 368–9).
4 See Beetham, D., Bracking, S., Kearton, I. and Weir, S. (2002) *International IDEA
Handbook and Democracy Assessment*, The Hague, London, New York: Kluwer
Law International.

## BIBLIOGRAPHY

Anderson, B., Shiraishi, T. and Siegel, J. T. (1999) 'Current data on the Indonesian
military elite January 1, 1998-January 31, 1999', *Indonesia*, 67: 133–47.
Antara (2003) 'Serious efforts needed to build civil society, says professor',
24 September 2003. Online. Available ProQuest doc. ID: 411349481 (accessed
5 January 2006).
—— (2004) 'Democracy, human rights must not become absolute goals: Minister',
10 January 2004. Online. Available ProQuest doc. ID: 523253981 (accessed
5 January 2006).
—— (2004) 'ICIS holds workshop on Islam and civil society', 10 November 2004.
Online. Available ProQuest doc. ID: 764063691 (accessed 5 January 2006).
Antlöv, H. (2003) 'Village government and rural development in Indonesia', *Bulletin
of Indonesian Economic Studies*, 39 (2): 193–214.
Aspinall, E. (1996) 'The broadening base of political opposition in Indonesia', in
G. Rodan (ed.) *Political Oppositions in Industrialising Asia*, London, New York:
Routledge.
—— (2000) 'Political opposition and the transition from authoritarian rule: The
case of Indonesia', PhD thesis, Research School of Pacific and Asian Studies,
Australian National University.
BAPPENAS (2005) 'Overview of the Indonesia's medium-term development plan
2004–2009 by Sri Mulyani Indrawati'. Online. Available HTTP: <http://www.bap
penas.go.id/pnData/news/200501/01_Overview_of_RPJMN_2004-2009_-
_CGI_2005_-_final.pdf> (accessed 20 January 2006).
Budiman, A. (ed.) (1990) *State and Civil Society in Indonesia*, Clayton: Centre of
Southeast Asian Studies, Monash University.
—— (1999) 'New Order old school', *Inside Indonesia*, 58: 7.
—— (2001) 'Negara dan Masyarakat Madani' [The state and civil society], in
S. Sularto (ed.) *Masyarakat Warga dan Pergulatan Demokrasi* [Civil Society and
the Struggle for Democracy], Jakarta: Penerbit Buku Kompas.
Choi, N. (2004) 'Local elections and party politics in post-reformasi Indonesia: a
view from Yogyakarta', *Contemporary Southeast Asia*, 26 (2). Online. Available
InfoTrac OneFile article: A122163888 (accessed 8 January 2006).
Cohen, J. L. and Arato, A. (1992) *Civil Society and Political Theory*, New Baskerville:
MIT Press.
Culla, A. (1999) *Masyarakat Madani. Pemikiran, Teori, dan Relevansinya Dengan
Cita-cita Reformasi* [Civil Society. Thought, theory, and its relevance to the aspir-
ations of reformasi], Jakarta: RajaGrafindo Persada.
Dhakidae, D. (2001) 'Sistem Sebagai Totalisasi, Masyarakat Warga dan Pergulatan

Demokrasi', in S. Sularto (ed.) *Masyarakat Warga dan Pergulatan Demokrasi*, [Civil society and the struggle for democracy], Jakarta: Penerbit Buku Kompas.

Emmerson, D. K. (1990) 'The military and development in Indonesia', in J. S. Djiwandono and Y. M. Cheong (eds) *Soldiers and Stability in Southeast Asia*, 2nd edn, Singapore: Institute of Southeast Asian Studies.

Fatah, E. S. (2004) 'The 2004 presidential election: possible outcome', paper presented at the 'The Indonesian Presidential Elections 2004: Up Close and Up to Date' seminar, Jakarta: Centre for Strategic and International Studies, 13 May 2004.

Ford, M. (2000) 'Continuity and change in Indonesian labour relations in the Habibie interregnum', *Southeast Asian Journal of Social Science*, 28 (2): 59–88.

—— (2001) 'Challenging the criteria of significance: lessons from contemporary Indonesian labour history', *Australian Journal of Politics and History*, 47 (1): 101–14.

Ghoshal, B. (2004) 'Democratic transition and political development in post-Soeharto Indonesia', *Contemporary Southeast Asia*, 26 (3). Online, Available ProQuest Doc ID: 782065371 (accessed 15 January 2006).

Global Information Network (2005) 'Indonesia: Yudhoyono loosens the reins on press, civil society', 14 October 2005. Online. Available ProQuest document ID: 911541931 (accessed 5 January 2006).

Habib, A. (2001) 'Posisi dan Peranan Militer' [The position and role of the military], in S. Sularto (ed.) *Masyarakat Warga dan Pergulatan Demokrasi* [Civil society and the struggle for democracy], Jakarta: Penerbit Buku Kompas.

Hadiz, V. (1994) 'Challenging state corporatism on the labour front: working class politics in the 1990s', in D. Bourchier and J. Legge (eds) *Democracy in Indonesia: 1950s and 1990s*, Clayton: Monash University.

—— (1999) 'Contesting political change after Suharto', in A. Budiman, B. Hatley and D. Kingsbury (eds) *Reformasi: Crisis and Change in Indonesia*, Clayton: Monash Asia Institute.

—— (2000) 'Retrieving the past for the future? Indonesia and the New Order legacy', *Southeast Asian Journal of Social Science*, 28 (2): 10–33.

Hamilton-Hart, N. (2001) 'Anti-corruption strategies in Indonesia', *Bulletin of Indonesian Economic Studies*, 37 (1): 65–82.

Harkrisnowo, H. (2001) 'The perspective of legal ethics on political condition and its predictions to legal system', paper presented at the 'International Seminar on the Political Condition in Indonesia: Its Impact on Macro Economic Investment', Brisbane: Griffith University, 21 September.

Hefner, R. W. (2000) *Civil Islam. Muslims and Democratization in Indonesia*, Princeton and Oxford: Princeton University Press.

Hikam, M. (1995) 'The state, grass-roots politics and civil society: a study of social movements under Indonesia's New Order (1989–1994)', PhD dissertation, University of Hawai'i.

—— (1996) 'Islam and the empowerment of Indonesian civil society', *The Indonesian Quarterly*, XXIV (1): 31–7.

—— (1999) *Demokrasi dan Civil Society* [Democracy and civil society], 2nd edn, Jakarta: Pustaka LP3ES.

Honna, J. (2001) 'Military ideology in response to democratic pressure during the late Suharto era: political and institutional contexts', in B. R. O. G. Anderson (ed.) *Violence and the State in Suharto's Indonesia*, New York: Cornell Southeast Asia Program Publications, Ithaca.

HRW (Human Rights Watch) (2001) *Indonesia: Abdurrahman Wahid's Human Rights Legacy*. Online. Available HTTP: <http://www.hrw.org/press/2001/07/wahidlegacy0726.htm> (accessed 10 January 2006).

Indobizlaw (Indonesian business law on the Internet) (2004) 'Legislation List'. Online. Available HTTP: <http://www.indobizlaw.com/default.asp?form=legislation> (accessed 15 January 2006).

*Jakarta Post, The* (2004) 'Political Outlook 2004'. Online. Available HTTP: <http://www.thejakartapost.com/outlook/political> (accessed 1 May 2004).

—— (2005) 'Political Outlook 2005'. Online. Available HTTP: <http://www.thejakartapost.com/outlook/political> (accessed 15 December 2005).

Jenkins, D. (1984) *Suharto and His Generals. Indonesian Military Politics 1975–1983*, New York: Cornell University Press, Ithaca.

Katjasungkana, N. (2001) *The Indonesian Legal System and the Empowerment of Women*. Online. Available HTTP: <http://www.law.unimelb.edu.au/news/assets/NursyahbaniPaper.doc> (accessed 25 November 2005).

Kleden, I. (1999) 'Tantangan Ganda Untuk Masyarakat Madani: Catatan Mengenai Politik Pasca Soeharto' [The multiple challenges for civil society: commentary about post-Suharto politics], *Diponegoro*, 74 (8): 6–17.

Lane, M. (1999a) 'Mass politics and political change in Indonesia', in A. Budiman, B. Hatley and D. Kingsbury (eds) *Reformasi: Crisis and Change in Indonesia*, Clayton: Monash Asia Institute.

—— (1999b), 'Interview with Indonesian labor leader Dita Sari', *Green Left Weekly*, 11 August. Online. Available HTTP: <http://www.greenleft.org.au/back/1999/371/> (accessed 30 November 2005).

Leifer, M. (1995) 'The challenge of creating a civil society in Indonesia', *The Indonesian Quarterly*, XXIII (4): 354–60.

Lubis, T. M. and Santosa, M. A. (1999), 'Economic regulation, good governance and the environment: an agenda for law reform in Indonesia', in A. Budiman, B. Hatley and D. Kingsbury (eds) *Reformasi, Crisis and Change in Indonesia*, Clayton: Monash Asia Institute.

Machali, R. (2001) 'Women and the concept of power in Indonesia', in S. Blackburn (ed.) *Love, Sex and Power. Women in Southeast Asia*, Clayton: Monash Asia Institute.

MacIntyre, A. and Resosudarmo, B. (2003) 'Survey of recent developments', *Bulletin of Indonesian Economic Studies*, 39 (2): 133–56.

Mangunwijaya, Y. B. (1999) 'Not reformasi, transformasi! Student demands have been far too timid', *Inside Indonesia*, 58: 10.

McAdam, D., McCarthy, J. and Zald, M. (1996) *Comparative Perspectives on Social Movements. Political Opportunities, Mobilizing Structures, and Cultural Framings*, New York, Melbourne: Cambridge University Press.

McBeth, J., Vatikiotis, M. and Cohen, M. (1998) 'Into the void', *Far Eastern Economic Review*, 4 June: 16–18.

—— (2001) 'Lost labour, lost reform', *Far Eastern Economic Review*, 15 March: 22–24.

McRae, D. (2001) *The 1998 Indonesian Student Movement*, Monash Working Papers on Southeast Asia No. 110, Clayton: Monash Asia Institute.

Montaperto, R., Przystup, J. J., Faber, G. W. and Schwarz, A. (2000) 'Indonesian democratic transition', *Strategic Forum*, April 2000 (no. 171). Online. Available HTTP: <http://www.ndu.edu/inss/strforum/sf171/forum171.html> (accessed 20 December 2005).

Nyman, M. (2002) 'Indonesia in Transition: The Challenges of Civil Society in the Era of Reformasi', MA dissertation, University of Southern Queensland.

—— (2006) *Democratizing Indonesia. The Challenges of Civil Society in the Era of Reformasi*, NIAS Report No. 49, Copenhagen: NIAS Press.

Pakulski, J. (1991) *Social Movements: the Politics of Moral Protest*, Melbourne: Longman Cheshire.

Panjaitan, M. (2001) *Gerakan Warganegara Menuju Demokrasi* [Citizens' movement towards democracy], Jakarta: Restu Agung.

Porter, D. (2002) 'Citizen participation through mobilization and the rise of political Islam in Indonesia', *The Pacific Review*, 15 (2): 201–24.

Rahayu, R. I. (1996) 'Politik Gender Orde Baru: Tinjauan Organisasi Perempuan Sejak 1980-an' [New Order gender politics: observations of women's organisations since the 1980s], *Prisma*, 25 (5): 29–42.

Rodan, G. (1996) 'Theorising political opposition in East and Southeast Asia', in G. Rodan (ed.) *Political Oppositions in Industrialising Asia*, London: Routledge.

—— (1997) 'Civil society and other political possibilities in Southeast Asia', *Journal of Contemporary Asia*, 27 (2): 156–78.

Scholte, J. A. (2000), *Globalization: A Critical Introduction*, London: Macmillan.

Sen, K. (1999) 'Women on the move', *Inside Indonesia*, April–June 1999: 14–15.

Shaw, M. (1994) 'Civil society and global politics: beyond a social movements approach', *Millennium: Journal of International Studies*, 23 (3): 647–67.

Sherlock, S. (2003) *Conflict in Aceh: A Military Solution?*, Current Issues Brief, No. 32 2002–2003. Online. Available HTTP: <http://www.aph.gov.au/library/pubs/CIB/2002–03/03cib32.htm> (accessed 20 December 2005).

Singh, B. (2003) 'The 2004 presidential elections in Indonesia: much ado about nothing?', *Contemporary Southeast Asia*, 25 (3). Online. Available InfoTrac OneFile article: A112411703 (accessed 8 January 2006).

Soesastro, H. (1999) 'Civil society and development: the missing link', *The Indonesian Quarterly*, XXVII (3): 256–66.

State Secretariat of the Republic of Indonesia (2005) 'State address of the President of the Republic of Indonesia and the Government statement on the state budget for the 2006 fiscal year and its financial note before the plenary session of the House of representatives on 16 August 2005'. Online. Available HTTP: <http://www.thejakartapost.com/sby_speech 2005.asp> (accessed 18 November 2005).

Sularto, S. (ed.) (2001) *Masyarakat Warga dan Pergulatan Demokrasi* [Civil society and the struggle for democracy], Jakarta: Penerbit Buku Kompas.

Sumartana, T. (1999) 'Towards the building of co-operation between religious groups in a time of national crisis, in A. Budiman, B. Hatley and D. Kingsbury (eds) *Reformasi: Crisis and Change in Indonesia*, Clayton: Monash Asia Institute.

Suryakusuma, J. (1996) 'The state and sexuality in New Order Indonesia', in L. Sears (ed.) *Fantasizing the Feminine in Indonesia*, Durham and London: Duke University Press.

Tanter, R. (1990) 'The totalitarian ambition: intelligence and security agencies in Indonesia', in A. Budiman (ed.) *State and Civil Society in Indonesia*, Clayton: Centre of Southeast Asian Studies.

Tarrow, S. (1994) *Power in Movement: Social Movements, Collective Action and Politics*, Cambridge, New York, Melbourne: Cambridge University Press.

—— (1996) 'States and opportunities: the political structuring of social movements', in D. McAdam, J. McCarthy and M. Zald (eds) *Comparative Perspectives on*

*Social Movements*, Cambridge, New York, Melbourne: Cambridge University Press.
Törnquist, O. (2000) 'Dynamics of Indonesian democratisation', *Third World Quarterly*, 21 (3). Online. Available Academic Search Premier, item: 3325509 (accessed 15 May 2002).
—— (2004) 'Labour and Democracy? Reflections on the Indonesian Impasse', *Journal of Contemporary Asia* 34 (3). Online. Available ProQuest document ID: 681316491 (accessed 6 January 2006).
Törnquist, O. *et al.* (2004) 'Executive Report January 28, 2004. 1st Round Study of the Problems and Options of Indonesian democratisation', DEMOS. Online. Available HTTP: <http://www.sum.uio.no/publications/pdf_fulltekst/tornquist.pdf> (accessed 12 January 2006).
Törnquist, O. *et al.* (2005) 'Executive Report January 20, 2005. Towards an Agenda for Meaningful Human Rights-Based Democracy', DEMOS. Online. Available HTTP: <http://www.demos.or.id/xc_summary_eng.htm> (accessed 12 January 2006).
Transparency International (2005a) 'Global Corruption Report 2005'. Online. Available HTTP: <http://www.globalcorruptionreport.org/gcr2005/download/english/country_reports_a_j.pdf> (accessed 10 January 2006).
—— (2005b) 'Report on the TransparencyInternational Global Corruption Barometer 2005'. Online. Available HTTP: <http://www.transparency.org/policy_and_research/surveys_indices.pdf> (accessed 10 January 2006).
—— (2005c) 'Corruption Perceptions Index 2005'. Online. Available HTTP: <http://www.transparency.org/layout/set/print/policy_and_research/surveys_indices/cpi> (accessed 10 January 2006).
Uhlin, A. (1997) *Indonesia and 'The Third Wave of Democratization': The Indonesian Pro-democracy Movement in a Changing World*, New York: St. Martin's Press.
—— (2002) 'Development and the external dimension of regime transitions. Illustrations from Indonesia', in O. Elgström and G. Hyden (eds) *Development and Democracy. What Have We Learned and How?*, London and New York: Routledge.
Wagemann, M. (2000) 'Indonesian women between yesterday and tomorrow', in M. Oey-Gardiner and C. Bianpoen (eds) *Indonesian Women. The Journey Continues*, Canberra: Research School of Pacific and Asian Studies.
Winters, J. A. (2000) 'The political economy of labor in Indonesia', *Indonesia*, 70: 139–49.
YLBHI (Yayasan Lembaga Bantuan Hukum Indonesia) (2001) 'Hand in hand with the people for democracy' – objectives, vision and mission statement, Jakarta: LBHI.

## INTERVIEWS

ACILS (American Centre for International Labor Solidarity) and *Dewan Pimpinan Pusat Federasi Serikat Pekerja Farmasi dan Kesehatan Reformasi* (Pharmaceutical and Health Workers Union 'Reformasi'), Jakarta, 9 January 2002.
Adnanya, K., former chairman of STSI Student Senate, Denpasar (*Ketua Senat Mahasiswa STSI Sekolah Tinggi Seni Indonesia*, Advanced College of Indonesian Arts), Ubud, Bali, 1 February 2002.

Hidayat, P., former KB-UI student activist at the University of Indonesia, Jakarta, 15 January 2002.

Kapal Perempuan (*Kapal Perempuan – Lingkaran Alternatif untuk Perempuan*, the Circle of Alternative Education for Women), Jakarta, 11 January 2002.

LBH APIK (*Lembaga Bantuan Hukum Asosiasi Perempuan Indonesia untuk Keadilan*, Legal Aid of Indonesian Women's Association for Justice, Jakarta, 11 January 2002.

Sisbikum (*Saluran Informasi Sosial dan Bimbingan Hukum*, Social Information and legal Guidance Foundation), Jakarta, 10 January 2002.

Sobary, M., social and political commentator at the national news agency Wisma Antara and the daily newspaper *Kompas*, Jakarta, 14 January 2002.

Soesastro, H., Executive Director of the Center of Strategic and International Studies (CSIS), and board member of the civil society organisation Tifa Foundation, Jakarta, 15 January 2002.

Solidaritas Perempuan (*Solidaritas Perempuan Untuk Hak Asasi Manusia*, Women's Solidarity for Human Rights), Jakarta, 8 January 2002.

Yakoma-PGI (*Yayasan Komunikasi Masyarakat – Persekutuan Gereja-Gereja di Indonesia*, the Association for People's Communication – the Council of Churches in Indonesia), Jakarta, 9 January 2002.

YLBHI (*Yayasan Lembaga Bantuan Hukum Indonesia*, the Indonesian Legal Aid Foundation), Jakarta, 14 January 2002.

# 12 From 'heroes' to 'troublemakers'? Civil society and democratization in Indonesia [1]

*Bob Sugeng Hadiwinata*

## INTRODUCTION

Following the third wave of democratization around the globe, concepts relating to civil society have been intensively discussed and debated. Regarded as a cure for the ills of state-led modernization, civil society has attracted international acclaim as the winning 'idea of the late twentieth century' (Khilnani 2001: 11). However, theorists have disagreed as to whether or not civil society can be treated as a distinct and specific area of analysis. Some have argued that civil society occupies a distinct space or inhabits the 'third sphere' comprising non-state and non-commercial groups – located somewhere between state and family – influencing the structure and rules of the political game. Other observers claim that civil society is part of the state as its existence depends on political – legal frameworks which can only be provided by the state.

When democracy has been added to the debate, theorists have typically failed to reach agreement on any possible links between civil society and democracy. One group of scholars, who can be called liberal-normative theorists,[2] draws a logical link between civil society and democracy. Including scholars like Putnam, Schmitter, Cohen and Arato, Diamond and Whitehead, these liberalists believe that a strong and vibrant civil society is a precondition for an effective democracy.[3] Defining civil society as the realm of organized social life that is open, voluntary and self-generating, they believe that civil society can increase the performance of representative governments and broaden the political participation of citizens. For the liberalists, civil society plays a crucial role in the different phases of democratization. In the liberalization phase, civil society may provide for individual rights and public space. In the transition phase, the role of civil society is in ousting authoritarian governments and drafting new constitutions which guarantee a public sphere. In the consolidation phase, civil society works to increase the transparency and accountability of government and ensure democracy survives as the 'only game in town'.

In contrast to the liberal-normative theorists, historical-empiricist theorists argue that civil society may not necessarily be supportive towards democracy.

Scholars such as Khaviraj and Khilnani, Chandhoke, Alagappa, Kopecky and Mudde, argue that associating civil society with liberal democracy is an incorrect assumption. Historical-empiricists regard civil society as both the solution and problem with respect to representative democracy (Chandhoke 2003; Alagappa 2004b, and Kopecky and Mudde 2003: 1–14). Defining civil society as space, site and agency[4] in the juncture of relations with other spheres, which may include power struggles, conflicts of interest and the construction of a counter-hegemonic narrative, the historical-empiricists believe that civil society is not necessarily immune to contamination from the state or from 'uncivil' elements in society: ultra-nationalist groups, extreme religious groups, recalcitrant militias, thugs and mafia organizations, all carrying predatory interests. Viewed in this context, civil society can play a role in potentially expanding as well as contracting democratic space. Expansion results when civil society supplies the means to resist, limit and curb excesses of the state and any uncivil elements, while also cultivating civic virtues, establishing democratic norms and generally spreading democracy (throughout society) (Alagappa 2004b: 41). Contraction of democratic space occurs when civil society is tainted by extremism, jingoistic exuberance, unruly behaviour and predatory interests promoting conflict within society and generally contributing to social disorder.

New democracies provide a range of examples of relationships between civil society and democracy which can support an ambivalent standpoint. Although civil society organizations may be at the forefront of peoples' movements to overthrow authoritarian regimes, as were subsequently vindicated in the cases of the Philippines in 1986, South Korea in 1987, African countries like Benin, Cameroon, Nigeria, Ghana, Kenya, South Africa, Zambia and Malawi during the late 1980s and mid-1990s, and finally Indonesia in 1998,[5] it is not clear as to whether or not the resulting new governments will continue to commit to democratic norms and values or to vicious power struggles, exploiting ethnic and religious hatred within society and using violence to eliminate rivals. Referring to democratic transition in Eastern Europe, Kopecky and Mudde argue that ethno-nationalist groups played a crucial role in ousting communist regimes, being hailed as 'heroes' by the liberalists, only to suddenly turn into ferocious advocates of a jingoistic exuberance which resulted in the infamous ethnic cleansing of communities in the former Yugoslavia (Kopecky and Mudde 2003: 3–5).

This chapter examines how civil society develops attitudes towards democracy by looking at Indonesia's experience in consideration of examples of similar cases elsewhere in the world. Sharing a common ground with the historical-empiricists, it is argued that, in the realm of civil society, there are both desirable and undesirable elements which may affect the transition to and subsequent consolidation of democracy. While good civil society can be the champion of democracy, less positive examples of civil society can diminish any previous achievement of democratic space. The Indonesian context provides a perfect setting for this strain of argument.

Forces which act in self-interest and come to play an important role in an ousting authoritarian regime do not automatically qualify as 'good' civil society. Indonesia is a country faced with deep ethnic and religious tensions, where the 'heroes' of earlier mass movements against authoritarian regimes have tended to turn into 'troublemakers' during the transition period, adding to the difficulties involved in consolidating a fledgling democratic system. Their habitual use of violence and primordial sentiments to demoralize enemies have earned them notoriety as extremist, jingoistic and recalcitrant elements which threaten the democratic process. Their refusal to accept others and the majority view has impeded their ability to accept democracy. In post-New Order Indonesia, some radical Islamic groups and ethnically-oriented organizations are known to have been responsible for inciting ethnic and religious hatred in the lead-up to violent inter-community conflicts in the Moluccas and Central Kalimantan. These religious and ethnic conflicts show how conflict within civil society is often vicious and violent, indicating the potential bawdy character of post-authoritarian civil society.

## 'GOOD' AND 'BAD' CIVIL SOCIETY?

The revival of the concept of civil society has followed on from the third wave of democratization. What then, are the ideological tenets of civil society? The rediscovery of civil society during the 1970s and 1980s led to promises to strive for a better life for all through greater democracy, prosperity and autonomy. As Hawthorn argued, 'it can come conventionally to be said that economic liberalization is desirable, that its political corollary is liberal democracy, that liberal democracy requires a flourishing civil society [. . .]' (Hawthorn 2001: 269). Later, civil society came to be used by those who wish to sustain the project of 'post-modern utopianism' – who try to reconcile socialism with democracy – to supplement the perceived illegitimacies of representative democracy (Khilnani 2001: 16). For them, civil society can serve as an alternative to defective political representation of individual interests.

The tendency to perceive civil society as an ideal form of social interaction and transactions has rendered civil society a rigid concept with limited scope for manoeuvre. Schmitter, for example, argued that civil society must embody four conditions or norms: dual autonomy, collective action, non-usurpation, and 'civil' or legal nature (Schmitter 1995). Seen in this context, the concept of civil society would seem to have no room for extreme ethno-religious groups or mafia-type organizations since they make efforts to appropriate political power, frequently use illegal means to achieve their ends and typically display uncivil character. Although Schmitter does not deny the possibility of negative contribution to democracy by civil society, he insists that extreme and mafia-type organizations should not be included in civil society. This view is supported by Whitehead as he contends, 'various forms of religious fundamentalism may have to be tolerated within a democracy, but cannot be regarded as part of a modern liberal civil society' (Whitehead 2004: 35). Thus, civil society is confined to voluntary and autonomous groups which abide by the law and act within the constraints of generally accepted social norms and rules. Meanwhile, anti-social and extreme ethno-religious groups belong to a special category of what Whitehead terms 'uncivil interstices between civil and political society' (Whitehead 2004: 34–5).

This normative view of civil society seems to bother those who want to detach civil society from its liberal ideological ties. Elliott, for example, argued that in analysing civil society, emphasis on norms should not obstruct regard for the structural underpinnings of the concept of civil society, leading to the belief that modern Western society holds the ultimate model for the ideal civil society (Elliot 2003: 21). Writing in the context of post-communist Eastern Europe, Kopecky and Mudde argued that the separation of uncivil from civil groups in civil society is not only oversimplifying, but also leads one to an exclusive perception of civil society that renders inconsistency. For example, the nationalist movement in Slovakia during 1990–92 was generally described as uncivil and therefore excluded from ideas of 'real' civil society, but similar organizations and individuals were accepted as members of 'good' civil society only slightly earlier, in 1989 (Kopecky and Mudde 2003: 3). Moreover, the exclusion of radical, populist and extreme groups from civil society may obscure the fact that they also perform a role in serving their constituencies. In Eastern Europe, it can be argued that unlike many prominent 'civil' organizations which are elite-driven NGOs operating in environments detached from mainstream versions of society, many organizations considered 'uncivil' have been the true social movements representing grassroots interests (Kopecky and Mudde 2003: 4). Writing on the Indian context, Chandhoke shares a similar concern arguing that,

> if we confine our attention only to social associations that are beneficial to civic management, we not only engage in moral irresponsibility, we also achieve a distorted understanding of civil society. For if civil society consists of associational life per se, then we have to accept that associations of every stripe and hue exist in this space.
>
> (Chandhoke 2003: 255)

Applying the concept of civil society to developing societies where a strong liberal tradition does not exist should not see the label confined only to groups or organizations which are 'good' for liberal democracy. Mahajan pointed out that in India many associations and organizations that can be classified as comprising civil society are hierarchical and based on primordial ties, including caste, ethnicity and religion, giving them a very different moral weight compared to those in 'modern' societies with Western orientations (Mahajan 2003: 188). Consequently, voluntary organizations carrying religious hatred, extreme ideologies, ethno-nationalist sentiments and majoritarianism should still be included in civil society. However, the refusal by such groups to accept other identities and their tendency to use violence as a means to promote their agendas make them fall into the category of 'bad' civil society. So in analysing civil society and democratization in Indonesia, both 'good' and 'bad' elements of civil society must be accurately considered, for not only do both include voluntary, self-help organizations promoting the interests of their respective constituencies, but they also play their respective roles in expanding and contracting democracy.

## THE HEROES OF *REFORMASI*

Western-style pessimists and proponents of the unique features of Asian culture might wonder whether civil society, central to classical Western political theory, exists in Asia. Chan (1997), for example, maintains that there is no room for a Habermasian public sphere in a traditionally Confucian state such as China, where any attempt to find civil society is based on nothing more than wishful thinking (Chan 1997: 242–51). Similarly, Callahan (1998) argues that the concept of 'new social movements' is more helpful than the notion of civil society in understanding popular politics in China and South Korea (Callahan 1998: 277–322). Less pessimistically, Hawthorn compromises that one can only consider the 'possibility' of civil society in these societies. Even if it does exist, it is irremediably local and depends on a narrow constituency (Hawthorn 2001: 272).

Other scholars, however, believe that civil society does exist in Asia. Diamond argues that in a number of prominent cases, civil society has played a crucial role in generating a transition to democracy, as was evident in the Philippines, South Korea, Thailand and elsewhere in Asia (Diamond 1999: 237). In a similar vein, Alagappa maintains that organizations typifying civil society organizations not only exist in Asia but have achieved dramatic growth since the mid-1980s. In some cases these organizations boast long historical roots, signs of their cultural relevance and endurance under different political systems (Alagappa 2004b: 10). Indeed, defining civil society as comprising of voluntary, self-sustaining organizations not dependent on the state and characterized by groups of citizens working to achieve some common goal within the public sphere, the argument weighs heavily in favour of saying that civil society does indeed have a long history in Asia.

In Indonesia, since before the colonial era, the spirit of *gotong royong* (mutual help) has seen civil society exercised through voluntary community activities where collections of individuals work together with the aim of helping each other through various groups, such as *arisan* (credit-and-saving rotation groups), *lumbung paceklik* (food security groups), *kelompok kematian* (burial associations), *selapanan* (weekly meeting groups), and *beras perelek* (burial insurance groups). These activities continue to survive, especially in the rural areas of Java. While less conspicuous – since these groups' activities are typically limited to private welfare-type community matters rather than political activities with a relevance reaching further afield – their importance in helping individuals deal with everyday issues proves that they continue to provide solid support to the foundations of civil society in Indonesia (Hadiwinata 2003: 90). During Indonesia's colonial period some voluntary organizations operating at the national level existed, concerned with national-ist, social, economic and religious issues. Some organizations such as *Budi Utomo, Taman Siswa, Sarekat Islam, Nahdlatul Ulama,* and *Muhammadiyah* were active in promoting education, religious activities, health care and commercial activities (Hadiwinata 2003: 90). A new generation of mutual aid associations emerged during the late 1960s and early 1970s. NGOs such as *Bina Swadaya,* LP3ES (Institute for Social and Economic Research, Education and Information), LSP (Development Studies Institute), YLKI (Indonesian Foundation of Consumers Organization), YIS (Indonesian Wel-fare Foundation), YLBHI (Indonesian Legal Aid Foundation), *Dian Desa* and many others were formed, being dedicated to promote self-help activities among the poor. Throughout the New Order period, these organizations grew in number and served an important function in supplementing the state's development activities.

From the late 1980s, when cracks in the machinery of Suharto's New Order regime began to appear, the opening up of new private space saw some NGOs come to play an important role in what ended up proving to be the laying of the preliminary foundations for Indonesia's transition to democracy about a decade later. Organizations such as YLBHI, INFID (International NGO Forum for Indonesian Development), KPA (the Agrarian Consortium), CPSM (Centre for Participatory Social Management), Forum-LSM-DIY (Yogyakarta NGO Forum) and many others promoted political education, disseminating ideas of 'popular sovereignty', 'people's empowerment', and 'individual freedom' in their training programmes. They even occasionally mobilized workers and farmers, organizing protests and demonstrations which made demands for more political space, higher wages (in the case of workers) and better compensation (in the case of forced resettlements). These NGO activities were often joined by student organizations such as the SMID (Indonesian Student Solidarity for Democracy), PRD (People's Democratic Party), ALDERA (Alliance for People's Democracy), INFIGHT (Indone-sian Front for the Defence of Human Rights) and many others.

Despite intense pressure including intimidation from Indonesia's state security apparatus – which sometimes went as far as detaining, kidnapping, torturing and even murdering some activists – these organizations continued their activities. It was, inter alia, their tireless collective action that finally forced President Suharto to step down in 1998. The precipitous fall of the Indonesian currency in 1997 sparked severe inflation, leading to ongoing stu-dent demonstrations in major cities in Java, Sumatra and Sulawesi, and riots in Jakarta. This 'May 1998 revolution', as many Indonesians call this histor-ical chain of events, led to the resignation of Suharto as the country's second president. Dubbed by many Indonesians as *reformasi* (reform), these popular movements involved not only organizations that fall into the category of 'good' civil society but also extreme Islamic organizations, militias, and *preman* which instigated public disorder, including the May riots in Jakarta.

Prior to the 1998 revolution, hard-line military leaders, ultra-conservative Islamic groups and thugs joined forces and developed a conspiracy theory. They circulated a booklet entitled *Konspirasi Mengguling Suharto* (The Conspiracy to Overthrow Suharto). Allegedly published by ultra-conservative Muslims, the booklet announced a domestic and international conspiracy against Suharto, drawing upon detailed accounts of how the IMF, the United States, international Jewish business networks, Indonesia's Roman Catholic community, Indonesia's ethnic Chinese and pro-democracy activists were acting in unison to destroy the Indonesian economy and topple Suharto.[6] In its conclusion, the booklet urged Indonesian Muslims to be vigilant against allowing power to fall into the hands of Zionist agents or groups fearful of Islam. Acting on this self-styled justification, the *preman* enacted physical damage by perpetrating the May riots: shopping centres and Chinese-owned properties were set ablaze. There were reports that the *preman* raped and tortured Chinese Indonesians. Although the May riots and subsequent lootings of Chinese properties in Java's main cities of Jakarta, Tangerang, Solo, Surabaya and Banyuwangi cannot be linked solely to this sinister booklet, the involvement of these elements in civil unrest and other anti-social behaviour is evidence that in 1998, the *reformasi* involved extremist groups and *preman* bearing grudges among their predatory interests.

Sadly, many have subsequently denied a voice to the claims that this time of political change and transition to democracy in Indonesia provided shelter to *reformasi* tainted with anti-Chinese and anti-Christian sentiments. Despite internet as well as international media reports of rape and torture during the May riots, none of the masterminds responsible for this mayhem and related crimes has been brought to justice. Only a handful of thugs have been prosecuted and jailed on charges of looting and destroying property. Any discussion of the human rights violations which occurred during the May riots has typically been overshadowed by talk about the 'heroic' actions of pro-reform leaders and students in forcing Suharto to step down. Looting and land appropriation were swiftly afforded a level of understanding as the symbolic gestures of popular uprisings against long-resented authority. As Aspinall described:

> [I]n Tapos, West Java, where, within a few hours of Suharto's resignation on May 21, five farmers began to dig plots on land that had been taken from them some twenty-five years earlier to make way for a cattle ranch owned by President Suharto himself – and many more joined them over the following days. Eventually . . . hundreds of thousands of hectares of land were seized by farmers across the archipelago in the years following Suharto's resignation.
>
> (Aspinall 2004: 85)

It is clear that popular movements which have successfully brought an authoritarian regime to an abrupt end may involve different elements of civil society, good and bad. The heroic acts of movement leaders and the dramatic collapse of the regime tend to be events applauded and revisited in later years with fond nostalgia, while the involvement of anti-social and extremist groups is conveniently forgotten. During Habibie's presidency, while students, the urban poor and the unemployed continued to protest against the slow pace of reform and economic recovery, on the other side of the spectrum looting and indiscriminate killing[7] occurred sporadically all over the country. In order to maintain order and stability, the commander of the armed forces announced approved the formation of *Pam Swakarsa* (self-initiated security guards) which allowed communities to form their own security forces.

Importantly, this decision by Indonesia's military commander provided ample opportunity for ethnic and religious groups to organize efforts and participate in the struggle for political power. Indeed, during this period many radical Islamic groups such as *Laskar Jihad* (Jihad warriors), *Front Pembela Islam* (Islamic Defenders Front), *Majelis Mujahidin Indonesia* (Indonesian Mujahedin Council) and several others were formed. These groups, according to Yunanto and others, created radical wings whose members perpetuated numerous terrorist attacks across Indonesia, including the Christmas 2000 bomb attack and the Bali bombings of October 2002 (Yunanto, Farkhan and Djarot 2003: 26–8). Elsewhere, in areas like Kalimantan, where ethnic tensions were already high, groups carrying radical ethno-nationalist agendas signified by a general intolerance towards others were also formed.

## DEMOCRACY'S TROUBLEMAKERS

Transition theorists believe that for democracy to have a chance at consolidation, the commitment of significant political actors is necessary at both the elite and mass levels. With their firm belief that democratic institutions make for the best political system and the only viable norm, opponents will also come to regard democracy – including its corresponding laws, institutions and procedures – as the 'only game in town', the only realistically viable framework for governing and advancing the nation's various interests (Linz and Stepan 1996: 5). Any rejection of the legitimacy of the democratic system – what Linz calls the manifestation of 'disloyalty' – will result in fragility, instability and non-consolidation/'de-consolidation'. An infant democracy might not be able to withstand instability caused by organizations or movements that resort to force, fraud, violence or other illegal means to acquire power or influence government policies. In a consolidated democracy extremists who have no tolerance towards others are typically relegated to society's fringes where their ability to influence and gain input in mainstream processes is severely limited. As Diamond states,

Any democracy will have its share of cranks, extremists, and rejectionists on the margins of political (and social) life. If democracy is to be consolidated, however, these anti-democrats must be truly marginal. There must be no 'politically significant' anti-system (disloyal) parties or organizations.

(Diamond 1999: 67)

In burgeoning new democracies, although civil society organizations may have played a crucial role in helping to oust an authoritarian regime, they tend to be weak in the immediate post-regime phase when their lack of organization becomes increasingly apparent and sees them tend to be dominated by a minority elite (Alagappa 2004b: 39). Newly established democratic institutions and procedures face serious challenges especially when the new government, confronted with a legacy of social and economic problems as well as new demands from different sectors in society, is not effective in designing and enforcing needed laws, achieving public security and order or devising relevant policies. Societies sharply divided along ethno-religious lines tend to find their developing democratic institutions fall into jeopardy when extremist elements are able to dominate proceedings. Particularly poignant for Indonesia's case, Alagappa warned, 'The rise of religious fundamentalism is of grave political concern in several Asia countries, especially those with a Muslim majority' (Alagappa 2004b: 7).

In Indonesia, evidence of Linz-style 'disloyalty' has come from religious extremist groups and ethno-nationalist organizations established in the 1990s against the backdrop of growing religious and ethnic tensions throughout the country. Although many extremist Islamic organizations were formed after the collapse of Suharto's government in 1998, it was during the early 1990s that religious extremism began growing. The rise of Islamic extremism at that time can be linked to three factors: first, was the ethno-religious conflict taking place in the former Yugoslavia where thousands of Bosnian Muslims were wiped out as 'ethnic cleansing' was carried out by Christian Serbs during one of the bloodiest separatist conflicts of the post-Cold War era. Feelings of solidarity among Indonesians towards these, their Muslim brothers, quickly turned into anti-Christian sentiment, and saw several incidents of church burning take place as Muslim-Christian relations grew increasingly delicate. Second, a sense of 'majoritarianism' among Muslim leaders came to the fore. As a majority, Indonesian Muslims believed they deserved more of a say in political and economic arenas. Marking the formation of the ICMI (Association of Indonesian Muslim Intellectuals), a number of Islamic leaders and intellectuals started a campaign for Muslim control in social, economic and political spheres. Third, before being finally toppled in 1998, President Suharto's attempt to win Muslims' support for his re-election in 1997 led to a dramatic shift in his government's approach towards Muslim constituents. Suharto's pilgrimage to Mecca and subsequent rollback of controls over Islamic organizations allowed ultra-conservative Islamic organizations – previously suppressed under the New Order regime – to be revived and reorganized.

Ethnicity has also become an increasingly sensitive issue in Indonesia since the 1990s. Indicative of the negative consequences of the transmigration policy introduced (by the government) during the early 1960s, during 1995 and 1996 a bloody conflict in West Kalimantan between the indigenous Dayak and migrant Madurese left hundreds dead or wounded, and thousands homeless. Madurese settlers have developed a reputation for being bawdy and insensitive to local culture, which has not helped soften the stance taken by either side in stand-offs when fierce competition for control over local resources and other economic assets between the two ethnic groups is at issue, and tempers rise (Pudjiastuti 2002). In 2001, an armed robbery by a Madurese criminal gang was enough to incite Dayak retaliation, sparking a bloody ethnic conflict throughout Central Kalimantan. Although finally settled after intervention by the military and others in positions of authority, anti-Madurese sentiment had spread to other areas of the island, and many race-based/ethnic-oriented organizations driven by prejudiced racist ideologies were formed.

Muslim extremist movement *Laskar Jihad* (meaning 'holy war troops') and the extreme ethno-nationalist organization LMMDD-KT (Dayak Deliberative Council of Central Kalimantan) will feature in more detail as representatives of undesirable 'bad' civil society and its counterproductive impact on democracy. While qualifying as civil society insofar as they serve the interests of a particular constituency, are voluntary, self-supporting and independent of the government, their members include revanchists, chauvinists and fundamentalists. Despite such 'uncivil' character, they are not deemed necessarily illegal while their main agenda remains to 'lawfully' promote the interests of their supporters. All the same, their tendency to foster intolerance towards others, their attempts to establish religious and ethnic hegemony in government, and their use of violence to dissuade opponents have branded them enemies of democracy.

## Laskar Jihad and religious conflict in Moluccas and Poso

The formation and survival of *Laskar Jihad* (LJ) was directly related to growing religious tensions in the Moluccas. Frictions started as competition between indigenous Christians and Muslim migrants for jobs within the bureaucracy, as well as control over economic assets, intensified. During the Dutch colonial period, Christians formed the majority and made up a disproportionately large part of the KNIL (the Dutch colonial military force). However, the influx of Muslims from other islands changed the religious composition of the Moluccas. As the educational level of Muslims improved and they took on more roles in the local bureaucracy, military, police and economy, Christians felt a loss of control and reduced sense of security over their collective situation. As a result, the relationship between the two religious groups became increasingly sensitive. In January 1999, a quarrel between a Christian bus driver and two Muslim passengers in the city of Ambon triggered widespread violence. Within hours of the incident, fighting had spread throughout the city, moving to the nearby islands of Haruku, Saparua, Seram and Manipa.

LJ was established as the paramilitary arm of the *Ahlus Sunnah wal Jamàah* Communication Forum (*Forum Komunikasi Ahlus Sunnah Wal Jamaah* or FKAWJ), whose main purpose is to defend Muslims from violence perpetrated by Christians in the Moluccas. The FKAWJ was established in February 1998 by Ja'far Umar Thalib – an *ustadz* (religious teacher) of Arab descent who ran a small *pesantren* (traditional Islamic boarding school) in Sleman (Yogyakarta) – together with a number of conservative Muslims. The FKAWJ claimed to have opened 70 branches across Indonesia, having developed from a *salafiyah* religious organization specializing in Islamic preaching. The organization was strongly influenced by the teachings of the eighteenth-century Arab preacher Sheik Muhammad Abdul Wahhab, which focused on returning to the purity of Islam (Hadiwinata 2006: 128). The teaching of Sheik Abdul Wahhab – also known as Wahhabism – denounced the Islamic *fiqh* school's philosophy and mysticism so prevalent in the Middle East during the eighteenth century. Wahhabism was notorious for its use of force and violence in spreading its teachings (Yunanto, Farkhan and Djarot 2003: 87). Apart from waging a holy war in the Molucca islands, LJ's ultimate goal is to establish an Islamic state in Indonesia.

The massacre of at least 500 minority Muslims in the Tobero district of the island of Halmahera in December 1999 provoked calls by Muslims for a retaliatory jihad. Five months later, LJ dispatched more than 4,000 warriors to crush the Christians. In a rally in front of the presidential palace in Jakarta on 6 April 2000, FKAWJ/LJ leader Ja'far Umar Thalib declared, 'Jihad is the ultimate effort by Muslims to stop the Christians' rebellion in the Moluccas!' (ICG 2002: 6). Despite a warning by President Wahid against outsiders' involvement in the conflict,[8] LJ managed to land thousands of Muslim paramilitary troops equipped with AK-47s, handmade guns, grenades and rocket launchers. Christian militias, supported by sympathizers among the police, maintained the upper hand during the early stages of fighting. However, the arrival of LJ fighters succeeded in turning the tide against the Christians, and forced tens of thousands of people to flee their homes and properties which were subsequently destroyed (ICG 2000: 9). During the peak of the conflict during 1999–2000, it was estimated that no less than 5,000 people were killed, and roughly 500,000 people became displaced. When another outbreak of religious conflict flared in Poso, Central Sulawesi, in August 2001, LJ sent hundreds of fighters to the area. LJ together with other Muslim fighters decided on a self-styled 'ethnic cleansing' and launched a scorched-earth campaign on Sulawesi, destroying dozens of Christian villages, killing scores of Christians, including women and children, and forcing a surviving number of 50,000 refugees into the Christian-majority lakeside town of Tentena in the process.

Suspicion of likely military support for LJ activities spread among Indonesians. Military training for some 2,000 recruits was believed to have been conducted in Bogor, then moved to Sleman following pressure from political leaders, under the guidance of members of the Indonesian military 'in their private capacity, and not on behalf of the institution' (ICG 2002: 6). In the aftermath of the October 2002 Bali bombings, Ja'far Umar Thalib surprisingly announced the dissolution of LJ saying that their work was no longer needed. This (surprising) decision came just weeks after Thalib's brief detention for ordering the stoning to death of one LJ member who had allegedly committed adultery. But the disbanding of LJ did not stop the violence. Despite the government's success in bringing the conflicting parties to talks, resulting in peace agreements at the first Malino meeting to end the conflict in Maluku, and the second Malino meeting to end the conflict in Poso, sporadic attacks against Christian neighbourhoods continued to occur.

LJ was not only notorious for promoting anti-Christian sentiment, but was also renowned for its rejection of liberal democracy. Husni Putuhena (one prominent LJ figure in the Moluccas) argued that democracy is a Western concept and is not compatible with Islam (Yunanto, Farkhan and Djarot 2003: 74). Similarly, Muhammad Attamimy, an academic and LJ member in the Moluccas, maintained that modern democracy makes governments out of bandits. If a state is led by such people, its laws and rules will undoubtedly be corrupt and unjust (Yunanto, Farkhan and Djarot 2003: 75). Although this extreme anti-democratic sentiment has only a small following among Indonesian Muslims, their typically militant attitude and determination in imposing their extreme views on others poses a serious threat to democracy. Their belief that Islam and democracy are incompatible certainly does little to nurture Indonesian democracy, still in its infancy. If they are able to convince Islamic parties to carry the Muslim majoritarian agenda, a secular system of democratic government will be difficult to achieve and protect. The threat is real, given that many prominent figures within Islamic parties such as the PKS (Welfare and Justice Party), PBB (Star and Crescent Party), PPP (United Development Party), and PAN (National Mandate Party) regularly attended FKAWJ's annual meetings (Yunanto, Farkhan and Djarot 2003: 38).

## LMMDD-KT and ethnic conflict in Central Kalimantan

The LMMDD-KT (Dayak Deliberative Council of Central Kalimantan) was established during the final years of Suharto's reign when the growing weakness of the New Order government during the early 1990s came to light, encouraging Dayaks to take action in line with their growing belief that they should rightfully control more of their local society. Comprising roughly two-thirds of Kalimantan's population, Dayaks wanted more positions of power in the island's bureaucracy and other lucrative jobs in the local mining and forestry industries. Formed in 1993 by intellectuals and strongly supported by local founding fathers and elders, the Council's main purpose has been to reclaim Central Kalimantan for the indigenous Dayaks (van Klinken 2002: 72).

Ironically, the formation of this organization was facilitated by a number of environmental and community development NGOs which actively campaigned for the recognition of 'indigenous rights'. Also blaming the central government and other outsiders for unchecked illegal loggings, the devastation of the island's environment, and the marginalization of the indigenous Dayaks, these NGOs viewed LMMDD-KT as a self-organized effort by local people to free themselves from unfair outside domination and take charge of their own futures. This NGO support was hardly surprising, given the common belief that organizations such as LMMDD-KT truly represent grassroots interests as expressed in the concept of 'grassroots empowerment' and Paulo Freire's ideal of 'conscientization'.[9]

Yet, LMMDD-KT would never have become so influential without the driving force of KMA Usop, a prominent academic at the Palangkaraya University, who served as its main ideologue. A Muslim belonging to the majority Ngaju Dayak ethnic group, Usop was actively involved in drumming up mass support for demands that more positions in government and business be assigned to *putra daerah* (sons of the soil). Usop's 1996 book, *Pakat Dayak*, spells out his deliberate intent in promoting a Dayak identity. Appealing to pro-Dayak nationalism, Usop draws on the Banjar War against the Dutch (1859–63), which led to the Tumbang Anoi peace agreement in 1894; Usop glorifies the unifying of the Dayak chiefs that gave rise to the awareness of Dayak ethnicity and their subsequent success in forcing the Dutch to sign a peace treaty. In December 1998, this book inspired discussions at the LMMDD-KT second people's congress which led to a unanimous statement of direction, that 'Dayaks should become masters in their own country' (van Klinken 2002).

Ethnic awareness in itself may not be a sufficient factor in inciting ethnic violence. But when such awareness becomes entangled with political ambitions among local leaders and/or would-be leaders, or embroiled in debates over issues of socio-economic advancement of competing ethnicities, direct conflict is often the result in consolidating democracies. Snyder warns that in many new democracies, the ambitions of chauvinist politicians and others with the power to influence can see them promote ethnic hatred as a national cause. This will enable them to hijack political discourse and future leaderships, together with the transition to democracy, irrespective of the type or degree of ethnic violence that results, as happened in former Yugoslavia and post-communist Russia, as well as Rwanda and Burundi (Snyder 2000). In Central Kalimantan, Usop and many other community leaders used LMMDD-KT as a vehicle to mobilize support for taking control of local government and business. As a 2001 ICG report noted, 'anti-Madurese political rhetoric in recent times has been stimulated by rivalries between Dayak-led parties seeking Dayak votes' (ICG 2001: 18). Usop stood as the

PDI-P (Indonesian Democratic Party – Struggle) candidate in the January 2000 election for a provincial governor, competing against Asmawi Agani of Golkar (the Working Group). Although Usop eventually lost the contest, his anti-Madurese rhetoric was welcomed by Dayaks (ICG 2001: 6). The use of anti-Madurese sentiment by Dayak leaders indicates an 'ethnification of local politics' in Indonesia, whereby attempts to revive pre-colonial ethnic identities in fostering support for claims by indigenous groups for control of local resources are made (Jacobsen 2002).

Anti-Madurese sentiment among indigenous Dayaks has increased over the past decade on the back of a growing sense of marginalization among the Dayaks. Although Madurese migrants constitute only seven per cent of the total population in Central Kalimantan, they dominated key jobs in mining, logging, small business and transport. The first generation of Madurese migrants came to Kalimantan during the early 1960s as part of the government's transmigration policy. Their numbers increased significantly during the second influx of the 1970s and 1980s. Some Madurese became successful entrepreneurs running timber companies, petrol stations, hotels, retail shops, marine and land transport companies. However, Madurese prosperity often came at the expense of the indigenous Dayaks, who were forced to settle in rural areas (ICG 2001: 14–15). Indicative of how Jakarta's forced migration policy worked the redistribution of its own citizens, by 2001, when the city of Sampit became the flashpoint of regional ethnic strife, the Madurese constituted 60 per cent of the total population.

This bloody ethnic conflict started with sporadic brawls between the two ethnic groups. On 15 December 2000, a fight broke out in a karaoke bar in the town of Kereng Pangi which saw a Dayak die after being stabbed by three Madurese. In retaliation, Dayaks went on the rampage, destroying Madurese-owned properties and killing dozens of Madurese. In the wake of the unrest, about one thousand Madurese fled into the surrounding jungles while others sought protection from the local police. A few days later, Madurese launched attacks on Dayak residential areas, killing between 16 and 24 Dayaks. Tensions mounted, especially after Madurese youths held a 'victory' parade through the city of Sampit, and thousands of enraged Dayaks proceeded to storm Sampit, killing hundreds of Madurese – including women and children – and forcing tens of thousands to flee the area. During February and March 2001, the massacre continued, spreading to other cities, including Palangkaraya, Pangkalan Bun, and Kuala Kapuas. By April 2001, estimates suggested that more than four hundred Madurese had been killed, many of them beheaded, and that about 108,000 refugees had fled Central Kalimantan, most heading for Madura and other parts of East Java (ICG 2001: 5). This series of incidents became one of the bloodiest ethnic conflicts in Indonesian history.

What role was played by LMMDD-KT in the Sampit massacre? As mentioned earlier, the leadership within the organization played a crucial part in stirring up anti-Madurese sentiment among Dayaks. Usop was the chairman of LMMDD-KT's presidium at the time of the massacre. In mid-April, he was called to Jakarta for interrogation by the police, and was then arrested in relation to allegations that he had encouraged Dayak hatred against Madurese and had therefore indirectly instigated the riots (ICG 2001: 6). The allegations against Usop arose from police interrogations of LMMDD-KT's secretary in Sampit, Pedlik Asser, and his brother-in-law, Lewis. According to the police, Pedlik and Lewis had been implicated in the sectarian violence by a group of hinterland Dayaks who had earlier been arrested and convicted of killing five Madurese in Sampit on 18 February. Police claimed that both Pedlik and Lewis paid the group US$2,000 to carry out the murders (ICG 2001: 6). According to the police, Pedlik and Lewis had been disappointed at being passed over in a reshuffle of top positions in the district government as part of the nationwide implementation of the law on regional autonomy, No. 22/2000. In perpetrating the riots, LMMDD-KT leaders may not have originally intended a deliberate 'ethnic cleansing' of the Madurese, meaning mainly to cause embarrassment for local authorities. But amid the region's growing ethnic tension in the region, the consequences of their actions to incite violence against the Madurese proved to be horrendous, far worse than these 'provocateurs' might have earlier imagined.

In the aftermath of the massacre, some Dayak leaders expressed regret over what had happened. But some local leaders maintained their hatred. Cheered on by Dayak warriors, KMA Usop declared, 'We have won the war . . . If they ever come back they will face the same treatment!' (van Klinken 2002: 67). Others adopted a less blatant approach, refusing to blame Dayaks for the massacre. Governor Asmawi Agani told a traditional ritual gathering that he wanted all Dayak warriors who had been arrested for their role in the massacre to be released immediately. Asmawi also provided financial support for the LMMDD-KT's 'third People Congress' in June 2001, which held the Madurese responsible for the violence and iterated calls for them not to return to Central Kalimantan (van Klinken 2002: 83).

As tens of thousands of Madurese remained refugees in East Java, their continued absence meant that some Dayak leaders boasted that their orchestrated expulsion of Madurese had been successful in generating a sense of 'ethnic hegemony'. Such rhetoric not only proved a successful tactic in uniting otherwise fragmented Dayak interests under the LMMDD-KT banner, but also in sending a strong message of warning to other ethnic minorities – Banjarese, Javanese, Bugis, and Chinese – to acknowledge Dayak dominance. This attitude concerning feelings of ethnic hegemony is particularly worrying, in what should be a pluralistic society where the ethnic majority acknowledges and respects all minority groups. Democracy can only function in a pluralistic society if there is tolerance towards others and among all minority groups. Such a sense of tolerance certainly appears to be absent in the case of LMMDD-KT. What happened in Central Kalimantan during 2001 demonstrates how a civil society organization can develop anti-democratic behaviour, especially when it is used as a 'political vehicle' by local leaders to win support from one specific ethnic group at the expense of other ethnic communities.

## CONCLUSION

Indonesia's recent history is a case in point as to the need for the study of civil society in non-Western societies to take into account the primordial character of civil society organizations. Although primordial ties may not necessarily drag civil society organizations into what Whitehead calls the 'uncivil interstices between civil and political society' that produce less-than-ideal civil society, there is the chance that extremists, who delight in stirring up religious and ethnic hatred, might be able to use civil society organizations as vehicles for their extreme movements, seeing these organizations adopt anti-social agendas which could constrain democracy. As the examples of both LJ and LMMDD-KT suggest, civil society organizations have proven to be vulnerable in giving over to religious and ethnic sentiments that may turn them into agencies notorious for provoking violence. Both LJ and LMMDD-KT were not only able to encourage religious and ethnic hatred that led groups of individuals to commit violence, but they were also successful in promoting a sense of religious and ethnic hegemony. The militant behaviour of LJ warriors sent a strong message to Indonesian Christians and the government to acknowledge the local religious hegemony of Muslims. Similarly, the lack of remorse shown by LMMDD-KT leaders in the aftermath of the Sampit massacre conveyed a message to other ethnic minorities in the region that they must accept Dayak supremacy. This seems to support Chandhoke's argument that the enemies of democracy can exist within civil society itself (Chandhoke 2003: 255).

Indonesian experience illustrates how a vibrant civil society may not necessarily be totally supportive of democracy. There is support for the arguments of Chandhoke, Alagappa, Khaviraj and Khilnani and others who posit that some civil society organizations promote civic engagement that strengthens democracy, while other organizations weaken the domain of civil society, imposing ideas of hegemony over other senses of identity. Even some liberal theorists admit that civil society should not be associated with everything that is democratic, decent and good. To quote Diamond,

> an association may be independent from the state, voluntary, self-generating, and respectful of the law and still be not only undemocratic, paternalistic, and particularistic in its internal structure and norms but also distrustful, unreliable, domineering, exploitative, and cynical in its dealings with other organizations, the state, and society.
>
> (Diamond 1999: 227)

This view reflects a departure from the conventional understanding of civil society, saying that democracy needs civil society as much as civil society needs democracy. It may well be that a viable liberal democracy may not be possible in the absence of civil society. But as the Indonesian case has made clear, democracy may also be put in danger within the context a vibrant 'uncivil' society.

This rethinking of what constitutes and promotes civil society certainly benefits the study of democracy and its consolidation. Treating the achievement of civil society as a desirable goal whereby civil society organizations are scrutinized and evaluated on the basis of their contribution to democracy may not help to identify potential threats to a consolidated democracy that might arise from 'disloyal' elements within the same society. This may not be helpful in identifying fragility, instability, and de-consolidation of democracy. However, by adopting the concept of 'bad' civil society, manifestations of 'disloyalty', as expressed by extreme and anti-social groups in the public sphere, which could challenge and undermine democracy, may be better detected and acted upon. Studying the activities of groups which lie on the other side of 'civil' society boundaries, according to Whitehead, may contribute to a better quality and stability of democracy (Whitehead 2004: 36). While the past decade has provided an overwhelming volume of studies on how civil society has contributed to democratization and democratic consolidation, more studies are needed on examples of how civil society, bearing what Diamond calls a 'civic deficit', can threaten democracy to the extent that a de-consolidation of the democratic process results.

## NOTES

1 This chapter was prepared during the author's research fellowship visit to the Indonesia Research Unit (IRU) of the Justus-Liebig University in Giessen, made possible by the support of the Alexander von Humboldt (AvH) Foundation.
2 Some would call this group neo-Tocquevillean for they share Tocqueville's idea that such voluntary associations perform several key functions: meeting still unmet social needs, intermediating between personal need and the national common good, and preventing the tyranny of the majority.
3 See, for example, Putnam (1996), Schmitter (1995), Cohen and Arato (1992), Diamond (1999), and Whitehead (2004).
4 For a comprehensive definition of civil society as space, site and agency see Alagappa (2004: 33–4).
5 In these countries, the initial impetus for democratic change emanated from various autonomous actors in civil society, from which then stemmed the 'popular upsurge': students, churches, professional associations, trade unions, religious organizations, women's groups, human rights organizations, intellectuals, journalists and many informal networks.
6 For a more detailed account of the content of this sinister booklet, see Hefner (2000: 202–4).
7 Most notable among the indiscriminate killings were those in East Java and parts of West Java, where rumours of '*pasukan ninja*' (ninja troops) and '*pemberantasan*

*dukun santet'* (witchcraft bashings) resulted in dozens of individuals suspected of practising black magic being kidnapped and executed.
8 President Wahid ordered the military to prevent any extremists from entering the Maloccas/Maluku island.
9 During the early 1990s, NGOs were obsessed with the idea of 'people empowerment': the imposition of decentralized and self-organizing principles in the management of resources used for economic development, as well as 'conscientization', which refers to the importance of awareness building among the marginalized of their social milieu.

## BIBLIOGRAPHY

Alagappa, M. (2004a) 'Civil Society and Political Change', in M. Alagappa (ed.) *Civil Society and Political Change in Asia: Expanding and Contracting Democratic Space*, Stanford: Stanford University Press.
—— (2004b) 'Introduction', in M. Alagappa (ed.) *Civil Society and Political Change in Asia: Expanding and Contracting Democratic Space*, Stanford: Stanford University Press.
Aspinall, E. (2004) 'Indonesia: Transformation of Civil Society and Democratic Breakthrough', in M. Alagappa (ed.) *Civil Society and Political Change in Asia: Expanding and Contracting Democratic Space*, Stanford: Stanford University Press.
Callahan, W. (1998) 'Comparing the Discourse of Popular Politics in Korea and China: From Civil Society to Social Movements', *Korea Journal*, 38 (1): 277–322.
Chan, A. (1997) 'In Search of Civil Society in China', *Journal of Contemporary Asia*, 27 (2): 242–51.
Chandhoke, N. (2003) 'The Civil and the Political in Civil Society', in C.M. Elliott (ed.) *Civil Society and Democracy: a Reader*, Oxford: Oxford University Press.
Cohen, J. and Arato, A. (1992) *Civil Society and Political Theory*, Cambridge, MA: MIT Press.
Diamond, L. (1999) *Developing Democracy: Toward Consolidation*, Baltimore: The Johns Hopkins University Press.
Elliott, C.M. (2003) 'Civil Society and Democracy: a Comparative Review Essay', in C.M. Elliott (ed.) *Civil Society and Democracy: a Reader*, Oxford: Oxford University Press.
Hadiwinata, B.S. (2003) *The Politics of NGOs in Indonesia: Developing Democracy and Managing a Movement*, London: Routledge-Curzon.
—— (2006) 'From Reformasi to an Islamic State? Democratization and Islamic Terrorism in Post-New Order Indonesia', in A. Croissant and S. Kneipp (eds) *The Politics of Death: Violence in Southeast Asia*, Munster: Lit-Verlag.
Hawthorn, G. (2001) 'The Promise of Civil Society in the South', in S. Kaviraj and S. Khilnani (eds) *Civil Society: Histories and Possibilities*, Cambridge: Cambridge University Press.
Hefner, R. (2000) *Civil Islam: Muslims and Democratization in Indonesia*, Princeton: Princeton University Press.
International Crisis Group (ICG) (2000) *Indonesia: Overcoming Murder and Chaos in Maluku, ICG Asia Report No.10*, Jakarta and Brussels: International Crisis Group.
—— (2001) *Communal Violence in Indonesia: Lesson from Kalimantan, ICG Asia Report No.18*, Jakarta and Brussels: International Crisis Group.

——(2002) *Indonesia: the Search for Peace in Maluku, ICG Asia Report No.31*, Jakarta and Brussels: International Crisis Group.

Jacobsen, M. (2002) *Nation-making and the Politicization of Ethnicity in Post-Suharto Indonesia, Working Paper Series No.26*, Hong Kong: Southeast Asia Research Centre, The City University of Hong Kong.

Khilnani, S. (2001) 'The Development of Civil Society', in S. Kaviraj and S. Khilnani (eds) *Civil Society: Histories and Possibilities*, Cambridge: Cambridge University Press.

Kopecky, P. and Mudde, C. (2003) 'Rethinking Civil Society', *Democratization*, 10 (3): 1–14.

Linz, J.J and Stepan, A. (1996) *Problems of Democratic Transition and Consolidation: Southern Europe, South America and Post-Communist Europe*, Baltimore: The Johns Hopkins University Press.

Mahajan, G. (2003) 'Civil Society and Its Avtars', in C.M. Elliott (ed.) *Civil Society and Democracy: a Reader*, Oxford: Oxford University Press.

Pudjiastuti, T.N. (2002) 'Migration and Conflict in Indonesia', unpublished paper, Centre for Political Studies, The Indonesian Institute of Sciences (P2P-LIPI).

Putnam, R. (1996) 'Bowling Alone: America's Declining Social Capital', in L. Diamond and M.F. Plattner (eds) *The Global Resurgence of Democracy*, Baltimore: The Johns Hopkins University Press.

Schmitter, P. (1995) 'On Civil Society and the Consolidation of Democracy: Ten Propositions', unpublished paper, Department of Political Science, Stanford University.

Snyder, J. (2000) *From Voting to Violence: Democratization and Nationalist Conflict*, New York: W.W. Norton & Company.

van Klinken, G. (2002) 'Indonesia's New Ethnic Elites', in H.S. Nordholt and I. Abdullah (eds) *Indonesia: in Search of Transition*, Yogyakarta: Pustaka Pelajar.

Whitehead, L. (2004) 'Bowling in the Bronx: The Uncivil Interstices between Civil and Political Society', in P. Burnell and P. Calvert (eds) *Civil Society and Democratization*, London: Frank Cass.

Yunanto, S., Farkhan, M. and Djarot. (2003) *Militant Islamic Movements in Indonesia and Southeast Asia*, Jakarta: Friedrich Ebert Stiftung and the RIDEP Institute.

# 13 Two sides of the same coin? Separatism and democratization in post-Suharto Indonesia

*Felix Heiduk*

## INTRODUCTION: DEMOCRATIC TRANSITIONS AND CIVIL WARS

The aim of this book, as stated in the first chapter, is to give an overview of 'the difficult, multilayered and often contradictory results of the democratization process'. Within this context this chapter will discuss the impacts of the democratization process on regions of separatist conflict in Indonesia. Separatist conflict, as well as inter-communal conflict, has been haunting the country for decades. In particular, the provinces of Aceh and Papua have been prone to armed violence for more than 30 years. Despite the fall of the authoritarian Suharto-regime, the weakening of the central government and its security apparatus, decentralization processes and the draft of Special Autonomy laws for Aceh and Papua, little progress was seen between 1998 and 2005 to finally solve the aforementioned conflicts. Only the devastating effects of the Boxing Day tsunami at the end of 2004 led to the beginning of a peace process in Aceh, which for the time being cannot be described as fully consolidated, whilst the conflict in Papua is yet to be resolved through political means. Looking at the courses of these two conflicts, the fall of Suharto and Indonesia's transition could be interpreted as the causes of the new escalation of violence in Aceh and Papua from 1999 onwards. The fall of Suharto was followed not only by significant democratic reforms as well as a large-scale decentralization process of the country, but also by the secession of East Timor, the aforementioned outbreak of inter-communal conflicts and the escalation of the separatist conflicts in Papua and especially in Aceh.

While the level of violence had been relatively low in Aceh during the second half of the 1990s (the year 1998, for example, saw only seven clashes between GAM (*Gerakan Aceh Merdeka*, Free Aceh Movement) and Indonesian security forces), the number of clashes between the separatist guerrillas and the TNI (*Tentara Nasional Indonesia*, Indonesian Armed Forces) rose to 129 in 1999. Similarly, the number of deaths sprang up from 13 in 1998 to 360 in 1999 (Tadjoeddin 2002: 19). Parallel to Indonesia's transition to democracy, the number and intensity of internal armed conflicts steadily spiralled upwards, leading various analysts to the assumption that the break-up or the 'balkanization' of Indonesia was occurring:

> The upshot: consistent with trends in the rest of the world, we think that the balkanization of Indonesia is now underway. We can expect, at best, federated nation-states throughout the region in the next two decades. We can expect, as with balkanization in the [1990s], horrific slaughter in the disguise of ethnic cleansing, religious wars and just plain civil strife.
>
> The Atlantic Advisory Group (1999)

Thus scholars and politicians alike feared that post-Suharto Indonesia could disintegrate much like the Republic of Yugoslavia did in the early 1990s (Cribb 1999). There seemed to be a correlation between Indonesia's transition to democracy, on the one hand, and the escalation of separatist conflict in post-Suharto Indonesia, on the other.

On a more theoretical level, the perception of a correlation between democratization and an increase of secessionist conflict does shatter popular assumptions that democracy fosters peace (both within and between democratic states), or respectively that democratization brings about more peaceful 'civilian' policies in dealing with civil strife and internal uprisings – holding that democracies almost never go to war with one another. During the 1990s especially, 'promoting democracy' was widely equated with 'promoting peace'. Yet, according to various studies, the popular assumption that there is a correlation between democracy and peace and thus democratization supports the establishment of peace and security (both inside states and within the international system) so far lacks empirical verification. It is not only Indonesia that has been prone to a new or renewed outbreak of internal conflicts after the end of an authoritarian government in Aceh, Papua, Sulawesi or the Moluccas, similar situations were to be found in countries like the former Republic of Yugoslavia, Sri Lanka or the Caucasus region (Snyder 2000). Quantitative research on the interdependencies between democratic transition and war does point out that 'since the French Revolution, the earliest phases of democratization have triggered some of the worlds bloodiest nationalist struggles' and furthermore that 'transitions from dictatorship to more pluralistic political systems coincided with the rise of national independence movements, spurring separatist warfare that often spilled across international borders' (Mansfield and Snyder 2002a: 297). Quantitative analysis has shown that while democracies and autocracies both have a low probability of civil war, countries that recently have experienced political transitions have a significantly higher risk of experiencing civil wars, especially if the transition to democracy is slow and/or incomplete (Hegre *et al.* 2001). While Indonesia's internal conflicts never caused any spill-over effects, the 'coincidence' between the transition from autocracy to democracy and the escalation of civil wars seems obvious when conducting research on post-Suharto Indonesia (see above).

The theoretical literature explains the aforementioned 'coincidence' between democratization and war mainly through the weakness of governmental institutions – those providing governmental services and those regulating political participation. Mansfield and Snyder note that the danger of war grows when the transitional period results in a somewhat 'incomplete democratization' (Mansfield and Snyder 2002b) because a defective democratic system often lacks the appropriate mechanisms to integrate the contesting political ideas and groups.[1] 'Hence, none of the mechanisms that produce the democratic peace among mature democracies operate in the same fashion in newly democratizing states. Indeed, in their imperfect condition, these mechanisms have the opposite effect' (Mansfield and Snyder 2002a: 301). In addition to that, the authors state that while federalist and decentralization policies may create political benefits for stable democracies, they have the potential to weaken the central government to the extent that centre–periphery tensions over the distribution of political power may exacerbate the existing problems. Furthermore, the weakness of the governmental institutions creates the opportunities for political elites – especially for those excluded or at least not fully integrated into the new political system – to employ nationalist (or separatist) rhetoric to mobilize for mass support. It seems, with regard to post-Suharto Indonesia, that especially the decentralization of the state, understood widely as one of the key features of Indonesia's democratization process, has caused a weakening of the power of the state vis-à-vis centrifugal forces in the periphery. In addition to that, the general opening of the political sphere after the fall of Suharto opened up political space for separatist movements somewhat, so that they could gain significant support as well as vast hopes for independence. Coming from such a perception it seems clear that there is a correlation between the democratization of Indonesia and the escalation of the aforementioned separatist conflicts.

My assumption herein is slightly different. With regard to the situation 'in the field' in Aceh and Papua from late 1998/early 1999, it is my opinion that it is not so much dysfunctional political institutions or the weakening of the central government vis-à-vis centrifugal forces through the decentralization of the country that correlate with the escalation of conflict in Aceh and Papua. Rather, it seems to me that the correlation is to be found in the very limited and contested implementation of the Special Autonomy laws for Aceh and Papua, often paralleled and thus contradicted by military-dominated methods of conflict resolution. Therefore the policies of the now-democratic government in Jakarta towards Aceh and Papua differed only theoretically from those of the authoritarian Suharto era: on the ground the trickle-down effects of the democratization were far too often overshadowed by broken promises of the central government, repression and state terrorism as shown in this chapter's fourth section, 'Recent developments in Aceh and Papua'. Unfulfilled promises, lack of political and economic participation and the continuing impunity of (past and present) human rights violators all contributed to the sense of grievance and alienation in Aceh and Papua. This led to the escalation of the conflicts between 1998 and 1999. For the most part, these aforementioned issues remain unsolved until today, hindering the possible positive effects of the national democratization process from reaching the people in Aceh and Papua. On the other hand, any escalation of violence served as a blockade for possible democratic reforms in the provinces; a somewhat vicious circle. This chapter's argument will develop first by shedding some light on the historical perspective of separatist conflicts in Indonesia. Here the question will be asked why, during Indonesia's first experiment with democracy during the 1950s, had separatist challenges, with the exception of a Dutch-sponsored separatist uprising on the Moluccas, not been experienced? If there is no historic correlation between democratization and civil wars, where are the roots of the current separatist conflicts to be found? Then the policies of the post-Suharto (democratic) governments towards Aceh and Papua will be analysed before taking a more detailed look at how these policies were implemented and what effect their implementation (or the lack of) caused with regard to the separatist conflicts. Finally, it will be explained that it was not 'too much' democratization that triggered the conflicts in Aceh and Papua after 1998, but rather the lack of it. To resolve the conflict the implementation of Special Autonomy laws as part of the democratization process can therefore only be the first step, whilst in the second step the economic and social grievances that lie at the heart of the conflicts must also be addressed.

## SEPARATIST CHALLENGES OF THE INDONESIAN NATION-STATE IN HISTORICAL PERSPECTIVE

Indonesia has never been a homogeneous nation in terms of culture, language or ethnicity: what today is known as 'Indonesia' is an archipelago consisting of more than 17,000 islands, stretching more than 5,000 kilometres from the western tip of Sumatra to the eastern border with Papua New Guinea. The population structure of the archipelago has been in every way (that is, linguistically, religiously or culturally) extremely heterogeneous. The population is subdivided into hundreds of 'ethnic' and 'cultural' groups, different religions and more than 400 local languages and dialects. With such a point of departure it seems rather astonishing that secessionist forces were particularly weak after the country became independent and throughout Indonesia's first experiment with democratic rule. From the declaration of independence in 1949 until the end of the 1950s, secessionist conflict only appeared in the Moluccas where local separatists with the support of the Dutch declared independence for an entity that was to be the Southern Moluccas republic (*Republik Maluku Selatan*, RMS). Their struggle for independence was largely supported by the Dutch in order to weaken the newly independent Indonesian state. Eventually the RMS rebellion was crushed by the central government as it lacked the military capacity and public support. The rebellion had no spill-over effects on other provinces of Indonesia (Chauvel 1990). That is not to say that the rest of the country did not experience armed conflict during the 1950s and 1960s; a variety of armed uprisings occurred but these were not challenging the territorial integrity of Indonesia. The largest one, the *Darul Islam* rebellion ('House of Islam') that took place in parts of Sumatra, East Java and Sulawesi, was mainly driven by the idea of transforming Indonesia into an Islamic state. It did not attempt to enable parts of Indonesia to secede. Thus local uprisings during the 1950s and 60s were mainly challenging the character of the state (secular vs Islamic) or its political and economic system (communist rebellions). Most of them lacked popular support and were therefore easily disbanded by military repression as well as by granting forms of local autonomy to conflict-ridden areas. By the 1960s, all major uprisings against the central government had ended (Sukma 2003: 378). Thus the roots of Indonesia's current separatist conflicts do not lie in the era of Indonesia's first experiment with democracy.

With one exception – the Dutch-backed RMS rebellion – the internal conflicts during Indonesia's first experiment with democracy were not so much directed at challenging the territorial integrity of the state rather than challenging the character, ideological foundation and power structures within the state. Neither the secessionist movement in the southern Moluccas or the regional revolts in Sumatra, West Java and Sulawesi had strong local support, nor were they able to resist the central government for a long period of time. In addition, the early regionalist and secessionist movements were partly initiated and/or backed by external powers. Former colonial power, The Netherlands, supported the secessionist movement on the Moluccas in order to destabilize the now-independent former colony. The USA supported the regional revolts on Sumatra in order to challenge the Sukarno government, which was, in the context of the Cold War, considered as being 'left-wing'. Therefore the abolition of the early internal conflicts of the 1950s and 1960s by military force could be presented by Sukarno as a continuation of the struggle for independence inside the country directed against 'anti-national' forces, who were declared as 'pro-colonial' or 'pro-imperialist'. Furthermore, the relatively quick abolition of these conflicts helped to consolidate the new nation against the destabilizing influence of external powers. Consolidation thereby meant centralization of power in the hands of Indonesia's first president, Sukarno, and the undermining of democratic institutions. The proclamation of martial law in 1957 by Sukarno in order to preserve the territorial integrity and stability of the nation marked the end of Indonesia's first experiment with democracy. In 1959, Sukarno reintroduced the Constitution of 1945 which gave the president full powers, responsible only to a very weak Parliament. He later dissolved Parliament, banned the Masyumi (liberal Muslim) and Socialist (*Partai Sosialis Indonesia*, PSI) parties and ruled by decree. Ironically enough, these measures – officially undertaken to preserve the territorial integrity of the state – laid the structural roots for the emergence of the current separatist conflicts.

What followed the anti-regime conflicts of the 1950s was the expansion of the Republic of Indonesia, including first and foremost what was described by the ruling elites of this time as the liberalization of the western part of the island of Papua, which by the beginning of the 1960s was still a Dutch protectorate. According to the ruling elites of Indonesia, West Papua was considered an integral part of Indonesia as it had the same colonial past as the rest of the country. Due to mounting Indonesian political and military pressure, the Dutch removed the last of their troops in 1962. The UN backed down and considered Indonesia as being in charge of the administration of West Papua. Seven years later, Jakarta appointed 1,025 Papuan tribe leaders to vote for Papua's integration into Indonesia in a referendum mandated by the UN which was widely considered as being manipulated from the start in favour of Indonesian interests. A secessionist guerrilla group, the Organization for a Free Papua (OPM, *Organisasi Papua Merdeka*), was already formed in 1964 to fight for the independence of West Papua. It issued a proclamation about the independence of West Papua from Indonesia, though without any support from the international community (Chauvel and Bhakti 2004: 13).

The Indonesian takeover of West Papua was not to be the end of Indonesia's expansive foreign policy. In fact, after President Sukarno had to resign after what was portrayed by the military as a communist-led coup d'état,[2] his place was taken by Suharto, a military general, who continued to enlarge the republic following a vision of a greater Indonesia. When the former Portuguese colony East Timor declared its independence on 28 November 1975 after the pullout of the colonial power, Indonesian troops moved into East Timor, occupying the country. While the second territorial expansion of Indonesia in a decade was openly criticized by the UN, no direct sanctions were enacted and Indonesia's occupation of East Timor remained unchallenged and unpunished (Nevins 2002). In East Timor the Revolutionary Front for an Independent East Timor was formed (*Frente Revolucionario de Timor-Leste Independente*, Fretilin), resulting in a bloody civil war against the Indonesian occupants. An estimated 120,000–200,000 of the 650,000 East Timorese fell victim to the war – either in battle or through disease, famines and massacres committed by Indonesian troops and paramilitaries (Robinson 2003: 271).

These conflicts – as well as the conflict in Aceh (see later) – fully emerged under the rule of President Suharto (1965–98). Indonesia under Suharto, besides the continuation of expansionist foreign policy strategies, implemented comprehensive and rapid industrialization and modernization policies in an authoritarian political framework. The culmination of these policies was to secure Suharto's grip on power inside the country for decades. But what was to bring prosperity and luxury to some had devastating effects on the local economies of the outer provinces. The outer provinces were primarily regarded as providers of natural resources and therefore were aligned to the needs of the manufacturing industries on Java. In order to increase the production of industrial goods on Java, the resources required were to be exploited in the resource-rich outer provinces. The modernization and industrialization processes applied by Jakarta often left little place for local involvement, profit-sharing or for any kind of consideration of the needs of the local population. The profits made went entirely to the main island of Java, which increased the already existing gap in the standard of living and overall development between centre and periphery. Thus the existing political friction between periphery and centre, mainly a result of the centralization policies of the 1950s and 1960s, was heightened through the economic exploitation of the periphery and its population. The resource-rich provinces of Aceh (liquid gas, oil) and Papua (copper, gold) were severely affected (Leith 2003: 14).

As an outcome of these policies, three main separatist conflicts emerged and/or escalated in the Suharto era: Aceh, Papua and East Timor. While the separatist movements in Papua and East Timor mainly emerged because of forced integration (read: occupation) of the provinces by the Indonesian army, Aceh had been an integral part of Indonesia since independence was claimed in 1949. Industrialization and modernization and their side effects heightened tensions in Papua and East Timor, but the separatist movements emerged mainly for political reasons. In Aceh the situation was slightly different as the province had been a part of Indonesia for decades. Friction between the local population and the central government began to escalate due to the Jakarta-centred industrialization policies which left only five per cent of the profits made from the exploitation of Aceh's natural resources inside the province (Tiwon 2000). The subordination of the local economy according to the business interests of the central government and its side effects (impoverishment, environmental damage etc.) led to resistance within the Acehnese population. The Free Aceh Movement (GAM) was founded by Hasan di Tiro in 1976 and fought for an independent Aceh. GAM thereby referred to the sovereign past of the province before it was colonized by the Dutch at the beginning of the 20th century (Aspinall 2003).

The 'conflict resolution' policies applied by the central government facing the emerging separatist movements in Aceh, Papua and East Timor were all alike: Jakarta tried to smash any kind of opposition by means of military repression and social control in order to keep the territorial integrity of the nation. Tactics included military repression, mainly by launching dozens of military operations destined to 'wipe out' the guerrilla movements (as well as their supporters by use of extrajuridical killings, kidnappings, arbitrary arrests, etc.), and social control mainly by forced displacements and resettlement policies. These resettlement policies were named *transmigrasi* and had the goal of altering the population structure of the conflict-ridden provinces by resettling transmigrants from other provinces into Papua, Aceh and East Timor. Through this the population structure was to be changed drastically in order to withdraw popular support from the guerrillas by displacing the indigenous population. The *transmigrasi* programmes added another element to the existing friction because the 'new' population quickly took over key positions in the local administration and economy. In addition to cultural and religious differences between indigenous people and transmigrants, this increased the social gap further. Diplomatic interventions and peace talks with armed opposition groups did not take place in the Suharto era. The all-out war solutions led to decades-long, low-intensity conflicts with the civil populations suffering the most. Parallel to the escalation of the conflicts, noncombatants increasingly became targets of the armed groups (Sulistiyanto 2001: 441).

Three things can be seen as characteristics of the separatist conflicts in the Suharto era: their long duration on a low-intensity level, the increasing popular support for the secessionist movements, and the all-out war policies applied by the central government leaving little to no room for any realistic conflict resolution. Structurally, the centralization of all political and economic power on the main island, Java, and the policies of modernization and industrialization were the root causes of the conflicts. By modernizing and industrializing the nation, the gap between the centre and the periphery was widened and social as well as economic problems were increased. Suharto's promise to develop the nation as a whole, which was used to legitimize his authoritarian rule, was only held for certain parts of the population as it left out the outer provinces. The effects of the modernization in the outer provinces stood in sharp contrast to Suharto's promises and therefore led to contradictive developments in Aceh, Papua and East Timor. The development of the outer provinces was further hampered by the military repression of any kind of opposition, no matter if Islamist, socialist or secessionist in shape, which left no political space for any kind of opposition to the government other than one of armed violence. The gap between the centre and the periphery, resulting in social grievances among the populations of the resource-rich outer provinces, was further widened by the continuing state terror conducted by the Indonesian security apparatus after the establishment of separatist movements.

## AFTER 1998 – WHO OPENED PANDORA'S BOX?

Following the Asian economic crisis in 1997, a popular uprising emerged throughout 1997 and 1998, forcing President Suharto to withdraw from power in May 1998. His successor, former vice president Bacharuddin Jusuf Habibie, promised democratic reforms which were supposed to transform Indonesia from a centralist and autocratic dictatorship to a decentralized, democratic system. The initial democratic transition and reduced repression against the opposition calmed tensions on Java. The popular upsurge was directed at the political establishment in Jakarta and its system of autocratic policies, corruption, collusion and nepotism. With Suharto stepping back from power and democratic reforms being launched, their main political goal was reached. However, the situation in areas like Aceh or Papua was different: the opening of the political sphere made the establishment of many local NGO's and grassroots organizations possible, who in turn mostly demanded not only democratic reforms but an investigation into of the various human rights violations conducted by the state security apparatus under Suharto. Therefore various NGO's and journalists investigated hundreds of cases of extrajuridical killings, torture and rape, and made these cases public. This further decreased the already low legitimacy of Jakarta in the outer provinces. The public outcry to put an end to the impunity of human rights violators led Habibie to promise the investigation of the countless cases of human rights violations and the withdrawal of troops. According to Habibie, if found guilty legal action against members of the security apparatus would be taken. These promises never materialized for Aceh or Papua and again shattered the little trust the Acehnese and Papuans held in Jakarta. On the other hand, the successful secession of East Timor made independence seem a somewhat realistic option for Aceh and Papua. Parallel to the development of many civil society organizations in Aceh and Papua, GAM, and to a lesser extent, the OPM could start up again.

All of this led to growing support for the idea of independence among the people of Aceh and Papua. Networks of civil society organizations started lobbying for independence in Aceh and to a much lesser extent in Papua as well. The decrease in military repression, the result of a short weakening of the state during its transformation from autocratic to democratic institutions and processes, further strengthened the aspirations of the separatist guerrillas as they were able to regroup and arm their fighters in 1999 and 2000. GAM was especially able to re-organize its military powers within months of the fall of Suharto (Schulze 2004: 31). After East Timor's secession Pandora's Box seemed to have been opened and Indonesia to be becoming the next 'Balkans' at the beginning of the 21st century. As a response to the rapidly growing independence movements in Aceh and Papua that followed the collapse of the authoritarian regime of Suharto in 1998, the government in Jakarta drafted Special Autonomy laws in November 2001. Special Autonomy was seen as an offer to provincial elites to divert separatist demands for sovereignty and independence. It could function as a framework to address the grievances that had fuelled separatist conflicts in Aceh and Papua; particularly so because the laws enshrined basic minority rights, marking a significant change in the policies by which the central government was dealing with separatist and regional conflicts (McGibbon 2004). From a historical perspective, the draft of Special Autonomy laws was a distinct product of a special period of state weakness. Amongst its separatist challenges the Indonesian government faced various other crises. Central authority was weakened in the first phase of Indonesia's democratic transition: it was largely dependent on international financing, its institutions were challenged by mass protests and, in the wake of the East Timor crisis, the central authority faced serious international criticism for human rights abuses. In this context came the drafting of Special Autonomy laws for Aceh and Papua, both granting the provinces a dramatic increase in the provincial share of natural resource revenues, devolution of administrative power benefiting the provinces administration, direct elections of governors and district heads (for Papua this even included the establishment of a Papuan People's Assembly (MRP)), as well as various other points like the implementation of sharia law in Aceh (McGibbon 2004: 83).

While overcoming its weakness step by step in 2002 and 2003, the government's approach towards its separatist challenges began to change. By 2003 the Megawati government followed a different track by imposing martial law in Aceh and making efforts to divide Papua into three separate provinces. This was the start of a more coercive, militaristic approach as well as a signal of the reluctance of the central government to give up or devolve political authority within the policies of Special Autonomy. 'National leaders feared that granting special concessions would trigger a cascade of demands from other provinces and increase the prospect of further separatist challenges [. . .]'. (McGibbon 2004: 3). Besides this major reversal in Jakarta's policies, local factors diminishing the success of the Special Autonomy laws need to be addressed here as well. Weak and corrupt local governments in Aceh and Papua generally failed to implement the laws and as a result the benefits of the increased share of natural resource revenues failed to reach the people. GAM, who saw itself as the legitimate government of the Acehnese people, established parallel state structures in the areas under its control (Schulze 2003: 257) and therefore prevented the implementation of the Special Autonomy laws in these areas. Special Autonomy, being only very rudimentarily implemented in both provinces anyway, became virtually policy-irrelevant – especially in the face of the escalation of violence in both provinces and the continuing of widespread human rights abuses by the Indonesian security apparatus. While the OPM in Papua was not able to form serious military resistance, the GAM, consisting of over (an estimated) 5,000 armed and trained guerrilla fighters, posed a serious security threat to the army units operating in Aceh.

Whilst the violent clashes between the OPM and the Indonesian military in Papua had decreased since 2000, the conflict in Aceh escalated after two peace agreements in 2000 and 2002, brokered by the Swiss Henri Dunant Center, broke down. The reasons for the collapse of the peace agreements are to be found on both sides: GAM's uncompromising claim for independence, literally discrediting Special Autonomy as well as any peace agreement as a status prior to full independence, encouraged mistrust within the central government. In the end the political and economical interests of the Indonesian military and the lack of civilian control over the security apparatus led to the breakdown of the peace agreements (Aspinall and Crouch 2003: 43). One result of the ongoing conflicts in Aceh and Papua was the establishment of an irregular civil war economy. This system of informal and illegal economic activities, taking advantage of the lack of civil control in the conflict areas, is used by all parties to make tremendous profits. Through illegal logging, arms and drug trafficking as well as extortion it is possible for the chronically under-financed military to bolster its budget. Furthermore, political influence was regained by pointing out a possible disintegration of the country. The perpetuation of the conflict in Aceh and Papua enables the TNI to take back some of the praetorian guard functions it had under Suharto, meanwhile securing indirect political influence for the armed forces (McCulloch 2003).

## RECENT DEVELOPMENTS IN ACEH AND PAPUA

### Aceh – from all-out war and the 'little doomsday' to the current peace process

As a reaction towards the collapsed peace agreement of 2002, the central government declared martial law over Aceh in May 2003 and during the second half of 2003 deployed more than 40,000 troops to the province to 'wipe out' GAM. The entire province was to be under military rule – even the civil administration including the governor was put under military supremacy – making Aceh's military command the most powerful institution in Aceh. Foreign access to Aceh was very limited and Indonesian journalists could only report out of Aceh by embedding themselves into TNI units. Independent news and analyses of the situation in Aceh were hard to come by. The Indonesian military reported the killing of more than 2,000 GAM fighters during the time of martial law. This number would have reduced the estimated capacities of GAM by 70 per cent, although the rising number of armed clashes and constant GAM ambushes against TNI troops casts doubts over the data provided by the TNI (*Far Eastern Economic Review*, 01 July 2004: 21). Therefore, independent observers as well as human rights organizations drew the conclusion that the majority of the killed 'GAM fighters' were civilians. Due to the aforementioned restricted access to Aceh during the times of martial law, no examination of the numbers has been possible (Tapol 2004), although sporadic reports about extrajuridicial killings of suspected GAM members, arbitrary arrests of their family members and kidnappings have surfaced throughout the year of martial law (HRW 2003). Whole villages known as GAM strongholds were forcedly displaced and civilians were forced to openly pledge allegiance to the Republic of Indonesia and to withdraw support for GAM.

In May 2004 martial law was changed into a state of civil emergency, which re-installed a civil governor as the head of state in Aceh, but in reality did not alter the situation of the Acehnese for the better. During the civil emergency the militaristic approach to attempt to end the conflict stayed intact; arbitrary arrests, extrajuridicial killings and curfews were to continue throughout 2004.

Independent observers such as the International Crisis Group asserted that the strategy of the central government to militarily wipe out GAM had failed and the current policies of Jakarta were described as being highly erratic – an end to the conflict seemed to be out of sight (ICG 2003a). Jakarta, however, did not respond to its critics by a change of the Aceh policy, nor was there any response or statement from the international community pressuring Jakarta to find a solution for the Aceh conflict. Ironically, it was to be the Boxing Day tsunami that changed the 'all-out war' situation in Aceh. The natural disaster which devastated large parts of the province leaving more than 160,000 of its inhabitants dead put the adversaries under enormous political pressure to resolve the conflict. Facing one of the biggest humanitarian emergencies of all time and with billions of dollars of foreign aid floating into Aceh, GAM and the central government in Jakarta were pressured to quickly open up peace negotiations. In particular, the international donor community insisted that ending the war was a precondition for effective reconstruction (Heiduk 2005). After nine months of talks under the mediation of the Finnish NGO CMI (Crisis Management Initiative) a Memorandum of Understanding was signed in Helsinki by both parties on 15 August 2005, ending the decade-long war in Aceh.

Core points of the agreement were the transformation of GAM into a local political party, with GAM in exchange giving up its struggle for an independent Aceh. Under the compromise laid down in the agreement GAM representatives were allowed to stand as independent candidates in the local elections. The government in Jakarta furthermore enabled GAM to transform into a local party within 18 months of the agreement. The Special Autonomy law for the province, which was supposed to be in effect since 2001, has not been implemented due to the ongoing war in the province.[3] Other key points of the agreement include the establishment of a Truth and Reconciliation Commission, GAM's demobilization and a withdrawal of all non-organic TNI troops, as well as the release of hundreds of political prisoners. To have the peace process monitored independently, both parties agreed to set up an independent, unarmed observer mission composed of representatives of the EU and ASEAN.

Even after the successful conclusion of negotiations in 2005 some possible perils remain for Aceh. First and foremost, the Indonesian military remains an important factor in Aceh – especially due to the fact that the military-backed militias were not included in the demilitarization process. The failure of the two previous ceasefires was due not least to heavy resistance from the military. In these contexts military-backed militia groups acted as proxies of the military, undermining security and stability in Aceh (Aspinall and Crouch 2003: 40). However, it needs to be made clear that it was President Megawati's support for the attempted 'wipe out' of GAM after the peace talks of 2002 failed that was crucial for the escalation of the conflict. She declared martial law and backed the hard-line track of the military. Therefore the situation in

2005 was slightly different with directly elected President Susilo Bambang Yudhoyono trying to bring the military under civil supremacy by 'demilitarizing' politics, though it remains to be seen how far the President's reforms can succeed in the face of strong opposition in parliament. Without the necessary parliamentary majorities for some of the provisions of the peace agreement (for example, altering the special autonomy law for Aceh) even a perfect agreement between GAM and Jakarta would stand little or even no chance of implementation and therefore would be doomed to fail in the long term. Beyond the balance of power between the civil government and the military in Indonesia comes the disarming of GAM's military wing. Examples from other countries show that the challenge of reintegrating guerrillas into civilian life is not only a question of political but, above all, of economic integration as well. Over the years of civil war, war-torn Aceh has been turned into a lucrative source of income for GAM and the TNI. Illegal logging, extortion, drug-trafficking and smuggling generated huge sums of profits which are estimated to be an annual US$400 million for the TNI alone (Forbes 2005). This clearly shows the importance of a coherent strategy of social and economical reintegration for the province (Barron *et al.* 2005: 18). Although in the context of the MOU important steps towards an end of the three-decade-long conflict have been made, a peaceful future for Aceh cannot, in the face of the multiple challenges stated above, yet be taken for granted. With most international aid and reconstruction programmes ending in 2009, it remains to be seen if the prospects for a peaceful future of Aceh will stand their ground.

## Papua – three out of one?

In the face of the tsunami, the situation in Papua seems to be less extreme, but not necessarily less complex in nature. The OPM is fragmented by rivalries between different tribes and has been left without a leader after the assassination of Yustinus Murib by Indonesian soldiers in November 2003. A Papua Presidium Council (*Presidium Dewan Papua*, PDP) consisting of many different tribal leaders has been established, dedicated to a non-violent struggle for the independence of West Papua. But most local politicians are heavily dependent on Jakarta for money and power and therefore for the most part collaborate with the central government while lacking legitimacy within the Papuan population. Having delayed the establishment of a Papuan People's Assembly (*Majelis Rakyat Papua*, MRP) three times in the month of October alone, the central government's election committee announced the 42 MRP candidates at the end of October 2005. Prior to the announcement, Jakarta blamed disputes between local leaders and authorities regarding the MRP appointments as the reason for the delays. The election of 42 candidates for the MRP is part of the law on Special Autonomy (Law 21/2001), which mandates the central government and the Papuan administration to create the MRP. The MRP is supposed to function as the political body representing the different community groups of West Papua, including different tribes, religions and genders. The wide-ranging powers of the body include the sensitive issue of dealing with human rights violations in the province as well as development polices. Under the Special Autonomy law, the MRP furthermore has the power to approve candidates for the province's governorship and for membership of the People's Consultative Assembly (MPR) for Papua. Since Law 21/2001 does not give any detailed specification about the MRP's composition, the government has experienced recurring problems in finding a balanced composition for the MRP. This is in order to buy time as the central government seems reluctant to set up such a powerful body and give it wide-ranging powers. However, the final election of certain members of the MRP at the end of October 2005 has drawn criticism from opposition groups, as some of MRP's representatives were chosen by local administrations, excluding opposition groups from the election process (*The Jakarta Post Online*, 27 October 2005). The undemocratic formation of the MRP represents, in the eyes of opposition groups, the central government's fear of a secession of Papua once the Special Autonomy law is fully implemented. In addition, it was feared that the undemocratic selection process could, for the lack of strong opposition candidates, facilitate those running for the Papua governorship in November 2005.

Another political problem intensifying the already existing friction between the Papuans and the central government is the planned split of Papua into three provinces, destined to fractionalize and weaken civil society, non-armed opposition groups, as well as the OPM (ICG 2003b). The adoption of such a law saw a great deal of resistance within Papua through mass demonstrations and the provincial parliament's objection to such a law in 2003, but President Megawati by presidential decree announced the establishment of the province of West Irian Jaya (*Irian Jaya Barat*) (*The Jakarta Post*, 25 June 2004: 4). This openly contradicted the Special Autonomy law, according to which the establishment of new provinces and/or the splitting up of existing provinces have to be approved by the MRP and the provincial parliament. A plebiscite in West Irian Jaya showed that the majority of Papuans rejected plans for a split of the province. Thus the MRP in early 2006 refused to back the central government's plans and declared the establishment of the province of West Irian Jaya as not being in line with existing Special Autonomy regulations. Nevertheless, plans for a split of West Papua have not yet been abandoned by the central government. On 11 March 2006 elections were held in Irian Jaya Barat to elect the new governor of the province, although the province's legal status was still unsettled and it was clear that a majority of the Papuans saw the holding of elections as a violation of the Special Autonomy law. After the elections riots between demonstrators and security forces left three policemen and one soldier dead and resulted in many severely injured protesters (ICG 2006). Laws and polices contradicting the Law on Special Autonomy led to mounting concerns amongst the people of Papua, particularly regarding the credibility of the government's intention to grant full Special Autonomy for Papua in the near future.

In addition to failed policies and a delay of implementing the Special Autonomy law, the Indonesian security apparatus serves as a more direct tool of the central government to exercise social, political and economic control over the province. Firstly, the military, as well as dozens of military-backed militia groups, are responsible for most of the human rights abuses that have happened since the euphemistically called 'integration' of Papua into Indonesia. Furthermore, Wing and King state that military involvement is common in illegal and corrupt activity and manipulation of the local political and security situation to justify and enhance further penetration of TNI and its Jakarta-based business cronies into the decision-making processes and administration in Papua (Wing and King 2005: 2). Aimed at protecting mining firms, forest concessions and timber estates, to mention just a few of the economic interests of the TNI in Papua, the military's legal and illegal operations in Papua generate tremendous economic profit for its members as well as bolstering the political influence of the military (Council on Foreign Relations 2003: 62).

The deteriorating security situation in the province enables the military to influence local politicians and the administration. In addition, it led to an increased targeting of pro-independence activists and human rights defenders, and generally increased repression of civil society organizations, blaming them collectively as being in support of the separatist guerrillas (Tapol 2003). Throughout 2003 and 2004 this even led to the displacement of as many as 6,000 Papuans from their villages by the military (Wing and King 2005: 2). After the situation in Aceh significantly subsided – since the start of the peace process in August 2005 – Papua could realistically be the next trouble spot of the archipelago. Various reports by human rights organizations indicate that the problems between the central government and the people of Papua in 2006 were far from being resolved. In fact, five years after the implementation of Special Autonomy, the human rights situation in Papua has still not improved (Tapol 2007). Non-armed civil opposition, which still has a broad base within the Papuan population, could soon turn again into violent rebellion if demands for the implementation of Special Autonomy are not met and the impunity of the security apparatus continues to prevail as it does today (*The Jakarta Post*, 25 June 2004: 4).

## CONCLUSION

Looking at the status quo of the often contradictory efforts and policies of the Jakarta-based elites towards Papua and Aceh, it does appear that the civil strife and bloody conflict in these two outer provinces has been at least partly a reaction towards these policies. For the time being, the impact of Indonesia's democratization process on the separatist conflicts seems to be as hybrid as Indonesia's current political system itself. On the one hand, the democratization process facilitated the emerging of new political elites, party pluralism and free and fair elections on the national level. On the other, the at least formally successful implementation of democratic institutions, party pluralism, and free and fair elections on the national level has yet to be transferred to Papua and, in many ways, also to Aceh. Many of the areas prone to separatist or intra-communal violence in Indonesia show how heavily restricted, contested and often contradictory the processes of democratization have become. The power-politics of elites in Jakarta, the weakness of governmental institutions and a general sense of grievance among many people in Aceh and Papua endangers trust and future cooperation between Jakarta and the outer provinces.

The Special Autonomy laws, drafted as an effort to tackle some of the grievances that are seen as the root causes of the ongoing conflicts, have not been fully implemented. Most of the profits made by extracting the vast natural resources of Aceh and Papua still have not reached the majority of the population. On the contrary, laws contradicting the Special Autonomy (the split of Papua) or discarding it (declaring martial law/civil emergency on Aceh) are promptly implemented if they are thought be central to Jakarta's interests. The military under Suharto was the one institution that towered above all others, and made great political as well as economical use of the ongoing conflicts: politically, by being able to regain some of the excessive influence on state policies by presenting itself as the only force being capable of holding the nation together; and economically by benefiting from weak and ineffective state structures in the conflict regions and a general lack of civil control by extracting millions of US dollars annually out of the conflict regions through illegal logging, extortion, raising of illegal taxes, drug-trafficking and smuggling. Although human rights and even minority rights are enshrined within effective laws, most of the abuses committed by members of the armed forces and the state security apparatus in Papua and Aceh remain unpunished. Impunity seems, for the time being, the general pattern in dealing with human rights violations as there has not yet been a single case where members of the armed forces or security apparatus have been sentenced.

In general, the coercive approach towards separatist conflicts – which are still regarded as an internal threat to the security and stability of Indonesia – all too often did not differ much from the approaches and policies applied under the authoritarian rule of Suharto. After all, such approaches are still ideologically based on the vivid vision of a greater Indonesia (*Indonesia Raya*), where little (if any) room is left for contesting regional identities and politics. Hence, whilst institutions and governmental structures appear to have changed after the fall of Suharto, Indonesian nationalism and its vision of the unitary state have not. The disintegration of Indonesia is still regarded as Indonesia's primary security issue by large parts of the political elite. In this context, it needs to be mentioned that the nationalist vision of a homogenous Indonesia Raya has, to an extent, been contested by granting Special Autonomy to Aceh and Papua. The acknowledgement of diverse interests and legitimate ambitions for local autonomy could become a framework to further reduce the grievance that has been fuelling separatist sentiment for decades. But this can happen only in combination with a broad and consistent policy enabling the local populations to actively participate in local politics and economics. Special Autonomy laws are a first step, but alone have proven to be too fragile and easily revertible to function as the main, comprehensive approach to end separatist conflict (McGibbon 2004: 64).

When looking at the root causes of the separatist conflict, even solid reforms of the political system in favour of a more decentralized and democratic form of governance will potentially fall short if the social and economic grievances that lie at the hearts of the conflicts are not addressed. After all, it was not only the incomplete democratization of Indonesia and the policies of repression of the central government and the military that fuelled armed violence in Aceh or Papua, but economic exploitation, poverty and unemployment as well. Economic and social grievances will not entirely be reduced solely by institutional reforms or the establishment of local political parties, but through a redistribution of power and wealth from the top to the bottom of society. A 'peace dividend' for Aceh and Papua not only needs to include the sheer absence of armed violence, but also has to provide 'trickle-down effects' (read: social and economic prosperity) to the people of Aceh and Papua.

## NOTES

1 Within the 'democratic peace' debate these mechanisms can be broadly described as 'democratic norms' and 'democratic political structures/institutions'.
2 The apparent coup d'état on 1 October 1965, during which six generals were kidnapped and killed and in which the Revolutionary Council led by Lieutenant-Colonel Untung sought to seize power, is one of the most contended events in Indonesian history. Whereas coup leader Untung described the coup as an attempt to safeguard President Sukarno and the Indonesian revolution by forestalling a military-led coup d'état, the military, after crushing the Revolutionary Council, was quick to issue reports linking the attempted coup directly to the PKI (*Partai Komunis Indonesia*, Communist Party of Indonesia). In the context of deep political tensions between conservative (including many military officers) and the PKI and PKI-affiliated organizations, these reports triggered a 'wave of revulsion' against the communists that resulted in the massacres of 1965–66, during which between half a million and three million alleged communists were killed by military units and Islamic militias (Cribb 2007).
3 Quite the contrary: martial law was established in Aceh in 2003. With the implementation of martial law all political power was centred in the hands of the Indonesian military (ICG (2003a).

## BIBLIOGRAPHY

Anderson, B. (1991) *Imagined Communities: Reflections on the Origin and Spread of Nationalism*, revised edition, London and New York: Verso.

Aspinall, E. (2003) 'Modernity, history and ethnicity – Indonesian and Acehnese nationalism in conflict', in H. Aveling and D. Kingsbury, *Autonomy and Disintegration in Indonesia*, London: Routledge Curzon.

Aspinall, E. and Berger, M.T. (2001) 'The break-up of Indonesia? Nationalisms after decolonisation and the limits of the nation-state in post-cold war Southeast Asia', *Third World Quarterly*, 22 (6): 1003–24.

Aspinall, E. and Crouch, H. (2003) *The Aceh Peace Process: Why it failed?*, Policy Studies 1, Washington D.C.: East-West Center.

Barron, P. *et al.* (2005) *Conflict and Recovery in Aceh – An Assessment of Conflict Dynamics and Options for Supporting the Peace Process*, Jakarta: The World Bank.

Blum, W. (2004) *Killing Hope – U.S. Military and C.I.A. Interventions since World War II*, updated edition, Monroe: Common Courage Press.

Chauvel, R. (1990) *Nationalists, Soldiers and Separatists*, Leiden: KITLV Press.

Chauvel, R. and Bhakti, I.N. (2004) *The Papua Conflict: Jakarta's Perceptions and Policies*, Policy Studies 5, Washington D.C.: East-West Center.

Council on Foreign Relations (2003) *Indonesia Commission: Peace and Progress in Papua*, New York: Council on Foreign Relations.

Cribb, R. (1999) 'Not the next Yugoslavia – prospects for the disintegration of Indonesia', *Australian Journal of International Affairs*, 53 (2): 169–78.

—— (2007) 'The 1965 Massacres in Indonesia – Issues still unresolved', in E. Streifeneder and A. Missbach (eds) *Indonesia – The Presence of the Past*, Berlin: Regiospectra.

Forbes, M. (2005) 'Hope for peace as drums welcome Aceh deal', in *The Age*, 15 August. Online. Available HTTP: <http://www.theage.com.au/news/world/hope-for-peace-as-drums-welcome-aceh-deal/2005/08/14/1123957950641.html> (accessed 19 August 2007).

Hegre, H. *et al.* (2001) 'Towards A Democratic Civil Peace? Opportunity, Grievance, and Civil War 1816–1992', *American Political Science Review*, 95 (1): 33–48.

Heiduk, F. (2005) *Nine Months after the Tsunami: Hopes for Peace in Aceh*, SWP Comments 2005/35, Berlin: SWP.

Hobsbawm, E.J. (1990) *Nations and Nationalism Since 1780*, Cambridge: Cambridge University Press.

Human Rights Watch (HRW) (2003) *Aceh under Martial Law: Inside the Secret War*, New York: Human Rights Watch, Report No. 10.

ICG (2003a) *Aceh: How Not to Win Hearts and Minds*, Indonesia Briefing (23.7.2003), Jakarta/Brussels: ICG.

—— (2003b) *Dividing Papua: How not to do it*, Indonesia Briefing (9.04.2003), Jakarta/Brussels: ICG.

—— (2006) *Papua: The Dangers of Shutting Down Dialogue*, Asia Briefing No. 47 (23.03.2006), Jakarta/Brussels: ICG.

Leith, D. (2003) *The Politics of Power: Freeport in Suharto's Indonesia*, Honolulu: University of Hawai'i Press.

Mansfield, E.D. and Snyder, J. (2002a) 'Democratic Transitions, Institutional Strength, and War', *International Organization*, 56 (2): 297–337.

Mansfield, E.D. and Snyder, J. (2002b) 'Incomplete Democratization and the Outbreak of Military Disputes', *International Studies Quarterly*, 46: 529–49.

McCulloch, L. (2003) *Greed – the silent force behind the Aceh conflict*, Working Paper, Deakin University, Melbourne.

McGibbon, R. (2004) *Secessionist challenges in Aceh and Papua: Is Special Autonomy the solution?*, Policy Studies 10, Washington D.C.: East-West Center.

McVey, R. (1984) 'Separatism and the paradoxes of the nation-state in perspective', in L. Joo-Lock and S. Vani (eds) *Armed separatism in Southeast Asia*, Singapore: ISEAS.

—— (1996) 'Building Behemoth: Indonesian Constructions of the Nation-State', in D.S. Lev and R. McVey (eds) *Making Indonesia*, Ithaca: Cornell University Press.

Nevins, J. (2002) 'The Making of "Ground Zero" in East Timor in 1999 – An Analysis of International Complicity in Indonesia's Crimes', *Asian Survey*, 17 (4): 623–41.

Robinson, G. (2003) 'The Political Economy of Cross-Border Relations: The TNI and East Timor', *South East Asia Research*, 11 (3): 269–96.

Snyder, J. (2000) *From Voting to Violence: Democratization and Nationalist Conflict*, New York: W.W. Norton.

Sukma, R. (2003) 'The Acehnese Rebellion: Secessionist Movement in Post-Suharto Indonesia', in A.T. Tan and J.D. Boutin (eds) *Non-Traditional Security Issues in Southeast Asia*, Singapore: IDSS.

Sulistiyanto, P. (2001) 'Whither Aceh?', *Third World Quarterly*, 22 (3): 437–52.

Tadjoeddin, M.Z. (2002) *Anatomy of Social Violence in the Context of Transition: The Case of Indonesia, 1990–2001*, Working Paper, Jakarta: UNSFIR.

Tapol (2003) 'Military Sets Papua Agenda', *Tapol Bulletin*, 173/4.

—— (2004) 'Unlawful Trials and Prisoner Abuse in Aceh', *Tapol Bulletin*, 175/2.

—— (2007) 'No human rights improvement under Special Autonomy', *Tapol Bulletin*, 185, January.

The Atlantic Advisory Group, *Asia: The Risk of Political Risk*, Thinkpiece Series, Second Quarter 1999. Online. Available HTTP: <http://www.atlanticadvisory.com/TP_asia_risk.html> (accessed 28 June 2006).

Tiwon, S. (2000) 'From Heroes to Rebels', *Inside Indonesia*, 62. Online. Available HTTP: <http://www.insideindonesia.org> (accessed 22 September 2004).

van Dijk, Kees (1990) 'The Indonesian State: Unity in Diversity', in S.K. Mitra (ed.) *The Post-Colonial State in Asia: Dialectics of Politics and Culture*, New York: Harvester Wheatsheaf.

Wing, J. and King, P. (2005) *Genocide in West-Papua? Report of the West-Papua Project*, Sydney: Centre for Peace and Conflict Studies, University of Sydney,

# Index

Lightning Source UK Ltd.
Milton Keynes UK
UKOW06f1814150216

268416UK00004B/337/P